WHAT OTHERS

THE INDEPENDENT FILM P … ;UIDE

Se

By Gunnar Erickson, F

"If you are in the independent film business, you must read this book."

—Cassian Elwes, head of the Independent Film Division
William Morris Agency

"The future of film will be in the hands of independent producers. A guide to producing a film correctly, creatively, and on budget will be an invaluable tool for all creative talent looking to succeed in a very complex world. This guide can not only help filmmakers survive but by using the authors' techniques and suggestions, the prospects of success are clearly enhanced."

—Robert Dowling, editor-in-chief and publisher
The Hollywood Reporter

"Producing an independent film is a challenging enough endeavor without being waylaid by the legal pitfalls and business blunders that loom at every turn. The authors have produced a marvelous primer that actually delivers what it promises, and that is clearly the result of real experience and knowledge that comes from being among the select few who have each labored in the legal and business trenches of the independent area for over two decades."

—Geoffrey Gillmore, programming director
Sundance Film Festival

"This is a true bible for all aspiring-and active-independent producers."

—Jean Picker Firstenberg, director and CEO
American Film Institute

"A must read for anyone interested in embarking on the journey toward making a movie."

—Renee Missell, producer and former artistic director
Santa Barbara Film Festival

"This book is a must for anyone looking for clear concise information on navigating the often daunting business of film. The authors have pulled together a comprehensive guidebook that is as compelling to read as it is indispensable as a reference."

—Ira Deutchman, founder
Fine Line Features

"What should you be asking a lawyer when making an independent film? Among other answers, this comprehensive guide provides wonderfully detailed information for the ever-growing number of indie producers."

—Annette Insdorf, professor
Columbia University

"This book is an invaluable how-to-do guide which belongs on your bookshelf if you produce independent film."

—Jonathan Dana, Producer's Representative

THE INDEPENDENT FILM PRODUCER'S SURVIVAL GUIDE

A BUSINESS AND LEGAL SOURCEBOOK

GUNNAR ERICKSON
HARRIS TULCHIN
MARK HALLORAN

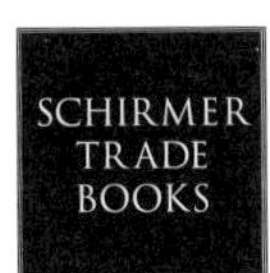

A Part of **The Music Sales Group**
New York/London/Paris/Sydney/Copenhagen/Berlin/Tokyo/Madrid

Schirmer Trade Books
A Division of Music Sales Corporation, New York

Exclusive Distributors:
Music Sales Corporation
257 Park Avenue South, New York, NY 10010 USA

Music Sales Limited
8/9 Frith Street, London W1D 3JB England

Music Sales Pty. Limited
120 Rothschild Street, Rosebery, Sydney, NSW 2018, Australia

Order No. SCH 10157
International Standard Book Number: 0-8256-7318-6

Cover Design: Josh Labouve

Cartoons courtesy of *The New Yorker*

Printed in the United States of America

Library of Congress Cataloging-in-Publication Data
Erickson, J. Gunnar, 1946-
The independent film producer's survival guide : a business and legal sourcebook / Gunnar Erickson, Harris Tulchin, Mark Halloran.— 2nd ed.
p. cm.
Includes index.
ISBN 0-8256-7318-6 (pbk. : alk. paper)
1. Independent filmmakers—Legal status, laws, etc.—United States. 2. Motion pictures—Law and legislation—United States. I. Tulchin, Harris. II. Halloran, Mark E. III. Title.

KF4298.Z9E75 2005
344.73'099—dc22

2004016968

TABLE OF CONTENTS

To Barbara, Kyle and Brent.
Gunnar Erickson

I would like to dedicate this book to my parents, Abraham and Natalie, my wife Carla, my children, Skyler, Talor, and Brett, my brother David, my mother and father-in-law Fred and Joyce Cowan, my aunt Thelma, Uncles Eli and Bernie, and all my other aunts, uncles, nieces and cousins, my brothers-in-law Keith and Robby, my sister-in-law Aline, and all my loved ones, friends, and business colleagues who have supported and motivated me throughout my life. Thank you for exhibiting compassion and honesty and for setting examples that I have tried to follow. My deepest love and thanks.
Harris Tulchin

To Gordon Stulberg, who taught me that keeping your ethics and achieving success in Hollywood are not incompatible, and to Ashley and Jessica Halloran, who taught me that love and family are more important than career success.
Mark Halloran

Acknowledgements

This book is a distillation of an aggregate of over 60 years of entertainment law practice. Through this journey certain clients and business people have been inspiring and helpful.

Teaching comes in many guises. Gunnar Erickson wants to acknowledge what he has learned from Hank West, Al Franken, Reg Gipson, Ron Bass, Alan Levine, Peter Locke, Beth Polson, Orly Adelson, Rod Taylor, Kate Johnson and his two coauthors.

Harris Tulchin would like to thank his coauthors for their inspiration and sharing their knowledge and expertise over the course of their careers along with Nick Stiliadis, Barry Hirsch, George Hayum, Geoff Oblath, Phylis Geller, Jonathan Dana, Mike Holzman, Jeffrey Ringler, Greg Bernstein, Mark Litwak, and Ron Merk, for believing in him and giving him opportunities to learn and excel.

Mark Halloran thanks Bob Geary, Jonathan Dana, Bart Rosenblatt, Al Corley, Bill Bernstein and Tom Pollock.

This book could not have come to fruition without the help of our publisher, Schirmer Trade Books, especially Steve Wilson, Dan Earley, Larry Birnbaum, Andrea Rotondo, and Len Vogler.

Special thanks go to Igor Meglic and Ron Merk for staging, arranging and photographing the authors.

Thank you to *The New Yorker* for permission to license some of their wonderful cartoons.

In putting the book together we also faced the gargantuan task of putting the text and forms together. Our thanks go to Kelly Choo at Halloran Law Corporation; to Monica Danner at Manatt Phelps & Phillips; and to Paul Hazen, Devin Valdesuso, Josh Ryan, Robert Yu, Ed Brancheau, Simon Newfield, Hart Comess-Daniels, and Jenny Ao at Harris Tulchin and Associates.

For more information on the book and for contracts on CD, please visit our Website *www.medialawyer.com.*

About the Authors

From left to right: Harris Tulchin, Mark Halloran, and Gunnar Erickson.

Gunnar Erickson

Gunnar Erickson currently practices entertainment law with Manatt, Phelps & Phillips in Los Angeles. He is a graduate of Stanford University and Yale Law School. He has been active with the UCLA Entertainment Law Symposium and taught Entertainment Law at Pepperdine Law School. He frequently speaks and writes about entertainment matters.

Harris Tulchin

Harris E. Tulchin is founder and Chairman of Harris Tulchin & Associates, Ltd., with affiliated offices worldwide. He is a graduate of Cornell University and Hastings Law School and has specialized in entertainment production, finance, distribution, communications, and multimedia law since 1978. He has lectured extensively at forums such as UCLA, the American Film Institute, Independent Feature Project, The Sundance Producer's Conference, the Cannes, Toronto, Los Angeles Independent, Hollywood, Venice, Edinburgh (Scotland) and numerous other film festivals, and has published numerous articles on entertainment law. He has served as Senior Vice President of Business Affairs and General Counsel for Cinema Group; General Counsel and Head of Business Affairs for KCET Television; Senior Counsel for United Artists; Director of Business Affairs at MGM Television; and Counsel for American

International Pictures and Filmways Pictures. In addition, Mr. Tulchin acts as an expert witness in entertainment litigation, is an adjunct professor of law at Southwestern University Law School, is an American Film Marketing Association arbitrator, serves as a producer's representative on scores of completed films, as well as film projects, and has served as Executive Producer of nine feature films, including the critically acclaimed *To Sleep With Anger*, distributed by Sony and Goldwyn, and *Guy*, financed and distributed by PolyGram.

Mark Halloran

Mark Halloran is a principal of Halloran Law Corporation. In his studio days, Mark was Vice President, Feature Business Affairs at Universal Pictures, and Business Affairs Counsel at Orion Pictures. In private law practice, Mark was a founding partner of Alexander, Halloran, Nau & Rose, and Erickson, Halloran & Small. Mark specializes in entertainment financing, production, and distribution, and acts as an expert witness in film, television, and music litigation. Mark is co-author of *The Musician's Guide to Copyright* (Charles Scribner's Sons) with Gunnar Erickson and Ned Hearn, and the current *The Musicians Business and Legal Guide* (Jerome Headlands Press/Prentice-Hall). He is co-chair of the SC Institute on Entertainment Law and Business and serves on the Board of Directors of the Los Angeles Chamber Singers.

INTRODUCTION

The rise of independent films has led to an explosion of possibilities for independent producers. Mel Gibson's *The Passion of the Christ* may have been the most profitable to date, but from *Blair Witch Project* to *Sex, Lies and Videotape* to *The Usual Suspects* to *Crouching Tiger, Hidden Dragon* to *My Big Fat Greek Wedding*, some of the most original, interesting, and profitable films in recent memory have come from independent producers based in the United States and abroad.

Each of us has been practicing entertainment law in Los Angeles for more than 25 years and we have been involved in the legal and business aspects of the production of hundreds of motion pictures, television programs, and video productions. We practice a very specialized, arcane area of the law. Despite growing interest in independent film production outside Hollywood, we have never seen a book that explains the nuts and bolts of the legal and business aspects of independent film development production and distribution. This is our effort to share the basic building blocks and some of the secrets.

In this book, we do not try to guide you in terms of your artistic quest and we do not deal with the technical mechanics of filmmaking. We do try to help you through the difficult task of handling the legal issues and mastering the business side of film. Balancing the inevitable tug between art and commerce is your job, but without film commerce, your art will never come into existence, much less reach an audience.

We write with some trepidation because the legal issues involved in motion pictures are very complex. It is easy to foresee situations where readers who blindly rely on this guide, in inappropriate circumstances, would suffer terrible results.

Nonetheless, we know that thousands of student films, independent features, and other motion pictures are produced every year on shoestring budgets and Visa cards by producers who cannot afford what it costs to have experienced motion-picture lawyers handle the necessary legal work. There are students who are just learning to handle a camera and are clueless about the legal requirements in making a film. We know that there are inexperienced lawyers who find themselves involved in the legal side of movie making and have few practical resources to help them. We also have come to realize that there are thousands of people who are professionally involved in filmmaking, but who have never had a clear understanding of the business and legal processes; they have had to suffer what seem to be pointless delays and annoyances at the behest of lawyers.

This guide is designed for all of these readers, but it is not a do-it-yourself kit. We beg you to get experienced advice to supplement it. While it may give you the tools to do some of the work, we hope this book will help you to understand when you need professional assistance. It can guide you to use lawyers more efficiently. As we lead you through the processes, we will point out areas where it would be shortsighted not to rely on experienced lawyers or other professionals who comprise your film-business team.

Some Latin jargon survives in the legal trade, particularly when no English term expresses the idea quite as precisely. "Caveat" is one of those terms, which can be crudely translated as a cover-your-back warning. We have a couple of caveats to using this guide.

First, we practice entertainment law in the Los Angeles area. The advice here reflects custom and practice in the entertainment industry here. As the independent film business has internationalized, we have increasingly needed to supplement our own knowledge with advice from lawyers from Rio de Janeiro to Tokyo to Munich. Some legal principles discussed here will not apply outside California and more will be inapplicable outside the United States. You must make certain that the advice you get covers where you are making your film and where you plan to exploit it. In the United States, statutes (legislative law) and case law (reported cases published in legal books) regulate contract law, which is the dominant set of legal principles that govern entertainment practice. They operate on a state-by-state basis, so New York law may be different from California law in ways that will impact your picture.

Second, we have also simplified much of what we say here. There are exceptions and nuances to much of what we write, which we have ignored for clarity and brevity. We emphasize the most common situations, and we apologize in advance to our legal brethren who will recognize where we have turned our back on subtleties in an effort to keep this guide as simple and as practical as we can.

In order to make this book more useful, we sometimes discuss films and the specific transactions that we were involved in as examples. As lawyers, we are constrained by attorney-client privilege, which prevents us from disclosing the specifics or details of matters that our clients do not want us to disclose, or which are not public knowledge. We apologize for occasionally being vague about the specifics of an example.

This guide starts with a discussion of the many functions that define an independent film producer. We then proceed through the steps involved in putting a film together. The emphasis is on the deals that need to be made. We give you an idea of the nature of various deals, point out the critical issues and provide parameters that deals typically fall within and how they are documented.

The discussion generally assumes that the production is an independent theatrical movie. But the legal production work is much the same for television programs, Internet productions, animation, and any other audiovisual productions. This book also includes the basic forms that are required in the course of doing the legal production work for most motion pictures. These forms are helpful to understand typical deals in detail. They can also be adapted for use on your picture. In fact, we offer these forms and additional forms on a CD-ROM available at *www.medialawyer.com.* But we strongly advocate that you engage an experienced entertainment lawyer to assist you in all the legal work. The stakes are high. Complications and thorny legal problems invariably arise in the real world. But understanding all of these deals and issues will help you to make better use of your lawyer. In our own practices, we are delighted to have knowledgeable clients. We hope this book can raise the level of sophistication of independent producers and result in more and better independent films being financed, produced, and distributed.

One last thought. Although in many cases we paint the bad results that can come from not properly managing the legal and business aspects of independent film, we have tried to balance these with stories of success. The one basic rule is this: Better to face your legal and business challenges than ignore them. Making an independent film is one of the most challenging and rewarding tasks anyone can undertake. We wish you great success and hope that this book adds to it.

—Gunnar Erickson, Harris Tulchin, Mark Halloran

MAKING AN INDEPENDENT FILM

Since this book is written for independent film producers, we are led to a threshold question: What is an independent film producer?

Any definition of "film producer" is inexact at best. But there is a reason for this. Producers, like others involved in the film business, are defined by what they do. Producers have many functions and their contributions are simultaneously more complex and more ephemeral than the functions of actors and directors.

Even the courts have had a difficult time defining "producer." While at Orion Pictures, Mark—one of the authors of this book—was the lawyer in charge of the legal production work for the Richard Gere/Francis Ford Coppola film *The Cotton Club,* released in 1983. A disgruntled "coproducer" of that film tried, at the last moment, to block the opening of the film because she had not received a coproducer credit. The coproducer filed an action in Federal Court in Los Angeles seeking a court order to prohibit the release of the film in theaters. She argued that the public would be misled if the film were released without her credit. The Orion lawyers argued, and the Federal Court agreed, that the public would not be misled since no one knew what a producer (or coproducer) did! The result would have been different, the court said, if Orion had launched the film with the credit "An Alfred Hitchcock Film," and Hitchcock had not directed the film.

When we discuss independent films, we are referring to pictures designed for release in movie theaters that are not produced, financed, and distributed throughout the world by one of the eight major studios: Disney, Dreamworks, Fox, MGM, Paramount, Sony, Universal, and Warner Bros. Typically, independent pictures are financed by "pre-sales" contracts from distributors that are discounted and cash flowed by a bank, and often supplemented by private money. And, if they qualify, from subsidies and tax incentives. The budgets range from tens of thousands of dollars to over $30 million, but the vast majority are produced for $200,000 to $10,000,000.

Independent film producers are a relatively recent phenomenon. Up until the 1960s, virtually all films were produced by major studios. With the advent of non-studio films (such as *Billy Jack* and *Easy Rider*), independent film producers began to supplement studios in terms of producing movies (but the major studios continued to dominate development, financing, and distribution). Today there are an estimated 1,500 independent films produced each year in the United States.

The most important difference between an independent producer and a producer who works on a studio picture is that the independent producer is responsible for handling an entire additional set of legal, business, and financial roles that are customarily handled by studios on pictures produced, financed, and released by the majors. Failing to understand those added roles can lead to disaster. One of us recently had an interview with potential clients who had produced a parody of a recent film phenomenon and had done so on a shoestring budget. They had an offer for ten times their negligible investment from a British video distributor, but there were a few problems. The title was not available for use without potential legal jeopardy to the video distributor. There were no written agreements with anyone involved, so the potential clients could not establish the chain of title. Additionally, with the title problems and chain of title problems, the production could not qualify for errors and omissions insurance, which the U.K. video distributor would surely require. The film was, in a word, undistributable. To go back and fix the problems may have been possible, but would have cost the filmmakers substantially more than the movie cost itself. They went away, sadder but wiser and with no hope of having their film distributed.

A great idea for a movie is worthless without proper business and legal implementation. In implementing the business and legal management of producing a movie, there are seven primary functions the independent film producer has: (1) business owner/manager, (2) project developer, (3) project packager, (4) project financier, (5) physical film producer, (6) distributor/distribution arranger, and (7) distribution and asset manager.

1. *Business Owner/Manager.* If you have never set up and operated a business, you will be dazed by the myriad rules, regulations, and forms to fill out. You additionally face legal risks of being sued by third parties, employees, and independent contractors. In Chapter 6, Finance Agreements, we discuss the basic steps in setting up your business. A fundamental management function of an independent producer is making deals. In Chapter 4, Getting the Green Light, we discuss the basics of deal making, including the necessary terms to negotiate and what paperwork is required.

2. *Project Developer.* You must develop your project to the point when it can be produced and financed. Your job in this role is to write or supervise the writing of a screenplay that can attract a director, cast, and financing. If your screenplay is to be based on material owned by someone else, you must option or acquire the rights. If you are partnered with, or hiring writers, you must own the screenplay that is created. Legal representation is mandatory at this stage. The development process is discussed in Chapter 2, The Development Process.

3. *Project Packager.* Once you have a completed screenplay, you must package the film and secure the financing. The film package consists of the script, director, producer (you), and cast, as well as the budget and production schedule. The budget and schedule are malleable to some extent and can be changed and adapted as time goes by. However, it is a good idea to have a budget range in mind during the development process. You cannot shoot a huge action piece with special effects and costumes on a $2 million budget.

   The most difficult part of the packaging process is attaching the director and actors. Although it is simpler to act or direct yourself, it is unlikely that your directing and acting talent will attract financiers. The fundamental issues are when and how to get talent. Chapter 4, Getting the Green Light, gives some guidance on appropriate strategies.

4. *Project Financier.* Once you attach a director and star, you still need production financing. Sources of independent financing are family and friends, equity investors, distributors (domestic studios and foreign distributors and sales agents), banks, foreign subsidies, and tax incentives; all are discussed in Chapter 5, Financing. You absolutely need a lawyer during this process to navigate through the financial minefields.

5. *Physical Film Producer.* Once you have a script, director, cast, and financing, you are in a position to make your movie. In Chapter 6, Finance Agreements, we discuss how to set up the production, including setting up your production company, hiring employees or engaging independent contractors, setting up accounting and payroll services, becoming signatory with the talent and craft guilds, finding your locations, and clearing the script and title. These events occur during

the very hectic preproduction process, which is typically the last six to eight weeks before principal photography starts.

Once photography starts, it is your responsibility to get the best performances from your director, cast, and crew and to keep your eye on the money and the clock. Your financiers and the completion bond company will expect no less of you.

In postproduction, your job is to take the shot footage, help edit it into a storyline within your time frame (usually 90 to 120 minutes), and add and balance the music and sound effects, all the while keeping your finger on the money pulse. As discussed in Chapter 16, Delivery, it is imperative that you create and safely store all the physical elements you will need for delivery, as well as the legal documentation needed for delivery to distributors.

6. *Distributor/Distribution Arranger.* Independent producers do not act as distributors of films. Distribution is still dominated by the Hollywood-based major studios that generate more than 90% of U.S. box office, but there are also scores of smaller distributors and independent sales agents who handle independent productions. Your job is to secure the right ones for your particular film. We discuss that process in Chapter 5, Financing, and Chapter 6, Finance Agreements.

7. *Distribution and Asset Manager.* Once you have a distribution deal in place, you still have to deliver the film as discussed in Chapter 16, Delivery. "Delivery" is a technical term and consists of supplying the physical elements such as the interpositive, internegative, sound tracks, video masters, stills and slides, and the legal elements (copyright registration, rights documents, insurance, copyright and title searches, and talent agreements that meet the distributors' requirements). You may think you have finished the film but until you have supplied all of the delivery elements, you will not be paid.

   Once the film is delivered, there is still the job of managing the distribution. It is likely you will be involved in advertising and marketing decisions. You'll have input on the trailer, marketing and publicity campaigns, one-sheet (a slick poster-size sheet that includes the artwork and credits for your film), and other advertising materials, and, in some cases, how the picture will be released in theaters. You must also make sure that your foreign sales agent makes appropriate deals, delivers the film to its subdistributors, collects the money, and remits your share to you. There are also accounting functions you must provide during distribution. If you make a worldwide deal, your worldwide distributor will typically assume the tasks of paying guild residuals and profit participations. More likely, however, you will have the accounting job and will have to account to profit participants and pay residuals.

After you deliver your film, you must monitor the accounting statements from the distributors and manage the remaining assets that are not being managed by the distributor. Music publishing is an often overlooked asset. If you own the music in your film, and there is a soundtrack album, or the film is exploited on television, you can receive additional revenues as the owner of the music. Again, managing this asset is best done by professionals (preferably a music publisher). This is discussed in Chapter 13, Music in Film.

Another asset to manage is the right to prepare "derivative" productions that stem from your movie, such as remakes, sequels, and television programs. Often your domestic distributor (but rarely your foreign sales agent unless they put up financing) will have a negotiation position on these rights. Unless your production is a hit, it is unlikely these assets will be worth anything. Still, a film relatively unknown outside of France, *La Cage aux Folles,* spawned both a stage play and a successful remake *(The Birdcage).*

The Hollywood Studio Deal for Producers

The job of the independent producer is perhaps the hardest and least appreciated in the film business. That leads to the question of why do it, or more specifically, why not try to produce through a studio. There are several advantages to producing pictures for a major studio. First, the amount of money available to make the film probably increases more than tenfold. The best cinematographers, costumers, and other technical personnel, not to mention stars, come within your reach and, of course, the picture will get a theatrical release commonly backed by millions of dollars in advertising and promotion. Also, your fee will be substantial and guaranteed. These are undeniable advantages and most successful independent producers aspire to move into studio pictures. For example, Joe Roth, who ran both Disney and Fox, got his start in the film business producing *Kentucky Fried Movie,* a quintessential independent film.

But the studio route has several downsides for tyro producers. The first is that it is difficult to get access and be taken seriously by a studio unless you have a track record. The second is that Hollywood drives very tough deals for inexperienced producers. The typical deal for a producer fortunate enough to control a book or script that a studio wants, is for the producer to receive a $25,000 development fee. One-half is paid when some defined conditions, such as having the underlying motion picture rights (such as to a novel or comic book) assigned to the studio, hiring a writer (and making sure the contract is signed), and signing your contract, are satisfied. The other half is paid when the studio either abandons the project or decides to make the picture. The development fee is credited against a producer fee of probably $100,000 to $250,000, which only gets paid if the studio chooses to make the picture (the odds of this are about one in ten). You will also get a modest share of profits, typically 2.5% to 10%. We discuss net profits at length in Chapter 14, Profits.

Your studio agreement will also include an almost inconceivably harsh provision called the "pay-or-play" provision that allows the studio to remove the producer at any time and the producer gets no credit, no profits, and just the producer fee (and in egregious cases, just the producer's development fee). Additionally, because studios are major conglomerates and the bottom line is king, they continually set up obstacles that require you to prove to them that your movie will be a financial hit when it is released. Unless you have the skill and tenacity to maneuver their roadblocks, your movie will probably be one of the thousands that languish in "development hell" and never get made.

Finally, in the majority of cases, other producers will join the picture, either assigned by the studio or accompanying the stars or director. Any producer credit to the first-timer will be diluted. The actual control of the film is usually taken away and placed in the hands of others and decisions will be made without a serious effort to involve the novice producer.

There is little remedy to this treatment. Charm, brazen enthusiasm, and political adeptness can help, but in retrospect most successful Hollywood producers chalk up their first studio producing experience as paying their dues. Even more experienced producers who set up development deals and ultimately earn their $25,000 development fee, rarely make a movie. So, despite the small budgets and the many challenges of the independent film world, it is still a place where you can be a real filmmaker and where you can keep a meaningful piece of the profits on a commercially successful project.

The Entertainment Lawyer

The balance of this book is devoted to the business strategies and legal mechanics of producing an independent film, but before we start the step-by-step, we are going to give you some candid information about entertainment lawyers and some advice on when and how to use them.

A harsh reality of working with entertainment lawyers is that they are expensive, and often, when you need them most, you are not yet making money. It is endemic to independent filmmaking that money is always in short supply. We will talk about legal fees a bit below, but we want to tell you some even more important things first. There are only a tiny number of entertainment lawyers in the entire world who have both the experience and connections to be able to do a first-class job for an independent film producer, and many of them are not going to be enthusiastic about representing you, regardless of whether you will pay their fee.

Fewer than 25 law firms in the United States have attorneys who really know how to take an independent film producer all the way through the process from development through distribution. The best lawyers who work in the independent film arena not only know how to draft contracts, but also the business and the players. They know which sales agents can actually sell and which ones do not pay. They know what kind of backend (profit participation) a powerful agency like Creative Artists Agency will ultimately accept, as opposed to ask, for its star clients. They know which completion bond companies get nervous and are prone to take over a picture, and they know thousands of other invaluable bits of information.

These lawyers are subspecialists within a small legal specialty. Most entertainment lawyers and law firms represent actors, writers, and directors who make Hollywood studio pictures or work in television or music. They may have pretty good ideas of how independent pictures are put together, but because most struggling independent producers never do more than struggle and never succeed in getting their film made, most entertainment lawyers choose not to represent them. Those few who specialize in independent films are very selective about the projects they represent. We certainly are.

You should be aware of the criteria we apply when we analyze a submitted project, because our approach will be shared by other experienced counsel. If it is a completed film, it is easy—we meet the filmmakers and screen the film with a view as to whether we could add enough value via our services in the marketplace to make it worthwhile for the client. If it is an undeveloped project, the process is more complicated. At a minimum, we need to know the idea or underlying work, who is attached, how much financing is available, and the ultimate marketing and distribution plan. When meeting with potential lawyers at the development stage, you should be prepared to discuss your long-term strategy to show you know what you are doing.

You should always deal with someone who is knowledgeable and respected in the independent film world, or whatever you pay them will be a double financial disaster for you. You will waste the money you pay them in fees, and you will waste at least part of the development or production money you spend under their guidance. If your lawyers cannot save you more money on your movie than they receive in fees, you have the wrong lawyers. For example, one of us recently did a quick survey of the international market value of a proposed independent film for a client who was asked to guarantee $1 million in offers to two stars. We found that the stars' name value would not support the budget of the picture, so we saved our client from throwing $1 million into a black hole.

It would be improper for us to provide a list of recommended law firms or lawyers, but virtually all of them are in Los Angeles and New York, with several in Toronto and in London. We suggest contacting other independent producers and asking for suggestions. But remember, just as there are a lot of wanna-be film producers and movie actors, there are a lot of wanna-be entertainment lawyers. While your Uncle Ralph may be a brilliant corporate lawyer, he is probably not the guy to help get your film made.

You should also note a basic distinction. Entertainment lawyers who do what we do are called "transactional" or "contract" lawyers. However, there are also entertainment litigators who file lawsuits and appear in court. There are an elite group of perhaps five or six top entertainment litigation law firms in Los Angeles that dominate the high-stakes entertainment litigation landscape. Most entertainment lawyers do not combine the two specialties, although there are a few.

Ideally, you will have found your lawyer before you start the development process, but because of cost factors and inaccessibility, you may not get to the lawyer until you are trying to conjoin the talent and financing. At that time, you may have a couple of names and telephone numbers for suggested lawyers. We urge you to be prepared before making the call. Lawyers, particularly good lawyers, get calls from prospective clients all the time. Their assistants' most important job is to protect their bosses from wasting time, so you first have to get past assistants. Saying truthfully that so-and-so (another client or a recognizable lawyer in the independent film world) suggested you call, can be helpful.

When you speak to a lawyer, you must succinctly explain: (1) who you are and what your film background is; (2) the nature of your project (for example, independent film with a $2- to $3-million budget); (3) what creative elements are involved (e.g., Ron Bass wrote the script based on a Raymond Chandler story, Luis Brunuel has committed to direct, and Ray Liotta has read the script and expressed interest); (4) the status of the financing (e.g., you have an equity investor who is considering putting up half the budget); and (5) what you want the lawyer to do (e.g., negotiate the director deal, make a deal for Liotta, and help find a sales agent). Although your job in the initial call is to sell yourself, you should remember that lawyers are trained to detect deception and inexperience. Deception is more heavily penalized than inexperience.

Have your act together. The lawyer will size you up and want to see how you handle yourself. If you are poised and convincing with him or her, you can be poised and convincing with agents, bankers, and others. The lawyer is also going to calculate the odds of your picture being made. Unless it is a very intriguing project, those odds will have to be much better than fifty-fifty, or the lawyer will probably offer you polite encouragement; suggest that you come back once it is closer to production; and wish you "good luck."

Fee arrangements can take several forms. Hourly billing is the most traditional. Hourly fees range from around $200 per hour to $500, but often, hourly charges bear little correspondence to results. One lawyer could spend eight hours drafting a contract from scratch while another would pull a better form from his word processor and draft the contract in an hour. One lawyer may have spent 20 years to develop the relationships and credibility to make a crucial five-minute call while another churns fruitlessly for hours. A $400-per-hour lawyer may—or may not—be cheaper than a $200-per-hour lawyer, so do not let the hourly rate be your sole criterion.

The second common fee arrangement is a flat fee. You can expect to pay $25,000 to $100,000 (as part of the budget) for competent legal production work on an independent picture depending on the complexity of the production. There can be additional charges for the financing and distribution work. Complicated financing structures are often separate, additional fees. If you make a flat fee arrangement, it is important for you and for the lawyer to have a written understanding of what legal work is included within the flat fee. Litigation, immigration work, tax matters, and other nonentertainment specialty work is not normally included, but you should get a clear understanding of who will handle areas such as music clearances and clip clearance.

The third fee arrangement is a percentage deal where the lawyer gets a percentage of the revenues from the film. This is most common where the lawyer helps find distribution and is typically combined with an hourly or flat fee component. For example, the lawyer might agree to do the legal work on the film for a fee of $30,000, plus 5% of the distribution revenues.

The fourth arrangement is the so-called reasonable fee, where the lawyer sets the fee after assessing the work and result. This arrangement is atypical and only works when there is a great level of trust and the fee is hard to set up front.

In addition to fees, your arrangements will require you to reimburse the attorneys for their expenditures on your behalf. These will include filing fees, copyright and title searches, messengers, long-distance telephone calls, photocopies, and faxes. Costs can be significant and producers can reduce them by using their own runners for deliveries and other cost-saving efforts. Another common provision which avoids surprises on cost is for the client to approve all costs which exceed a theshold.

Three specific tips for dealing with lawyers are—pay your bills on time, and never say a call is urgent unless it really, really is, and never call his or her cellphone on weekends unless it's really, really urgent.

How you work with your lawyer will depend on your experience and personality. The entertainment lawyer's expertise in making contract language precise and covering virtually all eventualities designates the lawyer as the person to handle those tasks. Either the producer or lawyer can do the negotiating. We get into that process in Chapter 3, Deal Making. Regardless of who negotiates the deals, the producer makes the key decisions, and the more you understand the process and the issues, the better your decisions will be. In addition to a lawyer, you will hire other people to handle many aspects of the production, but it is important that you understand what they are doing and why. You can think of yourself as CEO or captain of the ship; it all does come back to you. That is the simultaneously wonderful yet frightening part of being an independent producer.

A bedrock issue, which you must always keep in mind, is that communication is a two-way street. Most lawyers do their best to make sure that they have efficient phones, cell phones, faxes, e-mails, messenger services, and couriers. You should have the same. Always have call waiting on your home phone and cell phone. When you are traveling, do not expect your lawyer to track you down. Fax or e-mail your complete itinerary with all pertinent information and maybe even a gentle reminder as to time zone changes. Important decisions sometimes need to be made quickly in this business, so you want to make certain that you and your advisors can always reach each other.

THE DEVELOPMENT PROCESS

The development process consists of getting a screenplay to the point where it can be presented to financiers, directors, and actors in hopes of getting a green light: That all important conjunction of money and talent that signals that your movie is definitely going to be made. By far the simplest form of development is when you write the screenplay yourself, without any cowriters or partners, and you base your screenplay on your own original idea. Then, the legal aspects of the development process are easy.

The situation becomes more complicated when you base your screenplay on a preexisting work, such as a newspaper article, book, someone's life, a stage play, or videogame. That raises the initial question of whether you need to obtain rights in the underlying work or life-story rights. If the answer is 'yes,' you proceed to the question of how do you obtain those rights.

Public Domain

We will start with the first question. If you want to base your screenplay on a book, short story, play, or other literary or copyrightable work, you need permission from the copyright owner (unless the work is in the public domain). Copyright is a limited-duration monopoly and artistic works fall into the public domain and become freely usable by anyone once the copyright term runs out. For example, many of James Fenimore Cooper's books have been made into movies, and you need not ask permission from his descendants to write a screenplay or to do a movie based on *The Deer Slayer.* If, however, you want to adapt a John Grisham thriller into a movie, you need permission from Grisham or whoever controls the motion-picture rights to his book.

How do you find out if a work is in the public domain? There are books that purport to list public domain works. Unfortunately, these lists cannot be relied upon with confidence. Those books may be out of date and probably do not deal with copyrights outside the United States. Determining copyright duration is complicated and best left to your lawyer, but here are the basics. Under the 1909 Copyright Act (which was in effect until January 1, 1978), the term of the copyright began when a work was first published and continued for an initial term of 28 years and if properly renewed, a renewal term for 28 years, for a maximum copyright duration of 56 years from publication. Then the work went into the public domain. U.S. copyright law has undergone a series of changes in the last 25 years all works created or published before 1923 are public domain in the United States. Works now have a copyright duration commencing on their creation (not publication) extending 70 years after the death of the author, and there are some complicated transition issues on works created before the changes in the law. Other countries vary in the scope and duration of the copyright protection they offer. Since you must have rights throughout the world before proceeding, you must be sure the underlying work is public domain throughout the world. Some books are public domain in the United States but protected by copyright outside the United States.

If you are considering using an older work as the basis for your screenplay, a first step in determining if it is in the public domain is finding out when the author died. You can usually get this information from public libraries or from Internet research. You can also do searches of the records of the United States Copyright Office *(www.loc.gov/copyright)*. The rule of thumb is that the work is in the public domain if the author has been dead for 100 years or more.

Copyright Reports

If there is an iota of doubt about the copyright status, you must obtain a copyright report (or have your lawyer do it) from a copyright report service and have your lawyer analyze it. Three such services are Thomson & Thomson, 8383 Wilshire Boulevard, #450, Beverly Hills, CA 90211, (800) 356-8630, fax (800) 431-4031; Dennis Angel, 1075 Central Park Avenue, #306, Scarsdale, New York 10583, (914) 472-0820, fax (914) 472-0826; and Federal Research, 400 Seventh Street N.W., Suite 101, Washington, D.C. 20004, (800) 846-3190, fax (800) 680-9592. The cost of a copyright report is generally $300 to $400. These reports are not opinions as to whether or not a work is subject to copyright protection and they are not guarantees, but they do provide essential information, which is publicly available, about the author and the history of the copyrighted work that allow a lawyer to assess the copyright status.

Here are portions of a Thomson & Thomson copyright report to give you an idea of the kinds of information they provide:

COPYRIGHT REPORT — LADY CHATTERLEY'S LOVER

A search of the records of the Copyright Office, the card indices of the Library of Congress, and the records and files of this office reveals that the novel entitled *Lady Chatterley's Lover* by D.H. Lawrence was originally printed privately for the author by the "Orioli" version, and was apparently distributed in 1,500 copies. We find no record of copyright registration or subsequent renewal for this work.

Another version was published under the title *Lady Chatterley's Lover* in 1959 by Grove Press. The preface by Archibald MacLeish was registered for copyright in the name of Grove Press, Inc. as of a publication date of May 4, 1959, under entry No. A:390913. We find no record of renewal for this copyright registration.

DERIVATIVE WORKS

A French motion picture entitled *Lady Chatterley's Lover*, a work in approximately 100 minutes running time, produced by Gilbert Cohn-Seat for Regie-Orsay Film, directed by Marc Allegret, and starring Danielle Darrieuxx, was released in Paris, France in January, 1956, by Columbia Pictures under the title *L'Amant de Lady Chatterley*. We find no record of copyright registration or subsequent renewal for the subtitled version of this work.

RECORDED INSTRUMENTS

By Order Appointing Receiver in the case of *Colubmia Pictures Corporation v Lyric Theatre Corporation, Jack Linder and Seymour Linder,* Municipal Court of Los Angeles, dated May 4, 1959, recorded August 31, 1959, in Vol. 1051, pages 110-112, the Court appointed R.E. Allen as Receiver and ordered the defendants to assign to the Receiver all of their right, title and interest in the novel *Lady Chatterley's Lover*, any version thereof and any work of this title of which Jack Linder is author or proprietor, including certain rights granted to the defendants by Samuel Roth Publishing Company.

By Mortgage and Assignment of Copyright dated January 15, 1981, recorded January 27, 1981 in Vol. 1826, pages 306-317, Cannon

International, Inc., Cannon Group Inc., Cannon Films, Inc., Cannon Releasing Corporation, Cannon Productions, Inc., Cannon Television Corporation, Cinema 405, Inc., Cannon Happy Distribution Company, Inc., Cannon Sequel Corporation, and London Cannon Films, Ltd., mortgaged and assigned the copyright in the film *Lady Chatterley's Lover* to Slavenburg's Bank, N.V., as security for a loan. All rights assigned were released and cancelled by Credit Lyonnais Bank Nederland N.V., formerly known as N.V. Slavenburg's Bank, by instrument dated January 11, 1985, record April 25, 1985 in Vol. 2085, pages 334-352.

NEWSPAPER AND TRADE NOTICES

In 1933, it was reported that a French film company purchased an option on the picture rights in the novel and this option was renewed twice, but finally dropped when the company learned its contemplated picture could not be shown in the United States. *The Hollywood Reporter*, issue of October 19, 1977, reported that *Lady Chatterley's Lover* would be produced as a two-hour NBC World Premiere Movie staring Joanne Woodward, with production to start early in 1978 in England for presentation on NBC-TV during the 1978-1979 season with George Englund as executive producer and Michael Jaffe as producer for Henry Jaffe Eneterprises in association with George Englund Production and NBC-TV. *The Hollywood Reporter*, issue of February 17, 1978, reported that Michael York and James Mason would costar in this production.

Obtaining Rights

If you utilize an underlying literary work as the basis for your screenplay and you find that it is not in the public domain, you will have to get written permission from the copyright owner to create a screenplay and to produce and distribute your film. We emphasize that the permission must be in writing. This is one area where the law requires that you obtain the rights evidenced by a document signed by the owner of the rights. Some of our clients have been surprised that oral permission is worthless.

That written consent, together with the agreements signed with everyone who writes on the screenplay and the music composer and anyone else who contributes copyrightable material to the movie, comprise what is called the "chain of title." From a legal standpoint, the chain of title is the most important aspect of the whole movie-making process. Without a complete and satisfactory chain of title, no one will finance or distribute your picture.

If you have determined that the underlying work is protected by copyright, you must contact the rights holder and try to make a deal. There are two routes to tracking down rights in a literary work: You can try to reach the author directly or you can contact the publisher. Today, most book authors retain the movie rights to their books when they make publishing deals, so finding the author directly eliminates a step and can help you foster a personal and creative relationship with the author. We have found, however, that authors are sometimes difficult to track down and once found, are often slow to respond. Publishers are businesses and are usually responsive to producers who inquire about motion-picture rights. The copyright search firms we mentioned above will try to find a contact address for the author and include it in the copyright report. If that does not lead you to the author, we suggest trying one of the Internet people-finder services or contacting major author organizations such as the American Society of Journalists and Authors *(www.asja.org)* or the Authors Guild *(www.authorsguild.org)*. Publishers are relatively easy to find through telephone information. You should talk to their subsidiary rights department about optioning a book. A telephone call or e-mail often gets a quicker response than a letter. Please note that just because you cannot find the author, you cannot say, "I tried," and proceed. This is not a defense.

Fact-Based Stories

Before we go into a discussion of how deals for acquisition of rights are structured, we want to talk about a situation where the screenplay is not based on a copyrighted work, but on real events. *Monster* is an example.

To most people, it seems that the law is etched in stone: Static and hard-edged. But in reality, some areas are in flux and murky, more like gravy than granite. The law that governs the right to make motion pictures based on real people and events is in this semi-congealed state.

It used to be a legal maxim that "nobody can own history," and accordingly anyone could freely depict real people and re-create real events. It is hard to imagine publishing a newspaper if the publisher had to get everyone's consent before writing a news article. The constitutional rights of a free press were relatively sacrosanct, and the only legal limitation was that the depictions could not defame anyone or invade their right of privacy. These are two legal principles that had well-defined meanings based on many judicial cases interpreting them. A corollary to these two principles was that they only applied to living people. The dead had no right to protection against being defamed or having their privacy invaded and, in the United States, their heirs had no grounds for lawsuits.

Until recently, the legal analysis of whether there were any problems in making a movie based on real people started with seeing who was still alive. If they were still alive, you looked to see if the portrayal was unflattering or negative (which suggested that it could be defamatory) or whether it revealed personal information not previously disclosed that could be embarrassing, which sent up a red flag as to invasion of privacy. Even those problems could be overcome if the person signed a proper release. There were also possible defenses to these claims of defamation or invasion of privacy that might protect the film from damaging lawsuits.

Things have become murkier in the last two decades. There have been many well-financed lobbying efforts to pass state legislation to protect the "publicity" rights of famous people who are deceased. The State of Tennessee, for example, has legislation to protect against unauthorized uses of Elvis Presley's name and likeness. A Georgia law protects Martin Luther King, among others. Fred Astaire's widow successfully lobbied for legislation in California that expanded the rights of celebrities such as her late husband. Unlike copyright law, which is the same throughout the United States, privacy law is a patchwork quilt of many colors.

Because federal law trumps state law, state legislators are not free to infringe on the First Amendment rights of free press. Cases have held that the right of free press includes the right to report on real events and real people. That right extends beyond just newspapers to television reporting and, since there is no clear dividing line, further to protect docudramas and movies based on real people. The countless Kennedy family miniseries and movies like *Erin Brockovich* and *The Right Stuff* are examples. The courts have further bolstered this First Amendment protection by showing more tolerance for defamation and invasion of privacy towards people they call "public figures" than towards "private figures." Public figures include politicians, government officials, celebrities, and other people who voluntarily put themselves in the public spotlight. The courts think that one price of fame is needing a thick skin. Nonetheless, the rash of celebrity protection legislation has pushed against these free speech principles. Making a movie today based on famous deceased celebrities such as Marlon Brando or Marilyn Monroe is likely to involve legal claims.

A second relatively new legal complication in this area is what are called "Son of Sam Laws." These derive from an infamous 1977 serial murder case in New York. The convicted perpetrator, David Berkowitz, who used the moniker "Son of Sam," tried to sell the exclusive story of his life to a book publisher. The public outcry against a murderer profiting from selling an account of his crime prompted the New York legislature to pass a "Son of Sam" law that gave crime victims or their heirs the right to seize any money a criminal might generate by selling the story of the crime. A majority of states quickly put similar laws on their books.

These laws suffered a setback in 1991 when the U.S. Supreme Court reviewed a case involving Henry Hill, a criminal whose story formed a basis for Nick Pileggi and Martin Scorsese's *Goodfellas.* The court struck down the New York "Son of Sam" law as an infringement of free speech rights, but New York quickly reworked its law in a way to avoid the constitutional objection, and again most other states followed suit. California's "Son of Sam" law has been challenged in a case involving the kidnapper of Frank Sinatra, Jr., so this is a rapidly changing area of the law. The upshot is that it can be legally very tricky to make a deal with someone convicted of a crime to portray them in a movie. That is not a problem for producers who abhor the idea of paying money to a Charles Manson or Tonya Harding, but for many projects, it can pose a problem. Even criminals can be defamed if they are portrayed falsely.

Because of those various pressures, the law is sliding towards less freedom to make movies based on real people and some foreign countries particularly those in Western Europe, provide legal protections beyond those found under United States law. If you want to base a film on real or thinly fictionalized real people, you must get competent legal advice at the earliest stage of your project.

When you fill out the application for errors and omissions insurance, which will be required by your financiers and distributors, you will be asked whether the picture depicts any real people or disguised versions of real people. Changing real people's names to fictitious names in and of itself does not guarantee immunity. If your script depicts real people, the insurance company will subject the application to special scrutiny. They will engage an outside lawyer who will read your script and will want to discuss the clearance issues with your lawyer. The insurance company will want the writer to supply an annotated script that lists the factual references that support the events portrayed in the script. They will want line-by-line footnotes that indicate whether the action is based on fact (with documentation of proof) or is fictional. In addition to the annotated script, they will want a list of all the characters that indicates which are entirely fictional and which are based on real people. As to the real people, they will want confirmation that you have signed releases from everyone or failing that will expect a convincing explanation of why a release is not necessary.

In order to be prepared for the errors and omissions application process, you must think about those issues at the inception of your project. Before anyone even prepares the earliest treatment for the script, you have to work with a lawyer to analyze where you need releases and what errors and omissions problems you face. You want to get the releases early, and not after-the-fact when you have less leverage. The easiest releases to get are from the good guys—the people who may be the most central to the story and have heroic-type roles. The difficult releases are from the bad guys—not just criminals, but people like allegedly corrupt cops, callous business moguls, and incompetent doctors. These people are unlikely to sign releases that allow you to defame them. They will sue in a heartbeat. An experienced entertainment lawyer can help you shape a fact-based story in a way that gives you the creative freedom to tell a powerful story, but avoids the danger of developing a script that cannot be insured.

Satire and Parody

Believe it or not, judges sometimes have a sense of humor and there are well-established legal principles that permit parodies and satire of both people and copyrighted material. Think how less interesting our culture would be without Weird Al Yankovich and *Saturday Night Live.* There are limits, of course, and you run into particular trouble if your parody or satirical piece suggests that it originated from the same source as the work that it is based on.

This is an area where you should talk to a good lawyer early in the process to get guidance. Do not assume that just because you make fun of a character protected by copyright (like James Bond) that this is a "fair use" for which you do not need permission. There are no hard-and-fast rules in the parody and satire area, and a prophylactic talk with a lawyer is a necessity, not a luxury.

We have now discussed situations where you want to develop a screenplay based on underlying literary works and on life rights. Occasionally there is a combination of the two: You want to base your movie on a nonfiction book about real people. *Seven Years in Tibet* and *The Right Stuff* are examples. In these situations, you must make a deal for the the motion picture rights in the book and also do a careful analysis and get any necessary life rights. You cannot assume that the book author or the publisher cleared the life rights and that you automatically get the benefit by acquiring motion-picture rights to the book. It is very rare that a book author obtains life releases that will allow a film producer to make a picture that depicts the real people in the book.

Optioning Rights

The custom in the motion-picture business is that when a project is based on an existing property or life story, the production company initially options the underlying rights. The reason for this is simple economics; the cost of the option is lower than the cost of buying the rights, and at the development stage you do not know if the movie will be made or not. When the underlying work is copyrightable, the option agreement must be in writing and must be signed by the person who owns the underlying work. Since life-story rights are not protected by copyright, there is no formal requirement under copyright law that life-story rights be signed. However, in order to complete the chain of title, financiers, insurance companies, and distributors will insist that life-story rights agreements are, in fact, signed or that you demonstrate that you can proceed without permission.

Unless the underlying work is covered by the Writers Guild of America Basic Agreement, discussed below, there is no minimum legal requirement as to how much money must be paid for an option. You can option a book for a dollar or the mere promise that you will try to make the book into a movie. There is also no legal requirement that the option price be a certain percentage of the ultimate purchase price. The rule of thumb, which has countless exceptions, is that 10% of the ultimate purchase price is paid per year for the option. So you might make a deal to option a book and negotiate a purchase price of $100,000 with a payment now of $10,000, which gives you a year to decide whether you will purchase the rights. You could have a further option to pay an additional $10,000 and extend your time to decide for another year.

One issue in options is whether the initial payments reduce the ultimate purchase price. Again, there are no hard-and-fast rules. Commonly, the initial option price is deductible from the purchase price, but additional payments for extensions of time are not applicable against the purchase price. In our example, if the initial $10,000 option fee was applicable against the purchase price, you could exercise the option and acquire the rights by paying a further $90,000. If it was not applicable, you would have to pay $100,000 to purchase the rights, so the final cost of the book would be $110,000.

The term of options is usually a minimum of one year, but can be two to three years. The convention at Hollywood studios, these days is for an initial 18-month option with an 18-month extension. This may seem like a long time, but time passes quickly and a producer does not want to run out of time on the option before the picture gets a green light.

There are no rules for setting the price for underlying rights. It can depend on prior deals for the same writer, the subject matter, other producers' interest, or myriad other factors.

Independent producers usually option screenplays rather than books because it is hard for them to compete with studios on bestselling books and it is usually expensive to hire a writer to adapt a book. Optioning a screenplay also gets you closer to a green light faster. At the time you negotiate an option, you may have no idea what the ultimate budget will be or how much financing you can raise. One formula for independents is to set the purchase price as a percentage of the budget. The typical range is 1% to 3%. The definition of the budget should be set forth with particularity and include details of whether it includes contingency and finance charges. It is also common to set a "floor" (minimum price to be paid) and a "ceiling" (maximum price to be paid). For independent pictures with budgets in the $2- to $3-million range, the floor purchase price on an optioned screenplay hovers around $50,000 to $75,000 and the ceiling around $150,000 to $200,000. The range for books is broader: Perhaps $10,000 to $250,000. If you are making a mini-digital video picture for less than $100,000, you have to negotiate a much lower floor.

One tricky issue on these percentage deals is handling the exercise of the option if the budget has not been completed. We recently saw a 2% deal where there was no floor. The producer tried to buy the rights for $800 by claiming the budget was $40,000 even though the picture was not ready to shoot and the $40,000 figure was absurdly low. The agent sent the check back. The failure to deal with this can be fatal. One simple solution is to provide that the floor amount is paid upon exercisee of the options as an advance against the ultimate purchase price and the difference is paid once the budget is determined.

In addition to the cash purchase price, an option agreement will provide for a percentage of profits to be paid. This is usually in the range of 2.5% to 5% of the net profits for a book or 5% for a screenplay if the writer gets sole writing credit or 2.5% if shared credit. This is discussed in detail in Chapter 14, Profits.

If an option is not exercised, the producer has no further rights in the underlying work, but does continue to own any screenplays the producer has commissioned. However, the producer cannot use any part of the screenplay that is based on the underlying work without reacquiring rights in the underlying work, so those screenplays are essentially "sterile," and are often called "naked" scripts.

Most formal option agreements for copyrighted works include a Short-Form Option Agreement and Short-Form Assignment. These documents are designed to be recorded with the United States Copyright Office and not to reflect the material financial points agreed to by the parties. Recording the Short-Form Option Agreement gives the world notice that the producer has an interest in the underlying work. The recordation of the Assignment puts the world on notice that the transfer of motion-picture rights has taken place. If these formal requirements are accomplished and there is a competing transfer that is recorded later, the producer who recorded first should prevail.

Instead of an option agreement, a producer can negotiate a quasi option agreement, which is called an "Exclusive Representation Agreement." Under this sort of agreement, the producer is exclusively authorized to "shop" the underlying work; that is, the producer gets the right to go out to studios and financiers to see if he can find someone who wants to develop or produce the property, with the producer being "attached." Typically, the producer and the owner of the underlying material then work out their deals independently with the third party. They both have to be satisfied with their deals since each deal is dependent on the other deal closing. This type of agreement is used as a stop-gap when the parties do not want to go to the trouble and cost of extensively negotiating an option agreement and then finding no one who will finance development or production. The risk of these deals for the producer is that the rights holder may be unreasonable in his or her demands and blow the deal. A producer does not take this risk with an option, since it effectively controls the underlying work, so we prefer that producers option underlying works, even if it is a little more trouble and cost.

At the end of this chapter, we have included an Option/Purchase Agreement for a novel and a Life Rights Agreement. The life rights agreement includes waivers of claims of defamation and invasion of privacy. It also has other provisions that are essential to releases such as this and the form is virtually inviolate. A seemingly small change to either the option or life-story rights form would render it ineffective and worthless, so we warn you not to try to negotiate any changes on your own. If changes must be negotiated, use a lawyer who is very experienced in this area.

Writer Deals

Unless you write yourself, or have acquired a ready-to-shoot screenplay, you will have to hire a writer to adapt your underlying property into a screenplay or do revisions to your existing screenplay. The threshold question you will face in hiring a writer is whether their services will be governed by the Writer's Guild of America (WGA). The WGA is a labor organization that represents virtually all professional Hollywood writers in negotiations of a collective bargaining agreement with the major studios and independent production companies. The WGA prohibits its members from selling or optioning literary material to, or writing for any company that has not agreed to be bound by and signed the WGA Theatrical and Television Minimum Basic Agreement (WGA-MBA). That agreement contains very detailed provisions that govern most aspects of employment of a writer; everything from the minimum fees for writing, to the form of screen credits, to the format of the title page for a script. If you intend to hire a WGA member to write, you can start the process of becoming a signatory by contacting the WGA at (323) 782-4514. They also have a very informative web site at *www.wga.org*. Becoming a WGA signatory involves taking on serious responsibilities for reporting and paying residuals and otherwise carefully adhering to the requirements of the WGA-MBA. But, it is the only way to access the skills of established writers. It is crucial at this juncture to consult a lawyer regarding what entity you want to use to sign. Once a company is a WGA signatory it generally must adhere to the WGA-MGA for all of its projects regardless of whether the writer is a WGA member or not.

Whether you hire a WGA member or a nonmember, you must determine what services they will render and what you will pay. The WGA-MBA defines writer's services with some very specific terms, and it will be useful for you to know them and use them when you specify the services you want a writer to render. They are found in the WGA-MBA, but we will paraphrase them here.

"Story" is literary or dramatic material indicating the characterization of the principal characters, and containing sequence and action. A story typically runs 10 to 20 pages.

"Treatment" is an adaptation of a book, short story, play, or other literary work in a form suitable as the basis for a screenplay. It is essentially a "story" adapted from an underlying work.

"First Draft Screenplay" means the first complete draft of a script with individual scenes in continuity and with full dialogue.

"Rewrite" is a revision to a screenplay that entails significant changes in plot, storyline, or interrelationship of characters.

"Polish" is a revision to a screenplay that involves less significant changes than a rewrite.

There is not a clear line between a rewrite and a polish, but the WGA minimum payment for a polish is about half the minimum payment for a rewrite, which suggests the relative amount of work involved. It is common to engage a writer to do a "set of revisions." That normally means a rewrite, but since both a rewrite and a polish are revisions, it is better to specify a rewrite or a polish. A "dialogue polish" is a polish that focuses on dialogue changes but is not recognized as a separate species of writing step by the WGA.

The most common package of services is to hire a writer to write a first draft screenplay and a rewrite. The production company then has options to hire the writer to do a second rewrite and sometimes a polish for additional compensation.

The WGA-MBA does not allow a writer's payment to be conditioned on the producer's approval of the writing. If the writer writes the first draft screenplay and the producer does not like it, the producer still is obligated to pay the writer (unless the writer submits 90 pages of "x's"). Similarly, the WGA prohibits "speculative writing" where a writer is asked to write something and the producer agrees to pay only if he likes it or gets financing for the picture, although this rule is widely ignored.

To limit their financial exposure and to protect themselves against disappointing results from writers, producers sometimes structure "step deals." In these situations, only the first writing step is committed, and the producer has the option, but no obligation, to have the writer do the additional steps. Not unexpectedly, most writers and their agents resist these kinds of deals, but they have become more commonplace in the studio world. The WGA-MBA allows step deals but discourages them by making the minimum compensation higher if the writing is broken into optional steps than if the producer commits to a full package of writing steps.

The WGA-MBA sets minimum fees for writers' services. It does provide for lower rates for projects intended to be very low-budget films. Since the rates for low- and high-budget projects generally change on at least an annual basis, we will not list them here. When you become a signatory to the WGA-MBA, the Guild will provide you with a current schedule or you can go to the WGA Web site or call them for current minimums.

In addition to the writing fees, the producer must make a contribution to a health and welfare and pension fund on behalf of WGA writers and must pay residuals or reuse payments when the film appears on videocassettes or on television. The WGA-MBA sets forth all these in detail. Pension, health, and welfare payments generally run about 14.5%, so if you guarantee a writer $50,000 you have to pay $7,250 or so to the pension and health funds.

If you are not a WGA signatory and the writer is not a WGA member, you can freely negotiate the fees and other terms of employment. For both WGA and non-WGA deals, the typical structure is for the writer to be paid a negotiated, flat amount for the specified writing services with options for the producer to order additional revisions. That flat amount and any additional money paid for further writing is deducted from a production fee or credit bonus that is paid if the movie is made and there have been no other writers who receive credit. For example, a writer might receive a guaranteed $125,000 to write the first draft and rewrite, with a production fee or credit bonus of $275,000. If the movie is made and there have been no other writers who receive credit, the writer would receive an extra $150,000 ($275,000 less $125,000). The typical deal provides that the production fee or credit bonus is reduced by half if the writer shares credit with someone who revised his or her script. In our example, the bonus would then be $75,000. It is typical for a writer to also receive 5% of net profits for sole writing credit or 2.5% for shared credit.

The guaranteed writing fee is paid over the course of the writing. How it is broken down over the writing steps is individually negotiated but influenced by custom. Generally, 50% of the money for each step is paid on commencement of the step and 50% is paid on delivery.

The writing periods are usually scheduled with interim periods called "reading periods" that allow the producer to review what was delivered and to provide guidance on changes for the next writing step. Writing periods for a first-draft screenplay usually range from eight to ten weeks. For rewrites, the range is six to eight weeks, and for polishes, it is two to four weeks. Reading periods are usually four weeks. Sometimes the producers want more time between steps. Writers often agree to allow more time, provided they are paid the installment to start the next step at the end of the four week reading period even though the writing will be delayed until the producer provides notes. This is termed "pay and postpone."

There are basically three types of writing credit given to film writers, "Story By," "Screenplay By" and "Written By." Under the WGA-MBA, the "Screenplay By" credit is used in combination with "Story By" credit if the writer of the story is different from the writer of the screenplay or if there is an underlying work, such as a book. In these situations, the author of the book would also get a credit along the lines of "Based on the Book By." If both the story and the screenplay are written by the same writer, then the writer receives "Written By" credit.

Where there is more than one writer, the WGA-MBA has some very esoteric credit rules and woe to a producer who violates them. If you want to find out whether an entertainment lawyer really knows his stuff, ask him what the difference is between a credit that reads "Screenplay By Joe Ezterhaus and Ron Bass" and one that reads "Screenplay By Joe Ezterhaus & Ron Bass" ("and" and ampersand distinguish whether the writers wrote separately and sequentially (and) or as a team (ampersand).

If you are a signatory to the WGA-MBA, then credit is accorded pursuant to the WGA. You are required to send the WGA a Notice of Tentative Writing Credits, which is also sent to all the writers who contributed to the screenplay, as well as their representatives. The writers are then given an opportunity to challenge the credit determination. The WGA has a panel of writers who read all the materials and determine credit if there is a dispute.

If you are not a signatory to the WGA Agreement, then you must legislate how credit will be determined. There is wide variance in the credit determination mechanism in independent writer agreements. The simplest and most common is that credit will be accorded by the producer "in good faith." In other instances, there is a WGA-like mechanism that is appended to the agreement. Otherwise, the WGA credit determination mechanism is sometimes built into non-WGA agreements.

Writers' deals contain several other provisions. If the writer and producer are located in different areas, transportation and living expenses must be negotiated. The WGA requires that the producer furnish first-class transportation. Hotel and living expenses are usually tiered, based on whether the location where the writer is rendering services is low-cost or high-cost. A typical range for studio pictures is $1,000 per week at the low end to $3,000 on the high end. In the alternative, hotel accommodations are provided and the writer receives a per diem (daily cash stipend).

It is traditional that writers are "attached" and receive compensation when a derivative production that utilizes the characters created by the writer is produced. With respect to theatrical sequels and remakes, it is common for the writer to be accorded a right of first negotiation to write the screenplay, and possible payment if he does note write the screenplay For theatrical sequels, the writer typically receives a possible payment of one-half of his cash compensation and profits. For theatrical remakes, the writer typically receives one-third of the compensation and profits, based on what was received in the original deal, even if the writer does not write the screenplay.

Writer agreements also contemplate the possibility of a television series based on the movie. It is rare, but *The Fugitive* is one example. Generally, a royalty is negotiated based on the running time of the episode. A typical royalty would be $2,500 for a 30-minute episode, $2,750 for a 60-minute episode, and $3,000 for an episode over 60 minutes. The WGA legislates minimum royalties. On movies for television and miniseries, there is an hourly rate plus a cap. A typical royalty would be $10,000 per hour for the first two hours of running time, not to exceed $80,000 as the cap.

At the end of this chapter, we include a writer agreement that contains the provisions that are typically found in an agreement between a WGA signatory production company and a writer for an original screenplay that is not based on any underlying work.

Certificates of Engagement

You can see from the form that a full-scale writer agreement is a moderately lengthy document packed with legalese. Even where there is a clear agreement on the money and other basic points of the writer's deal, there will be negotiations of some of the finer points and the language. This takes time and since producers, by nature, must always be in a hurry, the entertainment business has developed short cuts to keep the legal side moving at the same pace as the creative process. We discuss deal memos and short-form agreements below, but one device is particularly prevalent in writer deals. It is called a certificate of engagement (or certificate of employment) and we provide that form at the end of this chapter.

There are some legal questions about who owns a screenplay—the producer or writer—in the absence of a signed agreement. The certificate is designed to settle the ownership issue before the writing starts, since the writer often starts writing before the formal agreement is signed. Predictably, that issue and several others are settled by the certificate in favor of the producer, but they are settled in the same manner as the formal agreement normally will settle them. It is traditional to pay the initial installment of the writing fee when the writer signs the certificate. So, certificates of engagement are common. We do, however, have some misgivings about them that we discuss in Chapter 4, Getting the Green Light.

At this stage in the development process, we assume you have obtained any necessary underlying rights and hired your screenplay writer. We want to cover two more topics before talking about packaging the movie: copyright registration and titles.

Copyright Registration and Recordation

From the earlier discussion on the public domain, you know that in the United States today the term of copyright commences when a work is created. It does not begin when the work is registered in the Copyright Office in Washington D.C. In fact, there is no requirement that a work be registered for copyright, but there are two important reasons to register. The first is to take advantage of a number of legal presumptions and benefits that come into play if there is litigation over copyright infringement, and the second is to have a public location to post your chain of title.

The Copyright Office registers and maintains records on a number of matters, including the initial registration of a copyright, notices of transfer, and any liens or other claims on the copyright. It is essentially the county recorder of documents. It provides a specific form called Form PA, which it requires to be used to register a copyright in a literary work such as a screenplay. It will also record transfers of the copyright and other documents as they are provided to it. To establish and protect your chain of title during development, you must record each link.

If you option a book, you will have the author sign the Short-Form Option we discussed earlier and send it to the Copyright Office for recordation. You can get the details on how to do that from the Copyright Office's Web site at *www.loc.gov/copyright*. Since everything registered with the Copyright Office becomes public, the entertainment business uses the Short-Form Option because it does not disclose any confidential terms such as the purchase price.

Presumably, the author or book publisher will have already registered the book with a Form PA. A copyright report by Thomson & Thomson, Dennis

Angel, or the Federal Research Corporation should show first the book registration and then the option of motion picture rights in the book to you.

You record the Short-Form Assignment once the option has been exercised and the rights purchased. Life-story rights (as opposed to books or articles written about real people) are not literary works, and Life Rights Agreements are not registered in the Copyright Office.

You must register the copyright in any screenplay that is written for you. When you hire a writer to write as your employee, or as an independent contractor to create a "specially commissioned work," the screenplay is what is called "a work made for hire" and you are considered the author of the screenplay for copyright purposes. (Since you are the author from the beginning you do not need an assigment of the screenplay.) You use Form PA for this registration even if the screenplay is based on a book or other copyrighted work. When you review Form PA, you will see that it asks if there is an underlying work and what new material the Form PA is to cover.

To extend our previous example, a copyright report would show the registration of the book, your recordation of the option, and your registration of your screenplay. If you exercised the option, the report would also show the assignment of motion-picture rights in the book to you. These are the key links in the chain of title that you have to provide to your financier and distributor. Once the film has been completed, you must register the copyright in it and again use Form PA.

Titles

Titles are interesting legal phenomena. To the surprise of many people, they are not copyrightable. Because titles do not contain sufficient artistic content, they are not eligible to be copyrighted and, in fact, the same titles have been used multiple times for songs, television episodes, short stories, books, and movies. Because of the value of well-known titles and the potential confusion to consumers, other legal doctrines, notably trademark and unfair competition, have been recruited to protect titles. In addition, the major studios and some other production companies have, by contract, established their own system for avoiding title disputes among themselves. They have a complicated registration process that allows members to reserve titles, establish priorities of use, and mediate disputes. All of the members are bound by their procedures but nonsignatories such as independents are not.

An independent filmmaker usually obtains a "title report" from Thomson & Thomson or Dennis Angel as part of the process of getting errors and omissions insurance. These reports are different from the copyright report discussed earlier, and they are based on searches for other uses of the same or similar titles in movies and otherwise in the entertainment world and also searches of trademark records to look for possible conflicts. The distributor and the insurance company want to see a clear title report on the final title selected for the movie. Title reports range in cost from $200 to $500.

OPTION/PURCHASE AGREEMENT

(Date)

(Writer)
(Agent)

Re: (Production Company)/"(Book Title)" by (Author)

Dear ______________

This will confirm the terms of the agreement between you and __________ ("Producer") relating to the published novel written by you entitled "__________" (all present and future drafts, versions and adaptations thereof are referred to collectively as the "Property"). All of Producer's obligations hereunder are subject to and conditioned upon Producer's review and approval of the chain of title of the Property, which such review and approval shall not be unreasonably withheld or delayed.

1. OPTION.

1.1 Option. Upon Producer's receipt of this agreement executed by you, you hereby grant Producer the exclusive and irrevocable option (the "Option") to acquire exclusively, perpetually and throughout the universe, all of the rights referred to in the Rights paragraph below, including the right to develop and produce one or more motion pictures or programs based upon the Property (the first of which shall be referred to as the "Picture").

1.2 Option Payment/Option Period. As consideration for the Option, Producer shall pay you the sum of **Seven Thousand Five Hundred Dollars ($7,500)** ("Option Payment"), payable promptly following the full execution of this agreement and exhibits hereto. The Option Payment shall be applicable against the Purchase Price, as denned below. The option period will initially extend from the date of your execution of this agreement for twelve (12) months ("Option Period").

1.3 First Extension of Option. Producer shall have the right but not the obligation to pay you the additional sum of **Seven Thousand Five Hundred Dollars ($7,500)** ("First Extension Payment") on or before the expiration of the Option Period in which event, the Option Period shall be extended for an additional **twelve (12)** months. The First Extension Payment shall be not applicable against the Purchase Price.

1.4 Second Extension of Option. Producer shall have the right but not the obligation to shall pay you the additional sum of **Seven Thousand Five Hundred Dollars ($7,500)** ("Second Extension Payment") on or before the expiration of the extended Option Period in which event the Option Period shall be further extended for an additional **twelve (12)** months. The Second Extension Payment shall be not applicable against the Purchase Price.

1.5 Further Option Extension. The Option Period, as it may be extended, will be automatically suspended and extended without the necessity of formal notice (provided notice shall be given to you as soon as reasonably practicable following the commencement of any such suspension or extension) by any period during which development and/or production activities based on the Property are materially interrupted, postponed or hindered by any occurrence of force majeure or during the pendency of any third-party claim that materially hampers or interrupts the development of the Picture provided, however, any such suspension or extension shall not exceed six (6) months.

1.6 Preproduction Activities. During the Option Period, as it may be extended, Producer shall have the right to engage in preproduction activities based on the Property including, without limitation, the right to seek a so-called development deal with a studio, network or other financier and/or distributor in connection with the development, production and distribution of the Picture.

1.7 Rights Frozen. Notwithstanding anything to the contrary contained herein, during the Option Period, as it may be extended, you may not "Transfer" (as defined below) any of the "Granted Rights" (as defined below) in any "Author-Written Sequels" (as defined below). Notwithstanding the foregoing, for the avoidance of doubt, you may exploit the "Publication Rights" (as defined in the Rights paragraph below) in any "Author-Written Sequels" at any time.

2. COMPENSATION.

2.1 Option Exercise/Purchase Price. Producer may exercise the Option by giving you written notice prior to the expiration of the Option Period, as it may be extended. If Producer exercises the Option, you shall be paid **two and one-half percent (2-1/2%) of the direct cost budget of the Picture with a floor of Seventy-Five Thousand Dollars ($75,000) and a ceiling of Two Hundred Fifty Thousand Dollars ($250,000) (less the Option Payment)** (the "Purchase Price"). "Direct cost budget" shall be the final production budget approved by the Producer and the completion guarantor, exclusive of bond, insurance, contingency and finance fees and shall be inclusive of the Purchase Price (provided, however, for purposes of calculating "direct cost budget" hereunder, the Purchase Price shall equal **Seventy-Five Thousand Dollars ($75,000)** irrespective of the actual Purchase Price paid to you). If the "direct cost budget" is not determined at the time of exercise of the Option hereunder, Producer shall pay you the sum of **Seventy-Five Thousand Dollars ($75,000)** as an advance against the ultimate Purchase Price as calculated upon determination of the direct cost budget. The Option shall be exercised by written notice and payment on or before the expiration of the Option Period, as same may be extended, but in any event no later than commencement of principal photography of the Picture.

2.2 Contingent Compensation. If the Picture is produced, you will receive an amount equal to **five percent** (5%) of one hundred percent (100%) of Producer's "Net Proceeds." "Net Proceeds" shall be defined, computed and accounted for in accordance with the standard net proceeds definition provided by the worldwide distributor for the Picture.

3. SUBSEQUENT PRODUCTIONS.

If Producer produces the Picture and you are not in material breach hereof, then you shall additionally receive:

3.1 For each theatrical sequel to the Picture which Producer produces, if any, an amount equal to fifty percent (50%) of the Purchase Price and Net Proceeds, with the Purchase Price payable promptly following the commencement of principal photography of the applicable sequel.

3.2 For each theatrical remake of the Picture which Producer produces, if any, an amount equal to thirty-three and one-third percent (33 1/3%) of the Purchase Price and Net Proceeds, with the Purchase Price payable promptly following the commencement of principal photography of the applicable remake.

If Producer produces a television series based on the Picture:

(i) A one (1) time only series sales bonus of **Twenty-Five Thousand Dollars ($25,000)** ("Series Sales Bonus"), payable promptly following Producer's receipt of a written, binding and noncontingent agreement with a studio or television network for the production of at least thirteen (13) episodes of such series based on the Picture, reducible prorata if less than thirteen (13) but six (6) or more episodes are ordered.

(ii) A per-episode royalty in an amount equal to **One Thousand Five Hundred Dollars ($1,500)** for each episode of thirty (30) minutes or less, or **Two Thousand Five Hundred Dollars ($2,500)** for each episode of sixty (60) minutes or less but more than thirty (30) minutes, or **Five Thousand Dollars ($5,000)** for each episode of more than sixty (60) minutes, payable promptly following broadcast of the applicable episode.

(iii) An amount equal to twenty percent (20%) of the one-time, per-episode royalty paid pursuant to the preceding paragraph for each episode of the applicable series, payable for each of the first five (5) free broadcast television reruns of such episode in the United States payable promptly following broadcast of the applicable rerun.

3.3 The royalties payable pursuant to the foregoing paragraphs, as applicable, shall be reduced by fifty percent (50%) for each episode or production which is not initially broadcast on U.S. primetime network (i.e., ABC, CBS, NBC or Fox) free television.

4. CREDIT.

You shall, subject to the provisions of any applicable guild or union agreements, be accorded credit on the Picture in substantially the form of "Based on the novel by ____________ (**Author**)" (if the title of the Picture is the same as the title of the Property) or "Based on the novel ____________ '(**Book Title**)' by ____________ (**Author**)" (if the title of the Picture is not the same as the title of the Property), in size and style of type equal to that of the screenwriter(s),
(a) on screen, on a separate card, in the main titles (if the screenwriter receives credit therein), and
(b) subject to customary exclusions and exceptions, in all paid ads issued by Producer or under its control, in which the screenwriter receives credit. If Producer incorporates any character from the Property created by you in a sequel, remake or television series, subject to applicable guild or union agreements, you shall receive credit in substantially the form "Based On the Character(s) Created by ____________ (**Author**)." All other matters relating to your credit hereunder shall be subject to Producer's sole discretion. No casual or inadvertent failure by Producer to comply with this paragraph, nor any failure by third parties, shall constitute a breach hereof. If Producer fails to accord you credit pursuant to the terms of this agreement, promptly following receipt of written notice setting forth in detail such failure. Producer agrees to use reasonable efforts to prospectively cure such failure, but nothing shall require Producer to cease using or to replace prints, negatives or other materials then in existence. Producer shall advise third parties of the credit provisions of this agreement.

5. RIGHTS.

5.1 Granted Rights. If Producer exercises the Option, then, excepting only those rights reserved under the following paragraph, all motion picture, television and all other audiovisual rights (now known or hereafter devised), and allied and ancillary rights (collectively, the "Granted Rights"), in and to the Property shall be deemed immediately, automatically, exclusively and irrevocably assigned to Producer, in perpetuity and throughout the universe. Such rights, whether now known or hereafter devised, include, without limitation, all theatrical, television (whether filmed, taped or otherwise recorded, and including series rights, subscription, pay, cable and satellite television rights), CD-ROM and interactive rights, cassette, disc and other compact device, sequel, remake, advertising and promotion rights (including the rights to broadcast and/or telecast by television and/or radio or any other process, any part of the Property or any adaptation or version thereof, and announcements of and concerning same); all rights to exploit, distribute and exhibit any motion picture or other production produced here-under in all media now known or hereafter devised; any and all so-called rental rights or lending rights; all rights to make any and all changes to and adaptations of the Property (and you hereby waive all moral rights); the right to publish up to 7500 words from the Property for advertising, publicity and promotion but not in a form for sale to the public; additional publication rights but only in connection with all productions based upon the Property (e.g., "making of," children's, picture and coffee-table books; character, merchandising, commercial tie-in, soundtrack, music publishing and exploitation rights; the right to use your name, approved likeness (with such approval not to be unreasonably withheld or delayed) and approved biographical material (with such approval not to be unreasonably withheld or delayed) in and in connection with the exploitation of the rights granted hereunder (provided, however, that there shall be no use of your name, likeness or biographical material for commercial endorsement purposes without your prior consent); and all other rights customarily obtained in connection with literary purchase agreements. You acknowledge and agree that Producer and/or its successors, assigns and designees shall own all right, title and interest, including the entire copyright, in and to any and all works produced pursuant to the rights granted by you hereunder.

5.2 Reserved Rights. Notwithstanding anything to the contrary contained in the foregoing paragraph, you hereby reserve the following rights (the "Reserved Rights") in the Property: all print, audio and electronic text publication rights (the "Publication Rights"); radio rights (subject to Producer's right to utilize radio in connection with the advertising, publicity and promotion of the Picture and any other productions based on the Picture); legitimate stage rights (not including the right to record and exhibit the recording of such stage play except the right to record for noncommercial, archival purposes); soundrecord rights (i.e., single or multiple voice audio readings/text only recordings) and all rights, including the Granted Rights, in "Author-Written Sequels" (i.e., book-length literary material other than the Property, including prequels, written by you or licensed or otherwise authorized to be written by you, using one or more of the main characters or other elements of the Property in different events from those found in the Property and the plot of which is substantially new); provided, however: you shall not use, exercise, license, dispose of or otherwise transfer (collectively, "Transfer") any of the Granted Rights in Author-Written Sequels at any time before the expiration of the period (the "Holdback Period") ending three years after the initial release or exhibition of the Picture, or five years after the exercise of the Option, whichever is earlier; and if, thereafter, you propose to Transfer any of the Granted Rights in Author-Written Sequels, you shall so notify Producer in writing. If Producer elects to negotiate for said rights, then Producer shall have an exclusive fifteen (15) business-day first-negotiation period after receipt of notice from you to negotiate with you respecting the terms and conditions relating to such rights. If you and Producer are unable to agree upon the terms and conditions thereof, then you shall be free to offer such rights to any third party, but you shall not, without first giving written notice to Producer setting forth the identity of the offerer and the terms of such third party's offer, be entitled to grant such rights to any third party on terms and conditions less favorable to you than your last offer proposed to Producer in writing, in which event, Producer shall have five (5) business days to accept such offer. If Producer fails to accept such offer, you shall be free to grant such rights to such third party. It is understood that Producer has to meet only those terms and conditions contained in an offer that shall be readily reducible to a payment of a determinable sum of money.

(i) After the expiration of the Holdback Period, and provided you have complied with the first negotiation/last refusal provisions of the foregoing paragraph, you may Transfer the Granted Rights in any Author-Written Sequel, subject to the following:

(A) You shall be entitled to Transfer the Granted Rights in only one Author-Written Sequel at a time;

(B) Such Transfer shall be conditioned upon and subject to your obtaining in writing, for your benefit (and for Producer's benefit as an express third-party beneficiary), the purchaser's express agreement not to use any "specifically identifiable elements" from the Property. For purposes hereof, "specifically identifiable elements" shall be those elements newly created by or for Producer not contained in the Property, which would identify a motion picture or other production to the general public as a sequel to, or based upon or related to any Production;

(C) Except as otherwise provided herein, each such Transfer by you of the Granted Rights in any Author-Written Sequel shall be of all such rights and not in part; and

(D) No such Transfer of the Granted Rights shall entitle the purchaser thereof to produce more than one motion picture in exercise of such Granted Rights.

(ii) After the Transfer of the Granted Rights to such one Author-Written Sequel (whether to Producer or not), provided you have again complied with the first negotiation/last refusal provisions of the preceding paragraph, you may, in accordance with subparagraphs (i)(A) through (D), Transfer (whether to Producer or not) the Granted Rights in any other Author-Written Sequel, but not until the earlier of the date three years after the first general U.S. exhibition of the first motion picture produced in exercise of the last Granted Rights Transferred or the date five years after the date of Transfer, if any, of such last Transfer of Granted Rights.

(iii) If Producer purchases the Granted Rights to one or more Author-Written Sequels and Producer, its licensee or assignee produces a Production based in whole or in part on any such Author-Written Sequel, then you shall not be entitled to any payments pursuant to the Subsequent Productions paragraph hereof respecting such Production.

(iv) You hereby acknowledge and agree that, if you assign, license or authorize any third party to write any literary material using one or more of the major characters or other elements of the Property: (a) the first-negotiation/last refusal provisions shall apply to all such literary materials, and (b) such assignments, licenses and/or authorizations shall be conditioned upon and subject to your obtaining in writing, for your benefit (and for Producer's benefit as an express third-party beneficiary), the third party's express agreement to comply with such provisions.

5.3 Confidential. You recognize the confidential nature of the terms of this agreement, and agree that neither you nor any representative on your behalf will issue written or oral publicity indicating the Option or Purchase Price, although you may announce Producer's purchase of the rights herein for an undisclosed sum. Provided such monetary terms are not disclosed, it is acknowledged that you may make incidental nonderogatory references to this agreement in connection with any publicity concerning primarily you. You may also disclose the monetary terms hereof for customary quote purposes within the context of a business deal.

5.4 General Rights. The rights granted by you to Producer hereunder are in addition to, and this agreement, whether ever executed or not, shall in no way limit, the rights (if any) with respect to the subject matter of this agreement which Producer may now or hereafter enjoy as a member of the general public.

6. REPRESENTATIONS AND INDEMNITIES.

6.1 Representations and Warranties. You represent and warrant that you are the sole and exclusive owner throughout the universe of all rights (including all rights of copyright), title and interest of every kind and nature in and to the Property; that you have the full and sole right and authority to enter into this agreement and make the grant of rights made herein; that no third party has the right (and you shall not, except as provided in this agreement, grant the right to any third party) to produce any production based, in whole or in part, upon the Property; that the Property is wholly original with you and that you are the sole author thereof; that no claims or litigation exist relating to the Property or purporting to question or adversely affecting the rights granted herein; and that, to the best of your knowledge (or that which you should have known in the exercise of reasonable prudence), the Property will not violate the rights of privacy of, or constitute a libel or slander against, or violate any common law or other rights of any person or entity; you have not entered into and shall not enter into any agreement, and that you have not made and shall not make any grants of any nature whatsoever, which would or might in any way prevent, conflict or interfere with Producer's full and complete exercise and enjoyment of each and all of the rights granted or agreed to be granted to Producer hereunder, nor shall you in any way encumber or hypothecate said rights or any of them, or do or cause or permit to be done any act or thing by which said rights or any of them might in any way be impaired.

6.2 Indemnities. Each party agrees to and shall defend and indemnify the other (and the other's licensees, successors and assigns) against and from any and all liability, loss, cost (including reasonable outside attorneys' fees) and damages incurred as the result of any breach of any representation, warranty or agreement made by the indemnifying party under this agreement. Excepting any matter arising out of or related to your breach of any representation, warranty or agreement hereunder or arising out of or related to any intentional tortious acts committed by you, Producer shall indemnify and hold you harmless from and against any and all liability, loss, cost (including reasonable outside attorneys' fees) and damages incurred arising out of or related to (1) any material added to the Property by Producer or at Producer's request, and (2) the development, production or exploitation of any production produced here-under. The Option Period and the Holdback Period shall be automatically suspended and extended during the pendency of any claim or litigation involving or relating to any representation, warranty or agreement made by you hereunder; provided that the Option Period and the Holdback Period shall not be suspended and/or extended for more than one year in connection with any claim for which an action is not commenced within one year from the notification of said claim (it being agreed that the Option Period and the Holdback Period shall be suspended and extended if an action relating to said claim is at any time commenced).

7. MISCELLANEOUS.

7.1 **No Partnership/No Obligation to Produce.** Nothing contained in this agreement shall be construed to make you and Producer partners, joint venturers or agents of one another, or (except as expressly provided herein) give you any interest whatsoever in any of the results or proceeds derived from the exercise of the rights granted or agreed to be granted hereunder. Nothing contained herein shall be deemed to obligate Producer to produce the Picture or make any other use of any right, title or interest in and to the Property acquired by Producer hereunder.

7.2 **Further Instruments.** You agree to execute and deliver to Producer such further documents as may be required by Producer (and provided to you) to further evidence or carry out the purposes and intent of this aqreement (including, without limitation, the Short Form Option and the Short Form Assignment attached hereto), and you hereby irrevocably appoint Producer as your attorney-in-fact (which appointment is coupled with an interest) with full power of substitution solely to execute, verify, acknowledge and deliver any documents you may fail to promptly execute, verify, acknowledge and/or deliver within five (5) business days after Producer's request therefore. Upon your request, Producer shall provide you with copies of documents executed by Producer on your behalf pursuant to this paragraph 7.2.

7.3 **Termination Rights.** If at any time you or any other party succeeding to your termination interest, or otherwise claiming by or through you or any other party so empowered by law, is deemed to have any right to terminate any or all of Producer's rights hereunder (the "Subject Rights") pursuant to the Copyright Act or any other laws of the United States or any of its subdivisions or of any foreign country, nothing in this agreement shall be deemed to preclude you from freely exercising said right to terminate; provided, however, to the extent allowable by law, you hereby agree not to sell, license or otherwise dispose of the Subject Rights to any party (other than Producer) on terms less favorable to you than those terms contained in your last offer to Producer, unless you first have offered such less favorable terms to Producer in writing and Producer has not, within fifteen (15) days after the offering of such terms to Producer, accepted them by written notice to you. Producer shall not be required to meet any nonmonetary terms that are not as readily performed by Producer as by any other party.

7.4 **Payments/Notices.** All notices to either party (unless and until written notice to the contrary is received) shall be given to the addresses set forth above. The date of mailing or facsimile transmission or delivery to a telegraph office or personal delivery, as the case may be, shall be deemed the date of service.

7.5 **Limitation on Remedies.** In the event of any failure or omission by Producer constituting a breach hereunder, your rights and remedies shall be limited to the right, if any, to obtain damages at law, and you shall have no right in such event to seek or obtain injunctive or other equitable relief or to rescind or terminate this agreement or any of Producer's rights hereunder. Producer shall not be deemed in breach of this agreement unless and until Producer receives written notice from you specifying the alleged breach and unless Producer fails to cure such breach within 10 business days after receipt of such notice.

7.6 **Successors and Assigns.** This agreement shall be binding upon and inure to the benefit of your and Producer's respective licensees, successors and assigns. Producer may assign or transfer all or any part of Producer's rights and obligations under this agreement to any person or entity; and, if and to the extent such assignee is a major studio, network, parent or entity acquiring substantially all of Producer's assets, Producer shall be relieved of its obligations hereunder.

7.7 **Reversion.** If Producer does exercise the Option and pay the Purchase Price to Owner in accordance with the terms hereof but principal photography on the Picture does not commence within five (5) years after such exercise and payment, all rights in and to the Property shall revert to Owner subject to a lien in favor of Producer for the Purchase Price plus interest repayable to Producer on or before the commencement of principal photography of the first production based thereon. Interest under this paragraph shall be calculated at 125% of the applicable U.S. prime rate.

7.8 **E&O.** If the Picture is produced, you shall be included as an additional insured under Producer's errors and omissions policy, if any, subject to the terms, conditions and limitations of such coverage. You acknowledge that if Producer elects to self-insure, then there shall be no obligation to obtain or maintain any coverage for you by a third-party insurer. You further acknowledge that any such coverage shall not in any way limit or restrict your agreements, representations or warranties hereunder.

7.9 **Videocassette/DVD.** Provided you are not in material breach or default hereof, you shall be provided with one (1) VHS videocassette copy of the Picture and one (1) DVD copy of the Picture (if made) upon commercial availability to the general public for your private, noncommercial use.

7.10 Premiere. Provided you are not in material breach or default hereof, you (and a guest) shall be invited to one (1) celebrity premiere (if any) of the Picture. If such premiere is more than seventy-five (75) miles from your principal residence, you (and a guest) shall be provided with reasonable hotel accommodations in connection with such premiere.

7.11 Entire Understanding. This agreement sets forth the entire understanding between you and Producer, cannot be modified except by a writing signed by the party to be charged, and shall be construed in accordance with the laws of the State of California applicable to agreements entered into and to be performed in that state; and the parties hereto hereby submit to the exclusive jurisdiction of the courts located in Los Angeles, California.

Please indicate your agreement to the terms of this letter by signing in the space provided below. If you will kindly return four (4) copies of this agreement signed together with executed exhibits, I will arrange for counterexecution and will provide you with a fully signed original. I am simultaneously sending this to our client and must reserve the right of further change and comment.

Very truly yours,
(Attorney)

AGREED AND ACCEPTED:

____
(Author)

Social Security #: ________________

Date of Execution: ___________, 200_

(Production Company)

By:____________________________
Its Authorized Signatory

PUBLISHER'S RELEASE

KNOW ALL MEN BY THESE PRESENTS: That in consideration of the payment of One Dollar and other good and valuable consideration, receipt of which is hereby acknowledged, the undersigned hereby acknowledges and agrees, for the express benefit of ______________ **(Production Company)** ("Purchaser"), and its assigns, successors, licensees and transferees forever, that the undersigned has no claim to or interest in the universe-wide motion picture rights (silent, sound, talking and/or musical), television, radio, phonograph record, merchandising and/or commercial tie-up rights or, without limitation, to any other rights of any nature or kind whatsoever, other than printed publication rights heretofore granted to the undersigned, in or to that certain literary work published by the undersigned and described as follows:

TITLE: ______________

AUTHOR: ____________

PUBLICATION DATE: ____________

COPYRIGHT REGISTRATION #: ____________

The undersigned hereby consents to the publication and copyright by and/or in the name of Purchaser, its assigns, successors, licensees and transferees forever, in any and all languages, in any and all countries in the world, and in any form or media of excerpts, dialogue and/or summaries, not exceeding 7,500 words in length each, of the said literary work and/or any motion picture, television or other version thereof based in whole or in part upon the said literary work, for the purpose of advertising, publicizing and/or exploiting any such motion picture, television or other versions.

IN WITNESS WHEREOF, the undersigned has executed this instrument as of__________,200_.

____

(Publisher)

By:___________

Its:___________

SHORT-FORM OPTION AGREEMENT

KNOW ALL MEN BY THESE PRESENTS: That in consideration of the payment of One Dollar and other good and valuable consideration, receipt of which is hereby acknowledged, the undersigned, ____________ (**Author**), does hereby grant to ____________ ("Producer") and its assigns, successors, licensees and transferees forever, the exclusive and irrevocable right and option to purchase from the undersigned all audiovisual rights of every kind, now known or hereafter devised, including, without limitation, the sole and exclusive motion picture (silent, sound, musical and/or talking), television, phonograph record, merchandising and commercial tie-up rights, and all allied and ancillary rights, throughout the universe, in perpetuity, in and to that certain original, published novel described as follows:

TITLE: _______________

AUTHOR: _____________

COPYRIGHT REGISTRATION #: _____________

The undersigned and Producer have entered into that certain literary option/purchase agreement (the "Agreement"), dated ________, relating to the transfer and assignment of the foregoing rights in and to said literary work. Without limiting the generality of the foregoing, this Short-Form Option Agreement shall be deemed to include, and shall be limited to, those rights of whatever nature which are included within the Agreement, which is not limited, added to, modified or amended hereby, and this Short-Form Option Agreement is expressly made subject to all of the terms, conditions and provisions contained in the Agreement.

IN WITNESS WHEREOF, the undersigned has executed this instrument as of _____________,200_.

____

(Author Name)

SHORT-FORM ASSIGNMENT

KNOW ALL MEN BY THESE PRESENTS: That in consideration of the payment of One Dollar and other good and valuable consideration, receipt of which is hereby acknowledged, the undersigned, ______________ (**Author**), does hereby sell, assign, grant and set over unto ______________ ("Producer") and its assigns, successors, licensees and transferees, all audiovisual rights of every kind, now known or hereafter devised, including, without limitation, the sole and exclusive motion picture (silent, sound, musical and/or talking), television, phonograph record, merchandising and commercial tie-up rights, and all allied and ancillary rights, throughout the universe, in perpetuity, in and to that certain original, entirely fictional, published novel described as follows:

TITLE: ____________________

AUTHOR: ________________

COPYRIGHT REGISTRATION #: _______________,

including all contents thereof and the theme, title and characters thereof, everywhere throughout the universe.

The undersigned and Producer have entered into that certain literary option/purchase agreement (the "Agreement"), dated as of __________, relating to the transfer and assignment of the foregoing rights in and to said literary work. Without limiting the generality of the foregoing, this Short-Form Assignment shall be deemed to include, and shall be limited to, those rights of whatever nature which are included within the Agreement, which is not limited, added to, modified or amended hereby, and this Short-Form Assignment is expressly made subject to all of the terms, conditions and provisions contained in the Agreement.

IN WITNESS WHEREOF, the undersigned has executed this Assignment on

____

____

(Author Name)

ACKNOWLEDGMENT

STATE OF CALIFORNIA
) ss.
COUNTY OF LOS ANGELES)

On ____________, 200_, before me, __________________, personally appeared ________________________________, personally known to me (or proved to me on the basis of satisfactory evidence) to be the person(s) whose name(s) is/are subscribed to the within instrument and acknowledged to me that he/she/they executed the same in his/her/their authorized capacity(ies), and that by his/her/their signature(s) on the instrument the person(s), or the entity(ies) upon behalf of which the person(s) acted, executed the instrument.

WITNESS my hand and official seal.

____
Signature of Notary

OPTIONAL
Though the data below is not required by law, it may prove valuable to persons relying on the document and could prevent fraudulent reattachment of this form.

CAPACITY CLAIMED BY SIGNER **DESCRIPTION OF ATTACHED DOCUMENT**

☐ INDIVIDUAL

☐ CORPORATE OFFICER

______________________ ______________________________
TITLE(S) TITLE OR TYPE OF DOCUMENT

☐ PARTNER(S) ☐ LIMITED
☐ GENERAL NUMBER OF PAGES________

☐ ATTORNEY-IN-FACT
☐ TRUSTEE(S)
☐ GUARDIAN/CONSERVATOR
☐ OTHER:________

DATE OF DOCUMENT ________

SIGNER IS REPRESENTING:
NAME OF PERSON(S) OR ENTITY(IES) ______________________________
SIGNER(S) OTHER THAN NAMED ABOVE

____

____

LIFE RIGHTS AGREEMENT

(Producer)
(Address)

Re: ________________ **(Namc of Story)**

Ladies and Gentlemen:

I understand that you plan to develop, produce and exhibit one or more theatrical and/or television motion pictures (collectively "Picture") based upon, adapted from, and suggested by the above-referenced life story and experiences (the "Story"). I further understand that the Picture may portray or otherwise refer to events involving me, as well as events involving other persons. In consideration of your payment to me of the sum of $________ and other good and valuable consideration, receipt of which I hereby acknowledge, I hereby agree as follows:

1. I hereby irrevocably consent and agree that you, your successors, assigns and licensees forever and throughout the universe, will have the exclusive right to portray, represent and impersonate me (or persons resembling me) under fictitious names or under my own name, and may make use of any episode, personal experience or incident of my life relating directly or indirectly to the Story, in and in connection with the Picture and any subsidiary, allied, and ancillary rights in the Picture and in remakes, sequels or television programs based thereon, which may be produced, distributed, exhibited or exploited in any and all media now known or hereafter devised throughout the universe in perpetuity, and in connection therewith in publications, advertising and publicity material of any and all kinds for use in any and all media. I agree that you shall have the right to use such personal experiences or parts thereof in historical, factual, or fictionalized form or in any combination of the foregoing, to add to, subtract from, dramatize, fictionalize, change, interpolate and adapt such personal experiences or parts thereof and to use them, whether in historical, factual or fictionalized form in conjunction with other material or property of any description, in the transmission, production, distribution, exhibition, exploitation, advertising and publicizing of the Picture. I understand that the Picture may contain dialogue, incidents, characters and written or visual material that may or may not be based upon or suggested by actual events.

2. I hereby release you, your agents, directors, shareholders, employees, successors, licensees and assigns, and their heirs, executors, administrators and assigns, and each of them (collectively "Producer") from and against any and all claims, liabilities, demands, actions, causes of action, costs and expenses (including without limitation attorneys' fees), whatsoever, at law or in equity, known or unknown, anticipated or unanticipated, suspected or unsuspected, which I ever had, now have, or may hereafter have by any reason, matter, cause or thing whatsoever, arising out of your use of the consent and/or rights herein granted or otherwise in connection with the Picture and I hereby agree that I will not assert or maintain against Producer any claim, action, suit or demand or any kind or nature whatsoever that I may now or hereafter have, including but not limited to those grounded upon invasion of privacy, property, publicity or other civil

rights, defamation, libel or slander or for any other reason in connection with the Picture or your use of the consent and/or rights herein granted to you. I agree that in the event of a breach by you of this agreement, my only remedy shall be for damages, if any, in an action at law, and I shall not be entitled to restrain the exercise of any rights granted or to be granted under this agreement, or to enjoin the use or exploitation of the Picture. As between you and me, you shall own all right, title and interest in and to the Picture and all elements thereof, and you shall have no obligation to me in connection therewith.

3. I grant you the foregoing rights with the knowledge and understandings that you will incur expenses and/or undertake commitments in reliance thereon and that in the granting of the foregoing consent and rights, I have not been induced so to do by any representation or assurance by you or on your behalf relative to the manner in which any of the rights or licenses granted hereunder may be exercised. I agree that you are under no obligation to exercise any of the rights or licenses granted hereunder.

4. This agreement is executed by me on behalf of myself and my heirs, executors, administrators, next of kin, personal representatives, successors and assigns and shall be binding upon each and all of them. This agreement is our entire understanding with respect to the subject matter hereof, cannot be amended except by a written instruments signed by the parties, and is to be construed in accordance with the laws of the State of California.

Yours very truly,

____

(Signature)

Name: ________________________

Address: ______________________

____

____

Date signed: ________________________

WRITER AGREEMENT

Dated as of ________

(Writer)
(Address)

Re: ________________ **(Name of Picture)**

Dear Sirs:

This will confirm the agreement between _____________ ("Writer") and ____________ ("Producer") regarding Writer's services in connection with the proposed theatrical motion picture tentatively titled "________________" (the "Picture") as follows:

1. Employment.

1.1 Committed Services. Producer hereby employs Writer to prepare a first draft teleplay (the "First Draft"), and a first set of revisions (the "First Rewrite") which together with any other writing performed hereunder by Writer are collectively referred to as the "Material").

1.2 Optional Second Rewrite. Producer shall have the option to engage Writer to write a second rewrite ("Second Rewrite").

1.3 Optional Polish. Producer shall have the further option to engage Writer to write a polish ("Polish"),

2. Writing Services.

2.1 Schedule.

(a) **First Draft.** Writing period of twelve weeks and reading period of four weeks.

(b) **First Rewrite.** Writing period of six weeks and reading period of four weeks.

(c) **Second Rewrite.** Writing period of six weeks and reading period of four weeks.

(d) **Polish.** Writing period of four weeks.

2.2 Other Terms. Writer shall deliver the Material to Producer at (address) or at such other location which Producer may designate). The person authorized to request rewrites of the Material is ___________. It is acknowledged that time is of the essence of this agreement. Writer shall render services instructed by Producer in all matters including those involving artistic taste and judgment, whenever and wherever Producer may reasonably require, but there shall be no obligation on Producer to actually utilize Writer's services or to include any of Writer's work in the Picture or otherwise, or to produce, release or continue the distribution of the Picture; and, if, at any time, Producer elects not to use Writer's services, Producer shall have satisfied its obligations hereunder by payment to Writer of the amounts provided in the following paragraphs, subject to and in accordance with the terms of this agreement. Writer's services shall be exclusive to Producer during all writing periods and nonexclusive, but first priority, during all reading periods. Notwithstanding anything to the contrary contained herein, Producer shall have the right to postpone the writing of any portion of the Material to such time as Producer may designate; provided, however, that no such postponement shall affect Writer's right to receive compensation as though such postponement had not taken place.

3. Writing Fees. Provided Writer is not in material breach hereunder and this agreement is executed, Producer agrees to pay to Writer, as full consideration for Writer's services and the rights granted by Writer herein compensation of:

3.1 For the First Draft and First Rewrite: The sum of $_____ accruing on delivery of all Material but payable:

(a) $_____ on commencement of Writer's services on the First Draft

(b) $_____ on delivery of the First Draft

(c) $_____ on commencement of the First Rewrite

(d) $_____ on delivery of the First Rewrite

3.2 For the Second Rewrite, if required: The sum of $_____ payable:

(a) $_____ on commencement of the Second Rewrite; and

(b) $_____ on delivery of the Second Rewrite

3.3 For the Polish, if required: The sum of $_____ payable:

(a) $_____ on commencement of the Polish; and

(b) $_____ on delivery of the Polish

4. Additional Consideration.

4.1 Studio Setup. If Producer enters into a development agreement with a major studio which contemplates the studio's financing and distributing the Picture, Writer shall receive a setup payment of $_____ payable promptly following execution of Producer's development agreement with the studio.

4.2 Sole Credit. Provided the Writer keeps and performs all of Writer's material obligations and agreements hereunder, and satisfactorily renders and completes all services required by Producer hereunder, then if Producer produces the Picture and it is finally determined pursuant to the WGA Agreement, but not Paragraph 7 of Theatrical Schedule "A" thereto, that Writer is entitled to receive a sole "Screenplay By" or "Written By" credit for the Picture ("Sole Credit"), Writer shall be entitled to receive additional consideration as follows:

(a) Bonus Compensation: $_____ less the aggregate of all sums previously paid to Writer pursuant to paragraphs 3 and 4.1 above ("Sole Credit Bonus").

(b) Contingent Compensation: An amount equal to ___ percent (__%) of one hundred percent (100%) of the "net profits," if any, of the Picture.

4.3 Shared Credit. Provided that Writer keeps and performs all of Writer's material obligations and agreements hereunder, and satisfactorily renders and completes all services required by Producer hereunder, then if Producer produces the Picture and it is finally determined pursuant to the WGA Agreement, but not Paragraph 7 of Theatrical Schedule "A" thereto, that Writer is entitled to receive shared "Screenplay By" or "Written By" credit for the Picture ("Shared Credit"), Writer shall be entitled to receive additional consideration as follows:

(a) Bonus Compensation. One-half of the Sole Credit Bonus.

(b) Contingent Compensation. An amount equal to __ percent (__%) of one hundred percent (100%) of the "net profits," if any, of the Picture.

4.4 If it is finally determined pursuant to the WGA Agreement that Writer is not entitled to receive Sole Credit or Shared Credit for the Picture, no additional consideration shall be payable to Writer hereunder.

4.5 The Sole Credit Bonus or Shared Credit Bonus payable pursuant to this paragraph 4, if any, shall be payable to Writer within ten (10) business days following Producer's receipt of the final WGA determination of credits.

4.6 For purposes of this Agreement, "net profits" shall be defined, computed, accounted for and paid as net profits are defined, computed, accounted for and paid pursuant to the provisions of the standard net profits or comparably similar definition of the production, financing and/or distribution entity with whom Producer enters into an agreement ("P/F/D Agreement") with respect to the Picture. In the event that Producer does not enter into a P/F/D Agreement, Writer's share of "net profits" shall be defined, computed, accounted for and paid in accordance with Producer's standard definition of net profits. Writer acknowledges that Writer's share of net profits, if any, provided hereunder shall not be a lien upon or claim against any of the rights granted herein, the Picture or any other exploitation of the rights granted herein.

5. Subsequent Productions.

5.1 First Negotiation. Provided Producer produces the Picture, Writer is not in material breach hereof, Writer receives sole "written by" credit and sole separation of rights on the Picture, Writer is then actively engaged as a writer in the motion picture industries and Writer is available to render writing services as, when and where required by Producer, then, if Producer desires to produce a sequel or remake (collectively, a "Subsequent Production") within five years after the release of the Picture, Producer will negotiate in good faith for Writer's services with respect to the first Subsequent Production on terms to be negotiated in good faith and in accordance with industry standards for comparable engagements; provided, however, that in no event shall the financial terms of Writer's deal be less than those terms contained herein. If such negotiations do not result in an agreement within twenty (20) days from the commencement thereof, Producer shall have no further obligations to Writer under this subpara-graph. The provisions of this subparagraph apply only to Writer personally and not to any heirs, executors, administrators, successors or assigns of Writer.

5.2 Passive Payments. In the event Producer produces the Picture, Writer is not in material breach hereof, Writer receives sole separation of rights or sole "written by" credit on the Picture upon final determination, and Writer does not render writing services on the Subsequent Production, then Writer shall be paid the following amounts, if any:

(a) If Producer produces a "sequel" (as such term is customarily understood in the television industry in Los Angeles), Fifty Percent (50%) of the Writing Fee and Sole Credit or Shared Credit Bonus (as applicable) for such sequel (payable promptly following the completion of principal photography thereof), plus a percentage of net profits equal to Fifty Percent (50%) of the percentage payable to Writer on the Picture (for this purpose net profits shall be defined, computed and accounted for as for the Picture).

(b) If Producer produces a "remake" (as such term is customarily understood in the television industry in Los Angeles), Thirty-Three and One-third Percent (33-1/3%) of the Writing Fee and Sole Credit or Shared Credit Bonus (as applicable) for such remake (payable promptly following the completion of principal photography thereof), plus a percentage of net profits equal to Thirty-Three and One-third Percent (33-1/3%) of the percentage payable to Writer on the Picture (for this purpose net profits shall be defined, computed and accounted for as for the Picture).

5.3 All sums paid to Writer pursuant to this paragraph for subsequent productions shall be credited against any corresponding sums required to be paid by the WGA

Agreement in respect of any such rights or services, and any corresponding sums paid to Writer pursuant to such guild provisions shall be deducted from any amounts thereafter payable to Writer pursuant to the provisions hereof.

6. **Rights.** Writer acknowledges that the Material was created within the scope of Writer's employment and, as such, is a "work made for hire." Accordingly, Producer shall be the sole and exclusive author and owner of the Material, the results and proceeds of Writer services hereunder and all rights of every kind and nature now known or hereunder created for all purposes throughout the universe in perpetuity. To the extent, if any, that ownership of the Material does not vest in Producer solely, exclusively and automatically by virtue of this agreement, Writer hereby assigns to Producer all rights (including without limitation, all rights of copyright and any so called "rental rights") of every kind and character in and to the Material and the results and proceeds of Writer's services. Producer and Writer acknowledge and agree that 3.8% of sums payable hereunder are in consideration of and are equitable remuneration for rental rights and that if under applicable law, any different form of compensation is required to satisfy the requirement of equitable remuneration then the grant to Producer of rental rights remains effective and Producer shall pay and Writer shall accept the minimum additional equitable remuneration permitted under applicable law. Writer hereby waives all "moral rights." Producer shall have the right to make such changes in the Material or to combine the Material, or portions thereof, with other material, and to make any and all uses of the Material (including, but not limited to, ancillary, subsidiary and derivative uses), all as Producer may determine, without any further payment to Writer, except as may be required by the WGA Agreement.

7. **Warranties and Indemnities.**

7.1 Subject to Article 28 of the applicable WGA Agreement, and except to the extent based upon materials furnished to Writer by Producer, Writer represents and warrants that: Material shall be wholly original (or, in minor part, in the public domain) with Writer and that Writer shall be the sole author thereof; Writer has the full and sole right and authority to enter into this agreement and make the grant of rights made herein; Writer is, and throughout the term hereof shall remain, a member in good standing of the WGA; and, to the best of Writer's knowledge (or that which Writer should have known in the exercise of prudence), the Material will not violate the rights of privacy of, or constitute a libel or slander against, or violate any common law or other rights of any person or entity. The approval by Producer of all or any part of the Material shall not constitute a waiver of such representations and warranties.

7.2 Producer warrants that it owns or controls (or will own or control) all rights necessary to develop, produce and exploit a motion picture based upon the Property, and that Producer is a signatory to the applicable WGA Agreement and the terms thereof shall be applicable hereto, except to the extent the terms hereof are more favorable to Writer and Producer shall pay any WGA pension; health and welfare contributions required of employers in connection with this agreement.

7.3 Writer shall indemnify Producer and its parents, subsidiaries, affiliates, successors, licensees, assigns, officers, agents and employees against all loss, cost, damages, liabilities and expenses (including reasonable outside attorneys' fees) they may suffer in connection with any claim which arises out of any breach of any of Writer's obligations, representations or warranties set forth herein.

7.4 Excepting any matters which are subject to Writer's indemnification and excepting any matters arising out of Writer's tortious acts or omissions or Writer's breach of any representation, warranty or agreement hereunder, Producer agrees to indemnify and hold Writer harmless from and against any claims, liability, loss and expense, including reasonable outside attorneys' fees, Writer may suffer by reason of (a) any materials furnished by Producer hereunder, (b) any material breach of any representation, warranty or agreement made by Producer in this agreement, or (c) the development, production or distribution of the Picture.

7.5 Writer shall be added as an additional insured under Producer's errors and omissions policy, if any, while Writer is rendering services for Producer within the scope of Writer's employment hereunder, subject to the terms, conditions and limitations of such coverage. Writer acknowledges that if Producer elects to self-insure, then there shall be no obligation to obtain or maintain any coverage for Writer by a third-party insurer. Writer further acknowledges that any such coverage shall not in any way limit or restrict Writer's agreements, representations or warranties hereunder.

8. Writing Credit. Writer's credit on the Picture, if any, on screen and in paid advertising, shall be in accordance with the applicable WGA Agreement. All other aspects of any such credit shall be at Producer's sole discretion. No casual or inadvertent failure by Producer to comply with this paragraph, nor any failure by third parties, shall constitute a breach hereof. If Producer fails to accord Writer credit pursuant to the terms of this agreement, promptly following receipt of written notice setting forth in detail such failure, Producer agrees to use reasonable efforts to prospectively cure such failure, but nothing shall require Producer to cease using or to replace prints, negatives or other materials then in existence.

9. Annotation. If the Material is based in whole or in part on actual events or real people, Writer shall annotate the Material in accordance with the guidelines provided by Producer. Concurrent with delivery of each step of the writing services hereunder, Writer shall provide a full annotation identifying the source of all factual material contained in the Material which concerns any actual individual, whether living or dead, or any "real life" incident or place. Writer shall cooperate with Producer and with Producer's counsel and insurance carrier, as may be reasonably necessary for the purpose of permitting Producer and its insurance carrier to evaluate and eliminate the risks involved in using the Material.

10. Suspension or Termination. Producer shall have the right to suspend Writer's employment and compensation hereunder during all periods: (a) that Writer does not render services hereunder because of illness, incapacity, default or other similar matters; or (b) that development of the Picture is prevented because of force majeure events. Unless this agreement is terminated, the period of employment provided for above shall be deemed extended by a period equivalent to all such periods of suspension. If any matter referred to in (a) above other than default continues for longer than ten (10) business days, or if any matter referred to in (b) continues for more than five weeks, or in the event of a material default on the part of Writer, Producer may terminate this agreement. Notwithstanding anything to the contrary contained herein: (a) Writer shall not be in default hereunder unless Writer fails to cure any such default within three business days after Producer's request (provided that there shall be no right to cure nor any cure period with respect to, any default which is incurable); and (b) in no event shall Producer be entitled to suspend this agreement more than once in connection with any particular event of force majeure. If, as a result of one or more events of force majeure, Producer suspends this agreement for a period of eight consecutive weeks or more, then Writer may terminate this agreement by giving Producer written notice at any time during the continuation of such suspension; provided that if, within one week after Producer's receipt of such notice, Producer elects to end such suspension, then such notice and such termination shall not be effective.

11. Assignment. This agreement will be binding upon and inure to the benefit of Writer's and Producer's respective licensees, successors and assigns. Producer may assign or transfer all or any part of Producer's rights under this agreement to any person or entity; and, if and to the extent such assignee is a major studio, network, parent entity acquiring substantially all of Producer's assets or a financially responsible party who assumes Producer's obligations in writing, including by executing an assumption agreement in accordance with the applicable provisions of the WGA Agreement, Producer shall be relieved of its obligations hereunder.

12. Services Unique. It is mutually agreed that Writer's services are special, unique, unusual, extraordinary, and of an intellectual character giving them a peculiar value, the loss of which cannot be reasonably or adequately compensated in damages in an action at law and that Producer, in the event of any breach by Writer, shall be entitled to seek equitable relief by way of injunction or otherwise.

13. Name and Likeness/Publicity. Writer hereby grants to Producer the right to use Writer's name and approved likeness in connection with the Material and the Picture and in advertising, exploiting and exhibiting same, but not as an endorsement of any product or service other than the picture. Writer shall not issue or permit the issuance of any publicity or make any public statements whatsoever concerning this employment, Producer the Picture; provided that Writer may make incidental, nonderogatory mention, of same in publicity primarily concerning Writer.

14. Transportation, Accommodations and Per Diem. If Producer requires Writer to render services on the Picture more than one hundred miles (100) away from Writer's principal residence (a "Distant Location"), then Producer shall furnish Writer with first-class round-trip transportation (if available and if used) and, while Writer is at such Distant Location at Producer's request, reasonable hotel accommodations, ground transportation and a per diem to be negotiated in good faith within Producer's customary parameters for comparable engagements.

15. Miscellaneous. No termination of this agreement or Writer's employment shall extinguish, limit or curtail any of Producer's right, title, interest or privilege in, to, or in connection with the Material or the results and proceeds of Writer's services or Writer's name and likeness. The rights and remedies of Writer in the event of any breach of the provisions of this agreement by Producer shall be limited to the rights, if any, to seek damages in an action at law, and in no event shall Writer be entitled, by reason of such breach, to rescind or terminate this agreement or to seek to enjoin or restrain the broadcast, exhibition, distribution, advertising, exploitation or marketing of the Picture or any other use of the Material or any part thereof. Producer and Writer agree to perform such other further and reasonable acts and to execute, acknowledge and deliver such other further and reasonable documents and instruments, including, without limitation, certificates of authorship with respect to all material furnished by Writer hereunder, as may be necessary or appropriate to carry out the intent hereof, and to evidence Producer's ownership of the results and proceeds of all services rendered pursuant hereto and a completed and certified Employment Eligibility Verification (1-9) in compliance with the Immigration Reform and Control Act of 1986. This agreement contains the full and complete understanding between the parties with reference to the within subject matter, supersedes all prior agreements and understandings, whether written or oral, pertaining thereto, and cannot be modified except by a written instrument signed by each party. Writer acknowledges that no representation or promise not expressly contained in this agreement has been made by Producer or any of its agents, employees or representatives. All notices which either party shall be required or desire to give to the other pursuant to this agreement shall be in writing addressed to the party receiving said notice at the addresses first set forth above for each party, or such other address which either party may hereafter give similar written notice. Three days after the date of mailing or the date of receipt of confirmation of facsimile transmission or the date of personal delivery, as the case may be, shall be deemed the date of service. Unless Producer receives written notice from the Writer to the contrary, all payments to Writer shall be made payable and delivered to Writer at the address set forth above. This agreement has been made in the State of California and shall be governed by and construed in accordance with the laws of the State of California.

Until and unless a more formal agreement containing customary terms and conditions relating to agreements of this nature in the motion picture industry consistent with the terms and conditions set forth herein is executed, this agreement will constitute a valid and binding agreement between the parties.

Please arrange to have four (4) copies of this letter agreement signed below where indicated and returned to me. I will provide you with a fully executed copy countersigned by our client.

Very truly yours,

ACCEPTED AND AGREED:

By:____________________________

Social Security #: ________________

By:______________________

Its:_________________________

ANNOTATION GUIDE

Annotated scripts should contain for each script element (whether an individual, entity, event, setting or section of dialogue within a scene) notes in the margin which provide the following information:

1. Whether the element presents or portrays

   A. fact, in which case the note should indicate whether the individual's or entity's name is real, whether he or she is alive (or it is existing) and whether he, she or it, as the case may be has signed a release;

   B. fiction, but a product of inference from fact; or

   C. fiction, not based on fact.

2. How the element differs and/or is the same from fact (for example, describe in detail how a character is the same as and is different from the actual person upon whom such character is based).

3. Source material for each element whether book, newspaper or magazine article, recorded interview, trial or deposition transcript or other specified source. Source material identification should give the name of the source (i.e., New York Times article), page reference and date. To the extent possible, identify multiple sources for each element. Retain copies of all materials, preferably cross-referenced by reference to script pages and scene numbers. Coding may be useful to avoid repeated, lengthy references. Descriptive annotation notes are helpful (e.g., the setting is a hotel suite because John Doe usually had business meetings in his hotel suite when visiting Las Vegas -New York Times; April 1, 1991; page 8).

CERTIFICATE OF ENGAGEMENT

(Name of Picture)

The undersigned ______________ ("Artist") hereby certifies that Artist has rendered and will continue to render services in connection with the motion picture project currently entitled ________________ ("Picture") within the scope of motion picture employment pursuant and subject to all of the terms and conditions of that certain agreement between Artist and _________________ ("Producer"), entered into as of _________ **(Date)** of underlying Agreement ("Agreement"). In connection therewith, I hereby represent, warrants and agrees that (a) services are rendered for good and valuable consideration, the receipt and sufficiency of which are hereby acknowledged; (b) the results, proceeds and product of such services are being specially ordered by Producer for use as part of a motion picture or other audio visual work; (c) such results, proceeds and product shall be considered a "work made for hire" for Producer; and (d) Producer shall be considered, forever and for all purposes throughout the universe, the author thereof and the sole copyright owner thereof and the owner of all rights therein and of all proceeds derived therefrom and in connection therewith, with the right to make such changes therein and such uses and disposition thereof, in whole or in part, as Producer may from time to time determine as the author and owner thereof, together with all neighboring rights, trademarks and any and all other ownership and exploitation rights now or hereafter recognized in any territory, including all rental, lending, fixation, reproduction, broadcasting (including satellite transmission), distribution and all other rights of communication by any and all means, media, devices, processes and technology, and all rights generally known as the "moral rights of authors." Artist further represents and warrants that, except with respect to materials supplied to me by Producer and materials in the public domain (which shall not be a material or substantial part of the results, proceeds and product of Artist's services), (i) the results, proceeds and product of services hereunder are and will be original with Artist and (ii) the results, proceeds and product of Artist's services hereunder do not and will not defame, infringe or violate the rights of privacy or any other rights of any third party and are not the subject of any actual or threatened litigation or claim. Artist shall indemnify Producer, its affiliated entities, assigns and licensees against any loss, cost or damage (including reasonable attorneys' fees) arising out of or in connection with any breach of any of the aforesaid representations, warranties or agreements, and Artist shall sign such documents and do such other acts and deeds as may be reasonably necessary to further evidence or effectuate Producer's rights hereunder. The Agreement may be assigned freely by Producer and such assignment shall be binding upon the undersigned and inure to the benefit of such assignee and, provided such assignee assumes all of Producer's obligations in writing, such assignment shall be deemed a novation forever releasing and discharging Producer from any further liability or obligation to Artist, except that if such assignment is to other than a major motion picture company, Producer shall remain secondarily liable.

IN WITNESS WHEREOF, this document has been signed this _________ **(Date of Certificate)**

____
"Artist"

AGREED TO:

(Production Company)

By:______________________
Its: Authorized Signatory

DEAL MAKING

We have now taken you through development, but before we go into the specifics of making deals for financing and securing talent deals, we want to discuss the deal-making process itself.

Hollywood Deal Making

To explain how deals are made in the entertainment business, we need to start by explaining how entertainment companies are organized. Since making deals is such a large component of the movie business, a specialized occupation called business affairs has arisen. Deal makers are usually, but not always, lawyers, whose job it is to negotiate on behalf of studios and production companies. In addition to business affairs departments, studios also have legal departments that prepare formal written agreements and negotiate their terms.

On the other side of the deal from the business affairs executive are the manager, agent, and lawyer who represent the creative talent. Each member of this trio has a subtly different role in the life of their client. In California, no one except licensed talent agents are permitted to procure employment for entertainers. In addition to being licensed by the State of California, talent agencies also enter into franchise agreements with the major entertainment unions—the Writers Guild of America, the Screen Actors Guild, and the Directors Guild—in order to represent members of those unions. Among other restrictions, the unions generally impose a ceiling of 10% on the commission that agents can charge their clients.

Personal managers in California are not licensed by the state or franchised by the entertainment guilds, and there is no cap on the commissions they charge. The norm is 10% to 15%, with the high range 15% to 20%. Managers are technically prohibited from trying to find jobs for their clients, but many tread into this area. Until recently, personal managers tended to be small companies, often a single person who lavished attention on a few clients. Talent agencies were often much larger and sometimes had hundreds of clients. Many entertainers, particularly actors, had both a manager and agent who worked together. Recently, managers have expanded their roles in three ways. They have aggressively pursued actors, writers, and directors as clients with notable success; they have formed production companies that produce movies and television programs utilizing their clients; and some procure employment and their clients have dismissed their agents entirely.

Entertainment lawyers, many of whom work on a 5% commission basis for their talent clients, are also involved in the deal-making process for talent. Their fortes are doing the nitty-gritty details in complicated deals and playing the "bad cop" role in the classic "good cop, bad cop" routine that is often used in negotiations. Sometimes they do not become involved until the verbal deal has been closed by business affairs and the agent and a written agreement has been drafted. Sometimes they are actively involved much earlier, which is our preference. Business managers are seldom involved in the negotiations of deals. They are generally accountants who handle financial matters on behalf of actors, directors, and other individuals.

The typical Hollywood studio deal starts with conversations between the studio's business affairs department and the talent's agent or manager. The conversations may be in person, but more commonly are by telephone. We have done multiple deals over the course of years with people we have never met face-to-face. After some number of back and forth discussions, a verbal agreement is reached on the deal terms (the deal is "closed"), or a deal cannot be made and the deal "blows." If the deal closes, the process of creating written documents that reflect the agreement starts. We call this "papering the deal."

Independent Film Deal Making

The deal-making process in the world of independent films is similar to the Hollywood structure, but you, the producer and your entertainment lawyer and—to some extent—your production staff, must divide the business affairs role since you, not the studio, are doing the hiring. Exactly what you do and what your lawyer does depends on your experience and preferences. Some producers prefer to negotiate the terms for the director, the stars, and other principal agreements themselves, sometimes coached by their lawyer. Others prefer to have the lawyer do all the negotiating, and the producer approves the terms. The paperwork is almost always handled by the lawyer in consultation with the producer. Line producers normally negotiate the more straightforward deals like location agreements, crew deals, and facilities. Casting directors often make deals for secondary cast members. In some cases, these deals are made with agents or managers who represent the talent. Other times, particularly in the independent world, they are made directly with the person hired.

Contracts

Regardless of who makes the deal, from a legal perspective, a contract is being formed. Entertainment law is largely a specialized version of contract law. Because contracts are so crucial in the film business, we want to explain some legal rules that govern them.

Contracts are legally enforceable exchanges of promises. I will do this, if you pay me that, for example. What makes contracts potent is that our legal system is designed to support contracts by providing a mechanism—lawsuits—to enforce them if one side does not fulfill its promise. The bank lends you money and you agree to pay it back. If you do not pay, you get sued. As flawed as our court system is, it is certainly better than people burning down each other's houses when they renege on deals. However, courts are picky about what deals they will enforce.

Material Terms

One essential that judges require before enforcing a deal is that there really was agreement on the main (material) terms. If there is doubt about what terms the parties agreed to or whether they ever created a contract by simultaneously agreeing on the terms, a judge is unlikely to enforce the deal. How can he? He does not know what the parties agreed to and the law forbids judges from speculating or filling in the blanks. The risk of not meeting this standard of establishing a clear agreement falls on the party trying to enforce it.

Over the years, we have had many people send us paperwork—often signed by the parties and often created by lawyers—that fails the essential test that the material terms must be agreed. The most typical variety is what we call "an agreement to agree." An example is a "contract" to buy a screenplay with the purchase price to be negotiated "in good faith" when the producer wants to buy the rights. Even though there may be a piece of paper signed by both sides, there is no legally enforceable agreement. The most critical provision—the amount of money to be paid—is missing and no competent judge is going to set the price. The people who guilelessly sign this kind of paperwork undoubtedly think they have a contract. They may go forward and when the movie producer wants to buy the rights, they may amicably agree on the purchase price. But if they disagree over what the price should be, woe to the producer for trying to make a movie without a chain of title.

For the typical movie employment contract, the minimum essential terms (deal terms) are usually services, money, and credit; what services are rendered, starting when and for how long; how much money is paid; and what credit goes on screen or in advertising. There may be other essential terms, and the contract forms of this book can serve as checklists for other terms.

Oral Agreements

Sam Goldwyn was quoted as saying "a verbal contract isn't worth the paper it is written on." But with all due respect to one of Hollywood's most colorful moguls, he exaggerated. Oral agreements, with or without the symbolic handshake, are often legally binding and enforceable agreements. There are two limitations to oral agreements. One is practical and the other is legal. On the practical side, it is often hard to prove the terms of an oral agreement. Most disputes over oral agreements have the opposing sides claiming different versions of the deal or one side claiming the deal closed and the other denying it. "He said" versus "he said" is a chancy lawsuit, particularly where the court will not enforce the oral agreement unless it is satisfied that both sides did agree on the material terms.

The legal limitation on oral contracts comes from the fact that, as a matter of law, some contracts must be in writing to be enforceable by a court. State laws require agreements for the sale of land and certain long-term agreements to be in writing. But for the movie business, the most important agreements that must be in writing are agreements transferring copyright. A verbal agreement with an actor or director or costumer can be enforceable. A verbal understanding, however, is worthless when it comes to transfer of copyright. Federal law supersedes state law in the realm of copyrights and it demands that any transfer of exclusive rights must be reflected in a written agreement signed by the party giving up the rights.

Mark was an expert witness in the lawsuit brought by Mainline Pictures over *Boxing Helena.* Kim Basinger never signed her acting contract, yet the court found it was enforceable and awarded Mainline millions of dollars in damages. Since then agents and lawyers have become more careful as to when their clients are actually committed since a signed agreement is not required for any actor's deal to be binding.

Offer, Counteroffer, and Acceptance

The process of reaching an agreement often goes through a number of steps with one side making proposals, the other side accepting some and countering others in an ongoing back and forth process. The law of contracts has established some ground rules for this process that are worth becoming familiar with. In legal terms, if you propose the material terms of a deal to the other party, you have made an "offer." The other party can close the deal by "accepting" those material terms exactly as proposed and within any time limit and by the means specified in the proposal. For example, you could send Jim Carrey a letter offering to hire him to star in your independent picture. The offer has the essential terms and says that if he accepts the terms, he needs to send you a letter by Friday agreeing to the deal. You can "rescind" your offer by telling Mr. Carrey that you are withdrawing it before he has accepted your proposal, but if he has accepted before you have rescinded, you are stuck with the deal.

If Mr. Carrey likes most of your proposal, but instead of the $5,000 you offered for the role, he writes that he "accepts" for $6,000, then as a legal matter he has "rejected" your offer with his "counteroffer." At that point, your original offer goes away. Mr. Carrey cannot later unilaterally resurrect it by changing his mind later and agreeing to the $5,000 you originally offered. Reciprocally, you can agree to "accept" his counteroffer by agreeing to exactly what he proposed. If you counter to his counter, then his offer to do the picture for $6,000 comes off the table. Any counteroffer is a rejection of the prior offer or counteroffer and extinguishes it. It is important to understand that neither side remains obligated to its prior proposals once there has been a counteroffer.

Another point to note is that the offer or counteroffer can impose deadlines and specify the terms of acceptance. The form of acceptance could be signing an agreement or it could be reporting for work by 7:00 a.m. on the first day of shooting. The person making the offer can control what has to be done to accept. The essential point to remember is that to create a legally binding and enforceable contract, there has to be an offer and a valid acceptance of that offer.

Forms of Paperwork

As we have discussed, most verbal agreements are legally binding and a contract is formed at the moment of verbal agreement, but as we have also discussed, it is reckless to rely just on a verbal agreement. So the typical practice is to follow up the verbal deal with paperwork that sets out the terms.

The nature of film production demands that things happen fast—much faster than the painstaking, excruciatingly slow pace that traditional lawyers feel comfortable working. So, the entertainment business has created some specialized forms to meet its needs. By tradition, almost all of this paperwork is created by those acquiring rights or employing talent: production companies and studios.

Reliance Letters

We call the first form "reliance letters." This is one party's version of the terms that were verbally agreed upon and it is sent to the other party with an admonition to the effect that "you had better object quickly if you have a different understanding because we are moving ahead in reliance on this deal." In this situation the other party is not asked to sign the letter, but is given an opportunity to object. This approach embodies two strategies. First, it creates a written version of the deal so both sides can quickly see if they agree on what was agreed. Often there are innocent misunderstandings or differing recollections about the verbal discussions and the reliance letter process highlights these areas. Second, the reliance letter takes advantage of legal doctrines that lend a higher level of enforceability to agreements that have been at least partially performed and provides defenses to belated claims by a party that remained silent while the other side proceeded. There is, however, a legal maxim that "silence is not assent" and the reliance letter is not as legally strong as a signed agreement. Unlike the other forms we will discuss, the representatives of talent sometimes send reliance letters, not just studios or production companies.

Short-Form Agreements

A second kind of paperwork is the short-form agreement. These are agreements to be signed by the parties that contain the material deal points and anything else that was agreed upon in the verbal negotiation. They sometimes go further than deal points and contain provisions considered routine or implied that may not have been discussed but are included in agreements by custom. A provision that makes it clear the actor has no ownership interest in the movie would be an example.

Short is a relative term and short-form agreements can run many pages. Their self-defining characteristic is that they close with a provision either to the effect that the parties will subsequently enter into a more formal agreement or that the agreement incorporates standard terms and conditions that are referenced but not attached. They anticipate a subsequent and expanded written agreement. As a practical matter, no matter what it says about entering a more formal agreement, the short-form agreement is often the end of the paper trail for movie agreements. In many instances either no formal agreement is ever prepared or if prepared, it never is signed. Still, so long as they cover all material points, short-form agreements are legally enforceable documents.

Deal Memos

Many years ago, a custom grew up in some studios for the business affairs negotiator who made the verbal deal to send the other side a copy of his memorandum to the legal department within the studio that directed the studio lawyers to prepare a formal agreement. That "deal memo" advised the legal department that "I have concluded" a deal and outlined the terms. By sending it to the other side, it served the same purpose as a reliance letter. Deal memos or IHCs (from "I have concluded") are still in common use and sometimes take this form, although they now often have lost their character as internal memoranda and serve more like reliance letters and are selected by studios, production companies, independent producers, and agents. Sometimes deal memos are prepared and sent to the other party for signature. Under our classification, this latter form of deal memo is a short-form agreement.

Certificates

Another category of paperwork is labeled "certificates of authorship" or "certificates of results and proceeds" or "certificates of engagement." We discussed the latter in the development chapter. These are notable by their almost complete omission of the deal terms. They do not have the money terms and other actual provisions that would make them enforceable contracts. Their goal is more narrow: They ask a writer (in the case of a certificate of authorship) or someone who renders other services (in the case of a certificate of results and proceeds or engagement) to sign them to certify that the production company or studio owns the copyright and other rights resulting from the deal and to waive any right to interfere with distribution of the picture. These certificates are designed as links in the chain of title to help establish that the production company or studio has all the rights necessary to exploit the picture.

Because these provisions are usually uncontested, it is relatively easy to get certificates signed, but we think they have serious limitations if misused. Our first reason is a belief that it is better for everyone to know as soon as possible if there is a mutual understanding of what the deal is and the second is that there seems to be a serious question of whether they really give the legal protection they try to obtain.

Unless they are supplemented by other signed paper, there is a strong legal argument that these certificates are not enforceable unless an underlying oral agreement can be proven. In a well-publicized case, Francis Ford Coppola signed a certificate of authorship in which he acknowledged that Warner Bros. was owner of a project he was working on called *Pinocchio.* A crude summary of the case is that Warner Bros. did not proceed with the project fast enough for Mr. Coppola's liking and he went to Columbia Pictures, which apparently was ready to make the movie if only it were not for that pesky certificate of authorship that clouded the chain of title. Warner threatened to sue Columbia if it went ahead, and electing prudence over valor, Columbia did not make *Pinocchio.* Mr. Coppola convinced a jury that although he had signed the certificate for Warner Bros., there really was never an underlying deal and Warner Bros. never had any rights in the project. Verdict: $60,000,000 to Mr.

Coppola. That case was ultimately reversed for other reasons on appeal. Nonetheless, our reluctance to expose our clients to the Warner Bros. experience makes us disinclined to rely solely on certificates to evidence the transfer of rights.

Letters of Intent

Letters of intent are an odd species of paperwork that sometimes appear because there is no agreement yet on the material terms. Producers often seek something along these lines from a "name" actor so that they can use it with distributors and financiers to prove that the actor is committed to doing the movie. These can be helpful during the packaging phase.

Whether there is a legally enforceable commitment depends on what the letter says: If it says the actor agrees to do the movie subject to approving the final script and his financial deal, it is not a contract; it is an unenforceable agreement to agree. Nonetheless, it may still serve the producer's needs since it at least shows the actor is aware of the project and has some interest in it. Actors' names have been used in vain without their knowledge countless times by producers of the hustler ilk and a letter of intent—even if unenforceable—helps the distributors and financiers sort total hype from the merely optimistic. Still, with only rare exceptions, letters of intent are not binding contracts.

Formal Agreements

The final category of paperwork is the formal agreement. It is the whole deal down to the details in a single written document signed by the parties. It is often called the "long-form agreement" with justification often being that it is both long in pages and long in negotiation. Like suits and ties, it is somewhat out of favor. We do not like neckties, but we do like formal agreements. We believe that agreements can be written succinctly that cover all but the most improbable eventualities and that the pages of language that have accreted over 75 years of movie contracts add no appreciable precision or protection to either party. The advantage of the formal agreement is that it leave few, if any, points open. There are no additional terms left open to cause problems.

Standard Terms

Standard terms and conditions are the fine print that lawyers are so famous for. They, of course, are not standard. They are drafted in favor of the party who is preparing the agreement and they cover the nondeal points. They must be reviewed with a fine-tooth comb. In many cases, they may even take away or undermine points that were agreed upon in the basic deal. So, be very careful with these terms. Standard terms and conditions can run 10 to 20 pages and consist of issues, among many others, as where lawsuits must be filed; assurances that there are no impediments to the services being performed; waiver of rights to enjoin distribution of the picture; and other topics of excitement to few but lawyers. There is not a specified set of issues that are covered and no uniformity as to what is considered part of the standard terms and what is considered part of the principal agreement. These provisions are sometimes called "boilerplate," the notion being that they provide reinforcement and backing to the principal terms.

Standard terms can be included in the body of the agreement or attached as an exhibit to the agreement. There is no legal difference and we prefer to attach them as exhibits simply as a matter of style and to get them out of the way of the deal terms.

Since we are on the subject of "standard," many times in a negotiation when one party is trying to hold the opposing party to a particular term, the argument will be: "This is absolutely standard." While there may be customs and general practices, remember that each deal and each situation is different and points are not standard. Whenever someone tries to tell you something is standard just respond by saying, "nothing is standard." You may not succeed in changing the point, but nothing should be off-limits for discussion.

Letter Agreements

Perhaps because it seems a bit friendlier, it is common for agreements in the entertainment business to be drafted in the form of a letter instead of the more traditional form of a legal contract, which even today still starts with a couple of "whereas" clauses and is signed "In witness thereof." We tend to use the letter form, but you should know that the choice of letter form or traditional form has no legal significance. It is what the words say that counts not whether it starts with "Dear Jim" or "Whereas."

One-Sided Agreements

Most people assume with some justification that all legal agreements are designed to be sneaky and overreaching, and many studio agreements are flagrantly one-sided. The one-sided agreement approach can result in signed agreements from the naïve and stupid or those without good legal resources. It can also result in resentment and leads to long, embittered negotiations when the other side has skilled lawyers and clout. Our experience has also been that blatantly one-sided agreements are difficult to enforce since judges and juries often are not sympathetic in such situations. We think the most effective approach is to use clear agreements and be respectful to the other party's objections and desires, but be firm on the points that are important to you.

We advocate using the deal negotiation as the time to bring out all the thorny issues that may arise and to agree in advance on how they will be resolved. That is not a natural instinct. Most people prefer smooth non-controversial negotiations. After all, the parties are getting ready to work with each other and to create distrust and hostility at the onset of the relationship can start a downward spiral between the parties. The sides may agree on a couple of points and knowingly, or unwittingly, defer some tough but important issues. As an example, a producer could involve a neophyte director to help rewrite a screenplay and agree to pay him for it. The producer and director expect him to direct it if they get financing, but what if a big name director wants to take over? Do you argue it out now? If you raise the issue with the director, will he feel the producer is getting ready to dump him—even if he really does expect him to direct? Some negotiators defer issues for strategic purposes because they know that as the deal is performed, the leverage will tip to their client. They know they can get their way later even though they would lose the issue if it were negotiated up front. Studios are known for this kind of negotiation and hold the money until they get their way.

Contracts are sometimes analogous to blueprints: guides subject to modification and clarification as the project progresses. It is unrealistic to expect that all eventualities can be foreseen, much less fully negotiated in advance. So, in the very practiced mold of movie making, many issues have to be worked out as things go along.

Because of the staggering volume of agreements in the movie business, the deals have evolved into common patterns, and industry custom and practice govern many aspects. A shorthand lingo has evolved with such terms as "pay or play" and "first refusal." It is used by negotiators as a way to efficiently express concepts. This body of how things are usually done can be very helpful to fill in minor details and courts are authorized to draw on it when interpreting ambiguous provisions. Confusion and difficulties arise when the terms are bandied about by people who do not know what they mean or when they are casually or ambiguously applied to cover an issue. We will discuss some of these terms later in the context of specific deals.

Studios have increasingly been brought under attack lately for their one-sided agreements. In one case, a producer accused the studios of conspiring to deprive producers and talent of a meaningful share of profits. In another, involving Art Buchwald's claim to profits in Eddie Murphy's hit *Coming To America,* Buchwald's contract was sought to be overturned because it was overreaching. Despite the challenges, most studios rarely change their contracts in significant ways, except for talent with proven track records.

Precedent

The American legal system is derived from the English system. The cornerstone of that system is precedent. Back in the Dark Ages, English judges decided cases by applying legal principles to particular fact situations and those decisions were then considered precedential and governed the outcome of later cases that involved the same principles and similar facts.

Law students today still spend most of their time in law school reading cases and learning precedents. Most Hollywood dealmakers are lawyers and are big believers in precedent. For them, precedent means what was done on prior deals. The studios and producers will only agree to certain terms because they want to preserve their precedents. Talent agents usually start their negotiations with the fee their clients last received as the precedent or "quote." Precedent takes on almost mystical power and both sides to a negotiation insist on not breaking theirs. Objectively, there is little reason that prior deals should control a new negotiation, but you will waste a lot of time trying to convince any Hollywood dealmaker to throw away their precedents. The advantage of a precedent-driven deal system is that the number of issues that are negotiated is relatively small and the range of those negotiations is relatively narrow. That makes for more predictable and faster deal making.

As you move into the production phase of your picture, you and your lawyer will have to figure out the procedures you will use to make your deals and how they will be papered. For independent pictures, we generally suggest not using reliance letters, deal memos, or short-form agreements. Do the paperwork once with formal agreements and do it right.

"So many indie films, so little time."

4

GETTING THE GREEN LIGHT

It takes a great script to get an independent picture made, and it must be great in three different dimensions. It certainly needs to be a well-crafted and compelling story. It also must be the kind of material that financiers and distributors in the United States and in the international territories believe will return their investment. So, it must have great commercial potential. Finally, and this is a dimension novice filmmakers sometimes do not fully appreciate, the script must include great roles for stars. All actors and particularly actors with the star power to get pictures financed want to play great roles. That is why ensemble pieces are often hard to finance. Think about it. Most Hollywood pictures are cast either with a male and female star or two star buddies. At $20 million or more for top actors, studios are judicious in the number of stars they hire, but stars are also choosy. Many even count the number of scenes for their role versus other roles when considering a script. Stars generally like to be heroic, witty, and sexy. They also want to play characters that have emotional range and depth. Stars all over Hollywood chased the *American Beauty* script for an opportunity to play a role, and they all cut their acting fees to get the part. We often see situations where an actor who loves a script jumps in to help the independent producer get the picture made. Our advice is not to even start the process of finding money and talent until you have the best script possible.

For this discussion, we are going to assume that you have completed the development process and have a script that meets all the criteria to be great. What is next? Obviously the two basic requirements are financing and the creative elements (director and actors). Getting these is the chicken and egg quandary that almost all independent producers must solve. The problem is that talent does not want to commit to do the picture and pass up other work opportunities unless they know the picture is going to be made and they are going to be paid. At the same time, distributors who will provide the money to make the picture will not commit to it unless they know the talent has committed. Independent producers must work both sides of this quandary simultaneously, but it is usually securing the talent that leads to the green light. We will dicuss how to do this before we delve into financing.

The Pay-or-Play Offer Strategy

In our experience, the strategy that has the best chance to get a binding commitment from talent is to use private funding or a foreign sales agent to back financial offers to stars. The strategy of using pay-or-play offers to actors is a bold one. Essentially, what you do is hire the actor to play the role in the movie, even though you do not yet have the movie fully financed and even though you will have to pay the actor even if you do not make the movie. There are several less risky variations on the strategy. Sometimes deals are made to "hold" an actor for a limited period of time ("holding deal"). Essentially, you get an option to use the actor's services for a negotiated payment. Another variation is to make an offer that is contingent on obtaining financing. These strategies tend to be less successful than unconditional "pay-or-play" offers. Agents and managers for actors generally prefer for their clients to do studio pictures. The salaries are usually higher and they do not have to worry about not being paid. Also, there is no skimping on production and the picture will get a major release backed by millions of dollars in advertising.

Unless the script is compelling and the role can create a breakout performance for their client, many agents and managers will discourage their major stars from agreeing to perform in an independent film. That is the main reason why anything less than a full unqualified offer to a star actor is likely to be rejected out of hand. Making a pay-or-play offer to a star actor separates your project from dozens of unfunded scripts that have been submitted. It makes your project real. You can expect the talent's agent to want proof that you have the money to back the offer and that is usually handled by a call from your banker or by depositing funds into an escrow account.

You only want to use a strategy like this for talent who will ensure financing: A so-called bankable star. Earlier, we mentioned that we once had advised a client not to invest $1 million to back offers to two stars because our research showed that the price distributors were likely to pay for the picture would not cover the costs. You must do your research in advance. You can destroy important relationships, as well as encounter legal problems, if you attach talent to a project and then find that they are unacceptable to financiers or distributors.

The Empty Handed Approach

If the private funding/foreign sales agent approach is not a viable method to get your talent, you will have to rely on ingenuity, creativity, political skill, bravado, and sheer persistence. While going through the front door to contact the star's or the director's agent is the most direct approach, you should understand that great scripts are sent to these agents all the time, particularly if their star can open a picture (generate substantial opening weekend box office). Talent agents are extremely busy and field hundreds of calls a day. They do not have a lot of time to listen to pitches and, in all probability, you will make your pitch to the agent's assistant or even the assistant's assistant. They are trained to weed out low-priority calls. Indeed, the first question you will hear after you make your pitch is: "Is this project financed?" These agents and their staffs have been down this road thousands of times, and in most cases they do not want to waste any time on a nonstudio, non-pay-or-play offer.

However, there are always exceptions and you may be able to fit your project into one of those exceptions. Maybe the star has recently complained about the quality and the caliber of the roles that he has been offered, and your material and the particular role in your project is just what their agent has been looking for. Maybe the director you want for your project wants to direct a different style of movie or a new genre and your project fits the bill. Maybe your project is set in Ireland in the summer and your desired star and director have summer homes there. Perhaps the star has had a string of flops released through the studios and the perception on the street is that he can no longer open a movie. Perhaps that star is looking for a comedy or a serious drama to reinvent his career. Perhaps the star or director is a sports enthusiast, an environmentalist, or secretly wants to conduct a philharmonic orchestra and you have the perfect role or project for that particular actor or director.

Read every trade paper and magazine about the movie business; surf the Internet; attend film markets, seminars, and festivals; and continuously network to equip yourself with more knowledge and information than other producers to make convincing arguments about why people should read your script and pass it on to the star, even without an offer, or with an offer that is subject to completion of the financing and not initially on a pay-or-play basis. (Film markets are essentially selling conventions where film buyers from all over the world come to meet with film sellers, view new product, and make deals. Three major film markets are The American Film Market, Cannes Film Festival, and MIFED.) If the star or director likes your material or the role he is going to play, you may be on your way to jump-start the financing for your movie.

Independent Divisions of Major Agencies

If, after using all of your charm, wits, ingenuity, and superior information, you are unable to get the star's agent to give you the time of day, there is a way to approach that same agency and, indirectly, that same agent through the side door. Most of the major agencies, including William Morris Agency, Creative

Artists Agency, International Creative Management, United Talent Agency, Endeavor, and a number of mid-size agencies maintain specialty divisions that spend their time arranging financing and distribution for independent films. The William Morris Agency has been a pioneer in this arena. The results are evident at each year's Sundance Film Festival where the William Morris independent film arm, William Morris Independents typically represents anywhere from eight to a dozen films that appear in the festival, which that agency has packaged and financed. Currently, Cassian Elwes, a former studio executive and independent producer, and Rena Ronson, a former senior international sales agent, head up William Morris Agency's independent division. Because of their experience and strong relationships within the creative community as well as the worldwide distribution business, William Morris Independent and other independent divisions of the other major agencies are capable of acting behind the scenes as an ad hoc producer or executive producer of your project. Often, they attach one or several of their actors or directors to a project, and then go into the international distribution community and assemble a package with sufficient distribution guarantees around the world to justify bank loans that green light the project.

It is important to know that the independent divisions of agencies do not exclusively work with their clients. They all recognize that the proper mix of writers, actors, directors, and producers often requires the talent of several agencies. Naturally, however, you are well served to use their clients since that provides work to the agency's clients and resultant commissions to the agency.

If you are able to attract the attention of one of the agents from an independent division at one of the major agencies, your project has a huge aura of legitimacy, having passed the scrutiny of various executives in that division, and your project will be viewed as viable by the entire industry. Now, when you approach the individual agent who represents a star or director who has ignored your project, you do so with the seal of approval of the independent division from that particular agency even though you may not be in a position to make a pay-or-play offer, and your project will be given the respect of one on the fast track to becoming a reality.

Conversely, if your target star or director is at another agency, the fact that an independent division of one of the other agencies is involved in the project and makes calls on your behalf to involve that star or director gives the perception that your film is close to becoming a go picture (a picture that has completed financing), and you are likely to get a quicker response and a willingness on the part of the agent to engage in a meaningful discussion.

Try to get the independent film financing divisions of the major agencies to champion your project.

Personal Managers

If you run up against a brick wall at the agencies, a more receptive facilitator for your project may be the star's or the director's personal manager. Managers typically have substantially fewer clients than agents do and spend more time on each client. Managers also tend to have more long-term views of their stars' or directors' careers and are generally more open to reviewing material even if there is not a pay-or-play offer on the table. Often, managers waive their commissions and instead serve as producers or executive producers on projects in which their clients star or direct. Since they are not regulated by the California Labor Commission as agents are (other than the fact that they are prohibited from procuring employment), managers have much more flexibility in how they structure their arrangements with their clients.

The manager's position as a producer in a project serves as a double benefit for their client. Less money comes out of the client's pocket for commissions, and the client also has an advocate on the project all the way from preproduction through production and distribution. Since managers tend to be intimately involved in their clients' lives, they have a comprehensive understanding of the long-term needs and goals of their clients, so it is understandable why it makes a lot of sense to approach the star's or director's manager instead of their agent. If your project is the perfect vehicle for the star's or director's next picture, the manager is often the best conduit to make sure that the star or director has the opportunity to read the script and decide whether to participate. Do not be afraid to make the manager a partner on the project. Generally, personal managers of major stars would not have their positions if they did not have excellent relationships in the creative community and with the business, finance, distribution, and marketing communities, as well.

Moreover, the manager may be in the perfect position to bargain with the studio and with major international financing sources to get your picture financed in exchange for their client's agreement to do a separate project, such as a sequel or a very commercial role that their client has done before and feels is not challenging. The manager is also in a pivotal position to assist you in attracting other stars to the project or perhaps a key director with whom the manager has a relationship. Enlisting a star's or director's manager as a friend of the project can serve as a major step to getting your project financed.

Entertainment Lawyers

Entertainment lawyers who represent talent can provide another conduit for your project. As a trusted business advisor of actors, writers, directors, and producers, as well as of their respective agents, business managers, and managers, an entertainment attorney's advice and opinions on a project are often given serious consideration. Many actors and directors do not make final decisions on projects until their lawyers are consulted. While most experienced entertainment attorneys are as busy as agents and managers, they are sometimes easier to approach.

Some entertainment lawyers also become involved in independent films as producers and assist in packaging a picture. Enlisting the assistance of an experienced entertainment attorney to jump-start your project is generally an effective and viable alternative to approaching managers and agents. Here is one example of the role a lawyer can play.

Several years ago Harris successfully arranged the financing for a production entitled *Mona Must Die* by serving in both the role of the production attorney, as well as an executive producer. A very successful television writer/producer named Donald Reiken approached Harris with a new project that he had written and that he intended to direct as his first theatrical feature. The writer/producer was willing to make the picture on a very modest budget so that he could get his directorial debut. The picture was designed to be shot at one location: At the producer's home on the ocean in Malibu, California. The shooting schedule was tight at three and a half weeks and the project was a European-style comedy about a dominating heavy-set woman named Mona who leaves her husband for a week to have liposuction.

This project obviously needed a well-known heavy-set actress to play Mona. Since it was determined that Roseanne Barr was unavailable, Harris suggested Marianna Sagebrecht, a German actress well-known for her roles in the critically acclaimed *Baghdad Café* and a major studio release, *War of the Roses.* Luckily, the producer knew a German gaffer who had worked in the United States and in Germany and knew Marianne Sagebrecht personally. The gaffer took the script to Germany, had dinner with Marianna and handed her the script. The next day Marianna called and said, "I love your movie and I want to play Mona." Harris quickly negotiated an agreement with Marianna's agent/manager, which did not require an up-front guarantee or pay-or-play commitment and Marianna became attached to the project. (It is important to note that generally, when dealing with stars from outside the United States, it is easier to deal with agents and managers because most non-U.S. actors really want to be in American movies. So, even if there is no cash commitment or pay-or-play offer up front, foreign actors are more willing than American actors to ride with the project until it gets financed. It is also important to keep in mind that in the United Kingdom, Europe, Canada, and Australia it is much easier to get directly to actors and directors through their personal relationships with gaffers, hair and make-up personnel, editors, composers, publicists, and the like. So, make friends with all of those people.)

Based on Marianna Sagebrecht's commitment to the project, the producer was able to secure a small number of equity investors to provide partial financing for the movie. Harris was able to secure an additional equity investment from a company that was involved in the recording and video industries and was in a position to assist in the domestic distribution of the movie. With a good portion of the financing in place, the producers and Harris were confident enough to begin to offer the other two key roles to lead actors in the United States and both agencies and managers were certainly willing to listen because a well-known star had already committed to the project.

Harris went to the Cannes Film Festival and spent the entire festival sitting at the German pavilion. He met with almost every German financier and distributor in the business. Since Marianna was extremely well known in Germany, Harris was able to secure five offers for a partial equity investment in the film as well as a German distribution guarantee for all media. Because the German deal was so lucrative, due mainly to Marianna's participation in the project, Harris and his partners were able to secure the entire financing needed for the project by selling the German territory and obtaining equity investments. Harris was asked to get involved less than five months from the time that the picture started production.

While all lawyers do not operate in this hybrid capacity, there are a few who do. Engaging a hybrid lawyer/producer can be a viable alternative when agencies and managers are not responding to your project.

Casting Directors

Casting directors can be crucial in attaching actors to your project and in assisting in getting your film financed. Casting directors spend all their business time casting movies and offering actors roles in movies. So casting directors are good people to know. They are constantly talking to, and negotiating with, agents, managers, lawyers, studios, financiers, and actors to put films together for production. They know who is hot and who is not; they know the up-and-coming talent, including those who are in hot studio movies that have not been released; and who is available and who is not. They know who really needs a picture and is open to any possibility and who is not interested in independent films. They know who is willing to travel and who will not shoot a move away from home. Casting directors know which distributors and financiers like what talent, who the directors prefer, and who the truly great actors are. Their job is to know who is right for each role in your project. Since casting directors have relationships with talent and their representatives on a number of different levels, they are ideal strategic allies to help you jump-start your project.

We discuss casting director deals in some detail in Chapter 9, Hiring Actors, but they typically work on a flat-fee basis ranging from $10,000 up to $125,000 and more per picture. They read scripts and prepare cast lists (lists of actors preferred for the principal roles, who are accessible within the producers timetable and budget) for anywhere from $1,000 to $2,500 or may do it on spec if you promise that they will be the casting director on the movie. Once the cast list is prepared, some casting directors can be enticed to continue to cast the project on spec or they may agree to a co-producer or other producer credit and fee in exchange for their casting expertise and relationships. Many former casting directors are now exclusively producers, and some currently functioning casting directors get co-producer, producer, or executive producer credits in addition to their casting director's credits. Often, the previously closed doors at the agencies and management companies will open and a star can be attracted to your project, which can set the financing in motion, if you have an experienced and well-known casting director on your team.

Experienced Producers

Another strategy to employ is to team up with an experienced producer or executive producer who is willing to work on independent films. Experienced producers and executive producers are typically experts in the packaging and financing process, having successfully arranged the financing for their projects numerous times in the past. As a result, they have ongoing relationships with financiers, distributors, studios, agents, managers, directors, and talent. When an experienced producer makes an offer to talent or a director, he or she does not always have to have the money in the bank or make a pay-or-play offer. The agents, managers, or lawyers who represent key talent know that when an experienced producer or executive producer (such as Jerry Bruckheimer, Dino de Laurentiis, Ed Pressman, Marshall Herskovitz, Ed Zwick, and many others) approaches their talent that the odds are favorable that the picture will get off the ground, so they are inclined to become proactive and pass the script on to their clients. Really experienced producers and executive producers have personal relationships with actors and directors and can usually get scripts directly to them without having to go through various gatekeepers. Moreover, if your project has one creative element attached but you have still been unable to lock down your financiers, an experienced producer or executive producer has the ability to attach the missing creative elements to round out the package. Finally, the financiers and distributors who have done business with the experienced producer or executive producer are more inclined to take your project seriously and commit to it when it is submitted through the auspices of that executive producer or producer. If you have not made a picture before or even if you have made one or two, the most effective way to get your project financed on a presale basis is to partner with an experienced producer or executive producer.

Harris was recently involved in such a situation. An award-winning documentary director had written a script, which he sought to finance in order to make his dramatic directorial debut. The project was called *Guy*; the script was well written and had a unique and meaty role for a lead actor. It was the story of a man, named Guy, who found himself being followed by a videographer who had inexplicably decided to make a movie about him. Guy was a regular guy, a used-car buyer, who found himself in the spotlight, pursued by a mysterious camerawoman. While he was initially incensed by the intrusion into every intimate detail of his life, he soon became enthralled with the camera and quickly fell in love with the photographer.

The script had bounced around for a while and had not procured any financing. Eventually it found its way to Harris and producer Renee Missel, who had produced the highly successful and critically acclaimed motion picture *Nell*, starring Jodie Foster and Liam Neeson, for Polygram. While Renee had experience producing studio and large-budget motion pictures, she had little experience producing smaller independent movies. She and Harris teamed to arrange the financing for *Guy*. Because of Renee's excellent relationship with various agencies, she was able to secure the services of Vincent D'Onofrio to play the lead role of Guy. Once Vincent's services were secured, the project was shopped around to various studios, independent distributors and financiers, and international sales companies. Initially, Polygram rejected the project; however, because of Renee's special relationship with the then chairman of Polygram and because she had previously delivered a highly profitable picture to the company on budget and on time, she was able to persuade Polygram to reconsider. Eventually the project was financed by an international coproduction consisting of Polygram, German distributor Pandora, and a German film fund out of Dusseldorf. Had it not been for Renee Missel's involvement in the project, *Guy* would never have been made. *Guy* was indeed ultimately produced and had its world premiere at the Venice International Film Festival. It had a small U.S. theatrical release through Polygram and was licensed by Polygram to many territories throughout the world.

Directors

In many cases, the best way to assemble the cast and financing for an independent project is to start with a director. Many companies that finance small specialty pictures such as Miramax and Sony Classics, are director-driven (rather than cast-driven) financing entities. They do not care about the cast initially. They want to know who the director is. The director will shape the vision of the project and see it through the production, editing, scoring, distribution, and marketing processes. Although writers would certainly disagree, film-festival officials and distribution entities in certain European territories view the director as the auteur or author of the film. It is for this reason that when a film is honored at a festival that the director is the individual who is invited to present the film (as opposed to the Oscars who give the "best picture" award to the producers).

Directors operate primarily behind the scenes and behind the camera and they do not have the huge entourages of support staff and gatekeepers that stars maintain. While they might have an agent or a manager and a lawyer, they do not have security guards, trainers, chauffeurs, hairdressers, publicists, make-up people, and the like. Most of them actually like to read. They regularly attend film festivals and participate on panels at educational symposia. In our experience, they are more easily approachable than some of the gatekeepers in the financing process. Directors can easily be found walking down the street at film festivals; sitting in cafés; standing in line to watch another director's work; participating in Directors Guild of America (DGA) educational events; and appearing on various panels, symposia, and workshops. We are not talking about first-time directors here, we are talking about directors who have made at least two or three films; have received critical or commercial recognition; have been honored at film festivals; and are on most of the studios', financiers', and distributors' approved directors lists. They have experience directing many actors and have their own personal relationships with those actors and their representatives.

Directors are uniquely positioned to slip a script to a well-known actor with whom he recently worked, or perhaps to someone with whom he has participated on a festival jury, workshop, or some other industry event. If you are lucky enough to get an established director excited about your project, the director can be the key person to help you assemble the cast. Once an established director is affiliated with the project, the agencies and managers start to pay attention because the project now has momentum and is closer to being a reality. That director's agent and manager will also be able to help you. Your calls to agents will start to be returned. Having also been involved in the financing, distribution, and marketing process, the director has his own unique relationships with financiers and distributors and he can help you to get them to pay attention to your project. An experienced director can also be in a position to help you attach a bankable producer to the project who can help secure the final financing to make your project a reality.

Here is another real-life example. One of us was recently involved in the production and financing process that utilized both the casting director and the director as the driving forces in securing the financing for the motion picture *Chinese Box.* Heidi Levitt, a well-known casting director, sent an established and critically acclaimed director, Wayne Wang, an article as a kernel of an idea for a movie that would take place during the transfer of control of Hong Kong from the English to the Chinese. Although there was no script when the financing of the project commenced, Wayne Wang's bankability as a director and Heidi and Wayne's abilities to attract high-level talent to the project, including Gong Li, Jeremy Irons, and Maggie Cheung, were key ingredients in obtaining financing for a budget of $12 to $13 million, even without a U.S. distribution deal in place.

Wayne Wang's agent, Bart Walker at ICM, was able to negotiate a deal with Canal+ to be the worldwide sales agent for the picture and to commit a significant portion of the budget with a distribution guarantee. The other financing was secured by an arrangement with an Asian equity investment firm based in London, which furnished an additional and significant portion of a budget in exchange for rights in various Asian territories. Bak Film, a French distributor, was given French distribution rights in exchange for a minimum guarantee of a significant portion of the budget, and Pandora, a German distribution company, obtained all German rights for a significant portion of the budget as well. With these four deals alone, and no domestic distribution deal, the production company had secured guarantees for the entire budget of the picture and was able to obtain a production loan from a British bank.

One key to the entire transaction was the fact that the production company was able to obtain over a million dollars in interim financing from the partners on the project pending the signing of long-form agreements and the closing of the bank loan, which did not close until well into the second week of principal photography. All of this was done on the basis of Wayne Wang's reputation as a bankable director and casting director Heidi Levitt's help in attracting a notable cast to the project. Even though the script had not been written when they committed to the project, the investors believed Wayne would be able to supervise the writing and deliver an appropriate script, attract talent, and direct and deliver a quality picture.

Actor Production Companies

A recent trend is for actors to form production companies that develop and solicit scripts for them. In some cases, the talent is partnered with a director or producer, and in some cases, the actor is looking for projects to direct or produce (Jodie Foster's or Mel Gibson's production companies, for example).

We have found that in many instances, the line is shorter at these companies than at the major talent agencies. It is often easier to get a script read and speak with someone who actually read your script. Additionally, many of these companies have inside entrée to the distribution behemoths, the studios.

So, if you cannot get the agent or manager interested, you might get the actor's production company interested. Although, if you do, you will be back at the agent's or manager's door to make the deal, but you will have a much different lever—the actor may actually tell their representative that they want to make the movie!

Film Festivals, Film Workshops, Seminars, and Grants

Another technique that has given producers a leg up in obtaining financing for their projects is getting involved in festival workshops, arts institution-sponsored workshops, or grant programs that assist the producer in further developing the property. Perhaps the most well-known and prestigious of these workshops is the Sundance Institute's writer, director, and acting workshops. Projects are selected based on originality, creativity, merit, and their prospects for being produced. Selected projects and their principals are invited to Sundance to further develop the project either from a writing, directing, acting, or producing standpoint. Professional actors and sometimes even well-known actors are invited to perform scenes from the project, which are filmed or videotaped during the workshop. Instructors are often well-known writers, directors, producers, and actors. Many of the projects selected for Sundance workshops ultimately get financed and produced and are invited to The Sundance Film Festival. A project that has received the seal of approval from The Sundance Institute is perceived, within the independent film community, as a project that is on the fast track.

Sometimes, the instructors who have participated in the development of the project at the Institute, be they actors, producers, or directors become attached to the project. Agents, managers, distributors, lawyers, and others are certainly more likely to return your calls and be willing to furnish their assistance to your project if it has been blessed by The Sundance Institute.

Another film festival sponsored workshop/market is the Rotterdam Cinemart. Producers who have projects that have some creative elements attached, either a director or actors, as well as partial financing, are invited to submit their materials to a competition sponsored by the Rotterdam Cinemart. The Cinemart customarily takes place in late January-early February. Projects that meet the criteria are selected from all over the world. The U.S. contingent is usually administered and selected by the Independent Feature Project. Financiers, co-producers, distributors, and sales agents from all over the world are invited to meet one-on-one or in groups with the producers of the various projects selected for the Cinemart. Typically, at Rotterdam, strategic alliances are made and many of the projects ultimately get produced. Insiders within the independent filmmaking community know that if a project has been selected for the Rotterdam Cinemart, it also has a leg up vis-à-vis other projects, and that makes it easier for your phone calls to be returned and for you to receive cooperation from the various gatekeepers in the business.

Grants and fellowships are available from such organizations as the Guggenheim Foundation, the MacArthur Foundation, and PBS and the Corporation for Public Broadcasting. If any of these institutions provides their money or support, it sets your project apart with the seal of approval of a prominent and selective organization, and it is certainly worth pursuing. Once you have obtained one of these seals of approval, you will find that the gatekeepers of the business will let you through their doors.

"Just tell him it's 'other people' as in 'other people's money.'"

FINANCING INDEPENDENT FILMS

We now turn to the other dimension of the chicken-and-egg quandary and discuss financing. We will first explore how private financing deals typically work and then turn to presales of distribution rights and introduce the people who can help you with that process. Then we discuss assorted techniques to supplement presale financing.

Private Funding

"Private funding" refers to either loans or equity investments from sources other than bank loans and money from distributors who acquire distribution rights in the picture. All private funding arrangements share some basic concepts. These are elementary, but they are key to understanding film financing. The first is the distinction between a loan and an equity investment. A loan carries an obligation to repay a fixed amount and yields a fixed rate of return—interest. With an equity investment, the person who puts in money gets a return in excess of their investment only if there are profits, however they are defined.

The original amount of a loan is called the "principal" and loans normally bear interest. "Simple interest" is calculated just on the principal. "Compound interest" is interest charged on the principal and the unpaid interest. In addition to interest, entertainment loans often bear other costs such as a commitment fee and the costs of having the bank's lawyers prepare and negotiate the documents. A loan is documented by a legal document called a "promissory note," which is a short-form document that spells out the interest rate, repayment and default terms of the loan, and a lending agreement that is a long-form formal agreement, which contains the terms set forth in the note and numerous other terms and conditions concerning the loan. These may include warranties, representations, completion bond requirements, collateral, security interests, takeover provisions, etc. The details of production loans from banks are covered in Chapter 6, Finance Agreements.

Normally, the person or company that signs a promissory note is obligated to repay it from all available assets, but film project loans almost always limit the source of money for repayment and the lender can look only to that source and not other assets. For example, if a note provides that it is to be repaid only from receipts from the film, it is called "nonrecourse" and no other funds of the borrower can be touched for repayment.

As a legal matter, loans are relatively simple and unregulated except that there are maximum limits on the interest that can be charged. These "usury laws" vary from state to state.

Experienced entertainment lawyers can help you structure your equity investment agreements so that they are not "securities." Common techniques are to grant investors approval rights over business and creative matters and have investors act as producers or executive producers. Although it is virtually impossible to make your investment deal bulletproof from a securities claim, granting a degree of control tilts the deal toward being a nonsecurity.

Equity investments are very heavily regulated by both state and federal governments if they are securities. Securities are investments under which the investors have no control over the business. The most familiar form of equity is stock in a corporation, but interests in limited liability companies and partnerships and many other forms of profit sharing are also securities. State and federal laws impose a very complex web of laws that regulate securities, although there are generally exemptions for investments by people who are actively engaged in managing the business and for small investments by family members and other closely related parties. Probably more than any other area covered in this book, you must get guidance from a lawyer before treading in this area.

Documenting equity deals is customarily more the domain of corporate lawyers than entertainment lawyers, and we will make only a few general observations about equity deals. First, the investment can be made in a corporation, partnership, or limited liability company or with an individual. Chapter 7 discusses these forms of business. Second, it is common in film financing deals for profits, however defined, to be divided 50% to "money" or the investors and 50% to "creative," which includes the producers as well as any actors, writers, and directors who share in profits. The term "point" is often bantered about in equity deals. It normally refers to one percent of the profits, but without a definition of profits, it is a meaningless term.

When you have met all of the state and federal regulatory requirements and are permitted to offer the investment to anyone, you have a "public offering," which is commonly sold through brokers. If you are restricted in whom you can offer to, typically only wealthy and sophisticated investors or people with whom you have a prior relationship, you have what is called a "private placement." Generally, an offer is accompanied by a document called an "offering circular" or "private placement memorandum" that describes the investment and potential risks.

There are also hybrid deals that have a loan component and an equity component. Some lenders get get an "equity kicker" in addition to interest. Equity deals are also normally structured so the investor gets a "preferred return," which is essentially repayment of the investment plus interest or a fixed bonus amount (e.g., 30%) and then a share in profits.

The key to structuring film financing is to maintain a clear picture of the order in which proceeds from the film will be paid out. We suggest that you make diagrams or speadsheets with simple examples. Where each party stands as the money is handed out should be indicated. You may have distributors, banks, investors, talent, completion guarantors, and guilds all jockeying to get their money first. You must make certain that everyone's place is clearly assigned.

In addition to the order of payment priorities "recoupment" specified in the various loan and investment documents and other agreements, there will be another line in which positions are controlled by the party's "security interest" priority. Bankruptcy laws establish the order of payment for creditors of a bankrupt individual or company. Some of the positions are governed by law—such as payment of taxes—but some can be controlled by the creditors by taking a "security interest," which insures them as "secured creditors" a priority in repayment over "unsecured creditors." Rest assured, any bank that lends money on a film will insist on a "first priority security interest" that puts it very near the front of the line. This bankruptcy law-imposed order of priorities overrides any contractual provisions. For example, an actor entitled to an unsecured "first dollar gross" from a bankrupt film would be paid, if at all, long after a bank note that had been secured by all of the proceeds of the film.

If you have potential sources of private financing for your movie project that are well-known to you, we urge you to find a lawyer who can help you work out those arrangements and competently document them. If, instead of people you know, your potential funding source is a referral or someone you meet at a cocktail party, we have some words of warning.

Avoiding Equity Financing Pitfalls—"Show Me the Money"

Through the years, we have had considerable experience in advising clients as to how to not waste their time and legal fees running after financing that appears enticing on the surface, but when closely analyzed, has no chance of happening.

Recently, a client of ours who was searching for equity financing for a motion picture was approached by a broker who claimed that our client had been "prequalified" for equity production financing. It is like receiving a preapproved credit card in the mail—they are hard to resist, but there is usually a catch (like 22% annual interest). The client provided us with the documents from the broker (which had the buzz words "specialized financing" on their letterhead). On the face of these documents, this broker was prepared to provide an equity line of credit (essentially a loan) repayable at the end of five years. Of course, there were a plethora of conditions, some of them so elastic (such as "prudent budget") as to be virtually meaningless. But here is the real kicker. In order to proceed, this company required a retainer exceeding $5,000, with no promise that the line of credit would ever happen.

Thankfully, the letterhead on the proposal letter included a Web site, and we investigated what kind of businesses this broker had provided financing to. The closest thing to an entertainment project was the financing of a drive-through restaurant in Peoria. In addition, when we spoke to the broker and asked him to provide some evidence that he had the money, he could not do so.

This is a common example. We estimate that the percentage of proposed equity financings that ultimately close and provide production financing is 1%, at best. However, if you follow the strategies below, you will substantially limit wasted time and money and increase the likelihood that you will get your project financed.

The first rule is deal with principals, not brokers. Hollywood is infested with all sorts of brokers, finders, producers, and other self-appointed money-finders, most of whom jeopardize your pocketbook. You may not need a broker to find what we call presale financing (money put up by companies in exchange for distribution rights). Just open the Hollywood Creative Directory (HCD), which lists every studio and production company. There is also the International Film Buyers Directory, which lists the foreign sales agents and many of the international territorial distributors, television networks, and video companies by country. Many of these companies know how to play the game, and they can be key to getting presale financing. However, we know of no person or company of any repute in Hollywood that makes a living from finding equity financing for independent films. It is just not a viable business.

The second rule is to find out all you can about the money source. Let us say you meet a guy at a cocktail party who brags that he has $300,000,000 in an insurance equity fund from some nebulous offshore company. You pitch him your project, and, guess what, it is just what he had in mind (brokers and finders tend to like everything). You might try these questions on the guy:

1. Are you a broker or a principal of the company?

2. Who is your lawyer?
3. Who are your accountants?
4. How many pictures have been actually produced and released with the funds from your insurance equity fund?
5. Who at your bank can I talk to in order to verify available funds?

It is best to get the bad news early. We had a bizarre experience a few years ago on a financing we were negotiating. Mark met with the purported financier and immediately was suspicious. He asked for the gentleman's business card and a few other details and immediately got authorization from the client to spend a relatively modest amount to check out the guy through a private investigator. In the meanwhile, the documentation from the financier's lawyer mutated from our client receiving money to our client giving the financier money.

The next day the private investigator called Mark and reported that the financier had eight different aliases and was wanted on both state and federal charges, including securities and computer fraud. Suffice it to say that our client backed out of the transaction. Unfortunately, this is not a rare occurrence.

How do you find out if the money is real? It is likely to be real if the company has invested it in the past. Companies that invest in the movie business and manage to stay in business either have some business savvy, strong financial backing, or luck. Also, the film business is quite a small community. A well-connected lawyer can probably check out a potential investor very easily if the investor has been involved in other film deals. Entertainment insiders protect each other from being involved with people who are untrustworthy, unsavory, or simply difficult, by trading very candid private assessments.

If an investor you do not know talks about providing money to your project, do not invest too much time before asking for a copy of a bank statement or other hard evidence that they have the money. Once you receive the bank statement or other documentation, follow up to make sure that it is real by speaking with the bank officer in charge of the account. Please keep in mind that in our computer age, it is very easy for crooks to doctor documents. A client of ours once sent us a letter of credit drawn on a Swiss bank to be used as collateral for a bank loan for production financing. Since we were not familiar with Swiss banks, we decided to check on the bank. It did not exist. The letter of credit was a complete forgery.

Here is another one of our favorite tests to separate the men from the boys—ask the potential investor for some up-front cash to cover costs. Our client used this in a recent transaction and had a $20,000 wire transfer the next day to cover our legal fees, without any paper whatsoever. That investor was real, and that financing came through. Sophisticated investors understand that they must pass the "show-me-the-money" test.

Family and Friends

The most common source of private financing for independent films, particularly smaller ones, is from family and friends. As we noted before, there are legal requirements connected with private financing that are securities, even with people you are very close to. We suggest that you are careful and professional. But when dealing with people who are ultimately investing based on their faith in you, there are other concerns. We have seen some very ugly situations and offer a few rules to apply when taking money from family or friends.

1. Be Professional. Treat the money as an investment. Have appropriate paperwork prepared and signed.
2. Risk. Make absolutely certain they understand they can lose their entire investment and satisfy yourself that they can afford to.
3. Full Disclosure. Stay in communication and do not hide bad news.
4. Ask for Help. Most people who can afford to put money in an independent film have some financial savvy. Do not be reluctant to go to them for advice, particularly if problems arise.
5. Use Experienced Professionals. Hire an entertainment lawyer at a minimum and perhaps a producer's representative.

Presales

After private funding, the next most important financing is presales of distribution rights in certain territories and media. You can do a worldwide presale, a domestic presale, or a foreign presale, but the most common is presale of foreign rights. A few independent producers have had great success preselling worldwide rights to a major U.S. studio prior to starting photography. These sales, however, involved major stars and substantial budgets and were for studio-type pictures. The rule of thumb is that with the right creative elements, after soft money contributions you can raise 60% to 70% of the remainder of the budget from foreign, and 30% to 40% from domestic rights. In reality, the domestic portion is harder to get because, except for microbudgeted pictures, only the major studios and major television players such as HBO and Showtime can put up the money to cover the 30% to 40% domestic portion. As a result, it is common for independent filmmakers to make their movie with a combination of equity money and foreign presales. They do not sell U.S. rights until the picture has been completed. We discuss how to sell a completed picture in Chapter 15. The keys to presales are usually international sales agents and producers' representatives.

Selling Spec Movies Before Completion to Domestic Distributors

Not all independent films are sold after they are completed. It is almost always advisable to seek and complete a deal for domestic distribution prior to commencement of principal photography if at all possible. By doing so, you insulate your risk that your movie will be noncommercial and not sell. A very few savvy producers have been able to lock in multimillions in profit by selling distribution rights prior to the commencement of principal photography, either on a worldwide basis or by splitting domestic and foreign rights and selling in each territory.

What makes a saleable picture? The alchemy of putting together independent films is an inexact science. Distributors like to think that the combined elements of a film will be turned into distribution gold. The main elements are the script, director and actors. In our experience, actors are by far the most important element in selling a film before principal photography.

The most important determination to make before selling a picture before completion is what you are going to show potential distributors. Before photography, with no footage to show, you sell the picture based upon the script and attached elements. One factor is whether you will show the budget to potential distributors. We like to keep the budget confidential and take the position that distributors are buying based upon value rather than on cost. It has, however, become increasingly difficult to maintain this position since domestic distributors are wary of producers "flipping" production and putting money in their own pockets. The current convention is that domestic distributors will contribute anywhere from 30% to 50% of the cost of a picture not covered by soft money. The domestic distributor will want to see a budget or at least the budget top-sheet (budget summary) and perhaps require contractually that you actually spend the money.

The acquisition of distribution rights based upon a percentage of the budget has its problems. It is always tempting for the independent producer to inflate the budget. Indeed, this was one of the main issues in the lawsuit of *Intertainment v. Franchise Pictures,* in which a foreign distributor, Intertainment, contributed a percentage of the budget cost of movies to Franchise Pictures, in return for certain distribution territories. Intertainment alleged that Franchise substantially inflated the budgets. Intertainment ultimately won the case. Although this case involved a foreign distributor, the same would apply in a domestic situation. One solution is that the domestic distributor pays the lesser of the budget or a percentage of the final negative cost. However, this can be problematic since there is no exact convention with regard to negative cost statements.

We recently sold a picture that was in postproduction. The picture was bought based on production stills and a very short product reel. There is also the controversial practice of selling pictures "blind" to distributors. Sometimes, not seeing footage is part of the cost a distributor must pay in order to acquire a film, especially in a bidding situation. However, if the distributor ultimately is disappointed with the film, they may seek to get out of the deal. Thus, it is important that the distributor not have the right to reject the film because of its commerciality, as opposed to its technical quality.

The odds of actually selling an independent picture for domestic distribution prior to principal photography are daunting. Many distributors pass by saying they will look at the movie when it is done. You should never interpret this as a sign of hope that in fact you will sell the picture after it is done—this is just a pass.

A word about the acquisition world: Virtually every major distributor, and especially their independent subsidiaries (such as Warner's Warner Independents and Sony's Sony Pictures Classics) track virtually every independent film that is in production, looking for the proverbial diamond in the rough. The acquisition executives are fiercely competitive and all seek to one-up each other by giving an early "look" at a film. You must be extremely careful in trying to keep a level playing field in dealing with the acquisition executives. Still, sale opportunities exist where the right distributor comes upon the right film at the right time. You may wish to allow a "preemptive" (exclusive and first) offer on your film. Producer reps are savvy at navigating the treacherous waters infested by distribution/acquisition executives and can be very helpful.

It has become extremely difficult to sell a picture prior to completion to a major distributor because the number of distribution slots has diminished in recent years and the cost of releasing has skyrocketed. The print and advertising expenditures (p&a) at the Motion Picture Association of America (MPAA) member companies increased faster than production costs over the last decade, hitting an average of almost $40 million in 2004. Thus, the distributors assess their investment and expected return and they are looking not only at your advance, but also at their p&a expenditures.

It is also important that you understand the process by which distributors look at films. Before acquiring a picture, the distributor will "run numbers." This consists of the distributor assessing the commercial value of the film and trying to project their financial return in various scenarios. Distributors are always looking for the slam-dunk where, with the minimum investment, they can achieve the maximum return. (Someone is always looking for another Blair Witch Project.) The higher the acquisition price and anticipated print and ad commitment, the better the film must perform in the marketplace before the distributor makes money. The internal evaluation of independent pictures at studios, from a financial standpoint, looks like this: After the acquisition executive brings in the film, the business affairs and financial teams get involved and build spreadsheets. They use Excel-type programs to assume various scenarios. They may create spreadsheets assuming a $2 million advance, a $5 million advance and a $10 million advance, and print and ad commitments of $5 million, $10 million, $15 million and $20 million. In some cases, the studios have "output" deals for pay TV, which are based upon box office but which have minimums and maximums. Thus, they can plug in numbers that correspond to box office performance of the film and accurately predict the resulting pay TV revenue. The home video departments will also give an estimate of revenues and costs. All of these assumptions are then built into spreadsheets, which show what the studio should make. The single most crucial point in the revenue stream is the studio's break-even point. Under our scenario above, the studio spreadsheets may indicate that the break-even point if they give an advance of $2 million will be $15 million in domestic box office, but if they give a $10 million advance, it may be $35 million. Obviously, the chances of reaching $15 million far exceed the chances of meeting $35 million, so the $2 million advance deal is much less risky and therefore more attractive to the studio.

While the studio runs its numbers, you should be running yours as well. In some of our negotiations, the studios or other buyers have been willing to share their revenue and costs assumptions so we can jointly figure out a deal that works for both sides. Sophisticated negotiators are always willing to discuss numbers although, in some instances, studios play the hide-and-seek game. When negotiators play hide-and-seek, the odds of a consummated deal are diminished greatly.

One very malleable cost variable is whether your production will be signatory to WGA, DGA, Screen Actors Guild (SAG), and International Alliance of Theatrical Stage Employees (IATSE)/Teamsters. Not only will the guild agreements increase your production costs, but also you will be responsible, unless the studio assumes and pays them, to pay residuals, which can be up to approximately 13% of the gross. This is a huge factor in how to calculate the profitability of a film.

What are the main points you will negotiate?

A domestic distributor will want to make sure that the film that they are buying, though uncompleted, is what they expect. They want the elements that are presented them to be the final product. Therefore, you will not be able to change the screenplay materially, your film must be shot with expected cast and director, it must meet the studio-mandated rating and perhaps you will have to financially conform to the budget.

The domestic acquisition price is the most important and usually the most heavily negotiated part of a domestic distribution deal. Prices can range from nothing to more than 100% of your anticipated production cost, but the norm hovers around 40% of the anticipated budget. In order for the domestic distributor to be convinced to pay your price, their numbers must indicate that they have a reasonable chance of earning back all of their costs and turning a profit. An alternative to the acquisition price structure is for the domestic distributor to not pay an advance but to pay you a substantial portion of the gross. The thinking behind these kinds of deals is akin to the *Twins* deal Mark negotiated, where Universal was insulated in case of poor performance, and the talent would make more than their quote if the picture were successful. Miramax reportedly structured such a deal at Sundance in 1999 on the picture Happy, Texas (although industry cynics believe Miramax announced it was a "gross" deal so as not to be viewed as overpaying on their advance). Gross deals are very rare in the independent world. Typically, producers have their investors or bankers breathing down their necks to get their money back, and the investors or bankers do not want to take the market performance risk and wait while interest accrues.

Domestic deals include North America. This customarily includes the United States, Canada and their territories and possessions along with the U.S. and Canadian military installations, airlines and ships. Although Mexico is geographically in North America, it is not part of North American deals. In some cases domestic distributors do hybrids between domestic and foreign deals by acquiring domestic rights and rights in some, but not all, foreign territories.

Studios seek to acquire as many distribution rights as possible and in perpetuity. Sophisticated producers may be able to shave off ancillary rights, including soundtrack album, music publishing and stage plays. In addition, it is customary for independent producers to reserve derivative production rights, including motion picture and television remakes and sequels. However, this reservation of right is almost always tempered by a right of first negotiation/last refusal to the domestic distributor.

In the independent world, whether or not there is a commitment to release a film in a minimum number of theaters, with an attendant print and advertising commitment, is often a hotly negotiated issue. If you are dealing with a studio, it is crucial that you get the attention and commitment from the marketing and distribution departments to assure yourself of their commitment to your picture. Actually, studios tend to focus on their in-house productions, where their average negative cost hovers at $50 million. Another strategy for the producer is to finance not only the production cost but also the print and advertising costs and negotiate a so-called rent-a-studio deal. This makes the deal more attractive to the studio since it lowers or eliminates their risk.

Naturally, the distributor's commitment with respect to screens and prints and ads must be tailored to each picture. Many independent pictures are of the art-house variety and the best way to release them is on a limited basis and expand that if they catch on. Still, there may be mainstream independent pictures that are best served in the marketplace by an initial release and substantial p&a spend.

We recently succeeded in negotiating that the print and ad commitment amount for the picture would be put in escrow, and to the extent not expended that our client was entitled to liquidated damages of 50% of the unexpended funds. Great lawyering, but the domestic distributor went belly up, did not distribute the film, and the clause became worthless.

The producer's backend negotiations on independent films are much more complicated than for a studio-employed producer. Studio-employed producers typically get 50% of the net profits, reduced by third-party participations to a floor, typically 20%. Star producers receive a percentage of the gross receipts payable at a point prior to net profits. The backend for producers of independent films utilizes the studio-employed model as a basis, but it varies widely, almost always to the benefit of the independent producer. This is fair since the independent producer has been, in effect, at the studio in packaging and financing the film. Here is where the action is to modify the studio producer model toward your benefit.

1. Home Video. Studios typically credit only 20% of the wholesale price of videocassettes to gross, and 20% of rental revenue, retaining the other 80% of income, although they do bear the costs. In the independent world, the trend has been to treat home video as akin to theatrical, with all receipts credited to gross. The studio takes a distribution fee, their expenses, and the remainder is credited to gross. Although home video costs have gone down, and DVD margins exceed those of VHS tapes for studios, it is traditional, if you use the distribution fee model, for the home video distribution fee to be higher than the theatrical distribution fee.
2. Distribution Expenses. It is sometimes possible to take out the customary 10% ad override fee.
3. Participations. It is likely that you, as a producer, have made commitments to profit participants, ranging from first dollar gross to net. You should always do your best to have the studio assume these obligations, not only because it benefits you economically, but also it removes you from the headache of reporting to the participants.

4. Interest. Studios love to charge artificially high interest rates of 125% of prime or prime plus 2.5% In some cases, on an independent film, you can get them to bring the interest rates down.
5. Acquisition Cost Overhead. Studios have traditionally charged a 15% overhead on negative cost. They sometimes try to stick to the same overhead figure on your acquisition price, even though they are not producing the movie. You should always try to resist this.
6. Talent Box Office Bonuses. Independent producers try to insulate themselves from the vagaries of Hollywood accounting by negotiating for fixed amounts of domestic box office bonuses at box office plateaus measured by *Daily Variety.* These bonuses are all over the board and we cannot point to any sort of consistency. There is one variable, however, to the fixed-point model. In some cases we have negotiated bonuses at multiples of acquisition cost, e.g., $100,000 at one and one-half times acquisition cost, $100,000 at two and one-half times negative cost, etc. One issue regarding domestic box office bonuses is whether or not the bonus can be applied against your profit participation. We have seen it both ways, although you can use the ability to apply the box office bonus against the profit participation as a selling point in trying to get box office bonuses.

One often overlooked point is whether you will be allowed to use the domestic distributor's promotional materials for your foreign deals. If you raise this point, you can win it oftentimes. If you do not, you are at the mercy of the studio, although some studios will sell the materials for a pro rata contribution to their creation costs.

The delivery date will be specifically negotiated because the domestic distributor will have plans to put the picture in one of their distribution slots. Always remember to leave yourself a little wiggle room and to provide for force majeure extensions(i.e. events out of your control like strike or terrorist attacks), usually capped at 60 to 90 days. It is also a good idea to provide that if the distributor requests changes to the film that the period of time necessary to input such changes delays the delivery date.

It is also important that you be involved in the discussions regarding initial theatrical release pattern and ad campaign. It is unlikely that you will get mutual approval; however, you will most certainly get consultation rights. We always like to insert a clause stating that the consultation rights will be "meaningful and continuous," including consultation regarding release of the picture, including trailers and one sheets, to all media and that the studio provide all materials on a timely basis so your acceptable comments can be implemented.

With respect to cutting rights, it is much more common on independent films for the directors and producers to have final cut notwithstanding the contract; however, the domestic distributor will push hard to have the most commercial version of the picture released. In some instances, the final cut can be determined by objective measures such as ratings at NRG screenings.

With respect to residuals, the majors are used to assuming guild residuals, and customarily do. However, it is becoming increasingly difficult with non-majors to have them pick up residuals. Please note that your production company will remain on the hook unless the distributor assumes the obligations and in fact pays the residuals.

Lastly, we always insist that there be a mutually approved press release. It is important that you put the proper spin on your picture. Always make sure that your agent, producer's rep and lawyer are identified in the press release. They will appreciate it.

With respect to documentation, we like to draft on behalf of our clients. However, the studios will not let you draft and there is always an arduous multi-month process in negotiating the studio form agreement. We have been successful in negotiating preapproved forms with some of these studios, however, and this is always the preferred route.

International Sales Agents

There are a large number of international sales agents who specialize in licensing motion picture projects and completed films on a territory-by-territory basis throughout the world. They scour the globe looking for new and unique ways to sell, license and finance motion picture product. They establish relationships with qualified buyers and distributors of entertainment product in all of the key territories around the world. They constantly research the market to determine what types of product will sell in different territories, which actor's work is saleable, which directors are important, and what genres are the most popular. They know who pays and who does not. The more active international sales agents attend at least six international markets around the world: National Association of Television Program Executives (NATPE), which is held at various locations in the United States in January; the American Film Market (AFM) formerly held in February/March and now holding its annual Santa Monica, California market in October; MIPTV held in Cannes, France in April; the Cannes Film Festival also held in Cannes, France in May; MIPCOM held in Cannes, France in October; and MIFED previously held in Milan Italy in October/ November, but considering changing its venue to Venice in September so as not to compete directly with the October American Film Market. There are also a number of mini-markets held in conjunction with other industry events such as the Venice Film Festival held in Venice, Italy in

September; the Sundance Film Festival held in Park City, Utah in January; the Berlin Film Festival held in Berlin in February; the Toronto Film Festival in Toronto in late September; and the L.A. television screenings held in Los Angeles, California in June.

Established, prominent sales agents are usually members of the Independent Film and Television Alliance (IFTA) formerly American Film Marketing Association (AFMA), which is located at 10850 Wilshire Boulevard, 9th Floor, Los Angeles, CA 90024, telephone number (310) 446-1000. IFTA is the independent sales agents' trade organization that runs the American Film Market and also does market research; helps international sales agents collect money due them from territorial distributors; conducts IFTA arbitrations when disputes arise between buyers and sellers; provides form international licensing agreements; and lobbies the state and federal governments to protect the interests of the independent filmmaking community. You can obtain a list of IFTA members as well as all companies that exhibit product at the American Film Market from IFTA. You can also consult the Hollywood Creative Directory's Distributor Directory for an extensive listing of international sales agents and distributors.

Since international sales agents make their living by charging sales agency fees, which range from 5% to 35% of the gross receipts from each territory, as well as recouping marketing and distribution expenses incurred in the licensing of product, it is in the sales agent's best interest to solicit, review and acquire new motion picture projects that fit their respective buyers' market profiles. The more established international sales agents have hundreds of clients throughout the world; excellent relationships with the entertainment lenders; and over the years have reinvested profits into new projects. Some sales agents have lines of credit at banks as well as capital reserves, which they can tap to provide interim financing to a project pending a bank loan. Most importantly, some sales agents have the financial resources to make or guarantee ("back") pay-or-play offers to actors. When an offer comes from an established sales agent who has credibility in the business or your offer is backed by that sales agent's good credit, you will be in a good position to secure the talent necessary to get your project financed. While these international sales agents are extremely busy, most have qualified acquisitions staffs who will promptly assess your project. It is extremely important to get to know the established foreign sales agents and their staffs.

The Producer's Representative ("Producer's Rep")

We will discuss the producer's rep further in Chapter 15, but since produce reps are so pivotal in the production, financing and distribution process, they are often involved in presales and can be instrumental in getting your project financed. The role of the producer's rep is not easy to define, since the typical rep is involved in so many different phases of the filmmaking and distribution process. In the broadest sense, they advise and consult with filmmakers in all phases of the financing, production, marketing and distribution process of the film. The producer's rep assists the filmmaker in establishing direct connections between the filmmaker and financiers, distributors, electronic media, journalists, press agents, critics and ultimately the audience.

Producers' reps have to be versatile. They act as backroom political strategists; sometimes they are cheerleaders; and other times Willie Loman-type salesmen, carnie barkers, publicists, negotiators, advertising designers and psychologists. The independent film business is a battlefield, and it is the producer's rep who serves as the field general to marshal the filmmaker's army of resources with campaigns, strategies and guerrilla techniques, to get the film financed, produced, distributed, exposed and ultimately recoup the filmmaker's investment. The route between the filmmaker, the financier, the distributor, and the audience is rarely clear, and there are numerous land mines (including—distributors buying your picture and deciding not to release it; not releasing your picture in the number of cities on the number of screens they originally said they would; not spending the amount of money they originally said they would spend; and many more) to avoid in achieving that direct connection.

Like a battle-worn veteran, an established producer's rep should have an array of skills, tactics and experience in helping filmmakers break away from obscurity to get their projects noticed, produced and making that connection with the audience. This experience includes involvement in all phases of the distribution process on a number of films and a knowledge of what sells to who and why, as well as what does not sell and why. Many producers' reps make it a point to spend 20% to 30% of their time on the road to attend the international film and television markets described above. In order to stay in touch with the current state of the marketplace for motion pictures, most producers' reps form strong personal relationships with many of the North American distributors (especially their acquisition executives) and international sales agents. This gives the producer's rep the opportunity to have first-hand knowledge of the personal tastes, genres, talent and styles of films the distributors and sales agents are attracted to. Buoyed with the knowledge of personal tastes and preferences of the various distributors and sales agents, along with an intimate understanding of each company's strengths and weaknesses, the producer's rep and the filmmaker can embark on the creation of a specific plan for the optimum presentation of the project to potential financiers, distributors and sales agents.

Since producers' reps are in constant touch with the distributors and sales agents with regard to the completed films they represent, they sometimes take on unproduced projects about which they are passionate and expose them to the appropriate distributors and sales agents in the hope of securing distribution guarantees that can trigger financing.

The producer's rep's endorsement of a project to a distributor and a sales agent will go a long way towards getting your project on the front burner, so get a producer's rep as early as possible. Producers' reps are relatively easy to find. They are listed at Independent Feature Project offices and you can find them at all the major film festivals, touting their clients' projects. A producer's rep generally charges a flat fee or a commission fee in the range of 5% to 20% of the financing or revenue they generate from the project, but these terms are negotiable depending on the budget, cast and director. Some producers' reps also charge a monthly fee either in addition to or against their percentage. Still others will take an executive producer fee from the budget of the picture as well as credit, if they are successful at setting it up.

Other Financing Sources

Even with your efforts and the efforts of the sales agent and producer's rep quite often there will be a deficit between the amounts guaranteed in presales and the cost of the picture. There are numerous other possibilities for bridging that gap. The following sections outlines various financing possibilities and when they come into play. We discuss the less traditional financing mechanisms listed on the chart below.

FINANCING YOUR INDEPENDENT PROJECT

Sources of Money	Development	Production	Distribution
Private Funding	Common	Common	Occasional
Lenders	Rare	Common	Rare
Presales	Rare	Common	Common
Tax Shelters/ Subsidies Incentives	Rare	Common	Occasional
Talent Deferrals	Common	Common	Rare
Producer Deferrals	Common	Common	Common
Soundtrack Albums	Rare	Occasional	Occasional
Music Publishing	Rare	Rare	Common
Product Placement	N/A	Rare	Rare

Soft Money

The term "soft money" comes up these days in any discussion of financing independent movies. That's because the traditional sources of money—equity investments and presales—are going through a dry spell. The ability to add so-called "soft money" to the traditional sources is now determining, for many projects, whether they can get made or not.

Soft money comes in many forms but the forms share a common feature. The motivation behind the funding is different from a traditional equity investment where the people putting in the money are concerned about getting the best return they can and different from a presale where the money buys distribution rights in the picture. The motive for providing soft money is usually to encourage production in a particular locale or facility or provide a tax benefit regardless of the ultimate profitability of a movie.

Governments are the biggest source of soft money. Within just the last twenty years, Canada, for example, has created a billion dollar film and television industry by offering soft money incentives to U.S. production companies. Generally filmmaking is regarded as a great business for the local area. The hotels and restaurants fill up. Local people get interesting, well-paying jobs. They, in turn, pay more taxes, buy more cars and DVD players and boost the local economy. Movie making creates no pollution and as a bonus, the mayor or governor or local bigwig gets to visit the set and maybe meet a star. So a variety of countries and many states within the United States have established programs to encourage moviemakers to come to their area and shoot.

A number of countries also believe it is in their interest to promote a national cinema that produces movies by and about their culture and country. While Hollywood has come to dominate the theatrical box office throughout the world, many other countries such as Australia, Russia, France, Spain, Italy, India, Mexico, the United Kingdom and Sweden, to name some of the most notable, have proud traditions of filmmaking and try to preserve and promote them.

This government support has taken many forms and we will discuss how they work below. This area, however, changes at an alarming rate. Government policies, particularly tax treatments, swing wildly back and forth between encouraging production and cracking down hard on what are sometimes thought of as wealthy and unworthy production companies and fat cats taking huge tax breaks. So, you will need to carefully investigate any specific program in a particular area before relying on it. The discussion below is intended to provide examples of how the mechanisms work, but the particular program may have changed by the time you are ready to explore using it while another practice may have come into being in the same locale.

Grants

The simplest form of soft money is a grant. Some non-profit groups occasionally provide grants to filmmakers, but usually to documentarians. It is worth exploring the McArthur Foundation, Guggenheim Foundation, The Corporation for Public Broadcasting and the Sundance Institute for support. A number of countries also have direct grant programs. Canada has had an extremely successful grant program for many years. Presently the Canadian Feature Film Fund and the Canadian Independent Film and Video Fund provide grants. In the United Kingdom there is the Film Council's Development Fund, Premiere Fund and the New Cinema Fund (see *www.filmcouncil.org.uk.*) Northern Ireland has funding through the Arts Council *(www.artscouncilni.org).* Wales has Arts Council funds *(www.acw-ccc.org.ukl)* and Scottish Screen provides some funds *(www.scottishscreen.com).* The Nordic Film and TV fund promotes production in Nordic countries by financing productions *(www.nftf.net).* The Film Finance Corporation Australia LTD has a sizeable amount of money it invests in co-financing projects. Other countries have their own funding vehicles.

You should be forewarned however that the money these funds have available is limited and they are very specific about the kinds of projects they will fund. As in many things, the insiders are more likely to know the intricacies and internal politics that surround these operations and they are the most likely to receive grants.

Production Assistance and Incentives

Another common form of soft money is to provide services or facilities for free or at a discount or to exempt productions from certain fees or taxes. Every state in the U.S. and most countries have a film commission that is charged with encouraging filmmakers to shoot in their area. Many offer a variety of incentives. Almost all film commissions, for example, often provide a library of photographs of locations and provide free assistance in contacting local suppliers, hotel operators and other production related activities. Some will fund scouting trips (for example, Minnesota). Hawaii has been known to assist in obtaining free or discounted air fares and hotel stays for productions.

Many states offer free or discounted location fees on government owned properties (e.g., Alaska, New Mexico and California). Minnesota offers free production offices. Productions often get exemptions or rebates on sales tax (Alabama, Georgia, Idaho, Illinois, Louisiana, Maine), Certain exemptions on hotel and lodging taxes are common (Alabama, Colorado, Illinois, Maine, Michigan, Montana, New Jersey and others) as are exemptions from fuel tax

(Arizona, Maine) and electricity tax (Maine).

A smaller number of states in the U.S. have rebate programs where money, usually calculated as a percentage of production funds spent in the state, is directly rebated to the production company. Oklahoma, for example, offers a 15% rebate on production money spent in-state *(www.otrd.state.ok.us/filmcommission/article.asp?a=7)*. New Mexico provides a fully refundable credit of 15% of eligible direct production costs (see *www.edd.state.nm.us/FILM/RESOURCES/resource.html*). North Dakota indicates that it will consider co-financing motion pictures shot primarily in North Dakota under certain circumstances (contact the film commission through *www.ndtourism.com*). *(See chart of state production incentives furnished by the Independent Film and Television Alliance. Reprinted with permission. Copyright 2004, 2005 I.F.T.A. All Rights Reserved.)*

Production Incentives From U.S. States

State	Sales Tax	Incentives	Contact Name	Phone	FAX	Contact Information
ALABAMA	10%	No lodging tax after 30 days. Sales and use tax abatements. Check website to determine eligibility. Right to work state. No state sales tax or income tax for individuals.	N/A	800-633-5898	334-242-2077	Alabama Film Office 401 Adams Ave., Suite 630 Montgomery, AL 36104 film@ado.state.al.us www.alabamafilm.org/
ALASKA	0%		Larry Hughes	907-465-2012	907-465-3767	State of Alaska Division of Trade and Development Alaska Film Program PO Box 110804 Juneau, Alaska 99811 alaskafilm@dced.state.ak.us www.alaskafilm.org
ARIZONA	5%	Single trip use fuel tax exemption for production vehicles crossing Arizona borders to deliver production business. No state tax on lodging after 30 days. 50% sales (transaction privilege) and use tax rebate on purchase or lease of tangible personal property for eligible productions spending $1 million or more in qualified spending in Arizona filming theater, TV, video, industrial or educational films or commercial advertising in a rolling 12 month period. Television commercials or advertising in commercials aired in two minutes or less must spend $250,000 or more to qualify for rebates. Nonresidents involved in motion picture productions exempt from wage withholding tax. Fee free filming on State Trust Lands. No cost state permits to film on state and federal highways.	Ken Chapa	800-523-6695 602-771-1193	602-771-1116	Arizona Department of Commerce Arizona Film Commission 1700 W. Washington Ste. 220 Phoenix, AZ 85007-2817 kenc@azcommerce.com www.commerce.state.az.us/Film/
ARKANSAS	5.125%	Production companies spending $500,000 within six months or $1 million within 12 months on the production of a film qualify for a gross receipts and use tax refund. This refund applies to purchases of property and services (including lodging). Potential sales & use tax refunds and income tax credits for hiring local crew (requires endorsement resolution from local governing authority) under Arkansas Enterprise Zone Program. Right to work state.	Joe Glass	800-Arkansas 501-682-7676	501-682-3456	One Capital Mall Little Rock, Arkansas 72201 jglass@1800arkansas.com www.1800arkansas.com/film
CALIFORNIA	8.25%	No state hotel tax on occupancy. No sales or use tax on production or post-production services on a motion picture or TV film. No sales or use tax on services generally (writing, acting...). Sales tax exemption(5%) on the purchase or lease of post-production equipment for qualified persons. Access to free or low-cost surplus state property (STAR - State Theatrical Arts Resources). Fee free permits on state property. Film California First Program is unfunded for 2004.	Amy Lemisch, Director	800-858-4749 323-860-2960	323-860-2972	7080 Hollywood Blvd. Suite 900 Hollywood, CA 90028 filmca@commerce.ca.gov www.film.ca.gov

COLORADO	3%	No state lodging tax after 30 days. No sales and use tax will be applied to film company services (exemption does not apply to personal property).	Stephanie B. Two Eagles	800-726-8887 303-620-4500	303-620-4545	Colorado Film Commission 1625 Broadway, Suite 1700 Denver, CO 80202 coloradofilm@state.co.us http://www.coloradofilm.org/
CONNECTICUT	6%	Sales and use tax exemptions (see website for qualifying costs). No lodging tax after 30 days. Five year exemption on local property tax on machinery and equipment used for the production of motion picture, video and sound master recordings. Fee free shooting at most public locations.	Guy Ortoleva	800-392-2122 860-571-7130	860-721-7088	805 Brook St. Building 4 Rocky Hill, CT 06067 info@ctfilm.com www.ctfilm.com/
DELAWARE	0%	No state sales tax.	Veronica Richardson	800-441-8846 302-739-4271	302-739-5749	Delaware Economic Development Department Film Office 99 Kings Highway Dover, DE 19901 veronica.richardson@state.de.us www.state.de.us/dedo/new_web_site/frames/film.html
FLORIDA	7%	Any qualified production company engaged in Florida in the production of motion pictures, made for television motion pictures, television series, commercial advertising, music videos or sound recordings may be eligible for an exemption from sales and use tax on the purchase or lease of certain items used exclusively as an integral part of the production activities in Florida. The production company must apply for a certificate of exemption to be presented to a registered Florida sales and use tax dealer when making purchases and rentals of qualified production equipment. No corporate income tax, no state property tax, no state personal income tax. A tax refund of up to $3,000 per new permanent full time job created by a new or expanding business in a qualified target industry. Right to work state.	Susan Albershardt	877-352-3456	850-410-4770	Governor's Office of Film and Entertainment Executive Office of the Governor The Capitol Tallahassee, FL 32399-0001 Susan.Albershardt@myflorida.com www.filminflorida.com
GEORGIA	5-7%	Production companies may apply for sales and use tax exemption (exemption will be applied at point of purchase). State lodging tax rebate after 90 days. Production Partnership Incentive Program. Right to work state.	Greg Torre	404-656-3591	404-656-3565	The Georgia Film, Video & Music Office 285 Peachtree Center Ave., NE Marquis Tower II Suite 1000 Atlanta, GA 30303 film@georgia.org www.filmgeorgia.org

HAWAII	4%	Income tax credit up to 4%, deductible from net income tax liability in state for film production. 7.25% deduction for costs incurred in state for transient accommodations. Must spend minimum $2 million (and satisfy other "use of Hawaii" requirements-see website) for motion pictures or $750,000 for TV pilot or MOW for maximum tax credits. If spend at least three million but integrate less "use of Hawaii" requirements then may claim 75 percent of the maximum tax credits."	Donne Dawson	808-586-2570	808-586-2572	250 S. Hotel St. Ste 510-B Honolulu, HI 96813 ddawson@dbedt.hawaii.gov www.hawaiifilmoffice.com
IDAHO	5%	All taxes are waived for lodging stays of more than 30 days.	Peg Owens	208-334-2470 800-942-8338	208-334-2631	700 West State St. PO Box 83720 Boise, Idaho 83720-0093 powens@idoc.state.id.us www.filmidaho.com
ILLINOIS	6.25%	Exemption from sales and use tax on products used for photoprocessing involved in commercial motion pictures. No state lodging tax after 30 days. The Illinois Film Production Services Tax Credit Act provides for an income tax credit of 25% for wages paid to each Illinois residents working on television and film projects shot in Illinois (limited to first $25,000 and productions of 30 minutes or more will have to spend at least $100,000 on Illinois labor).	Brenda Saxton	312-814-3600	312-814-8874	100 W. Randolph Suite 3-400 Chicago, IL 60601 info@commerce.state.il.us www.filmillinois.state.il.us
INDIANA	5%	Lodging tax waived for 30 consecutive days lodging. No permits required for most locations.	Chris Pohl Project Manager	317-232-8829	317-233-6887	Indiana Film Commission Dept. of Commerce Indiana One North Capitol Ave. Suite 700 Indianapolis, IN 46204-2288 filminfo@commerce.state.in.us www.filmindiana.com
IOWA	5%	No state lodging tax after 30 days. No permits required for most locations. Right to work state.	N/A	515-242-4726	515-242-4809	200 E. Grand Ave. Des Moines, IA 50309 filmiowa@ided.state.ia.us www.filmiowa.com
KANSAS	4.9%	Right to work state.	Peter Jasso	785-296-4927	785-296-3490	Kansas Film Commission 1000 S.W Jackson Street, Suite 100 Topeka, KS 66612-1354 eschroeder@kansascommerce.com www.filmkansas.com

KENTUCKY	6%	Sales and use tax refund on purchases in Kentucky for productions filmed or produced in the state during any 12 month period.500 Mero St.	Todd Cassidy	800-345-6591 502-564-3456	502-564-7588	Kentucky Film Commission 2200 Capital Plaza Tower Frankfort, KY 40901 Todd.Cassidy@mail.state.ky.us Dian.Knight@mail.state.ky.us www.kyfilmoffice.com/
LOUISIANA	4%	Investor Tax Credit - Tax credit for taxpayers domiciled and headquartered in LA- If total base investment is between $300,000 and $1 million, each taxpayer allowed a 10% tax credit of the investment. If the investment is more than $1 million, each taxpayer allowed a 15% tax credit. These tax credits are allowed against the income tax for the taxable period in which the credit is earned. If the tax credit exceeds the amount of taxes due, the unused credit may be carried forward 10 years. Labor Tax Credit - The credit is 10% of total aggregate payroll for residents employed in connection with production when total production costs in LA are between $300,000 and $1million during taxable year. The credit is 20% of total aggregate payroll for residents employed in connection with such production when total production costs in LA equal or exceed $1 million during the taxable year. Unused tax credits can be carried forward 10 years. State and use tax exclusion if report anticipated expenditures of $250,000 or more from a checking account in LA in connection with filming or production in LA w/in any consecutive 12 months.	Mark Smith	225-342-8150 888-655-0447	225-342-5349	Office of Film and Television Department PO Box 94185 Baton Rouge, LA 70804-9185 msmith@lded.state.la.us http://www.lafilm.org/
MAINE	5%	Sales tax exemption for producers. State lands are fee free locations for filming. Surplus state property program allows production company to borrow surplus state equipment. No state lodging tax after 27 days (lodging tax is 7%).	Lea Girardin	207-624-7631	207-287-8070	Maine Film Office 59 State House Station Augusta, ME 04333 lea.girardin@maine.gov filmme@earthlink.net www.filminmaine.com
MARYLAND	5%	Sales and use tax exemption for the purchase or lease of production or post-production equipment, services, supplies, props and sets used in the production of motion picture, television, video, commercials and corporate films. No state lodging tax after 30 days. Location fee free state lands and properties.	Jack Gerbes, Director Catherine Batavick, Deputy Director	800-333-6632 410-767-6340	410-333-0044	217 E. Redwood St., 9th Floor Baltimore, MD 21202 filminfo@marylandfilm.org www.marylandfilm.org
MASSACHUSETTS	5%	Fee-free state locations.	Jonathan Paris	617-624-1237	617-624-1239	Massachussetts Sports and Entertainment Commission c/o The Fleetcenter 1 Fleet Center Place, Ste 200 Boston, MA 02114 jparis@masports.org www.masports.org/film.html

MICHIGAN	6%	Hotel tax (ranging from 1% - 8%) is refunded after 30 days.	Janet Lockwood	800-477-3456 517-373-0638	517-241-2930	Michigan Film Office 702 W. Kalamazoo Lansing, MI 48909 jlockwood@mi.gov michigan.gov/filmoffice
MINNESOTA	6.5%	No sales tax on creative services and no lodging tax after 30 days.	Craig Rice	612-332-6493	612-332-3735	Minnesota Film and TV Board 401 N. 3rd St., Suite 460 Minneapolis, MN 55401 info@mnfilm.org www.mnfilm.org
MISSISSIPPI	7.25%	10% tax credit of the total aggregate payroll for employing Mississippi residents; 10% rebate on base investment;sales tax on machinery and equipment used in production lowered to 1 1/2%. Sales tax exemption expanded to include other equipment in production. Right to work state.	Ward Emling	601-359-3297	601-359-5048	Woolfolk Building 501 North West Street, 5th Floor Jackson, MS 39201 wemling@mississippi.org www.visitmississippi.org/film/index.asp
MISSOURI	4.25%	Tax credit up to 50% of expenditures in the state, amount of credit not to exceed $500,000 per project. Entire program is capped at $1 million annually, so pre-application process is available (tax credits can be set aside for a project). Hotel tax rebate after 31 days.	Jerry Jones	573-751-9050	573-522-1719	Harry S Truman Building 301 West High, Room 720 PO Box 118 Jefferson City, MO 65102 mofilm@ded.mo.gov www.ecodev.state.mo.us/film/
MONTANA	0%	No state sales tax. No property tax on out-of-state equipment used for motion picture or commercial production. No state lodging tax after 30 days.	Sten Iversen	800-553-4563 406-841-2876	406-841-2877	301 S. Park Street PO Box 200533 Helena, MT 59620-0533 sten@visitmt.com www.montanafilm.com
NEBRASKA	5 .5%	No state lodging tax after 30 days. Free usage of Nebraska Game and Parks Commission - controlled land and facilities. Right to work state.	Stu Miller	402-471-3680	402-471-3778	PO Box 98907 Lincoln, NE 68509-8907 info@filmnebraska.org www.filmnebraska.org
NEVADA	7. 5%	No corporate or individual income tax. Right to work state.	Charles Geocaris, Director	877-638-3456 702-486-2711	702-486-2712	555 E. Washington Ave., Suite 5400 Las Vegas, NV 89101 lvnfo@bizopp.state.nv.us www.nevadafilm.com

State	Tax	Incentives	Contact	Phone	Fax	Address
NEW HAMPSHIRE	0%	No state sales tax. Individual income tax on interest and dividends only. No property tax on machinery or equipment. No capital gains tax. Permit free locations.	Margaret Joyce	800-262-6660 603-271-2665	603-271-6870	172 Pembroke Road PO Box 1856 Concord, NH 03302-1856 filmnh@dred.state.nh.us www.filmnh.org
NEW JERSEY	6%	Sales tax exemption for film and video machinery and equipment (includes services of installing, repairing, and maintaining the equipment). Applies to use of equipment in production and post production of motion pictures, television, or commercials. The Film Production Assistance Program allows film projects to be eligible for loan guarantees through the New Jersey Economic Development Authority. Lodging tax exemption after 90 days."	Joseph Friedman	973-648-6279	973-648-7350	153 Halsey St., 5th Floor PO Box 47023 Newark, NJ 07101 NJFILM@njfilm.org www.njfilm.org
NEW MEXICO	5%	1) 15% tax credit on New Mexico based production expenses; No sales tax at point of sale for commercial filming 2) NTTC Program (gross receipts tax deduction); 3) No charge for filming at state-owned facilities 4) Workforce Training Program. For More details visit website at www.nmfilm.com	Frank Zuniga	800-545-9871 505-827-9810	505-827-9799	New Mexico Film Office PO Box 20003 Santa Fe, NM 87504-5003 film@nmfilm.com www.nmfilm.com
NEW YORK	4% - 8.5%	Sales and use tax exemption for machinery, equipment and services used in production and post-production activities for feature length films, television, music videos and commercials. No charge for permits in NY City. In order to qualify for the NY Film Production Tax Credit program, at least 75% of total stage work must be done on a qualified stage in NY. These productions will receive a 10% tax credit for eligible production costs including most production and post production costs such as: technical and crew costs, production props, makeup, wardrobe, film processing, camera, background talent, facilities, sound recording, set construction, lighting, shooting, editing and meals. It does not include costs for a story, script or scenario or wages or salaries for writers, directors, etc (except for background actors with no script lines. Qualified films include feature length films, television films, television pilots and/or each episode of a television series. Each calendar year will have a $25 million cap.	Katherine Oliver	212-489-6710	212-307-6237	Mayor's Office of Film, Theatre & Broadcasting 1697 Broadway #602 NYC, NY 10019 http://nyc.gov/film
NORTH CAROLINA	6% - 6.5%	Savings of 83% on sales and use tax on the purchase and rentals to motion picture production firms or cameras, films, set construction materials, as well as chemicals and equipment used to develop and edit film that is used to produce release prints. Exemption taken at the point of purchase. Full exemption for the purchase of film that becomes a component part of release prints sold or leased. The chemicals used to develop release prints and audiovisual master tapes used for production are also exempt from sales tax. Savings of 83% on state sales tax on items rented or purchased for filmmaking. Right to work state."	Bill Arnold	919-733-9900	919-715-0151	North Carolina Film Office 301 N. Wilmington St. Raleigh, NC 27601-2825 barnold@nccommerce.com www.ncfilm.com/

NORTH DAKOTA	"6%	Most cities and counties have no permit fees. Right to work state.	Mark Zimmerman	800-435-5663 701-328-2509	701-328-4878	North Dakota Film Commission 1600 East Century Ave Bismark, ND 58501 mzimmerman@state.nd.us www.ndtourism.com/Resources/viewArticle.asp?choice=&ID=62
OHIO	8%	No state lodging tax after 30 days. $10 state permit fees for most locations.	Christine Groxik-Cleveland Christine Erwin-Cincinnati	216-623-3910 (Cleveland) 513-784-1744 (Cincinnati)	216-623-0876 (Cleveland) 513-768-8963 (Cincinnati)	50 Public Square, Ste 825 Cleveland, OH 44113 602 Main Street, Suite 712 Cincinnati, OH 45202 cgrozik@clevelandfilm.com infro@film-cincinnati-org www.clevlandfilm.com www.filmcincinnati.com
OKLAHOMA	4.5%	A film company may be eligible to receive a 15% rebate by providing proof of completion bond and distribution agreement. Contingent on the availability of funds, the 15% rebate is on eligible costs for film production in the state (if an income tax return is filed there) with total payments not exceeding $2 million per fiscal year. Check website for further details. A production can get local and state sales tax combined returned in the form of a rebate. Sales tax exemption on sales of tangible, personal property or services for a motion picture or television production company to be used or consumed in connection with and eligible production. An "eligible production" is defined as all television productions (but no commercials) TV pilot or on-going series televised on a network or a feature-length motion picture intended for theatrical release. No state lodging tax after 30 days. Oklahoma is a right-to-work state.	Dino Lalli	800-766-3456 405-522-6760	405-522-0656	Oklahoma Film and Music Commission 15 N. Robinson, Suite 802 Oklahoma City, OK 73102 dlalli@otrd.state.ok.us www.oklahomafilm.org
OREGON	0%	No sales tax & waive lodging tax after 30 days. Case-by-case rebates from Governor's Strategic Reserve Fund, as available. Many government buildings and small towns are fee-free. Parking rebate Portland. Beginning July 2005: 10% rebate on all spending in Oregon, up program in to maximum rebate of $250,000 per movie or $30,000 per episode for a television series.	Veronica Rinard	503-229-5832	503-229-6869	Oregon Film and Video Office One World Trade Center 121 SW Salmon Suite 1205 Portland, OR 97204 shoot@oregonfilm.org www.oregonfilm.org/

PENNSYLVANIA	6%	If at least 60% of total production expenses are incurred in Pennsylvania, a film company may apply for a 20% Film Production Tax Credit. A taxpayer seeking the credit must submit an application to the Depart. of Revenue of the Commonwealth by February 15 for those production expenses incurred in the taxable year of the prior calendar year. Production expenses include: wages, salaries, editing, wardrobe, lighting, etc... It does not include film marketing and advertising costs. The taxpayer may also sell or assign the tax credits. For more info contact www.filminpa.com. Also, a 6% sales and use tax exemption for the purchase of props,sets, supplies, tools, production and post production services including processing, editing, etc. No lodging tax after 30 days.	Jane Shecter	717-783-3456	717-787-0687	Pennsylvania Film Office Commonwealth Keystone Building 400 North St., 4th Floor Harrisburg, PA 17120-0225 jshecter@state.pa.us www.filminpa.com/
RHODE ISLAND	7%	25% investment tax credit for film production companies who have an income tax liability in Rhode Island. Productions between $300,000 and 1 Million. Incentive to Producer.	Rick Smith	401-222-3456	401-273-8270	Rhode Island Film & TV Office Rhode Island State Counsel on the Arts One Capitol Hill, Providence, RI 02903 rsmith@arts.ri.gov www.rifilm.com/
SOUTH CAROLINA	5%	Sales and Use tax exemption on the supplies and equipment used in the production of motion pictures and television programs. Corporate and personal income tax exemptions for investments in South Carolina projects or production facilities. Right to work state.	Dan Rogers	803-737-0490	803-737-3104	South Carolina Film Office PO Box 7367 Columbia, SC drogers@teamsc.com www.scfilmoffice.com/
SOUTH DAKOTA	4%	No state income tax. 4% lodging tax for 28 days, exemption after that. No general permits required. Right to work state.	Chris Hull	800-952-3625 605-773-3301	605-773-3256	Media Services Center 711 East Wells Ave. Pierre, SD 57501 Chris.Hull@state.sd.us www.mediasd.com
TENNESSEE	9.25%	Sales and use tax refund for goods and services purchased or rented in Tennessee if an out-of-state production company spends at least $500,000 within a 12-month period. Right to work state.	David Bennett	877-818-3456	615-741-5554	Tennessee Film, Entertainment and Music Commission William R. Snodgrass - Tennessee Tower, 9th Floor 312 8th Avenue North Nashville, TN 37243 tn.film@state.tn.us david.j.bennett@state.tn.us www.state.tn.us/film/
4 TEXAS	6.25%	Sales tax exemption for most purchased and rented equipment or services. Services and equipment must be used exclusively in the production of a motion picture or a video recording for ultimate sale, license or broadcast. This includes cable broadcast. No state lodging tax after 30 days. Refund for fuel taxes for unlicensed, off-road vehicles, including generators."	Carol Pirie	512-463-9200	512-463-4114	Texas Film Commission PO Box 13246 Austin, TX 78711 film@governor.state.tx.us www.texasfilmcommission.com

UTAH	6.75%	No state lodging tax after 30 days. Right to work state.	Leigh von der Esch	800-453-8824 801-538-8740	801-538-8746	Utah Film Commission 324 South State Street, Suite 500 Salt Lake City, UT 84111 LVONDERE@utah.gov www.film.utah.org/
VERMONT	5%	No tax on hotel stays in excess of 30 days. Exemption of sales and use tax on products, goods and services used in the making of a motion picture, television program or commercial. Income tax rate on the performer's salary is based on the lower of Vermont's income tax or the performer's home state's income tax rate.	Danis Regal	802-828-3618	802-828-0607	Vermont Film Commission 20 Baldwin Street, Drawer 33 Montepelier, VT 05633 vermontfilm@state.vt.us www.vermontfilm.com
VIRGINIA	4.5%	Sales and use tax exemption for the purchase of production equipment, supplies and accessories. Hotel lodging tax rebate after 90 days. Many state-owned locations are available free of charge. Government Motion Picture Opportunity Fund offering a rebate of up to 15% on labor costs and 10% on production resource services. Right to work state.	Rita McClenny	800-854-6233 804.371.8204	804-371-8177	Virginia Film Office 901 East Byrd St. Richmond, VA 23219-4048 rmcclenny@virginia.org www.film.virginia.org
WASHINGTON	6.5% - 8.8%	Sales and use tax exemption for purchase or rental of production equipment and services used in motion picture or video production or post-production. No sales and use tax on vehicles used in production. Lodging tax exemption after 30 days. No state individual income tax.New fee of $25 per day for Master City Film Permits. Use of City property, including parks and facilities, as part of the film permit fee. Parking passes for location scouts. Increased availability of large, dedicated studio space at Sand Point, a former naval airbase. Support for low-impact productions. Streamlined permit process and costs.	Suzy Kellett	206-256-6151	206-256-6154	2001 6th Ave., Suite 2600 Seattle, WA 98121 wafilm@cted.wa.gov www.filmwashington.com
WEST VIRGINIA	6%	Certain incentives are determined on a project-by-project basis	Pamela Haynes	304-558-2200 x 382	304-558-1662	West Virginia Film Office c/o West Virginia Division of Tourism 90 MacCorkle Ave., SW South Charleston, WV 25303 phaynes@callwva.com www.wvfilm.com
WISCONSIN	6%	No film permits required.	Mary Idso	800-345-6947 608-267-0761	608-266-3403	Wisconsin Film Office 201 W. Washington Ave., 2nd Floor Madison, WI 53703 midso@filmwisconsin.org www.filmwisconsin.org/

WYOMING	4%	10% discount on various services & equipment with contracted vendors. No state lodging tax after 30 days. No state corprate or individual income tax. Right to work state.	Michell Phelan	800-458-6657 307-777-3400	307-777-2838	Wyoming Film Office I-25 at College Drive Cheyenne, WY 82002-0240 mphela@state.wy.us www.wyomingfilm.org
PUERTO RICO		40% rebate on shooting costs while in the country. Payroll subsidized up to 20% for local hires. No sales tax on hotel room after three (3) days.	Laura Velez	787- 758-4747 EXT. 2251	787- 756.5706	Puerto Rico Film Commission P.O. BOX 362350 San Juan, Puerto Rico 00936-2350 lavelez@pridco.com www.puertoricofilm.com/index_e.htm
DISTRICT OF COLUMBIA	5. 75%	No film incentives.	Crystal Palmer	202-727-6608	202-727-3787	Office of Motion Picture & TV 410 8th St., NW, 6th Floor Washington, DC 20004 crystal.palmer@dc.gov www.film.dc.gov
VIRGIN ISLANDS				340-775-1444		http://www.bvitouristboard.com /frames.php?page=/movies/information.php3

THIS INFORMATION IS PROVIDED FOR REFERENCE PURPOSES ONLY, IS SUBJECT TO CHANGE AND IS NOT INTENDED TO BE A COMPLETE DESCRIPTION OF EACH STATE'S INCENTIVE PROGRAM. PLEASE CONTACT THE LOCAL FILM COMMISSIONER FOR THE MOST CURRENT INCENTIVE INFORMATION.

Tax Shelters

Tax shelter soft money is particularly complicated, but we will try to give you an idea of how it basically operates. Both individuals and companies are subject to income tax and throughout the world, and legions of accountants, tax lawyers and advisers spend their lives trying to reduce the amount of income tax that their clients pay. Under most tax systems, income is reduced by deductions for costs incurred in generating the income. A grocery store, for example, deducts the cost of the products it sells along with rent and wages to employees in calculating the net income on which it is taxed. Clever minds have devised ways to use movie production to increase deductions and thereby reduce income tax.

Here is a much-simplified example in an imaginary country. A wealthy doctor has net income from her practice of $1,000,000. The income tax rate is 50% so the doctor's tax bill should be $500,000. But before the doctor writes the check and vows to move to the Cayman Islands, a tax shelter promoter comes along. This gentleman tells the doctor about an investment opportunity in an upcoming blockbuster movie and explains the tax consequences. The movie producer has a $1,000,000 budget and through presales and equity has raised $900,000. That leaves the producer $100,000 shy of what he needs to make the movie. The tax shelter promoter suggests that the doctor buy all rights in the yet-to-be-produced movie for $25,000 that goes directly into the tax shelter promoter's pocket. The doctor then hires the movie producer to shoot the movie and uses the $900,000 in presales plus $100,000 of the doctor's own money to complete it. She then licenses all distribution rights in the movie to the movie producer in exchange for a small, often illusory piece of net profits.

At this point in time, the producer has gotten the movie made, has received $100,000 in soft money from the doctor to help complete it and also has all the distribution rights back. The tax shelter promoter has made $25,000. So how is this such a great deal for the doctor?

The doctor has put up $125,000 in cash and may never see it again. But she also has produced a movie that cost $1,000,000. Her country has a tax policy that encourages new businesses and movies in particular, and under its laws, the entire cost of production can be deducted in the year the costs were incurred. (Most tax systems require expenditures for things like movies to be deducted gradually over a number of years.) So the doctor has a deduction of $1,000,000 that she can subtract from her $1,000,000 in net income from practicing medicine. That deduction wipes out all her income and thereby wipes out her $500,000 tax bill. In the end, the $125,000 she put into the movie saves her $500,000 for a nice, tidy savings of $375,000.

This sounds like a scam that would end up with the doctor, tax shelter promoter and the movie producer doing prison time. But when the intricate requirements of the tax system are satisfied, this approach is tolerated and even encouraged by various countries. The technique also is not unique to the movie business. The same basic structure has been used for everything from airliners to industrial machinery. In the 1980's Canada, for example, had several large tax shelter operations that were involved in other industries. At a chance meeting at a hotel swimming pool in Hawaii, a U.S. producer met the president of a Canadian tax shelter operation that was involved in other industries. One thing lead to another and within months, a major U.S. television mini-series was being shot in Canada under a tax shelter program. Scores of other U.S. movie and television projects then followed and a major new industry took hold in Canada. As discussed below, Canada eventually made a policy decision that it would be better and cheaper to cut out the tax shelter operators and to provide a more direct incentive to American film producers so it changed its tax regulations.

Today, the tax laws and regulations of Germany, the United Kingdom and Hawaii, among others, offer significant tax shelter programs for companies and wealthy individuals and these territories are important sources of soft money for the movie business. While there are strict provisions that govern what projects qualify and the benefits are less than the doctor in our fictional example received, tax shelters have resulted in big booms in production in these countries.

New U.S. Federal Tax Incentives

The United States has finally responded to the various foreign tax incentives by setting up its own incentives. After a full-court lobbying effort from the independent film production community and the entertainment guilds, The American Jobs Creation Act of 2004 ("Act") was signed into law on October 22, 2004. It includes a number of provisions designed to help independent producers by stimulating investment in the production films and television programs. The Act will have a major impact on the financing, production, structure, and taxation of independent films.

U.S. taxpayers may now write-off against income 100% of the qualified cost of production of motion pictures and television programs budgeted at $15 million or less (or up to $20 million if a significant amount of the production expenditures are incurred in certain low income or depressed areas in the U.S.) in the same year as those production costs were incurred. To qualify, the Act requires that at least 75% of the total compensation expended on the production (not including residuals and participations) be for services performed in the United States. Detailed regulations eventually will determine exactly what compensation can be counted towards the 75%, but it appears that at a minimum it will include the salaries for actors, directors, producers and crew.

Previous U.S. tax regulations generally required the taxpayer to write-off the cost of production of a motion picture using one of two methods: Either straight line over 15 years or under the income forecast method. The straight-line method limited the deduction of production costs to one fifteenth each year and was rarely used. Income forecast was designed to permit the same percentage of production costs to be deducted each year as the percentage of total income forecast to come in during the same year (e.g. if 50% of income was projected to come in year 1 then 50% of the production costs could be written off in year 1). In practice neither method allowed the entire cost of production to be deducted in the year the movie was made. The Act now accelerates that write-off for qualifying production costs into one year. These provisions went into effect in October 2004 and they are scheduled to expire at the end of 2008.

Another provision of the Act makes some important changes to the write-off method for productions that do not qualify for the 100% write-off. We, however, expect that most independent films shot in the U.S. will be able to qualify for the more generous provisions of the 100% write off.

The Act also creates a new deduction from income calculated as a percentage of qualified production activities income. This provision goes into effect in 2005 and the percentage deduction ramps up over time starting at 3% and reaching 9% in 2009. As with the accelerated write-off provision referred to above, only motion pictures primarily using U.S. labor will qualify. In this case, 50% of the qualified production costs must be paid to U.S. actors, producers, directors and production personnel rendering services in the United States. It is expected that creative producers and tax planners will quickly devise methods of allowing wealthy investors to get the benefits of these new deductions against income in exchange for investments in productions.

Although further implementing regulations will be promulgated to provide additional guidelines, we anticipate that independent producers will take immediate steps to avail themselves of the advantages brought by the Act. Many provisions of the Act will require very careful analysis because of their complexity; of course, expert legal and tax advice are essential to properly access these incentives. Nonetheless, early analysis of the Act suggests that the benefits could amount to as much a 25% of the production costs of a qualifying production (that is $2.5M on a $10M film). Such an immense contribution for hard-to-finance indie productions is expected to stimulate a new wave of U.S. production activities and retard the exodus of runaway productions to the foreign locales listed in this chapter that already have offered subsidies and tax relief.

Great Britain

England is well-known for its sale and leaseback transactions. This soft money mechanism has been widely used, not just for small independent films, but for major Hollywood projects as well. It is a refined form of the tax shelter deal described above with the doctor.

In simplified form, a filmmaker sells a completed but unreleased film to someone with a large British tax liability. In the past this was usually a major corporation such as a bank, but recently film investment partnerships have been formed and solicited funds from wealthy individuals. Those funds are estimated to have raised about U.K. 500 million in 2002 and 2003.

The transaction requires that the picture qualify as a "British Film" under the Films Act of 1985 either under Schedule 1 of that act or as a co-production. The acquirer then leases it back to the producer for a period of typically 10 to 15 years. The producer is then free to exploit the film for the period of the lease. In order that the acquirer does not have the burden and risk of collecting lease payments over a number of years from the producer, the discounted total of the lease payments are usually placed on deposit with a bank that then makes the periodic payments to the acquirer for an administration fee. At the end of the lease, the rights can revert to the producer.

Films that meet the criteria of Section 42 of the Finance Act are permitted to write off production costs over three years. Films that cost less than U.K. 15 million and qualify as "British" under the Films Act of 1985 can meet the criteria of Section 48 of the Finance Act. Those pictures are permitted to write off 100% of production costs in one year, which is a very attractive opportunity for someone fortunate enough to have a large tax liability.

In these transactions, the acquirer of the picture gets the deduction over either one or three years and then receives the lease payments over 10 to 15 years. The lease payments are taxable to the acquirer, so much of its benefit is tax deferral. It still pays tax, but is able to postpone the day of reckoning.

The discounted lease payments prepaid by the producer are less than the sale price and the difference represents the soft money benefit to the producer. The amount of the benefit depends on various factors including size of the film and competition for deals but is generally in the range of 9% to 14% of the cost of the film.

In 2002 and 2003, several British investment funds stepped outside the Finance Act and instead of utilizing the criteria of Section 42 or 48, they relied on an application of "generally accepted accounting practices" and provided more aggressive write offs to investors which could generate up to 45% of the budget for a qualified film. Inland Revenue, the U.K.'s tax authority abruptly shut down this approach in early 2004 leaving many projects in jeopardy. The legal and accounting wizards in London immediately commenced devising new financial products to fill new loopholes.

In the fall of 2004. the British Treasury Department issued new regulations covering tax treatment of British films under Section 48. Section 48 tax relief was to expire in July 2005, but now such tax relief will still be available through April 5, 2006 provided that principal photography of the applicable film commenced before July 2, 2005. Under the new regulations, which will commence on July 2, 2005, British tax credits will be available to fund 20% of qualified British film production costs compared to 15% under Section 48. The qualifying film must be intended for theatrical release in the U.K. or elsewhere. Additionally, films costing up to U.K. 20 million will be eligible for such tax treatment as opposed to up to U.K. 15 million under Section 48. The tax relief will apply to all production expenditure, not just the U.K. spend. A key new feature that will be welcomed by filmmakers is that the tax relief funding will be required to be paid directly to the filmmakers and not through third party intermediaries so that the system will be less open to abuse than previously. The maximum tax incentives available under the new system will rise to U.K. 4 million, as opposed to a cap of U.K. 2.25 million under Section 48.

The rules specify that production expenditure eligible for tax relief will not include: Expenditures incurred on financing for the film; deferments, profit participations, and any other payments that are dependent on the commercial performance of the film; reinvestments or similar circular flows of money; any expenditure on pre-existing material and on any rights beyond rights solely attributable to the production of the film; entertainment expenses; and general business overhead. The new regulations will not be limited to any time period, but will be monitored closely and re-evaluated. There will be a scheduled review of the new regulations in 2010 after five years of operation. Stay tuned and be aware of the ever changing world of soft money regulations and incentives in the U.K.

Canada

The Canadian government has long encouraged its film industry and has had a very successful grant program for pictures by and about Canadians. In the early 1990s the use of tax shelters encouraged many American television and movie producers to shoot in Canada for the soft money benefits those programs offered.

The Canadian government, however, took steps in the late 1990s to squelch the tax shelter programs and it substituted a federal program that was intended to provide a comparable incentive to U.S. production companies but at a lower cost to the treasury of Canada.

The program offered a refundable tax credit or rebate to production companies equal to 11% of the funds they spent employing Canadians working on a picture. That credit was increased to 16% of the qualified Canadian labor expenditures in the 2003 federal budget. The credit or rebate is structured so that it is not simply an offset against Canadian taxes. It was a cash payment to the production company. The federal program was designed to be supplemented by similar programs offered by provinces. British Columbia and Ontario, for example, initiated production services tax credit programs that provide a rebate of 11% of the qualified Canadian labor costs. Several provinces have offered even more generous rebates. Manitoba provides 35% and New Brunswick provides 40%. The provincial rebates can be combined with the federal tax credit.

The success of the Canadian soft money programs is marked by the nearly $5 billion in annual expenditures for film and television.

What makes the Canadian production services tax credit programs particularly attractive for U.S. producers is that there is no requirement that certain jobs be performed by Canadians or that a minimum percentage of production costs be spent in Canada. The production company is free to use an American director, but it gets a 20% rebate on the salary if it hires a Canadian one. Only pictures costing at least CN$1M qualify for the program. Producers of those pictures have the flexibility to spend a lot of the budget on Canadian labor or a little, but the production company has a significant incentive to employ Canadians which is the objective of the program.

Canada has a more restrictive program of refundable tax credits for films that meet the standard of having "Canadian Content" and being certified by the Canadian Audio-Visual Certification Office (CAVCO). To meet those criteria, either the director or screenwriter and one of the two highest paid actors must be Canadian. Points are awarded for other key Canadian production personnel and if the picture meets all the criteria and obtains the necessary points, it can receive refundable tax credits equal to 25% of the expenditures for Canadians.

Canada also is party to 56 bilateral film co-production treaties with other countries. There is, however, no co-production treaty between the United States and Canada and none is anticipated in the near future. As noted above, a co-production treaty offers qualifying projects the opportunity to take advantage of soft money mechanisms in more than one country on the same picture. The most frequent Canadian co-productions are with the United Kingdom and France.

Germany

Soft money in Germany is provided by a number of private media funds that collectively raised over U.S. $3 billion in 2003. These funds solicit private investors who receive a sheltering of income taxes through investing in closed end funds that co-finance a slate of pictures.

In order to qualify for the maximum tax deductions under German law, the individual investors must be regarded as "producers" and hence the money spent on the film constitutes "business expenses" for them. The German Ministry of Finance has tightened the standards for qualifying as an "investor" so the laws and regulations that govern the operation of these funds are strict and pose some difficulties for motion picture producers who choose to utilize them.

In most cases, the larger, well-established funds prefer to work with experienced production companies and on larger budgeted projects. They closely examine the budget. They require that some essential production (shooting, or post production) take place in Germany and that the picture contain some German technical and creative elements. They require significant presales with limits on the sales fees charged. The picture must have a completion bond and appropriate insurance and finally the fund must be at least co-owner of the copyright and must have a right of control over the production. These controls are exercised through an investor committee.

For productions able and willing to meet these criteria, the funds can provide up to 50% of the budget.

Other Territories

Movies are shot all over the world and where there are movies being shot, there is usually soft money. We have covered the territories where the most soft money production of English language pictures takes place, but we will mention and comment on several others that you may want to investigate if the location makes sense for your project.

Australia has tax incentive programs, but they are considered hard to access. France, Italy and Spain are active in co-productions primarily with other European countries although Spain also co-produces on many Latin American projects. South Africa has a persistent, if erratic, private tax fund program. There are film studios and production companies in Luxembourg, Romania, Russia and various East European countries that can provide fantastic facilities at astounding prices. Countries have even been willing to provide their armies as extras. India is the most voluminous movie producer in the world and a number of Los Angeles based production companies are now producing there with the assistance of soft money.

Given the current difficulty in raising production financing from U.S. equity sources and from presales of foreign rights, soft money is usually an essential ingredient in getting independent films made where the budget exceeds $2M. And these days by the time a producer delivers a movie, he or she likely will know far more about tax laws and regulations than they ever imagined.

Co-Productions

Many of the movies utilizing soft money are co-productions involving more than one country. The fact that multiple countries are involved does not provide any unique financing benefits that are not available to films made completely within a country, but it allows a production company to take simultaneous advantage of soft money benefits from more than one country on the same picture. So, for example, a Canadian/U.K. co-production can get both labor rebates provided under Canadian federal and provincial programs and also get the soft money benefits of a U.K. sale and leaseback transaction. Turning it into a ménage a trois by adding a French co-producer can add even more benefits.

Stacking these soft money benefits through a co-production can be lucrative but it is mind bogglingly complicated. The starting point is that the countries involved have to have a co-production treaty with each other. Those are very specific in what they provide, but in essence they agree to treat companies from each other's country the same as they treat companies from their own country. That allows the co-production to get the soft money benefits, provided they meet the qualifications set out in the treaty or regulations.

The U.K., for example, has co-production treaties with Australia, Canada, France, Germany, Italy, New Zealand, and Norway. Those treaties contain provisions that require that each of the co-producing companies meets certain levels of financial contribution and creative input. The United States unfortunately does not have motion picture co-production treaties with any other countries and American producers generally can only participate as minority partners with very limited involvement and credits.

In addition to formal co-production treaties, many European countries are signatories to the European Convention on Cinematographic Co-production that provides for co-productions among the member countries. Again, these co-productions have strict requirements concerning shooting, expenditures and creative input that must be met for a picture to qualify.

The most extreme stacking of co-production benefits we have seen involved three countries and allowed a producer to make a movie with a $200,000 presale and $800,000 in soft money. It is much more common for soft money to provide 10-30% of the cost of making a movie.

If you want to seriously pursue any of this funding, you will need to engage the services of local attorneys, accountants or fund managers who specialize in the area and can advise you on the intricacies. Often it takes a long time to qualify a production for soft money benefits and since regulations change often, a producer runs a risk of encountering an adverse change in one country while waiting for approval in another. You will need a specialist who has contacts and follows what is happening in several countries simultaneously to help you with co-productions.

Talent Fee Deferrals

Talent (actors and directors) fee deferrals are simple in concept, but complex in implementation. The basic notion is that you pay the talent less than their "studio quote" (last price on a studio picture) but give them an opportunity to earn more revenue as proceeds are derived from the picture. At the studios, talent deferrals have become much more popular as guaranteed fees for actors have skyrocketed up to $25 million and for directors over $10 million. Mark was involved in structuring one of the pioneering talent deferral deals on the Universal hit picture *Twins.* Arnold Schwarzenegger, Danny DeVito and Ivan Reitman deferred their traditional high salaries and received minimum scale payments, but were rewarded with very substantial first dollar gross backends. The appeal of the deal to Universal was that the production cost on *Twins* was drastically reduced. Thus, if *Twins* turned out to be a flop, Universal had succeeded in shifting a substantial portion of the production cost risk to the talent. However, if *Twins* were a hit, Universal would make less money because the talent had in effect invested in the picture and would receive amounts far in excess of their studio quote for their risk. Fortunately, *Twins* was a huge hit and grossed $216 million worldwide and everyone was happy.

The deferral concept also applies to independent films. If an actor makes $2 million per picture, and you offer him $100,000, he is looking to make up for that $1.9M from proceeds from the film, along with a premium on his risk investment. There are two ways to accomplish this. The first is to give the actor a deferral of the $1.9M by specifying that it will be paid contingent on the film generating sufficient revenue. The second is to give the actor a "first dollar gross deal." Assume you are willing to make a $100,000 payment against 10% of the gross from first dollar. Since the $100,000 is an advance against the first $1 million of income, you do not have to pay the actor anything further while you receive the first $1 million in revenue since he is earning out his advance. However, for every dollar after you receive $1M, you have to pay the actor

10%. Gross participations and deferments can become very complicated, heavily negotiated and sometimes they do not work, as the other investors and the distributors and equity investors want their money back first. However, talent deal deferrals are an integral part of independent filmmaking today, especially to attract star actors and directors who are used to studio prices.

Producer Fee Deferrals

Producer fee deferrals work very much like talent fee deferrals, with one fundamental exception. Typically, when producers defer fees, they have to wait for all the other investors, including the talent who deferred their fees, to get their money back before they get theirs. There are many independent films where the producers get no money until the picture is in profits.

One intermediate step is for the producer to defer a part of the fee and treat it as a part of the contingency. Sometimes, completion bond companies require this. Sometimes, studio producers get deferments based on salary cuts. For example, you may have a $500,000 producer from DreamWorks, who agrees to produce an independent film for $100,000. That producer would want to get that deferred $400,000 at the earliest possible moment in the stream of revenue, as well as a share of the profits.

Soundtrack Album

In the Chapter 13, Music In Film, we discuss the myth that soundtrack albums generate more income than the film. However, in appropriate circumstances, they can serve as valuable financing mechanisms. The typical studio strategy is to get an advance against soundtrack royalties from a record company and use the advance to augment the music budget and to finance the soundtrack album. We are aware of a few small independent films that were financed almost entirely on the soundtrack albums. These were so-called urban films starring rappers. However, this is outside the norm for independent films. There are two basic requirements to get a substantial soundtrack album advance from a record company. The first is to have top artists on the album. The second, and more difficult, is to have a major theatrical distributor. Usually, record companies demand a major U.S. theatrical release before they will pay an advance. If these elements are in place, you can augment your music budget by a very substantial sum.

Music Publishing

Presales of music publishing rights in pictures are almost nonexistent in North America. However, in Europe, the music publishing companies and record companies tend to be hybridized, and many European film producers who have less access to capital than do American producers, lay off the music budget on the music publisher/record company and give up all music rights other than the right to use the music in the film. Still, music-publishing presales rarely generate more than several hundred thousand dollars.

Product Placement

Product placement is a deal where a manufacturer loans or provides free product, or even pays the production company to prominently feature their goods in a motion picture. Product placement, although not unknown in the independent world, is common in the studio world, since the product licensor has confidence that its product will be exposed to a large audience.

Product placement agreements are very simple. Typically, the manufacturer will agree to provide the goods to be featured in the film and the products will be used as props in specific scenes. The manufacturer pays a flat sum and provides the goods.

With product placement, you must make sure that you maintain maximum flexibility in terms of how you edit your picture. There is a lawsuit currently pending against one of the major studios because the director cut the products out of a film after the studio had entered a product placement deal, which required that the products be depicted in the film.

Conclusion

There are limitless combinations of elements that comprise independent film financings. The key in putting them together is to be resourceful, open-minded and flexible. We do not have one easy answer on how to finance your picture, but if your heart is not in it, you may be better off writing novels. In your darkest hours of discouragement, you should remember that there are over 1,500 independent producers who manage to find financing for their independent features every year. The job may be hard, but quality projects, in the hands of determined and resourceful producers, get made.

FINANCE AGREEMENTS

In this chapter, we will discuss the various players and agreements and entries used to actually secure the financing and start the production funding flowing so you can actually go out and produce a movie.

Entertainment Bankers

Entertainment bankers are among the most knowledgeable, influential, and indispensable facilitators in the independent-film business. Prominent entertainment lenders include the Lewis Horwitz Organization, which was acquired by Imperial Capital Group; Comerica and its subsidiary Imperial Bank (not to be confused with Imperial Capital Group); Netaxie; Newmarket Capital; Mercantile Bank; City National Bank; Chemical Bank; Chase; Coutts; Guinness-Mahon; and Union Bank. In most cases when an independent film project is financed with presales, an entertainment lender is involved in the transaction. The lender will gather all of the distribution contracts on the picture from various territories throughout the world, a completion bond will be obtained, and the lender will make a loan for the production budget of the movie and take the distribution contracts for the picture as collateral. In many cases, there will be a gap between the amount of money that is guaranteed under the distribution contracts and the actual production loan for the film. Only very specialized and knowledgeable entertainment lenders make loans for the production budget where a gap is involved. They will do so only when they are confident the picture will ultimately be sold in the unsold territories and the monies ultimately collected will be sufficient to repay the loan. Gap financing is a risky proposition, but gap lenders spend their time assessing the credit worthiness of sales agents and distributors around the world.

Entertainment banking can be very profitable. Banks charge points (percentages) and origination fees to set up loans and charge healthy interest rates. If there is a gap involved, they charge a super or special interest rate in consideration of the extra risk. Banks stand to make substantial amounts of money on each motion picture financed. Origination fees range from one-half of a percentage point to three percentage points of the entire loan (plus seven to ten percentage points on the amount of the gap loaned).

Entertainment lenders have a substantial economic incentive to help you get your project financed and can help to move your project forward. They can introduce you to the foreign-sales agents and distributors with whom they have relationships. These are the sales agents who time and time again have delivered, to the bankers, on the estimates they have made for how much revenue their pictures would generate throughout the world. If a project receives a recommendation from an entertainment lender and it is sent to a sales agent or distributor, they are going to give it a lot of attention. Once a sales agent or distributor gets involved in a project in conjunction with an entertainment lender, the filmmaker may be in a position to make pay-or-play offers to talent and start production.

Entertainment lenders are not hard to find. They attend all of the film markets, many of the festivals, and they have their own suite of offices at the American Film Market, where they are listed under the designation of Affiliated Financial Institutions. Most are willing to talk to you about your projects, and we recommend that you get a banker involved as early as possible.

Production Loans

In discussing production loans, it is necessary that you understand a few basic concepts. The first is that you have to finance the entire cost of the movie. This includes not only the direct cost of making it, but also a completion guarantee fee on the direct cost (generally about 3%), a contingency of 10% on the direct cost, and the finance costs that range from 10% to 20% (and even higher) of the direct cost. Financing costs include the commitment fee on the loan; the interest costs based on the estimated interest on the money you are borrowing, along with an interest reserve of 2% to 3%; and bank legal fees, which can range from $15,000 to $50,000. Thus, on a $5 million direct cost movie you will have a completion guarantee fee of $150,000, a contingency of $500,000, and financing costs of $500,000 to $1 million. Some producers are astounded that a $5 million movie will require a loan approaching $6.5 million, but that is the reality.

A second basic concept is to avoid being personally liable on a production loan. Independent producers should set up new limited liability entities or single-purpose corporations to produce a film and be the borrower in the loan transaction. Your loan should always be "nonrecourse" as to your personal assets. The bank can take your film, but not your house.

Although many producers negotiate bank loans themselves, you are best served to have your lawyer either negotiate the deal or at least advise you on the terms. It is always best to negotiate with more than one bank to make them compete on pricing and have a backup in case a deal with a bank falls through.

Here are the most important issues involving motion picture production loans:

Interest Rate

Interest is usually pegged to a floating variable rate, such as LIBOR (London Inter Bank Offering Rate) or prime. LIBOR loans can get complicated, as you must choose the LIBOR rate for a stated period of time, typically 30, 60, 90, or 180 days. However, the LIBOR rate has run less than prime by an average of 2% or so over the last 20 years. Because LIBOR is a lower interest rate, the premium banks take on that rate is usually higher than prime. A bank may offer you a choice of LIBOR plus 2%, or prime plus 0.5%. It is best to seek the advice of your financial advisors to assess which rate you should take. In some instances, a bank will offer you the option of periodically choosing LIBOR or prime during the course of a loan. Although on the surface this seems like a good deal, it takes constant scrutiny and management. Most producers are so busy making movies that they ignore these details. Not surprisingly, the default rate if you do not make a choice is prime, which is usually more profitable to the bank.

Commitment Fees (Points)

Lenders are paid a percentage of the amount of the loan. In some cases, this can be a flat amount. Points are higher on smaller and riskier loans.

Legal Fees

Banks are always reimbursed for their legal fees for the preparation of loan documents. These fees range from $15,000 to $50,000. It is always a good idea to make sure that these fees are capped so you do not write the bank lawyers a blank check. Otherwise, the bank will request that you pay their legal fees whether or not the loan closes and sometimes require an upfront down payment on the legal fees.

Commitment Letters

The beginning of the documentation of a bank loan occurs when the bank sends its "commitment letter," which sets forth the elements of the production, the collateral, interest rate, commitment fees, and legal fees. They always end by stating that the bank is not in fact committed until all its conditions are met. In commitment letters, bankers often try to make the producer liable for the bank's legal fees even if the transaction does not close, and some bankers even ask for a legal fee deposit. Naturally, producers resist this.

Opinion Letters

Almost without fail the bank will request that the lawyer for the producer give an "opinion letter," which states that the loan documents are enforceable and the bank's security interest, so long as the formalities are met, is properly perfected. Some law firms have the policy of never giving these opinions, but if they represent producers, it is hard to avoid. We have developed forms with the various entertainment-lending institutions that include numerous disclaimers in the opinion letter. While we have never heard of a firm being sued for malpractice for issuing a faulty opinion letter, it can happen and one of the items you are paying for when you hire a law firm for a bank loan is the opinion letter. The banks want to know that as far as the producer's lawyer is concerned, all the information they have been given to use as the basis of the loan is accurate, complete, and that the corporation or limited liability company was properly formed and is a valid existing entity.

Security Interests

Security interests are one of the most complex and least understood parts of production loans. A security interest is a claim on a specific property (your motion picture) in order to enforce a contractual obligation. In title production loans, the bank takes a security interest in the physical film elements themselves, the rights, and all accounts and proceeds. If you do not perform (repay the loan), then the bank can foreclose on the picture and sell it to repay the loan. If your company becomes bankrupt, the bank has priority over the unsecured creditors, so it is paid first. An often fought-over issue is priority of security interests (who stands at the head of the line to collect first in the event of default or bankruptcy). SAG, DGA, and WGA all require security interests, as do equity investors and the completion guarantor. The guilds usually subordinate their interest to the banks, but not to equity investors. The completion guarantor usually subordinates to investors and the guilds.

Loan Repayment

The bank loan normally is repaid from the proceeds from the film, not from your personal assets. Banks always start from the position that 100% of all the revenue of the exploitation of the picture must be applied to repayment of the loan. If you have an equity investor who is putting up 50% and the bank 50%, it does not seem fair that the bank would not go pro rata with the equity investor, but they will not. Banks also try to make the foreign-sales agents, producers' reps, and lawyers all defer their percentage fees until the bank has been repaid. To avoid that, foreign-sales agents include as much of their distribution fees and costs in the budget as possible. For example, a foreign-sales agent with a 15% distribution fee might include $150,000 in the budget as an executive producer fee, which is an advance against their distribution fee. Sales agent costs are also budgeted sometimes. It is also necessary sometimes to set aside a portion of the payments from film revenue to pay guild residuals.

Documentation

Bank documentation is the most complex and time-intensive work in the independent-film business. Some lawyers who do "production legal" on behalf of independent producers also do bank documentation. It is usually a separate and additional charge and can range from $15,000 to $50,000 and more. This is the fee to have your lawyer do the documentation. You are also charged for the cost of the bank lawyer's legal work. The main agreements are as follows:

Loan and Security Agreement

This is the linchpin agreement. It will incorporate the provisions included in the commitment letter, along with seemingly endless bank boilerplate clauses. In addition to setting forth the economics of the loan, it also covers the grant of the security interest to the bank and attaches a draw-down notice (your request to the bank for the periodic amounts from the loan), a promissory note, and the power of sale. The power of sale allows the bank to sell the picture if you have not sold it by a specific date.

Notice of Assignment and Distributor's Acceptance

If foreign presale contracts are going to be discounted, the bank will require that those contracts be assigned to the bank and that the distributors sign this document to confirm that they will pay the bank directly and waive any defenses the distributor may have to avoid payment.

Interparty Agreement

This sets forth the rights and payment priorities among the producer, sales agent, the completion guarantor, and lenders and investors. It is the most heavily negotiated document because of the myriad competing interests and parties.

In negotiating production loans it is essential that you involve a lawyer. Wherever possible we start with prenegotiated forms to reduce negotiation time. Our main job is to make sure that the loan documents properly reflect the economics set forth in the commitment letter. Overnegotiating bank boilerplate is a waste of time. Banks have all the leverage and there is no getting around it.

Completion Guarantees

If you finance your film either through equity or a production loan (or a combination of the two), you will need a completion guarantee. The completion guarantor protects the financiers by assuring that the picture will be completed and delivered (even if it goes overbudget) or in the alternative, that investors and lenders will be repaid. The completion guarantor has three options if the picture runs overbudget. The first is to loan additional money to the producer to finish the picture. The second is to take over the picture and finish it. The third is to stop production and repay the investors and lenders, an option that is rarely, if ever, chosen.

In an independent motion picture financing transaction, financiers use presale agreements, which include the distributor's commitment to make payment on delivery of the picture, as collateral for the financing. If the picture is not capable of being delivered, the distributor will not pay and the financiers will never be paid. Production financiers are not willing to take the credit risk that distributors will not pay because of non-delivery, so they shift the risk for completion and delivery to the completion guarantor.

The completion guarantor usually obtains reinsurance from a third-party insurance company or insurance brokers (such as Lloyds of London). The reinsurance is a way for the completion guarantor to spread risk, since they may be on the hook for millions of dollars. If the completion guarantor is not itself an insurance company, it will arrange for a "cut through" certificate to be issued by a substantial insurer (such as Lloyd's of London) in an amount sufficient to cover the amount of the loan. The cut through permits the bank to go directly against the reinsurer and not be concerned with the financial condition of the guarantor.

The first job of a guarantor is to assess the project and determine whether the picture is likely to be made within the budget and schedule with the particular personnel involved. Completion guarantors have in-house production experts who specialize in analyzing motion picture and television projects. The completion guarantor also reviews all of the production documents, including the script, the shooting schedule, budget, postproduction schedule, insurance and actor, writer, rights, and director agreements and financing documents.

Once the guarantor determines that the direct cost budget is sufficient, it will also require a 10% contingency to the direct cost budget. In some cases, they will insist that the producers and director pledge a part of their fees against completion, especially if they do not have proven track records or if they have histories of going overbudget. The guarantor will also require that the producer and director sign off on the script, the budget, and production schedules and agree that they will follow the guarantor's instructions if the guarantor takes over production. These documents are carefully scrutinized by the lawyers who represent the producers and directors, to make sure that their clients are not personally liable for cost overruns.

Sometimes, a completion guarantor will have a representative at the film location with the cost paid from the budget. This representative will stay involved in the day-to-day production, review daily production reports, and report back to the guarantor if there are any problems. Even if no rep is on location, the completion guarantor will require a constant and ongoing monitoring of the production. Completion bonders will suggest approved line producers, production accountants, assistant directors, production managers, and postproduction supervisors.

If the completion guarantor has to put up money to finish the picture, it is entitled to a recoupment position for that money backed by a security interest in the picture. This recoupment position is nonrecourse against the individual producer (i.e., only revenues from the film can be used to repay the guarantor). Typically, the guarantor recoups after the main financier has recouped and charges interest as other investors do.

If the picture appears to be in danger of going overbudget or overschedule, the guarantor has the right to take over the production and call the shots. This includes taking an assignment of all the agreements, taking over the bank account, etc. The basis for takeover is usually a subjective standard that the completion guarantor uses to anticipate when the picture will go overbudget. In some cases, it is an objective standard (e.g., the picture is 10% or more overbudget on a projected basis) or the production schedule is behind by a certain number of days.

Completion guarantors do not take on every risk of the production. They exclude claims that arise from defects in the chain of title or failure to get an MPAA rating certificate. The completion guarantor does not guarantee the artistic content of the motion picture, but is only responsible for the technical quality of the motion picture. The distributors must take delivery of the motion picture notwithstanding its artistic quality. The completion guarantor does not provide coverage for risks based on the distributor's failure to pay, as long as the picture has been delivered. The completion guarantor is not obligated to fund the completion guarantee until the financier has put up all of the production financing, including the 10% contingency.

Completion guarantor delivery requirements mirror those contained in the distribution agreement with the domestic distributor, although they are limited to the "essential delivery items." If there is no domestic or foreign deal in place, then an anticipated schedule of delivery items will be attached.

Foreign-Sales Agent Deals

The most basic functions of the foreign-sales agent are to find foreign distributors for your movie and then negotiate and document the terms of the distribution agreements. Timing is very important. If you are trying to raise money to finance your film, the foreign-sales contracts must be negotiated and signed before a bank will make a production loan. The foreign-sales agent sells your picture through their contacts, arranges screenings, and prepares sales materials such as the trailer, brochure, key art, and advertisements. Another essential function of the foreign-sales agent is to deliver the film to each distributor and to collect the money due. Foreign distributors are notorious for late payment and sometimes even nonpayment. Smaller distributors come and go with regularity.

The functions of a foreign-sales agent are very similar to those of foreign distributors since the primary task of both is to sell your picture to foreign theatrical distributors, television networks, home video companies, and others. Sometimes the same company will operate as a sales agent on some pictures and distributor on others. The crucial difference lies in whether distribution rights, which are part of the copyright in the film, are transferred. A foreign-film distributor does acquire the distribution rights for itself and then transfers distribution rights for certain territories, media, and terms to the end users. With a foreign distributor, the agreements are made in the name of the distributor, and collections are made in their name. If the foreign distributor has financial or legal problems, the distribution rights are exposed to other creditors who may get the money from the sale of the film that by contract should go to you.

The foreign-sales agent does not acquire rights in the film. It is hired by the producer of the film to assist in making distribution deals. Distribution agreements are entered into between the production company that made the film and the foreign user, such as Canal+ for French pay television rights. However, when foreign-sales agents pay cash to the producer in the form of an advance or completion funding, they retain the right, in their contracts, to make the deals themselves, rather than in the name of the producer.

You can approach foreign-sales agents when your project is not completely packaged, once it is packaged, or after it is completed. The earlier in the process you submit your film, the more work will have to be done by a sales agent, the more costs they will incur, and the greater their expectations will be of how much they should get paid. If you approach the agent at an early stage, it is crucial to know what you expect of them. Some foreign-sales agents act as producers or executive producers and will help you package the film. In some cases, they make or guarantee pay-or-play offers to director or cast.

If you decide to approach a foreign-sales agent at an early stage, it is better to approach one who is established and has the connections and resources to make your project happen. Some of the larger companies, such as Summit and Intermedia/IEG, have the resources to back pay-or-play offers without having the project completely presold. The smaller agents do not have this financial ability.

In the past, foreign-sales agents did not get involved in development. However, a recent trend has been for some of the larger foreign-sales companies that have adequate capital backing to become involved in development. Some act as quasi-studios and have first-look deals with prominent filmmakers. But this still remains the exception, and it is unlikely that the foreign-sales agent will option your script, pay for the writer, or pay you a development fee. That arena remains dominated by the studios.

Once you approach a foreign-sales agent, what kind of deal can you expect? Here are the major deal points:

Producer Fees

Some foreign sales agents insist on having a producer or executive producer fee for their company's principals in the budget. This fee is separate from your budgeted producer fee. This is fair when the foreign sales agent is involved in packaging the film and makes pay-or-play offers. Often, this producer fee is treated as an advance against the sales commission or distribution fee, since banks sometimes make sales agents defer their fees until the banks are paid. There is no standard amount for the foreign-sales agent's producer fee, but you can expect it to be in the range of 2% to 3% of direct cost.

Expenses

Foreign-sales agents often have high overheads and spend substantial sums in selling pictures. These sums fall into two categories: The first are direct out-of-pocket costs (distribution costs) and the second are allocated market costs. The distribution costs consist of making and shipping videocassettes, creation of trailers, preparation of key art, advertising in trade publications, and setting up screenings. Knowledgeable producers negotiate for these amounts to be either capped, budgeted, or both. On small pictures, these costs can be $10,000 to $25,000; on midsize pictures, $75,000 to $100,000; and on larger pictures up to $400,000.

Foreign sales agents attend film markets, such as Cannes, MIFED, and the American Film Market. Many also attend the television markets such as MIP-

COM, MIPTV, and NATPE. The market costs include the cost of maintaining a suite at the market, market registration fees, airfares, hotel, and per diems for staff. Since sales agents generally represent more than one film at the market, they allocate their costs to the various pictures. There is no standard way of doing the cost allocation. Some companies do it pro rata based on the number of films they represent, and others do it pro rata based on sales they make for each particular film. Usually, foreign sales agents treat all the films they represent in a particular market on the same basis, so they are not over or under paid. It is always best to have a budgeted amount or a cap at each market. For simplicity of accounting, many agents now negotiate flat per-market costs for the first year of representation (e.g., $10,000 each for Cannes, AFM, and MIFED, as well as the other markets they may attend).

Territory

The next issue is to determine in which territories the foreign-sales agent will sell the film. If the sales agent will provide production financing or make pay-or-play offers, it will want to be the agent for the entire world, which is fair if they put up all of the financing. Otherwise, it makes more sense to have a separate agent/producer's rep for domestic sales, if you can get the foreign-sales agent to agree. Many foreign sales agents will not take on a picture unless they have the right to coordinate the worldwide sales. Obviously, you must make sure that your domestic and foreign distributors do not conflict. One recent area of hot debate has been the treatment of Internet distribution rights, since it knows no borders. The usual compromise is that the distributors in the various territories can obtain the Internet distribution rights and advertise on the Internet, but cannot distribute on the Net until there is adequate "border protection" to prevent access outside licensed territories.

Sales Commissions

Sales commissions are the most highly contested part of a foreign-sales agency agreement. In general, fees on uncompleted pictures are higher than fees on completed ones, especially where the foreign-sales agent provides financing. A typical deal on a picture where the foreign-sales agent takes worldwide rights and provides financing would be 25% on foreign and 10% to 15% on domestic. By "foreign," we mean the world outside the United States and Canada. Fees are sometimes lower for large-budget pictures since the perception is that they will generate more revenue. In some cases, commissions are tiered upwardly (e.g., 15% of the first $3 million; 20% from $3 million to $6 million; 20% thereafter). Conversely, sometimes the fees are tiered downwardly.

One area of concern is the impact of foreign withholding taxes, which can range from 5% to 25% of gross revenues. You have to make sure that the commission is taken on the net amount remitted by the foreign distributor, not the gross amount. Some foreign-sales agents have sophisticated structures whereby the monies are initially remitted to another country that offers favorable tax treatment, such as Hungary, the Channel Islands, and certain Caribbean territories, before being remitted to the United States, to take advantage of tax treaties.

Media

Foreign-sales agents focus on selling theatrical, home video, television, and Internet rights. When a foreign-sales agent finances a picture, it will also represent and commission the soundtrack album, music publishing, merchandising, and book-publishing rights. However these rights can be reserved by the producer.

Derivative Productions

Foreign-sales agents have an interest in these rights (such as remakes, sequels, and new television projects based on the original movie) only when they put up substantial financing. Unlike studios, which fully finance and own the rights, foreign-sales agents customarily have no rights, or at best, a right of first negotiation and last refusal with respect to derivative productions and are not necessarily contractually entitled to be involved.

Term

One area that engenders a lot of confusion is the negotiation of the "term." In an agency agreement there are actually two terms. The first is for how long the agent is authorized to sell the picture. This can be as short as a year or as long as 20 years. The second is the term of the distribution rights that the agent is authorized to sell. For example, a sales agent might sell German television rights for two, 12, or 20 years. If the foreign-sales agent acts as a distributor, it can sell the rights during the term of the distribution rights it has been granted. A typical range for a term of distribution rights is 15 to 25 years. If the foreign-sales agent puts up all of the financing, the term of the rights is usually perpetual. In some cases, there are extensions of the term if the foreign-sales agent has not recouped its costs (e.g., 20 years for distribution rights; and an additional five years if not recouped at the end of 20 years).

Guild Residuals

Another battlefield is which party will be responsible for the payment of guild residuals. Guild residuals are payable on the sums that are attributable to "supplemental markets," which are home video and television exploitation. At this time, the majority of income that is generated overseas comes from home video and television licenses. Producers who sign with the WGA, DGA, and SAG are contractually obligated, under their agreements with those guilds, to have all distributors assume the obligation to pay residuals for their territories. The guilds are also entitled to demand "adequate assurances" of ability to pay. However, few foreign-sales agents or distributors assume guild residuals. This leaves most producers in technical breach of their guild agreements. The practical, nonlegal solution is for producers to pay the residuals themselves. The guilds do not complain as long as the residuals are paid. The allocation of advances paid by foreign distributors can lead to some complicated accounting problems. It is common for a producer to allocate as much of the advances as possible to theatrical rights, since there are no residuals payable on theatrical revenue. In some cases, there is an allocation in foreign contracts of the advance towards the various media, which the guilds usually live with, if it is reasonable. The guilds have become more aggressive lately in trying to assure that their members are paid guild residuals. In some cases, they insist that there be an allocation from the budget to cover foreign residuals. In certain circumstances, this issue can make or break a picture, as there may be no money left in the budget to prepay these amounts. For now, the guilds are attacking this on a case-by-case basis, but you should not be surprised if the guilds try to make you set aside estimated residuals from your budget before they sign off and allow you to start production.

Approval of Sales

A key issue in any sales-agency agreement is whether the producer has the right to approve the sale in each market. If you have no controls, the results can be disastrous, such as the sales agent selling rights for $500,000 in the foreign market when $2 million is needed to repay the bank loan. Since many of the sales take place on a whirlwind basis at overseas markets, it is not possible for the foreign-sales agent to have each and every agreement approved by the producer. Before foreign-sales agents embark on selling, they do projections showing low and high, and sometimes medium asking and taking prices for each territory. The projection schedule, separated by territory, is appended as an exhibit to the agreement. The deal is that so long as the foreign-sales agent can meet the minimum projection in a particular territory they are authorized to go ahead and make the sale.

Form of Contracts

Another issue is the form of the contracts that are used by the foreign-sales agent. Most foreign-sales agents use standard Independent Film and Television Alliance (IFTA) formerly the American Film Marketing Association (AFMA) deal memos, although the long forms vary. It is always a good idea for you to preapprove the form of the contract used.

Accountings

Foreign-sales agents account on a quarterly basis for the first two years, semi-annually for the next two years, and annually thereafter. You should receive statements and payments no later than 60 days after the calendar close. The producer has the right to audit. You should make sure that you get copies of all contracts so you can align them with the statements to make sure you are being accounted to properly. Many foreign-sales agents agree that if they underreport by 5% or more, they will bear the cost of the audit.

Credit

Many foreign-sales agents now take producer or executive producer credit, especially when they provide financing. In addition, foreign-sales agents usually take a "presentation" credit in their territory and often utilize a logo. Producers rarely object to these credits.

Delivery

The negotiation of delivery schedules for foreign-sales agents is much like the negotiation for worldwide distributors, except the schedules are usually shorter. However, you should be prepared for some quirks with respect to foreign delivery, such as you will have to deliver a PAL master and special soundtracks that allow for dubbing and textless backgrounds for subtitling. As with the delivery schedules propounded by worldwide distributors, the schedules are often overinclusive. If you do not anticipate making theatrical sales, it does not make sense to deliver theatrical elements such as an interpositive, an internegative, and a check print, which can easily run $30,000. One solution is to promise to deliver the elements if they are needed for a theatrical sale and preferably agree that the sales agent will pay for those items from the proceeds of the theatrical sale. Another problem with respect to foreign delivery is signed contracts. Often, American contracts, especially with star directors and actors, are never signed. This can be a problem for foreign delivery, since many distributors require signed contracts. It is always a good idea to try to have your production lawyer get signed contracts.

Escrow Collection Accounts

Some foreign-sales agents agree to put the sales money in escrow at a bank.

Although the escrow costs money, both in terms of escrow fees and legal and transactional costs, you are more likely to get paid from an escrow than as a general creditor. Due to the numerous parties and territories now involved in the financing of an independent film, a new mini-industry in the form of companies offering "escrow" or "collection" services has arisen. Especially where there are numerous producers, co-financiers, and profit participants involved in a movie, it is prudent to involve a neutral third-party collection agent experienced in the collection and calculation of all participants payable in connection with a motion picture to undertake that daunting task. One of the leaders in this relatively new business is Fintage House *(www.fintagehouse.com).*

Cutting Rights

Foreign-sales agents are not as aggressive as studios in asserting a right to "final cut" of the film, but they insist on the right to cut for television broadcast and for censorship reasons. Always make sure that the cutting rights you grant are not inconsistent with the cutting rights of your director.

Marketing, Publicity, and Advertising

Experienced foreign-sales agents believe that they understand the international marketplace and how to properly market, promote, advertise, and publicize your film. Nevertheless, you probably know and understand all of the selling points of your film better than anyone else. While sales agents rarely grant you the right to approve the trailer, marketing campaign, advertising, and publicity, they will usually encourage you to give them your creative input and contractually give you consultation rights on those materials.

Distribution Agreements

Unlike most other motion-picture contracts which vary widely depending on the company or lawyer who is preparing it, the international film distribution agreement is very often a single form originated by IFTA formerly the AFMA (the AFMA International Multiple Rights Distributor Agreement) and utilized by its members. Since it is likely that you will see it and because it is such an important agreement, we will include a very detailed explanation of its provisions and the issues surrounding them. This is very dense reading and you may want to skim through it now. You can return to it as a resource when you are prepared to negotiate a distribution agreement.

IFTA International Multiple Rights Distributor Agreement
The IFTA International Multiple Rights Distributor Agreement, including the "Deal Terms" section (which is not reproduced in this book) may be purchased by visiting the IFTA Web site at *www.ifta-online.org* or by contacting IFTA at (310) 446-1000.

International Film Distribution Agreement: Explanation of Provisions

I. Basic License Terms

A. Picture. The Agreement will describe the particular motion picture licensed, the title, and the key creative elements such as stars, director, writer, and producer.

B. Territory. The Agreement will describe the country or territory to which the Motion Picture is licensed.

C. Agreement Term and License Period.

1. Term. The Agreement will generally provide for an overall term of years from availability of certain delivery materials, actual delivery of the motion picture, or the execution of the Agreement ranging from a low of one year to as long as 25 years or, in some cases, in perpetuity.

2. License Period. The Agreement may also provide for a specific License Period for particular rights that are licensed under the Agreement.

(a) For example: Cinematic Rights (which for purposes of this outline includes Theatrical, Nontheatrical, and Public Video exploitation) may be licensed for six to 12 months from initial Delivery of the motion picture or initial Theatrical Release of the motion picture. Video Rights (which for purposes of this outline includes Rental Home Video, Sell-Through Home Video and Commercial Video) may be licensed for five years from initial Delivery, initial Theatrical release, or initial Video release. Pay TV rights may be licensed on a specific Pay TV system for one to two years commencing one year after the initial Theatrical release. Free TV Rights (which for purposes of this outline includes Terrestrial Free TV, Cable Free TV, and Satellite Free TV) may be licensed on a specific TV station or network for three years commencing two to three years after initial Theatrical Release. Ancillary Rights (which for purposes of this outline includes Airlines, Ships at sea, and Hotel exploitation rights) might be licensed for two years from initial Theatrical Release.

D. Authorized Languages. The Agreement will specify which languages are authorized under the License Agreement in the particular Territory. For example, a license for the Territory of France will specify that its authorized language is French. The License Agreement will also specify whether the various media are to be licensed in dubbed versions or subtitled versions, subject to the approval of the Licensor for creative purposes, as well as for insuring that all talent agreements have been complied with. It is also important to note that Licensors will require that copyright ownership in all dubbed and subtitled versions of the motion picture be retained by the Licensor, despite the fact that the Licensee may have arranged for, paid for, and supervised the creation of any dubbed or subtitled versions.

E. Release Requirements. The Agreement will specify whether or not a Theatrical release is required, at what time (for example, not later than six months after Delivery) the Theatrical release is required to take place, as well as the minimum number of prints, the maximum number of prints, the minimum advertising commitment in U.S. Dollars, and the maximum advertising commitment in U.S. Dollars. Additionally, a date may be specified for the Video Release of the motion picture, along with a Holdback period, which would require that the Video release be not earlier than, say, three months after the initial Theatrical release of the motion picture and perhaps not later than six months after the initial Theatrical release.

II. Licensed Rights Terms

Motion-picture producers and copyright proprietors vigorously retain and defend their copyrights in their motion pictures. As a result, International Motion Picture Licensing Agreements license very few rights, other than the rights to distribute, exhibit, publicly perform, and duplicate the motion picture for a limited number of years, and in some cases for a limited number of exhibitions or performances in each Licensed Media subject to a number of strict approval rights, contractual restrictions and holdback provisions as described in more detail herein. The rights most commonly licensed are Cinematic Rights, Video Rights, Pay TV Rights, Free TV Rights, and Ancillary Rights. In some cases, International Motion Picture Licensing Agreements also include provisions for the licensing of Merchandising Rights, Interactive/New Media Rights, Music Soundtrack Album Rights, and Music Publishing Rights that arise from the licensed motion picture.

III. Financial Terms

The financial terms of each Licensing Agreement vary depending on the film—the budget, stars, director, and producer; the relative strength of Licensor; the relative strength of Licensee; and whether a theatrical release in the U.S. and elsewhere is contemplated. The following is a discussion of several types and key terms of financial arrangements between the Licensor and the Licensee.

A. Minimum Guarantee. The most common arrangement is the Minimum Guarantee, where the Licensee pays the Licensor a specified Minimum Guarantee for various rights licensed under the Agreement. Depending on whether or not the Motion Picture is in preproduction, production, or completed, various installments of the Guarantee may be payable upon execution of the Agreement, on the commencement of principal photography, on the completion of principal photography, on the Notice of Initial Delivery, on Additional Delivery, on Theatrical Release, on Video Release, or at some other time. It is important to note that the Minimum Guarantee deal is the type of deal frequently used to raise financing for the production of Motion Pictures because it provides security and collateral for banks to lend money against.

1. The foregoing installment payments are the guaranteed amounts that would be paid to the Licensor. Beyond the Minimum Guarantee, overages (amounts in

excess of the Minimum Guarantee, depending on the success of the Motion Picture in the particular Territory) will also be paid. These overages are discussed below.

2. Less common arrangements include the pure distribution deal where a Licensee provides no Minimum Guarantee, but advances the Distribution Costs, retains a Distribution fee and the Distribution Costs advanced and remits all or a negotiated portion of the remaining balance to the Licensor. Another type of arrangement is the Costs-Off-the-Top Deal that provides no Minimum Guarantee, where the Licensee advances the Distribution Costs, recoups them off the top, and remits 50% or some other negotiated percentage of the Gross Receipts to the Licensor.

B. Payment. Two principal payment methods are customarily specified in International Motion Picture License Agreements.

1. Wire Transfer. The first method is wire transfer, where the Licensee is required to pay various installments of the Guarantee or other payments due the Licensor by wire transfer of unencumbered funds, free of any transmission charges, to a specified account.

2. The Letter of Credit. In other circumstances the Licensee is required to pay the Licensor by irrevocable Letter of Credit, payable on presentation to the Licensor's bank of some or all of the following:

(a) Sight draft in customary commercial form indicating payment due,

(b) Invoice for payments then due,

(c) Bill of Lading, such as an air waybill evidencing shipment to Licensee of the Initial Delivery Materials.

(d) Completion Guarantor's Certificate certifying that technically acceptable Initial Delivery Materials are available for delivery, or,

(e) Laboratory Access Letter indicating that the required Initial Delivery Materials are available at a designated laboratory for use by the Licensee.

C. Allocation of the Guarantee. The Guarantee may be allocated among various licensed rights such as the following:

1. Forty percent (40%) to the Cinematic Guarantee for Theatrical, Nontheatrical, and Public Video Licensed Rights.

2. Five percent (5%) to the Ancillary Guarantee for Airline, Ship, and Hotel Licensed Rights.

3. Twenty-five percent (25%) to the Video Guarantee for Home Video and Commercial Video Licensed Rights.

4. Ten percent (10%) to the Pay TV Guarantee for Pay TV Licensed Rights.

5. Twenty percent (20%) for the Free TV Guarantee for Free TV Licensed Rights.

D. Talent Guild Residuals. It should be noted that the Allocation of the Guarantee to the various Licensed Rights is an important factor in the analysis of the profitability of an International Motion Picture Licensing Agreement because substantial residual payments are required to be made to talent guilds such as the Writer's Guild, the Director's Guild, and the Screen Actors Guild, based on Gross Receipts derived from International Video, Pay TV, and Free TV exploitation, whereas no residuals are paid for International Theatrical exploitation. Accordingly, many Motion Picture producers attempt to allocate as much of the Guarantee as reasonably possible to Theatrical exploitation in contract negotiations and documentation so as to reduce talent guild residual payment obligations and increase the profitability of their Motion Picture. It is for this reason that talent guilds often retain first priority security interests in the copyright of the Motion Picture and file mortgages of copyrights with the U.S. Copyright Office. Accordingly, rights granted under many International Motion Picture Licensing Agreements are granted subject to the prior interests of the talent guilds.

E. Recoupment of the Guarantee. Depending on the financial arrangements, the Guarantee may be cross-collateralized among the Licensed Rights.

1. If cross-collateralization is allowed, the applicable percentage of the Guarantee will first be recouped from the Licensed Rights to which it is allocated. Any shortfall with respect to one Licensed Right will then be defined and recouped in accordance with the cross-collateralization provisions outlined below.

2. Where no cross-collateralization is allowed, the applicable portion of the Guarantee may only be recouped from the Licensed Rights to which the Guarantee has been allocated. No "shortfall" as explained in the cross-collateralization provisions of Paragraph F below with respect to a particular Licensed Right may be recouped from the Gross Receipts from any other Licensed Right.

F. Cross-Collateralization. Cross-Collateralization is the means by which the recoupable portion of the Guarantee and the Recoupable portion of the Distribution Costs and sometimes the distribution fee, in one Licensed Media, (for example, Cinematic Rights), can also be recouped from revenue derived from another Licensed media (for example Video, Pay TV, or Free TV exploitation). In cases where a considerable amount of Distribution Costs are expended on the Theatrical Release, because of the substantial risk involved in an expensive Theatrical Release, it is customary for the Licensee to be able to recoup the shortfall in a less financially successful Theatrical Release from the Video revenue, Pay

TV revenue, Free TV revenue, and other Ancillary Revenue.

G. Disposition of Gross Receipts. Depending on the nature of the Motion Picture, creative elements, budget, relative strength of the Licensor and the Licensee, and whether or not an expensive Theatrical Release is contemplated, there will be various negotiated methods of the disposition or sharing of the Gross Receipts in the Licensed Media of the Territory. The following is a brief description of some of the more common methods the Licensor and Licensee will share Gross Receipts.

1. The Costs-Off-the-Top Deal. Under this arrangement, the Licensee will be allowed to recoup 100% of its Distribution Costs from the Gross Receipts in all Licensed Media. The balance remaining after recoupment of all the Distribution Costs will then be shared in a particular negotiated manner. (For example, after the Minimum Guarantee has been recouped, 75% to the Licensor and 25% to the Licensee). These negotiated percentages may apply across the board in all media or may be different in different Licensed Media. (For example, after recoupment of the Minimum Guarantee, the remaining Gross Receipts may be shared 65% to the Licensor, 35% to the Licensee in the Licensed Cinematic Media, 30% to the Licensor and 70% to the Licensee in Licensed Video Media, and 75% to the Licensor and 25% to the Licensee in Licensed Television Media).

2. The Distribution Deal. The Distribution deal is one in which the Licensor actually shares in the Licensee's Gross Receipts revenue stream from first dollar in a negotiated percentage. Thereafter the Distribution Costs will be recouped by the Licensee, then the Minimum Guarantee will be recouped by the Licensee, and then the Licensor and the Licensee shall share further in a negotiated percentage of the Gross Receipts revenue stream. (For example, the Licensor and the Licensee may agree that they will each receive 20% of the Gross Receipts from dollar one in each licensed media. The balance remaining, or 60% of the remaining Gross Receipts will be used to recoup the Distribution Costs, and the balance thereafter remaining will be used to recoup the Minimum Guarantee, if any, advanced by the Licensee. Once the Minimum Guarantee has been fully recouped, then the Licensor and the Licensee may agree to share the remaining balance on a fifty-fifty basis or in some other negotiated percentage.) All of these percentages and recoupment methods can also be negotiated in a different manner for each Licensed Media.

3. The Video Royalty Deal. In the late '80s and early '90s, worldwide Video Revenue achieved rapid and substantial growth and in many cases surpassed the revenue from theatrical and other media. As a result, many times Video rights were licensed separately, or, when licensed along with other rights, were accounted for separately. A typical Video Royalty deal could be structured as follows:

(a) Licensor's Royalty. The Licensor is accorded a royalty of 20% to 30% of the Home Video Rental Gross Receipts and 10% to 15% of the Home Video Sell-Through Gross Receipts. (Video Rental revenue is revenue that is generated by selling Videocassettes to retail stores for rental. Sell-Through Video Rental revenue is revenue generated by selling Videocassettes to wholesalers and stores for sale directly through to the retail customer.) The Licensee retains the balance of the Gross Receipts for purposes of recouping its distribution fee and its Distribution Costs.

(b) Recoupment of the Minimum Guarantee. If there was a Minimum Guarantee paid against Video exploitation, the Guarantee would customarily be recouped out of the Licensor's royalty or share of the Video Rental or Video Sell-Through Gross Receipts.

(c) After Recoupment of Minimum Guarantee. After the Guarantee has been recouped, the Licensor's share of the Home Video Rental and Sell-Through Gross Receipts might stay the same or it might increase to a higher percentage, depending on the particular arrangements between Licensor and Licensee.

(d) Minimum Pricing Terms; Free Goods. Often, the Licensor will insist that, for purposes of calculating the Video royalty, there be certain minimum prices that Rental and Sell-Through videocassettes and discs must be sold at in both the wholesale and retail channels. Additionally, there is customarily a limit on the amount of free goods that are allowed to be given away as promotional items in both the Rental and Sell-Through distribution channels.

IV. Delivery Terms

Because most Motion Pictures are delivered to the consumer in a number of different formats, i.e., theatrically in theaters, on videocassette, by satellite, by free TV, by pay TV, on videodisc, on DVD, and in other media, the delivery of materials necessary to enable the exploitation in all such media can be costly and complicated, particularly when different territories have different standards of technical acceptability of such delivery materials. International Motion Picture Licensing Agreements provide for different forms of Delivery Materials, depending on the relationship between the Licensor and the Licensee and the various exploitation requirements in the different Media licensed. For example, the Delivery items listed below may be furnished physically, by Laboratory Access, or furnished to the Licensee on loan for copying and then be returned, in other cases by satellite delivery, or in the form of the purchasing or lending of a video master. In most International Motion Picture Licensing Agreements, there is a multipaged list of Materials (including lengthy definitions and specifications) that are required for the complete delivery of a Motion Picture into a particular Territory. We discuss these in Chapter 16.

A. Outside Date for Delivery. The date upon which the Licensor is required to give notice to the Licensee that the Licensor is prepared to make Initial Delivery of the Motion Picture.

B. Licensee's Obligation to Pay For Delivery Materials. With respect to the Delivery Materials listed above, in many cases, the Licensee will be required to pay for the costs of certain of the Delivery Materials separate and apart from the Minimum Guarantee. These payment obligations for specific materials, such as an NTSC or PAL Video Master will be specified in the Agreement.

V. The Standard Terms and Conditions

A. The foregoing terms are the customary principal Deal Terms and conditions for International Motion Picture Licensing Agreements. There is also usually a 15- to 20-page Exhibit to the Agreement, which is entitled Standard Terms and Conditions. These terms and conditions outline Definitions of Terms; a more specific definition of the Motion Picture and the Key Creative Elements; a discussion of the various versions of the Motion Picture that are required to be delivered; provisions concerning when each Licensed Right is vested in the Licensee; provisions concerning the reservation of rights by the Licensor; a definition of Reversion with respect to each specific Licensed Right; Reversion as it applies to the overall term of the Agreement; more detailed definitions, terms, conditions, and provisions relating to the Territory, the Term, License Periods, Gross Receipts, Recoupable Distribution Costs, Payment Requirements, Accountings, Delivery and Return, General Exploitation Obligations, Theatrical, TV and Video Exploitation Obligations, Music Matters, Suspension and Withdrawal, Default and Termination, Antipiracy Provisions, Licensor's and Licensee's Warranties and Indemnities, and Assignment and Sublicensing; and other Miscellaneous Terms and Conditions. The following are some of the more important provisions contained in the customary Standard Terms and Conditions of International Motion Picture Licensing Agreements:

1. Credit, Advertising, Dubbing, Subtitling, Editing. The Standard Terms will usually include provisions that concern the exercise of Allied Rights, screen, and paid advertising requirements and the approval procedures of advertising materials by the Licensor. They also include the requirement that the Licensee comply with all screen, paid advertising, publicity, and promotional requirements, as well as actor, writer, and director name and likeness restrictions; Videogram packaging credit requirements; dubbing, subtitling, and editing restrictions pursuant to various guild agreements; and the specific contractual obligations relating to such issues with individual actors, directors, and writers.

2. Exercise of Allied Rights. The Standard Terms also include specific provisions that concern the exercise of Allied Rights, including the nonexclusive right to advertise, publicize, and promote the Motion Picture; to include in all advertising, promotion, and publicity the name, voice, and likeness of any person who renders materials or services on the Motion Picture; the restrictions on any commercial endorsements of any product or service other than the Motion Picture; the inclusion of the credit or logo of the Licensor at the beginning and end of the Motion Picture; the Licensor's right to change the title of the Motion Picture, but only after first obtaining the Licensor's approval of the change; the Licensee's right to dub the Picture, but only in the authorized language; the Licensee's right to subtitle the Motion Picture, but only in the authorized language; the Licensee's right to edit the Picture, but only in accordance with various censorship terms and conditions; and the Licensee's right to include commercial announcements in the Picture, but only at those specific points specified by the Licensor.

3. Restrictions and Limitations. The Licensee is customarily restricted from the following:

(a) Altering or deleting any credit, copyright notice, or trademark notice appearing on the Motion Picture, or

(b) including any advertisement before, during, or after the Motion Picture other than the credit or logo of the Licensee, an approved antipiracy warning, or commercials that are approved by the Licensor.

4. Territory and Region.

(a) Existing Political Borders. The definition of Territory is customarily the countries and territories listed in the Agreement as their political borders exist as of the date of the Agreement.

(b) Embassies, Government Installations, etc. The Territory generally excludes foreign countries, embassies, military and government installations, oil rigs and marine installations, airlines-in-flight, and ships at sea located within the Territory with respect to certain specified Licensed Media and includes the same with respect to other limited specified Licensed Media.

(c) Changes in Borders. If, during the Agreement Term, an area separates from a country in the Territory then the Territory will customarily nonetheless include each separating area, which formed one political entity as of the date of the Agreement. If during the Term an area is annexed by a country in the Territory, then the Licensee will promptly give Licensor notice whether the Licensor desires to exploit any Licensed Rights in such new area, the Licensor will then customarily accord the Licensee a right of first negotiation to acquire such Licensed Rights in the area for the remainder of its License Period subject to the rights previously granted to other entities in such area.

5. Parallel Imports. The Agreement customarily provides that the Licensor does not warrant that it has granted or can grant exclusivity protection against sale or rental in the Territory of Videograms embodying the Motion Picture imported from outside of the Licensed Territory. The Licensor nevertheless generally agrees that during the License Period for any Licensed Video Rights, it will not sell or authorize the sale in any authorized language of Videos embodying the Motion Picture that are sold in the region outside the Territory and intended primarily for consumer sale or rental within the Licensed Territory except that such a provision generally does not apply to sales of regional unsubtitled English language

Videograms even if English is an authorized language. The parallel import provisions apply specifically but without limitation in cases where the region includes any country in the European Union or European Economic Area.

6. Gross Receipts. The Agreement, generally, has a very broad definition of Gross Receipts with respect to each and every Licensed Right. This definition customarily includes without limitation all monies or other consideration of any kind (including all amounts from advances, guarantees, security deposits, awards, subsidies, and other allowances) received by, used by, or credited to the Licensee or any Licensee Affiliates, or any approved subdistributors or agents from the license sale, lease, rental, barter, distribution, diffusion, exhibition, performance, exercise, or other exploitation of each Licensed Right in the Motion Picture, all without any deductions whatsoever.

(a) Infringement Recoveries. Gross Receipts will also include all recoveries for infringement of any Licensed Right.

(b) Advertising Accessories. Gross Receipts will also include all monies received by or credited to the Licensee or any approved subdistributors or agents from any authorized dealing in trailers, posters, copies, stills, excerpts, advertising accessories, or other materials used in connection with the exploitation of any Licensed Right or contained on any Videograms in embodying the Motion Picture.

(c) Calculated "At the Source." The Gross Receipts are also generally calculated at the source without any deduction of any fee collected by any Licensee Affiliates, subdistributors, or agents. (For example, this means that Gross Receipts derived from theatrical exploitation would be calculated at the level at which payments are remitted from the theaters, or from television exploitation, at the level at which payments are remitted by broadcasters or cable systems without any deduction therefrom).

(d) Royalty Income. Certain royalty income, to which the Licensor is entitled, is generally excluded from the definition of Gross Receipts in the Agreement between the Licensor and the Licensee. The reason for this exclusion is that the Licensor generally has the right to collect these royalties directly and the licensee accordingly is not allowed the right to charge a distribution fee and to charge distribution expenses against such royalty income. This income generally includes all amounts collected by any collecting society, authors' rights organization, performing rights society or governmental agency that is payable to authors, producers, performers, or other persons, and that arise from royalties, compulsory licenses, cable retransmission income, music performance royalties, tax rebates, exhibition surcharges, levies on blank Videograms or hardware, rental or lending royalties, or the like. If any of these sums are paid to the Licensee, then the Licensee is required to immediately remit such sums to the Licensor with an appropriate statement identifying the payment and without any deductions therefrom.

(e) Rebates and Subsidies. Rebates and subsidies are generally excluded from the definition of Gross Receipts but are used to reduce recoupable Distribution Costs. Such rebates and subsidies include: print, publicity, and similar subsidies for the cost of releasing, advertising, and publicizing the Motion Picture; income from publicity tie-ins, freight, print, trailer, and advertising; and other cost recovery discounts, rebates, or refunds from approved subdistributors, exhibitors, or other persons or entities.

7. Recoupable Distribution Costs.

(a) The Agreement will generally have an extensive list of recoupable Distribution Costs, which the Licensee will be entitled to recoup from the Gross Receipts generated from the exploitation of the Motion Picture in various Licensed Media. Recoupable Distribution Costs will generally mean all direct, auditable, out of pocket, reasonable, and necessary costs, exclusive of salaries and overhead, and less any discounts, credits, rebates, or similar allowances, actually paid by the Licensee for exploiting each Licensed Right in arm's-length transactions with third parties, all of which will be advanced by the Licensee and recouped under the Agreement for the following:

(i) Customs duties, import taxes, and permit charges necessary to secure entry of the Motion Picture into the Territory.

(ii) Copyright registration, title registration, and import clearance costs.

(iii) Taxes including Sales, Use, VAT, Admission and turnover taxes, and related charges assessable against the Gross Receipts realized from the exploitation of any Licensed Rights. But these taxes will not include Corporate Income, Franchise, Windfall Profits taxes, Remittance, or Withholding taxes assessable against the amounts payable to the Licensor unless otherwise agreed between Licensee and Licensor.

(iv) Shipping and insurance charges for the Delivery of Delivery Materials to the Licensee.

(v) The cost of manufacturing of internegatives, interpositives, preprint materials, positive prints, masters, tapes, trailers, and other copies of the Motion Picture in an amount which is reasonably preapproved by the Licensor.

(vi) The costs of subtitling or dubbing, if authorized, and only in the authorized languages.

(vii) The cost of approved advertising, promotion, and publicity, which amounts are usually preapproved by the Licensor.

(viii) Legal costs and charges paid to obtain recoveries for infringement by third parties, but only to the extent reasonably preapproved by the Licensor.

(**ix**) Actual and normal expenses incurred in recovering debts from defaulting sublicensees.

(**x**) The costs of packaging for Videograms, but only to the extent reasonably preapproved by the Licensor.

(**xi**) Censorship fees and costs of editing to meet censorship requirements, but only as allowed under the terms of the Agreement.

(**b**) Limitations on Recoupable Distribution Costs. Generally, any specific costs that are not authorized or approved by the Licensor are not subject to recoupment by the Licensee. There are, customarily, specific restrictions against double deducting or recouping a Distribution Cost more than once. Unless otherwise agreed by the parties, recoupable Distribution Costs for one Licensed Right (i.e., for Theatrical exploitation) are not recoupable from the Gross Receipts that are generated from any other Licensed Right (i.e., Television exploitation) unless otherwise authorized under the cross-collateralization and recoupment provisions of the Agreement.

8. Payment Obligations. The Agreement will generally have extensive and detailed provisions regarding payment requirements. Many of these payment provisions are designed to give Banks, which have loaned production financing against the Minimum Guarantees, some level of comfort that payments will be made when due. These terms and conditions customarily include some or all of the following:

(**a**) Timely Payment. Timely payment is generally the essence of the Agreement, and payment is only considered made when the Licensor has immediate and unencumbered use of funds in the required currency, in the full amount due. The Licensee is generally required to use diligent efforts to promptly obtain all permits necessary to make all payments to the Licensor.

(**b**) Minimum Guarantee. The Minimum Guarantee is generally a nonreturnable but recoupable sum, in accordance with the recoupment provisions of the Agreement. The Minimum Guarantee is generally a minimum net sum payable to the Licensor and no taxes or charges of any sort may be deducted from it unless otherwise agreed by the parties. (For example, if an Agreement is made with a Japanese Licensee for a $400,000 Minimum Guarantee and there is a 10% Japanese withholding tax, it would be the Japanese Licensee's responsibility to pay the Japanese withholding tax so that the net amount remitted to the Licensor under the Minimum Guarantee would be $400,000 and not $360,000.)

(**c**) Installments. The Licensee is required to make all installment payments when due. When an installment is payable on events within the Licensor's control (e.g., the start or end of principal photography), the Licensor will customarily be required to give the Licensee timely notice of the event and the payment required. When any installment is payable on events within the Licensee's control (e.g., Theatrical or Video release within the Licensed Territory) the Licensee will customarily be required to give the Licensor timely notice of the event, along with all payments then due to the Licensor.

(d) Letter of Credit. If a payment is to be secured by a Letter of Credit, then the Licensee will customarily open the Letter of Credit at a bank in the Territory designated by the Licensor as a corresponding bank of the Licensor's bank. While open, the Letter of Credit will remain valid, negotiable, transferable, confirmed, and irrevocable; it will be automatically renewable for any period specified in the Agreement if the Licensor has not negotiated the Letter of Credit by its first date of expiration. All costs of the letter of credit are customarily borne by the Licensee, unless otherwise agreed by the parties.

(e) Limitations on Deductions. Unless otherwise provided in the basic Deal Terms, the Agreement will, generally, have a provision that limits the amounts of deductions from any payments due the Licensor as a result of any bank charges, conversion costs, sales, use or VAT taxes, quotas or any other taxes, levies, or charges. The Agreement will, generally, prohibit the deduction of Remittance or Withholding taxes from the Minimum Guarantee, but any such taxes paid by the Licensee are usually allowed to be recouped as Recoupable Distribution Costs after the Licensee provides the Licensor with appropriate documentation.

(i) Overages, Deductions. If the Licensee is required to pay any remittance or withholding taxes on overage amounts due to the Licensor in addition to the Minimum Guarantee, then the Licensee will, customarily, provide the Licensor with all documentation indicating the Licensee's payment of the required amount on the Licensor's behalf before deducting such payment from any sums due the Licensor.

(f) Blocked Funds. The Agreement will usually have a blocked funds provision, which provides that if a law in the Territory prohibits the remittance of any amounts due to the Licensor, then the Licensee will immediately give the Licensor notice and will then deposit such amounts in the Licensor's name for the Licensor's free use in a suitable depository designated by the Licensor in the Territory without any deduction for the costs of providing such service.

(g) Finance Charge on Late Payments. Generally the Agreement will provide for a late payment charge in addition to any other rights and remedies that the Licensor may have for the failure of the Licensee to make a timely payment. The AFMA Agreement provides for the finance charge to accrue from the date the payment was due until it is paid in full at three points over the three-month

LIBOR rate or the highest applicable legal interest rate, whichever is less.

(h) Exchange Provisions, Payment. The Agreement will usually provide for all payments to be made in U.S. dollars or such other freely remittable currency, which is designated by the Licensor. All payments are generally computed at the prevailing exchange rate on the date the payment is due at a bank designated by the Licensor. In the event of a late payment, the Licensor is generally entitled to the most favorable exchange rate between the due date and the payment date. The risk of devaluation of the U.S. dollar or other currency chosen by the Licensor against the currency of the Licensed Territory is at the Licensor's risk; and the risk of the devaluation of the currency in the Licensed Territory against the U.S. dollar or other currency designated by the Licensor is customarily at the Licensee's risk.

(i) Exchange Provisions, Recoupment. Many Motion Picture Licenses are made to a foreign Territory that includes a number of countries. (For example, when German language rights are licensed, the Territory generally includes all German language rights in Germany, Austria, and Switzerland.) The major country in that particular Territory is considered Germany. As a result, the calculation and recoupment of the Minimum Guarantee and the Recoupable Distribution Costs are generally made in the currency of the major country in the Territory, in this example, Germany. Therefore, any payments made for Recoupable Distribution Costs in Austrian currency or Swiss currency will be converted to the German currency for recoupment purposes, using the exchange rate on the date that the Minimum Guarantee was received by the Licensor or the date the Recoupable Distribution Costs were paid by the Licensee.

(j) Documentation. The Agreement will generally require the Licensee to undertake all reasonable efforts to obtain permits or clearances required to exploit the Licensed Rights in the Territory, such as certificates for local dubbing, copyright registration, quota permits, censorship clearances, the filing of author certificates, certificates of origin, music cue sheets, and the like, which are required to be filed with appropriate local authorities, as well as making payments therefore.

9. Accountings. The Agreement will generally have a number of detailed provisions concerning accounting issues. These issues include some or all of the following:

(a) Limits and Cross-Collateralization. Each Motion Picture is customarily licensed separately. Accordingly, no payment for one Motion Picture will be cross-collateralized with or set off against any amounts payable for any other Motion Picture licensed to the Licensee, whether included in the Agreement, another particular agreement, or otherwise. Any amounts due for the particular Motion Picture licensed may not be used to recoup amounts unrecouped for any other motion picture or vice versa.

(b) Limitations on Allocations. If the Licensed Motion Picture is exploited with other motion pictures, then the Licensee will generally be required to only allocate Gross Receipts and expenses between the Licensed Motion Picture and the other motion pictures, in a manner, which the Licensor has had an opportunity to approve in advance, in its sole discretion.

(c) Financial Records. The Licensee is virtually always required to maintain complete and accurate records, in the currency of the Licensed Territory, of all financial transactions regarding the Motion Picture in accordance with generally accepted accounting principles in the entertainment distribution business, throughout the Term of the Agreement and during any period while a dispute about payments remains unresolved. These records generally include all Gross Receipts derived, all Recoupable Distribution Costs paid, all allowed adjustments or rebates made, and all cash collected or credits received.

(i) Cash Basis—Maintenance of Records. All records are customarily maintained on a cash basis. If the Licensee permits any offset, refund, or rebate of sums due to the Licensor such sums will nonetheless be included in Gross Receipts. The Licensee will also keep complete and accurate copies of every statement, contract, voucher, receipt, computer record, advertising report, correspondence, and other writings, from all persons or entities pertaining to the Motion Picture.

(ii) Accounting Statements—Contents. The Licensee will generally have a number of reporting requirements under the Agreement including Accounting Statements in English (and if requested, supporting documentation) for the Motion Picture that identifies from the time of the immediately prior statement, if any, all Gross Receipts derived, all Recoupable Distribution Costs paid, identifying to whom payments were made and all exchange rates used.

(iii) Video Reporting. If any Video rights are licensed, the accounting statements will also include detailed information as to all Videograms manufactured, sold, rented, leased, returned, erased, recycled, or destroyed; the wholesale and retail selling prices of all Videograms; and all allocable deductions taken.

(iv) Multiple Country Reporting—Reserves. If the Territory contains one or more countries, the information is generally required to be reported separately for each country and consolidated for the entire Territory (e.g., the German speaking territories Germany, Austria, and Switzerland). The information will be provided in reasonable detail on a current and cumulative basis. Additionally, each accounting statement is usually accompanied by a payment of all monies then due to the Licensor. The Licensee may not withhold any Gross Receipts as a reserve against returned or defective Videograms for more than two consecutive accounting periods, and the amount withheld may not exceed 10% of the Video Gross Receipts derived for the two accounting periods for which the reserve is retained.

(**v**) Statements—When Rendered. Accounting Statements are customarily rendered monthly, quarterly, or as the Term progresses, semiannually. The AFMA Agreement provides that the Licensee is required to render statements for the following periods:

(**aa**) Each of the 12 months after the Theatrical release, or if there is none, the Video release.

(**bb**) Each calendar quarter or other quarterly periods designated by the Licensor during the entire Term of the Agreement and as long as, thereafter, any Gross Receipts are derived by the Licensee.

(**cc**) One month after the Video release, the first pay TV telecast of the Motion Picture in the Territory and first free TV telecast of the Motion Picture in the Territory. Each statement is customarily accompanied by payment of all monies then due the Licensor.

(**vi**) Audit Rights. The Licensor will generally have the right to audit the books and records of the Licensee relating to the Motion Picture with at least ten days prior notice. This examination may be conducted by the Licensor itself or through its auditors. The examination customarily takes place at the Licensor's expense, unless it uncovers an uncontested underpayment of more than 5% of the amount shown due to the Licensor on the statement audited, in which case the Licensee will customarily be required to pay the cost of the audit.

10. Delivery and Return. Because a Motion Picture has so many delivery elements required for its exhibition in different media, the Delivery of a Motion Picture will generally take place in stages. Certain Delivery Materials are delivered by actual physical delivery, other elements are delivered through access to the materials at a laboratory, other materials are delivered on loan, and some materials may be delivered by satellite transmission. There is usually an initial set of materials that is required to be delivered (Initial Delivery), and then, at a later time, an additional set of materials that is required to be delivered (Additional Delivery). The AFMA Agreement sets out the procedure for Initial Materials Delivery and Additional Materials Delivery as follows:

(**a**) Initial Delivery. The Licensor will generally give Licensee a "Notice of Initial Delivery" that the Licensor is prepared to deliver the Initial Materials by a specific date. Upon the notice, the Licensee is customarily required to immediately pay for such Initial Materials and their cost of shipment. Upon the receipt of the payment, the Licensor will ship the Initial Materials to the Licensee.

(i) Ordering of Materials. If the Licensor specifies the Materials that are available in the Licensor's Notice of Initial Delivery, then within ten days of receipt of the notice, the Licensee will give a notice to the Licensor stating the number of preprint items, prints, trailers, advertising and promotional accessories, support items, and other Initial Materials relating to the Picture that the Licensee requires subject to the Licensor's reasonable approval. The Licensor will then give the Licensee notice of the cost of the approved Initial Materials and their shipment to the Licensee, and the Licensee will immediately pay for such Initial Materials. The Licensor will then deliver such Initial Materials to the Licensee.

(ii) Outside Date for Initial Delivery. In all cases, the process of Initial Delivery of all approved Initial Materials must take place within two months of the Licensor's notice of Initial Delivery.

(b) Additional Delivery. Essentially the same process as described above will take place with respect to the Additional Delivery items. The Delivery Materials to be delivered during each phase of Delivery will be specified in the Delivery Terms section of the Agreement and each phase will include a number of the Materials listed above in Section IV, Delivery Terms.

(c) Delivery of Materials.

(i) Physical Delivery. When physical delivery is required, the Licensor will deliver to the delivery location specified in the Agreement the physical materials listed in the Agreement, which are required for use as or manufacture of necessary exploitation materials. Unless otherwise specified in the Agreement, the physical materials are customarily shipped to the Licensee by air transport.

(ii) Laboratory Access. Where laboratory access is specified in the Agreement, the Licensor will provide the Licensee with laboratory access to the physical materials needed for use as or manufacture of necessary exploitation materials. An approved Laboratory Access letter, which is customarily attached as an Exhibit to the Agreement, will provide the terms and conditions of access between and among the Laboratory, the Licensor, and the Licensee. The physical materials are customarily held in a recognized laboratory or facility in the Licensor's name. The Licensee may order prints and other exploitation materials for the Motion Picture to be manufactured from the accessible physical materials, all at the Licensee's sole cost and expense. The Laboratory Access letter will customarily provide that the Licensee is responsible for charges it incurs and the Licensor is responsible for charges it incurs, and that unpaid charges of either the Licensor or the Licensee shall not prohibit the other from further access to or the ordering of additional materials.

(iii) Loan Materials. Where loan of materials is specified in the Agreement, the Licensor will deliver on loan the required physical materials for manufacture of necessary preprint materials to the delivery location specified by the Licensee. These physical materials loaned will only be used to make new preprint materials at the Licensee's sole expense from which necessary exploitation materials can be made. These physical materials will customarily also be held in a laboratory or facility subject to the Licensor's reasonable approval and will be returned to the Licensor within a reasonable time that is designated by the Licensor.

(iv) Satellite Delivery. Where Satellite Delivery is indicated, the Licensor may deliver various Delivery Materials by satellite transmission. The Licensor is customarily responsible for all uplinking transmission costs. The Licensee is customarily responsible for arranging to receive this satellite reception and for all downlinking reception costs. The Licensee's failure to make suitable downlinking receiving arrangements, or the failure to receive a transmission of the Motion Picture due to technical downlink or reception failure is customarily not deemed a breach of the Agreement by the Licensor and will not affect the Licensee's obligations under the Agreement, including the obligation to make any payments. The Licensee will customarily pay the Licensor the cost incurred for each missed satellite feed.

(d) Delivery of Support Materials. Support materials include such items as stills, slides, color stills, video packaging art, poster art, one sheet (poster), press kit, press book synopsis, music cue sheets, video packaging credits, paid ad credits, main and end title credits, and other support items. In the event that the Licensee does not use any of the support materials created by the Licensor, the Licensee will be required to obtain prior approval by the Licensor for using any of its own servicing, advertising, promotional, or other support material, so as to insure that they meet all of the contractual requirements and restrictions of the Licensor.

(e) Evaluation and Acceptance. Because technical standards can be different in various Territories around the world, the Licensee must have an opportunity to review and evaluate Delivery Materials for technical suitability. The Agreement will usually provide for a prompt evaluation period. This period usually ranges from ten to 30 days. The AFMA Agreement provides that all Delivery Materials will be considered technically satisfactory and accepted by the Licensee unless within ten days after the receipt of the Delivery Materials, the Licensee gives the Licensor notice specifying any technical defect. If the Licensee's notice is accurate, then the Licensor will at its election either:

(i) timely correct the defect and redeliver the affected Delivery Materials; or

(ii) deliver new replacement Delivery Materials; or

(iii) exercise its rights of suspension or withdrawal under the suspension and withdrawal provisions included in the Agreement.

(f) Delay Tactics. Evaluation and Acceptance is often used as a delay tactic in the Delivery process, or as an excuse for not paying sums when due. As a result, it is customary to include a clause in the Agreement stating that in the event that the Licensor has undertaken a Theatrical or Video release of the Motion Picture, or has begun exploiting any Licensed Rights, then any alleged defect will be deemed waived by the Licensee.

(g) Ownership of Materials. Legal ownership of, and title to, all Delivery Materials customarily remains with the Licensor subject to the Licensee's right to use such Delivery Materials under the terms of the Agreement. The Licensee is also required to exercise due care in safeguarding all Delivery Materials and assumes all risk for their theft or damage while they are in the Licensee's possession.

(h) Payment for Delivery Materials. The Licensee will customarily pay for all Delivery Materials as indicated in the Deal Terms of the Agreement. All costs of Delivery and Return, including shipping charges, import fees, duties, brokerage fees, storage charges, and related charges will customarily be the Licensee's sole responsibility unless its otherwise specified in the Deal Terms of the Agreement.

(i) Ownership of Licensee Created Materials. When the Licensee creates its own materials such as dubbed versions, masters, advertising and promotional materials artwork, and the like, the Licensor is usually given free unrestricted to all such materials created by the Licensee. Once the alternate language tracks and dubbed versions are created, the Licensee is required to give the Licensor notice of each person or entity who prepares any such dubbed or subtitled tracks for the Motion Picture and of each laboratory or facility where the tracks or materials are located. Promptly after completion of any dubbed or subtitled version of the Motion Picture, the Licensee will also provide the Licensor with immediate unrestricted free access to all those dubbed and subtitled tracks. Additionally, the Licensor will immediately become the owner of the copyright in all dubbed and subtitled tracks, subject to a nonexclusive free license in favor of the Licensee to use such track during the Term of the Agreement solely for the exploitation of the Licensed Rights. If such ownership is not allowed under the law in a Territory, then the Licensee will grant the Licensor a nonexclusive free license to use such dubbed or subtitled tracks worldwide in perpetuity without restriction.

(j) Return of Delivery Materials. Upon the expiration of the Agreement Term, the Licensee will, at the Licensor's election, either:

(i) return all Delivery Materials to Licensor at the Licensee's expense; or
(ii) destroy all Delivery Materials and provide the Licensor with the customary Certificate of Destruction.

11. General Exploitation Obligations and Restrictions. The Agreement generally provides affirmative obligations on the part of the Licensee with respect to exploitation as follows:

(a) Holdback Periods. The Licensee will not exploit or otherwise authorize the exploitation of any Licensed Right before the end of a holdback period.

(b) No Discrimination. The Licensee will not discriminate against the Motion Picture or use it to secure more advantageous terms for any other Motion Picture product or service.

(c) Obligation to Furnish Information. Upon the Licensor's request, the Licensee is obligated to provide all information to the Licensee regarding the time and place of the first exploitation of each Licensed Right.

(d) Approval Rights. The Licensor is customarily given the following Approval Rights regarding the exploitation of each Licensed Right:

(i) License Agreements. The approval over the material terms of each license for the exploitation of the Licensed Rights; and

(ii) Subdistributors, Agents. The Licensor will also have prior approval of the material terms of each subdistribution agreement or agency agreement.

(e) Continuing Obligations. There is also customarily an affirmative continuing obligation for the Licensee to use all of its diligent efforts and skill in the distribution and exploitation of the Licensed Rights, to maximize the Gross Receipts, and to minimize the Recoupable Distribution Costs. The Licensee will also be obligated to distribute and exploit the Motion Picture consistent with the quality standards of first class distributors within the Territory and to maintain the Motion Picture in continuous release throughout the Territory for a period consistent with reasonable business judgment.

12. Theatrical Exploitation Obligations.

(a) Licensor's Approval Rights. The Licensor is generally given broad Approval Rights, on an ongoing basis, of significant aspects of the exploitation of the Cinematic Rights throughout the Territory, including the initial Theatrical release campaign, the distribution policy of the Licensee, execution of contract terms, the minimum and maximum print order, total amount and the specific items of the advertising and publicity budgets, the advertising and marketing campaign of release dates, the release pattern, the theaters in key cities, the marketing strategy, Gross Receipts allocations between the Motion Picture and short subjects, and any amendments or modifications to these matters. The Licensee is also required to submit each such item in a timely fashion to the Licensor for the Licensor's prior approval.

(b) Theatrical Release Obligations. The Licensee undertakes to place the Motion Picture in general theatrical release throughout the Territory in no less than a number of cities and theaters reasonably required by the Licensor and no later than the specified theatrical release date referred in the Agreement.

(c) Print Order. The Deal Terms will customarily specify that the Licensee will order and pay for no less than the minimum number of prints and no more than the maximum number of prints.

(d) Advertising and Marketing Commitments. The Licensee is also customarily required to comply with the advertising and marketing campaigns approved by the Licensor and to spend no less than the minimum advertising commitment and no more than the advertising budget reasonably approved by Licensor. Additionally, the Licensee will be required to give the Licensor reasonable advance notice of all premieres of the Motion Picture in the Territory.

(e) Festivals, Charity Premieres. The Licensee will customarily not enter the Motion Picture in any festival, charitable screening, or the like, without the Licensor's prior approval.

(f) Release Information. In addition to the accounting requirements, with respect to Theatrical exploitation, the Licensee may be required to give weekly notices to the Licensor, furnishing all information available regarding the results of the release including exhibition terms, box-office receipts as received, and expenses as incurred both on a weekly and cumulative basis.

(g) Exhibition Restrictions. The theatrical exhibition of the Motion Picture will also customarily be required to comply with the following:

(i) Separate Agreements. All exhibition agreements should be separate and independent from all other exhibition agreements for any other Motion Picture project or service.

(ii) Restricted Engagements. The Licensee should not authorize its first run to be exhibited on a flat license or on a four-wall (where the Licensee pays for the rental of the theater and keeps all the revenue) basis or as part of a multiple feature engagement unless the Licensor has preapproved same and all relevant terms of the exhibition, including the proposed allocation of box-office receipts to the Motion Picture as well as advertising costs, license fees, and film rental.

(iii) Allocations Among Motion Pictures. If the Motion Picture is required by law to be exhibited with another motion picture or short subject, there are stringent allocation requirements with respect to the box-office receipts that would apply to such an exhibition in order to protect the Gross Receipts to be allocated to the licensed Motion Picture.

(iv) Settlements. Any settlements with the theater owner should be submitted to the Licensor for approval and should be at rates no less than those comparable to other Motion Pictures in the Territory.

(v) Audit. The Licensee is customarily required to audit all exhibition engagements for the Motion Picture consistent with the practices of first-class distributors in the Territory and to promptly supply the Licensor with the results of such audits.

(vi) Maximizing Collections. The Licensee is also customarily required to undertake all actions reasonably necessary to maximize collections from the exhibitors as quickly as possible.

(h) Controlled Theaters. If the Licensee also controls the theaters in which the Licensee wishes to exhibit the Motion Picture, the Licensee is required to license the Motion Picture at an arm's-length basis and also provide the Licensor with copies of all exhibition agreements with the controlled theater.

13. Video Exploitation Obligations. The Agreement will customarily provide for the Licensee to release the Video no later than the specified Video Release Date in the Deal Terms and further provide that the Licensee will only exploit the Video in the formats for which it is authorized and will not authorize or advertise of the availability of Videograms to the public until two months before the end of any applicable Video Holdback Period.

(a) Efforts and Quality. The Licensee is also customarily obligated to use diligent efforts and skill in the manufacture, distribution, and exploitation of the Videograms of the Motion Picture and to meet quality standards at least as comparable as other motion picture Videograms commercially available through legitimate outlets in the Territory.

(b) Catalogue Availability. The Licensee is customarily required to make the Video of the Motion Picture available through its catalogue and not allow Videograms to leave normal channels of distribution for a commercially unreasonable period of time.

(c) Licensor's Video Ad Campaign Approval Rights. The Licensor is generally given the right of prior approval for the advertising and marketing campaign for the exploitation of Video Licensed Rights. All proposed advertising and artwork is submitted to the Licensor for approval before it is used, and, unless it is otherwise specified, the Licensor is given one month to object to the artwork and advertising.

(d) The Licensor's Packaging Approval Rights. The Licensee will generally provide the prototype copy of the Videotape and its packaging for the Licensor's approval, to be given within ten days of Licensor's receipt of said items. The

Licensor is also generally given ten free copies of each authorized format of the Videogram in its packaging for Licensor's own use.

(e) Limits on Included Material. The Licensee is customarily precluded from authorizing any advertising or any other material to be included on the Videogram without the prior approval of the Licensor.

(f) Minimum Retail Price. Where there is a Minimum Retail Price in the Deal Terms of the Agreement, the Licensee is not authorized to exploit the Videogram at a consumer price that is less than the Minimum Retail Price and accordingly, for purposes of calculating the Gross Receipts and amounts due to the Licensor, the Videograms will be deemed sold at retail for not less than a contractually specified Minimum Retail Price.

(g) Minimum Wholesale Price. Similar provisions, as noted above, with respect to the Minimum Retail Price apply to the Minimum Wholesale Price as well.

(h) Free Goods. Where there are a minimum number of free goods set forth in the Deal Terms (which are free copies of the Video used as promotions, gifts, or free samples), the Licensee agrees not to exceed that amount. In the event that the amount is exceeded, then all additional units are deemed to be sold at not less than the Minimum Wholesale Price specified in the Deal Terms for purposes of computing the Gross Receipt and amounts due to the Licensor.

(i) Sell-off Period. During the last six months of the Term, or the License Period for Video rights, the Licensee customarily agrees not to manufacture an excessive number of Video units reasonably exceeding the normal customer needs. During the three-month period following the end of the License Period, the Licensee will customarily have the nonexclusive right to sell off its then-existing inventory for Home Video exploitation only. At the end of the three-month period, the Licensee will either sell its remaining Videograms and their packaging to the Licensor at cost or destroy them and provide Licensor with a customary Certificate of Destruction.

(j) Import/Export Restrictions. The Licensee customarily agrees not to import or authorize the importation of Videograms into the Territory other than the Delivery Materials provided by the Licensor. The Licensee also agrees not to export or authorize the export of Videograms embodying the Motion Picture from the Territory.

14. Television Exploitation Obligations. In exploiting Television Rights in a Territory, the Licensee will customarily have the following release obligations:

(a) Advanced Notification. Licensor will be notified in advance of the first Pay TV and Free TV broadcast of the Motion Picture in the Territory.

(b) Dubbed and Subtitled Versions. The Motion Picture will not be broadcast on Pay TV or Free TV in dubbed or subtitled versions except as authorized in the Deal Terms of the Agreement.

(c) Authorized Runs and Playdates. The Licensee will not authorize the broadcast of more than the authorized number of Runs and Playdates set forth in the Deal Terms and if there are no specific Runs or Playdates authorized, then said numbers will be reasonably preapproved by the Licensor.

(d) Encryption. The Licensee will not broadcast or authorize the broadcasting of the Motion Picture in any form of Pay TV other than an encrypted form and will not sell, rent, export, or authorize the sale, rental, or export of decoders for such encryption outside the Territory.

(e) Reception Outside the Territory. The Licensee will not authorize the broadcast of the Motion Picture by any means including terrestrial, cable, or satellite from within the Territory, where such broadcast is primarily intended for reception outside the Territory or is capable of reception by more than an insubstantial number of home TV receivers outside the Territory.

(f) Run. A Run generally means one telecast of the Motion Picture during a 24-hour period over the nonoverlapping telecast facilities of an authorized telecaster, such that the Motion Picture is only capable of reception on TV receivers within a reception zone of such telecaster once during such period. A simultaneous telecast over several interconnected local stations (i.e., network) constitutes one telecast; a telecast over noninterconnected local stations whose signal reception areas do not overlap constitutes a telecast in each station's local broadcast area. In other words, a Run usually means one telecast during a 24-hour period.

(g) Playdate. A Playdate generally means one or more telecasts of the Motion Picture during a 24-hour period over the nonoverlapping telecasting facilities of an authorized telecaster, such that the Motion Picture is only capable of reception on TV receivers within a reception zone of such telecaster during such period. A Playdate may include more than one telecast during a 24-hour period.

(h) Usage Reports. The Licensee is generally required to provide the Licensor with each person or entity responsible for preparing a dubbed or subtitled version of the Motion Picture and the time and place of each telecast of the Motion Picture since the previous notice to the Licensor.

(i) Commercials. The Licensee is customarily only authorized to insert commercial announcements in the Motion Picture at those points designated by the Licensor. Additionally, the Licensee must require each broadcaster to broadcast all credits, trademarks, logos, copyright notices, and other symbols appearing on the Motion Picture as furnished by the Licensor.

(j) Conclusion of Run or Playdates. The License Period for each Pay TV or Free TV Licensed Rights will generally end on the earlier of the conclusion of the last authorized Run or Playdate or the end of the License Period specified in the Deal Terms. A License Period will not be extended because the Licensee failed to take all the authorized Runs or Playdates for any applicable License Right.

(k) Secondary Broadcast and Compulsory Licenses. Secondary Broadcasts are the simultaneous, unaltered, unabridged retransmission by a cable microwave or television system for reception by the public of an initial transmission by wire or over the air, including by satellite, of a Motion Picture intended for reception by the public. (When a Cable System transmits a Motion Picture simultaneously with the broadcast of the Motion Picture on a Free TV Station, a Secondary Broadcast exists.) In certain territories, compulsory licenses are required to be paid for such Secondary Broadcasts or royalties are payable or are required to be paid under local laws or through collective management societies or collective contractual arrangements. The Licensor customarily reserves all the rights to make, authorize, and collect royalties for a Secondary Broadcast in a Motion Picture in territories where broadcasters may grant or withhold authorization for a Secondary Broadcast of their primary broadcast. The Licensee is required to notify each broadcaster to abide by the Licensor's directions regarding Secondary Broadcasts including the prohibition of Secondary Broadcasts until after a date designated by the Licensor.

15. Music. Music is an important part of the motion picture licensing process. In order to exploit the Motion Picture properly in any Territory in the world, the Licensor must show that it has acquired all music rights with respect to music embodied in the Motion Picture. Once the Licensor is able to provide documentation of the Licensor's control of such rights, the Licensor will also be entitled to collect various royalties for the performance and the reproduction of the music in the Motion Picture within the applicable Territory.

(a) Cue Sheets. The Licensor will customarily supply the Licensee with cue sheets that list the composer, lyricist, and publisher of all music embodied in the Motion Picture. The Licensee is generally required to promptly file with the appropriate governmental agency or music rights society in the Territory such music cue sheets, without change.

(b) Synchronization. The Licensor generally authorizes the Licensee to exploit the rights to synchronize the music in the Motion Picture without charge in conjunction with its exploitation of the Motion Picture. The Licensor is, however, customarily responsible for paying all royalties and charges necessary to obtain and control such synchronization rights during the Term of the Agreement and will customarily hold the Licensee harmless from any payments in this regard.

(c) Mechanical Rights. The Licensor also represents that the Licensor controls all rights to make mechanical reproductions of the music contained in the Motion Picture, on all copies exploited by the Licensee in the Territory during the Term. The Licensor further authorizes the Licensee to exploit the mechanical rights, without charge, in connection with the Motion Picture. The Licensor is also customarily responsible for paying all royalties or charges necessary to obtain and control the mechanical rights during the Term provided that if a mechanical or author's rights society in the Territory refuses to honor the authorization obtained by the Licensor's mechanical license, in the country of origin of the Motion Picture, then the Licensee will become responsible for such licenses, royalties, or charges.

(d) Music Performance Rights. The Licensor customarily represents warrants to the Licensee that the nondramatic performing rights in each musical composition in the Motion Picture are:

(i) in the public domain; or

(ii) controlled by Licensor; or

(iii) available by license from the local music performance rights societies in the Territory affiliated with the International Confederation of Author's and Composer's Societies (CISAC). In such an event, the Licensee is usually responsible for obtaining a license to exploit the performance rights from such local music performance rights societies.

(e) Music Publishing Rights. As between Licensor and Licensee, the Licensor is generally solely entitled to collect and retain the publisher's share of any music publishing royalties that arise from the Licensee's exploitation of any of the Licensed Rights in the Motion Picture in the Territory.

16. Suspension and Withdrawal.

(a) Licensor's Right of Suspension or Withdrawal. The Licensor will customarily have the right to suspend delivery or withdraw the Motion Picture at any time if:

(i) the Licensor determines that it might infringe on the rights of others or violate any laws; or

(ii) the Licensor determines that the Delivery Materials are unsuitable for manufacture of first class commercial quality exploitation materials; or

(iii) as a result of events and force majeure; or

(iv) the Licensee refuses to accept delivery of the Motion Picture for any reason.

(b) Effect of Suspension. The Licensee will customarily not be entitled to claim any damages for lost profits for any suspension. Instead, the Term of the Agreement will be extended for the Term of the suspension, however, if any suspension lasts more than three consecutive months, then either party customarily may terminate the Agreement on ten days written notice, in which case the Motion Picture will be treated as withdrawn.

(c) Effect of Withdrawal. If the Motion Picture is withdrawn, then the Licensor customarily either substitutes a Motion Picture of like quality mutually satisfactory to Licensor and Licensee or must refund promptly all unrecouped amounts of the Minimum Guarantee paid to the Licensor and all unrecoupable Recoupable Distribution Costs. The sole remedy of the Licensee is customarily to receive the substitute Motion Picture or the refund. In most cases, the Licensee may not collect any lost profits or consequential damages.

17. **Default and Termination.** The default and termination provisions in the AFMA Agreement provide for customary default provisions for both the Licensor and Licensee, for failure to pay or failure to honor their respective obligations under the Agreement, as the case may be, for bankruptcy and similar debtor/creditor situations, breach of warranty, and other customary default terms.

(a) Licensee's Default:

(i) The License is in default if Licensee fails to pay any installment when due;

(ii) the Licensee becomes insolvent, makes an assignment for the benefit of creditors, or seeks relief under any bankruptcy law;

(iii) the Licensee breaches any material condition, term, condition, or covenant of the Agreement; or

(iv) the Licensee attempts to make any assignment, transfer, sublicense, or appointment, without first obtaining the Licensor's approval.

(v) Notice to Licensee. The Licensor will customarily be required to give Licensee notice of any claim of default. If the default is capable of being cured, the Licensee will have ten days after the receipt of notice to cure a monetary default and 20 days after receipt of notice to cure a nonmonetary default. If the default is incapable of cure or if the Licensee fails to cure within the specified time period, then the Licensor may proceed against the Licensee for available relief, including terminating the Agreement retroactive to the date of default, suspending Delivery of the Motion Picture, and declaring the Licensee in default.

(b) The Licensor's Default:

(i) The Licensor will be in Default if the Licensor becomes insolvent or fails to pay its debts when due.

(ii) The Licensor makes an assignment for the benefit of Creditors or seeks relief under any bankruptcy law or

(iii) The Licensor breaches any material Term, Covenant, or Condition of the Agreement. Any default by the Licensor is limited to the Motion Picture, and no Default by the Licensor as to one Agreement would be a Default as to any other Agreement with the Licensee.

(iv) Notice to Licensor. Licensee must give the Licensor notice of a claim Default. Licensor will have ten days after receipt to cure a monetary default and 20 days after receipt of default notice to cure a nonmonetary default. If the Licensor fails to cure within the time period provided, then the Licensee may proceed against the Licensor for all available relief, provided, however, in no case may the Licensee collect any lost profits or consequential damages.

(c) Arbitration/Litigation. All disputes under the AFMA Agreement are resolved by final and binding Arbitration under the Rules of International Arbitration of the American Film Marketing Association. Other agreements may provide for arbitration under the Commercial Arbitration Rules of the American Arbitration Association, while still other agreements may provide for disputes to be resolved in the applicable courts of the jurisdiction agreed upon by the parties.

18. Antipiracy Provisions. In order to protect the Motion Picture against pirates, a number of Antipiracy Provisions have been developed and are included in the AFMA Agreement. These Antipiracy Provisions include the requirement that the Licensee include copyright notices and antipiracy warnings on each copy of the Motion Picture, including all negatives, preprint materials, release prints, masters, tapes, cassettes, discs, videograms, and their packaging.

(a) Copyright Infringement. The Licensee is required to take all necessary steps to prevent copyright infringement of the Motion Picture and to prevent piracy. The Licensor may participate in any antipiracy acts or action using its own counsel, and the Licensor's expenses will be reimbursed from any recovery in equal proportion to the Licensee's expenses. If the Licensee fails to take any antipiracy action, the Licensor may do so and retain the entire Recovery for itself.

(b) New Technology. If new technology is developed which provides protection against unauthorized piracy or exploitation of the Motion Picture, then the Licensee is required to use any such technology in a reasonable manner and is entitled to deduct the cost of doing so as a Recoupable Distribution Expense after first obtaining the Licensor's reasonable approval.
(c) Cooperation Against Piracy. The Licensor and the Licensee each agree to use reasonable efforts to cooperate to prevent and remedy any act of piracy.

19. Warranties and Indemnities.

(a) Licensor Warranties. Licensor makes the customary indemnities with regard to title and the right to grant all rights licensed under the Agreement to the Licensee and that the Motion Picture is free and clear of all liens, claims, and encumbrances and that the Motion Picture does not infringe on the rights of any third party.

(b) Licensee Warranties. The Licensee makes the customary warranties as to the authority to enter into the Agreement and the financial ability to perform all obligations under the Agreement and that there are no existing or threatened claims of litigation that could adversely affect the Licensee's ability to perform and that the Licensee will honor all restrictions in the exercise of the Licensed Rights and will not exploit the Licensed Rights outside of the Territory before the end of its Holdback or after its License Period.

(c) Indemnity. Each of the parties indemnifies the other from the other party's claims, costs or expenses that arise out of breach of the indemnifying party's representations and warranties.

20. Assignment and Sublicensing.

(a) Licensee's Limitations. The Agreement is personal to Licensee. It may not assign or transfer the Agreement or sublicense or use an agent without the Licensor's approval.

(b) Licensor Assignment. The Licensor is entitled to freely assign and transfer the Agreement, but the Assignment will not relieve Licensor of its obligations under the Agreement.

(c) Licensor's Assignment for Financing Purposes. Customarily, in Motion Picture licensing transactions, the Agreement is assigned to a bank for purposes of obtaining production financing. Accordingly, the agreement is customarily used as a security for a lender, completion guarantor, or other financing entity. The Licensee is required, promptly on request, to execute a reasonable and customary Notice of Assignment or security document or similar instrument to establish and perfect the lending institution's security interest in the Motion Picture. The Licensee agrees to abide by consistent written instructions from the Licensor in making any payments otherwise due the Licensor directly, due the bank, or other lending institution. The Licensee further agrees not to assert any offset rights against the lending institution or assert any rights it may have against the Licensor to delay, diminish, or excuse the payment of any sums pledged or assigned to the lending institution. Instead, the Licensee agrees that it will only treat such offsets or other rights as a separate and unrelated matter solely between the Licensor and the Licensee.

21.Miscellaneous Provisions.

(a) The Agreement usually includes customary Miscellaneous provisions including Separability, Cumulative Remedies, Notices, Entire Agreement, Modifications in Writing, etc., which provisions appear in most International Motion Picture Licensing Agreements. The AFMA Agreement provides that the Agreement will be governed by and interpreted under laws of the State and Jurisdiction Specified in the Deal Terms, however, if none is specified, then California Law will apply. Additionally, if no forum is dictated in the Deal Terms, then the forum will be Los Angeles County, California, U.S.A., where disputes will be resolved. Other agreements may provide for alternative forums, venues, and jurisdictions for the resolution of disputes in accordance with the agreement of the parties.

SETTING UP THE PRODUCTION

Think of an independent picture as a one-time business. Although its life span is limited, it may employ 100 or more people and run through millions of dollars in expenses. As any business does, it must face issues about its legal structure, financial systems, and risk management. We will discuss those organizational aspects before turning to the next role of the independent filmmaker: Production manager.

The Form of Production Company

There are four forms by which you can do business as a motion-picture producer. The first is what is called a "sole proprietorship"—one person running his own business. The second is a partnership, when two or more people run the business. The third is a corporation, which is an entity legally separate from the individuals owning and running the business. The fourth, and most recently introduced form, is the limited liability company, which, like a corporation, is a separate entity from the people who own and run it.

Each of these ways of doing business has special features, which should be considered when you decide how to organize your business. The two most important features that impact a producer are insulation from personal liability for debts and taxation. We will give you general guidelines as to how each of these business forms work, but you should seek professional advice to determine the best form for your particular situation. The decision as to how you will run your production business should be made based on advice from your lawyer and your accountant.

Sole Proprietorship

Sole proprietorship is the most common form by which small businesses are conducted. It is also the simplest in that there is one individual owner. To start a sole proprietorship in California you need only prepare a few simple documents.

The first is a "Fictitious Business Name Statement," commonly called a DBA (doing business as). This document identifies you as the owner by your name, address, and the name under which you are doing business. Please note, however, that a DBA only has to be filed if you use a name other than your real name to do business. Mark Halloran Films is not a fictitious name if you are Mark Halloran. The DBA is filed with the County Recorder located in the county in which you do business. You can get the DBA forms from your local newspaper or the County Recorder's office. The cost of filing is usually around $20. In addition to filing, you must publish a legal notice in a local newspaper. Your County Recorder will tell you which newspapers publish these notices and their rates. Some local governments may require you to obtain a separate business license under your fictitious name.

As to your liability, you as sole proprietor are responsible for your own acts, and, in general, for the acts of your employees. For example, if you send your assistant out to deliver a script to a potential actor on your project and he is involved in a car accident, you could be responsible for compensating the injured parties in the accident. If you lose a lawsuit, then the person who won the suit can look to all your assets, including both your business and your personal assets to recover. Obviously, this is a risk for which you should be insured.

As a sole proprietor, you are considered self-employed and must file quarterly estimated income tax returns and make prepayment of anticipated taxes with both the IRS and your local state tax authority. You should consult your accountant to assist you in these matters.

Partnerships

If two or more people form a business and agree to share the profits and losses, they have a partnership. Ideally, your relationship with your partner is governed by a written partnership agreement, which details your respective rights and responsibilities. However, you can have a partnership even without a written agreement, and many people are in partnerships even though they might not realize it. If you and a friend write a script together that you co-own and jointly control, you are a partnership with respect to that script.

If there is an oral understanding but no written partnership agreement, then state law will control the relationship among the partners. That law generally gives each partner an equal share of profits and losses and an equal voice in decisions. Written agreements are particularly important when the partners have arrangements that are not the norm. The partners in a partnership can be individuals, other partnerships, corporations, other limited-liability companies, or any combination thereof. Sometimes very large and complicated companies operate as partnerships. Time Warner, for example, operated through a partnership before the AOL deal.

There are three kinds of partnerships: General partnerships, joint ventures, and limited partnerships.

General Partnerships

General partnerships are the most common. In a general partnership, each partner has an interest in all of the partnership property. The typical deal between two partners is fifty-fifty, although you are free to agree otherwise. Each partner has a duty to the other partners to take care of partnership property and not dispose of it without the consent of the other partners. Additionally, each partner may act on behalf of the partnership and bind the other partners. It has been a surprise to many of our clients that one of the partners can go out and make a deal on behalf of the partnership, not tell the other partners, and the innocent partners are on the hook. This is also true if a partner is involved in a car accident while on partnership business. Not only can the partnership be sued, but you can be sued individually. This unlimited personal liability for partnership debts is the biggest drawback of general partnerships.

In California, a partnership must file a DBA certificate (if all the partners surnames are not in the partnership name) and publish a DBA notice. The partnership must also file a form SS-4 with the IRS to obtain an employer identification tax number (EIN), even if the partnership does not employ anybody. These forms can be obtained from your local IRS service center or at *www.irs.gov.*

Unlike corporations, partnerships do not pay tax. However, partnerships are required to file informational tax returns. The losses or profits pass through the individual partners on their individual tax returns. As with sole proprietorships, the partners must file quarterly returns and make personal income tax prepayments.

Joint Venture

A joint venture is a partnership limited to a single or limited series of business transactions, rather than a continuous business. You may want to partner with someone for the purpose of producing one project, but do not want to be involved on a continual basis. Your partnership would be considered a joint venture, but everything else that applies to a general partnership would apply.

This joint venture form of partnership is very common in the entertainment business. Cowriters partner when they write a script together. Producers often jointly option properties. These are usually joint ventures, and even if the legal formalities of getting an EIN and filing tax returns are not undertaken (which in most cases they arc not), the same rules of coliability, right of one partner to bind, etc., still apply. Keep that in mind any time you embark on a movie project with others. A written understanding, as simple as a letter signed by the parties that sets out the ground rules, will be helpful.

Limited Partnership

A limited partnership is a form of partnership commonly used to raise investment money. It requires at least one "general partner," who runs the business. The "limited partners" contribute capital, but do not manage the business and have no liability beyond their investment in the partnership. Limited partners have to be careful not to become involved in the management of the business or they can lose their limited-liability status. Limited partnerships have been the legal form of choice for private investments in films because there were tax benefits available that were not possible through corporations. As discussed below, limited-liability companies have become the form of choice for most of these investments today.

Generally, a limited partnership exists for a set period of time and its rules of governance are set out in a written limited-partnership agreement. State and federal securities laws apply to limited partnerships that raise money from investors. This is a complicated arena and under no circumstances should you form a limited partnership without the help of a lawyer. If you do not set up the limited partnership properly and abide by the rules, you could be personally liable to your limited partners for up to three times their investment.

Corporations

Corporations are different from sole proprietorships and partnerships. A corporation is an artificial, separate legal entity formed under procedures set up by state law. A corporation can own, buy, or sell property in its own name, enter contracts, borrow money, and raise capital. A corporation is governed by a board of directors, which is elected by its shareholders. The directors appoint officers, such as a president and chief financial officer, to manage the corporation. Liabilities of the business are borne by the corporation. The shareholders' liabilities are limited to the amounts invested in the corporation and their share of profits. A corporate shareholder's personal assets are not at risk if the corporation cannot pay its debts. Corporations must file annual tax returns and pay taxes on their profits. Unlike partnerships, there is no passing of profits and losses from a corporation to the individual shareholders, unless the corporation is a Subchapter S corporation. With a Subchapter S corporation, the shareholders are treated like partners and their profits and losses are passed through to them for tax purposes, while they retain the benefit of the corporation's limited-liability status.

You form a corporation by filing a document known as "Articles of

Incorporation" with state authorities. Corporations are governed by bylaws, which are adopted at the beginning of the corporate life. Generally, the officers of the corporation have authority to deal with the affairs of the corporation, subject to the approval or disapproval by the board of directors, which in turn answers to the shareholders. The board of directors schedules periodic meetings to review the acts of the officers. The shareholders generally have an annual meeting to review the board of directors. The corporation's existence is perpetual unless the shareholders vote to terminate the corporation or the corporation cannot continue financially.

Shares of publicly held corporations are transferable from one owner to another on the open market. But with closely-held corporations, there is no ready market for the shares and there are legal restrictions on their transfer. Before transferring shares of a closely held corporation, you must talk to your attorney and accountant. Because of these restrictions on transfer and for other reasons, it is more common to give people profit participations in a movie than shares in the corporation that owns the movie. Profit participations are not ownership interests; they are a contractual right to receive money.

Limited Liability Companies

In the last dozen years, a new form of business entity has gained popularity in the movie business: the "limited liability company" (LLC), which is a hybrid of partnerships and corporations. An LLC is an organization in which the owners (members) are legally separate from the LLC. There are two types of LLCs: Member-managed and manager-managed. In member-managed LLCs, the members make management decisions; in the manager-managed LLCs, the members make only the major decisions (somewhat akin to a corporate board of directors) and leave the authority to exercise day-to-day management decisions to the managers.

LLCs provide limited liability for the owners just like corporations, but are treated as partnerships for tax purposes. The members of the LLC are not individually liable for the obligations and liabilities of the LLC. This also extends to the relationship among the members. So, while general partners have an obligation to contribute to the partnership and indemnify other partners for losses and obligations incurred, no such individual obligation exists for LLC members. Generally, the LLC will be required to indemnify members for obligations incurred by the members in carrying on the business of the LLC. However, if the LLC does not have sufficient assets to fully indemnify the member, the member may not look to the individual assets of the other members, as is true in a general partnership. LLCs are formed by filing of Articles of Organization (equivalent to Corporate Articles of Incorporation) and operate under written operating agreements that set out how they will function. We cannot emphasize enough that if you do not observe the corporate and LLC formalities, you will lose the insulation these entities provide. Although you can purchase Corporate and LLC do-it-yourself kits, there is no replacement for competent legal and accounting advice in these areas.

The form of business you utilize will depend on your individual situation and should be worked out with the help of an attorney and an accountant.

Business Accounting

When you organize your business, you will need an accountant. There will be income tax issues to be considered and you will become subject to several kinds of reporting requirements. Hiring people triggers a number of obligations. We will touch on the steps and highlight several of the issues that arise in the entertainment business.

The first step is to get a federal employer identification number (EIN). This is the number businesses use for federal and state tax reporting requirements, and you can obtain it through a simple application to the IRS.

When you hire employees, your business will be obligated to withhold Social Security tax, Medicare taxes, federal income tax, and other monies (such as state disability insurance amounts). These amounts have to be reported and paid to appropriate governmental agencies. When the employee is a guild member, such as WGA, there are also pension, health, and welfare fund payment reports to be made. If you or the people who work for you are not qualified to handle these responsibilities, you must arrange for your accountant to undertake them or use a payroll service.

Payroll services are companies that specialize in handling the accounting and reporting for employers, and they are very commonly used on independent films because people are hired rapidly and then laid off after the picture shoots. Several payroll service companies that are qualified to handle movie payrolls are DISC (818) 973-4525 and Entertainment Partners (818) 955-6299.

Independent Contractors or Employees

One tricky issue in the entertainment accounting area is whether to treat people who work for you as independent contractors or employees. It is tempting to treat someone as an independent contractor because independent contractors are responsible for their own withholding taxes, whereas employers pay an employer's share for an employee. This can amount to thousands of dollars per worker. However, there are very expensive repercussions for mischaracterizing someone as an independent contractor. The problem in the movie business is that some people fall into both categories.

The IRS lists a number of indicia as to whether or not someone is an independent contractor or an employee. Generally, if you have the ability to direct someone's work and you provide them with the tools (such as an office, computer, etc.) they are employees. There are no hard and fast rules. When there is a close call, you should treat people as employees.

It is clear that actors, directors, and most of the crew are employees. Most writers are treated as employees. However, some independent producers treat writers as independent contractors, and it is an arguable position since writers take only general instructions from you as the producer, and they do their work at home and with their own tools. You are well advised to discuss how to treat workers with your accountant.

Loanout Corporations

Most high-priced creative talent in Hollywood uses what are called "loanout corporations." These are corporations formed by the talent to employ their services. The corporations are given the right to loan the talent's services to other companies. For example, if Paramount wants to hire Richard Gere to star in a movie, they actually contract with his loanout company, which agrees to make his services available to Paramount. The payments are made to the loanout company.

From the talent's perspective, there are several advantages to this arrangement. As noted, the use of a corporation limits the shareholder's personal liability for debts. It can make tax-deductible retirement contributions. It may allow some adroit shuffling of income at the end of the fiscal year. It stymies the alternative minimum tax and eliminates the deduction on unreimbursed employee business expenses. The benefits are offset by some additional costs and even in the best case, the net benefits are not immense. Years ago, the loanout form did create enormous benefits but a focused series of changes in the tax laws have sharply reduced the economic benefit. Nonetheless, habit, zealous accountants, and a status symbol aura have combined with the remaining benefits to make loanouts de riguer for most Hollywood talent.

From the filmmaker's point of view, except for the cost of payroll taxes, which can be significant on high-priced talent, it makes little difference whether talent uses a loanout. Since it is customary for the loanout company to bear payroll taxes, it is cheaper for the producer if the talent designates a loanout. If they do, the agreement is entered between the production company and the loanout corporation. The individual talent signs what is called an "inducement letter" and agrees to perform the services and acknowledges that the loanout will be getting the money. There is no tax withholding from the payments to the loanout. The loanout corporation is responsible for payroll taxes and deductions for its employee. The loanout company receives an IRS Form 1099 at the end of the year, which reflects payments to it. Your accountant should handle that.

At the end of this chapter, we have provided a handy form that converts the personal service agreements in this book from agreements directly with talent into agreements with loanout companies. It is called a "wraparound." It is a short document that is attached on top of the normal employment agreement. All the deal terms in the normal employment agreement remain. In essence all the wraparound says is that: "Despite the fact that the normal employment agreement says it is directly with the talent, this agreement is really between the production company and the loanout company." This agreement is signed by the loanout company and the production company. The wrapping is completed by the addition of the inducement letter at the end of the package. The talent signs it and thereby agrees to perform all the services. The original employment agreement does not have to be signed by anyone. Technically, it becomes an exhibit to the wraparound agreement.

Production Accounting

The role of accounting in film production goes much farther than getting the EIN and calculating payroll deductions. Money, and a lot of it, moves very fast on a movie. The producers will have prepared a budget, but budgets are only estimates. Production accountants take over when the money becomes real and establish cash-flow schedules that project expenses and revenues on a weekly basis from preproduction through delivery. They will prepare weekly expense reports tied to the budget categories that show budgeted amount, money spent to date, estimated cost to complete, and projected overage or underage in the budget category. These are essential tools you need in order to manage your film and are required by corporate guarantors and lenders.

There is sophisticated computer software for all of this, but experience counts as well. We urge you to find a seasoned production accountant to help you. This may be your regular accountant, but only if he has experience in this specialized area. If not, your regular accountant will team with the production accountant. You can expect to pay $1,500 to $3,000 per week for production accounting for an independent feature in the $3,000,000 to $7,000,000 range.

The world of production accounting is ever changing, so we cannot offer specific recommendations. Many production accountants freelance from production to production and are not easily found in the Yellow Pages. Your best source to finding the right accountant is to talk to other filmmakers in your area to see whom they can recommend. Another good source is your completion bonder. They know all the efficient and honest accountants and often will designate one. Remember, however, it is foolhardy to hire anyone without personally checking at least three references.

Insurance

In addition to engaging accountants, you are also going to establish a relationship with an insurance broker. There are several kinds of insurance you will need: Worker's compensation to cover your employees, general liability to cover negligent injury or damage, auto policies for vehicles, and the like. Many general insurance brokers can help you assess your risks and get these policies. Those general brokers, however, are probably not the right ones to help you when your picture goes into production.

Providing insurance for movies is a specialized field and there are several brokers that concentrate on arranging for this coverage. We list three we have worked with many times. Although they are in Los Angeles, they can help arrange coverage for you wherever you shoot your picture.

For most productions, you will need four types of polices: Entertainment package, general liability, worker's compensation, and errors and omissions. The entertainment package is a collection of several policies that covers different risks. It is also called a Film Production Package and generally two to four insurance companies actively write the policies. The broker can guide you towards the company that offers the best rates for your production.

The entertainment package covers the following risks:

1. *Cast Insurance.* This covers the risk that the production is delayed or canceled due to the illness, injury, or death of a cast member. Enhanced coverage can provide protection during preproduction and postproduction. A specific endorsement is available under some polices to covers losses that arise because a cast member cannot work due to the unexpected death or injury to a member of their family. The director and other essential personnel can also be covered. Medical examinations are generally required before the coverage can go into effect.
2. *Negative.* This coverage protects against losses that result from damage to raw film, tape stock, exposed film, videotapes, and the like; from damage that results from faulty cameras, videotape equipment, or sound equipment; and from faulty developing or processing. We have had a number of situations where the negative was scratched during processing, which led to a combination of expensive reshooting and reprocessing. Negative insurance proved invaluable.

3. *Props, Sets, and Wardrobes.* This coverage protects against loss or damage to these items. Each policy will have limitations and restrictions. For example, it is common to have a dollar limit on the coverage for antiques, furs, and gems. Boats, cars, and other vehicles are usually not included in this coverage.
4. *Equipment.* This protects cameras, lights, sound equipment, and the like against damage and loss.
5. *Third-Party Property Damage.* This coverage protects you for loss or damage to someone else's property as a result of the production. Primarily, this insures locations and location owners will require proof that this coverage is in place as a condition of allowing you to use the location.
6. *Automobile.* This coverage insures property damage to cars used in the production. There is comparable coverage available for boats, airplanes, flying saucers, and any other moving contrivance filmmakers can conceive and launch.
7. Extra Expense. This coverage pays for delays that result from damage to locations or other facilities you utilize on the production or from loss of power or other utilities.

General liability is the second insurance policy you will need. Unlike the entertainment package, which generally pays you in the event of damage, general liability covers the production for damages to others for injuries they suffer. For example, if a light falls over and breaks a passerby's foot, you look to your general-liability insurance. You may have a general-liability policy already, but because filmmaking is very physical, you may want to raise your limits.

Worker's compensation insurance is required in virtually all states for every employer. It compensates employees for injuries suffered in connection with their jobs. If you have employees during the development stage, you must have this insurance. If not, it has to be put into place when you start employing people on your movie.

Errors and omissions insurance (E&O in Hollywood parlance) is the fourth policy. It insures against claims of defamation, libel, invasion of privacy, copyright infringement, plagiarism, and similar matters. It does not protect you from your breaches of contract. You will be required to fill out a detailed application before you can get this insurance and will be asked very specific questions about what rights you have obtained or not obtained. Your script has to be "cleared" before you will be ready to apply for E&O. This coverage is required by financiers and distributors. Many low-budget producers, trying to save a buck, purchase the Production Package, General Liability, and Worker's

Compensation Insurance but skimp on the Errors and Omissions Insurance policy. If at all possible, budget enough to get the Errors and Omissions Insurance policy as well. You will save money by purchasing all of the policies in one package. If you try to buy E&O later on, it will cost more, and if you do not have E&O, you will not be able to license or distribute your picture. Sometimes independent producers hope the distributor or sales agent will pay for the E&O insurance when they pick up the picture, but there is no guarantee they will be willing to do that and most resist it.

Insurance policies are contracts and you are only covered on what the policy says it covers. There is very little standardization of language or coverage and your insurance broker and lawyer will be your best guides to make certain that you are insured against the unavoidable risks. You will want to contact a broker early in the preproduction process to discuss the specific coverage your show will need.

INSURANCE BROKERS THAT SPECIALIZE IN MOVIES

Abacus Insurance Brokers, Inc.
12300 Wilshire Blvd., #100
Los Angeles, CA 90025
Tel: (310) 207-5432
Fax: (310) 207-8526
www.abacusins.com

AON/Albert G. Ruben
10880 Wilshire Blvd., 7th floor
Los Angeles, CA 90024
Tel: (310) 234-6800
Fax: (310) 446-7839
www.albertgruben.com

Truman Van Dyke
6255 Sunset Blvd., #1401
Los Angeles, CA 90028
Tel: (323) 462-3300
Fax: (323) 462-4857

Script Clearance

We mentioned that E&O insurance is essential to your production. In order to get that coverage, you have to do more than write a check for the premium, you have to "clear the script."

The focus of script clearance is to find and eliminate things that can trigger potential legal claims. There are three general areas of possible claims:

1. *Copyright Infringement.* If there are any copyrighted works that appear, you need written permission to use them. These can include quotes, music, and props. You must also be on the lookout for plagiarism.
2. *Chain of Title.* As we discussed in Chapter 2, The Development Process, you must prove through written agreements that you have every link in place concerning all of the rights in the underlying literary properties.
3. *Defamation and invasion of privacy.* If there are real people (or institutions) portrayed or mentioned, you need to analyze whether their rights may be infringed. Since even names that the writer intends to be fictional may be the same as real people, you need to use only clear names (those unlikely to give rise to claims).

PROFESSIONAL SCRIPT CLEARANCE SERVICES

Act One Script Clearance
210 South Kenwood St., Ste. 260
Glendale, CA 91205
Tel: (818) 240-2416
Fax: (818) 240-2418
www.actonescript.com

Joan Pearce Research
8111 Beverly Blvd., Ste. 308
Los Angeles, CA 90048
Tel: (323) 655-5464
Fax: (323) 655-4770
home.earthlink.net/~jpra

Marshall/Plumb Research Associates
4150 Riverside Dr., Ste. 209
Burbank, CA 91505
Tel: (818) 848-7071
Fax: (818) 848-7702
or

(East Coast Branch)
83 Wheelter Road
Marstons Mills, MA 02648
Tel: (800) 304-1179
Fax: (508) 428-1487
www.marshall-plumb.com

At least a month before photography is scheduled to start, the script must be reviewed for legal clearance. The production lawyer will read the script with the specific intention to focus on potential legal issues. We know from experience that even lawyers can become caught up in the plot and can easily slip into film-critic mode. This process cannot be a casual read, but should be undertaken with Post-it notes, pencils, and sharp-eyed intensity. The script should also be reviewed by a professional script-clearance service.

For fees of $1,500 to $3,500 (depending in part on how quickly you need the report), these companies have a professional—usually a nonlawyer/researcher—read the script and prepare a detailed written report. Their focus is less on legal issues like defamation and more on checking to see if the names of characters, businesses, telephone numbers, and the like are the same as real ones. If your fictional Mafia hit man's name is Bruce Bruno and the only real person in the United States with that name is a respected ornithologist in New Jersey, the script clearance service should point it out and will recommend a change. They can also suggest clear names that have no conflicts.

Once the lawyer has reviewed the script and made notes and the script-clearance report has been completed, a negotiation will ensue between lawyer and client. Filmmakers are inclined to defend their scripts from all attempts to change them, even the well-meaning efforts of lawyers. Some script-clearance recommendations are incontrovertible. It is irresponsible to use a copyrighted work knowingly in a film without permission, but others are judgment calls and issues of risk tolerance. Going back to the example of Bruce Bruno, if the script-clearance report shows there are 23 so-named men in the United States and none of them live in Chicago where the picture is set, and most importantly, the director loves the name, do you have to change it? The answer is an absolute "yes" if you want to eliminate all risk of claim, but the risk of a claim is probably small and the chances of one or more of the real Mr. Brunos actually winning a lawsuit are extremely small. In this case, the errors and omissions insurance policy on the picture will defend the claim as long as the producer stays within the bounds of normal clearance procedures and is not undertaking foolhardy risks.

Occasionally, we go to the errors and omissions insurance company during development and consult with them on whether an element of the script falls in the acceptable risk zone. Insurance companies are decidedly not prone to take chances. They give pretty conservative advice, but are often willing to issue insurance subject to minor script modifications. With those modifications, the producer knows that the insurance company will provide coverage if there is a claim.

There has to be a follow-up procedure to make certain that the necessary changes are incorporated into the script. You must also review later revisions to the script, and the film itself, for late-emerging clearance issues.

Fireman's Fund, which is a major underwriter of errors and omissions insurance for the motion picture and television business, includes its recommended script-clearance guidelines on its application. We reprint them below. You can see that they go beyond the areas of copyright, chain of title, defamation, and privacy we have just discussed. They also include guidelines on title clearance, minors' contracts, and some other topics we cover elsewhere in this book. This can be a helpful checklist to the production lawyer in script-clearance procedures.

CLEARANCE REPORT EXCERPT

1. The following cast names have been checked:

CAST	REFERENCE
Air Traffic Control p. 1	Not identified by name.
Copilot p. 1	As above
Mike Hogan p. 1	We find 36 men with this name, various forms (Michael, Mike) in Massachusetts, two prominent individuals listed with this name, one a judge in Oreg., born 1946, one a diversified company executive in Mo., born 1953. We find six licensed pilots listed as "Michael Hogan," none indicated as being in the New England area. Do not consider use here as name of pilot with fictional airline company to pose a conflict.
Flight Attendant p. 1	Not identified by name.

Arch Davis p. 2	We find no internationally prominent individual listed with this exact name. Consider to be clear for employee with fictional airline.
Mrs. Heatherton p. 3	Surname use only.
Katy Phillips p. 3	We find 19 women with this name, various forms (Kathy, Katherine, Cathryn, Catherine, Cathy, etc.), listed in Mass., prominent individual listed with this name, a "Kathye" Phillips, nurse in La., born in 1960. Do not consider use here as name for flight attendant with fictional airline to pose a conflict.
Catering Crewmember p. 3	Not identified by name.

The following items have been checked:

PAGE	REFERENCE
20	**Lost in his CD-player earphones**—Before taking off, there is always an announcement that ALL electronic devices, cell phones, and pagers must be turned off and cannot be turned on again until after an announcement comes from the captain and that those electronic devices which cannot be used during a flight will be listed in the onboard flight magazine.
21	**Power to N1 complete**—Presume navigational dialogue used here and throughout script will be confirmed by your technical advisor.

27	**Lockheed Tristar**—Reference in dialogue only to well-known style of Lockheed airplane.
31	**The in-flight magazines**—If wish fictional in-flight magazine title, the following have been cleared for use: "AirJets," "AirFlight monthly," "Air Elite," or "AirJet Corridors."
32	**Me…are gonna**—Presume typo for: "…my wife and I are gonna..."
48	**Keflavik International to Iceland**—Reference to an indicated location use of actual airport in Iceland.
49	**A Troll Doll**—Advise avoid emphasis of actual trade name brand of doll.
58	**Some GRAVOL PILLS**—Indicated featured prop use of trade name brand of anticholinergic, available by prescription in Canada.
59	**Twin-engine Comanches**—Commercial identification in dialogue only to trade name brand of airplane.
60	**Elite Club Member**—Consider name for speciality club within the fictional airline company of AirJet Atlantic to be clear. Our sources indicate no listing for any airline club with this exact name.
61	**Uses a Swiss Army Knife**—Advise avoid emphasis of actual trade name brand of jackknife.

Fireman's Fund Clearance Procedures

The following is a guide—not a complete checklist—for the applicant's attorney who should make certain that the undernoted points have been complied with prior to final cut or first exhibition of the production to be insured:

1. The script should be read prior to commencement of production to eliminate matter that is defamatory, invades privacy, or is otherwise potentially actionable.
2. Unless the work is an unpublished original not based on any other work, a copyright report must be obtained. Both domestic and foreign copyrights and renewal rights should be checked. If a completed film is being acquired, a similar review should be made on copyright and renewals on any copyrighted underlying property.
3. If the script is an unpublished original, the origins of the work should be ascertained—basic idea, sequence of events, and characters. It should be ascertained if submissions of any similar properties have been received by the applicant and, if so, the circumstances as to why the submitting party may not claim theft or infringement should be described in detail.
4. Prior to final title selection, a title report should be obtained.
5. Whether production is fictional (and location is identifiable) or factual, it should be made certain that no names, faces, or likenesses of any recognizable living persons are used unless written releases have been obtained. Release is unnecessary if person is part of a crowd scene or shown in a fleeting background. Telephone books or other sources should be checked when necessary. Releases can only be dispensed with if the applicant provides the insurer with specific reasons, in writing, as to why such releases are unnecessary and if such reasons are accepted by the insurer. The term "living persons" includes thinly disguised versions of living persons or living persons who are readily identifiable because of identity of other characters or because of the factual, historical, or geographic setting.
6. Releases from living persons should contain language which gives the applicant the right to edit, delete material, juxtapose any part of the film with any other film, change the sequence of events or of any questions posed and/or answers, fictionalize persons or events including the releasee, and to make any other changes in the film that the applicant deems appropriate. If a minor, consent has to be legally binding.
7. If music is used, the applicant must obtain all necessary synchronization and performance licenses.
8. Written agreements must exist between the applicant and all creators,

authors, writers, performers, and any other persons providing material (including quotations from copyrighted works) or on-screen services.

9. If distinctive locations, buildings, businesses, personal property, or products are filmed, written releases should be secured. This is not necessary if nondistinctive background use is made of real property.
10. If the production involves actual events, it should be ascertained whether the author's sources are independent and primary (contemporaneous newspaper reports, court transcripts, interviews with witnesses, etc.) and not secondary (another author's copyrighted work, autobiographies, copyrighted magazine articles, etc.).
11. Shooting script and rough cuts should be checked, if possible, to assure compliance of all of the above. During photography, persons may be photographed on location, dialogue added, or other matter included which was not originally contemplated.
12. If the intent is to use the production to be insured on video discs, tape cassettes, or other new technology, rights to manufacture, distribute, and release the production should be obtained, including the above rights, from all writers, directors, actors, musicians, composers, and others necessary therefore.
13. Film clips are dangerous unless clearances for the second use are obtained from those rendering services or supplying material. Special attention should be paid to music rights, as publishers are taking the position that a new synchronization and performance license is required.
14. Aside from living persons, even dead persons (through their personal representatives or heirs) have a "right of publicity," especially where there is considerable fictionalization. Clearances should be obtained where necessary.

Production Checklist

As you undertake actually producing your picture, you might find the following checklist helpful in remembering the legal and business tasks you will need to complete.

INDEPENDENT FILM PRODUCTION CHECKLIST

I. GETTING SET UP

Establish production company.
Legal formation.

Get federal employer identification number.
Set up tax withholding.
Get worker's compensation insurance.
Get general liability insurance.
Get production accountant.
Get legal counsel.

2. SCRIPT

Review chain of title.
Assign necessary rights to production company.
Register assignments in U.S. Copyright Office.
Obtain copyright report if any underlying work.
Obtain clearance report and revise script as necessary.
Register copyright in screenplay with the U.S. Copyright Office.

3. FINANCING

Negotiate distribution or sales agent agreements.
Negotiate bank load or other financing agreement.
Negotiate completion bond agreement.

4. PREPRODUCTION

Obtain production insurance:
(a) Entertainment package.
(b) Errors and omissions.
Complete guild affiliations.
Casting director deal.
Director deal.
Key Actor deals.
Producer deals.

5. PRODUCTION

Day Player and Extra deals.
Crew deals:
(a) Director of Photography.
(b) Editor.
(c) Assistant Directors.
(d) Miscellaneous Crew.
Location agreements.
Miscellaneous releases.

Equipment agreements.
Facilities agreements.
Film clip licenses.

6. POSTPRODUCTION

Title Clearance.
Laboratory agreements.
Music:
(a) Composer agreement.
(b) Music package.
(c) Outside music clearance.

7. DELIVERY

Register copyright or file with U.S. Copyright Office.
Delivery requirements.
Errors and Omissions Insurance Certificates.
Laboratory Access Letters.
Credit Requirements Lists for Advertisements and Screen.
Physical Delivery of Various Video and Sound Masters.
Key Production and Music Contracts
All Chain of Title Documents.
Copyright and Title Reports and Opinions.
Stills—Black and White; Colors and Transparencies.
Trailer (if available).
Key Art (if available).
Music Cue Sheets.
Certificate of Origin.
Rights Transfer Instrument or Assignment (if applicable).

Loanout Wraparound Agreement

Dated as of _______________, 200__

________________________ (Lender)
____
____
____

1. You agree to furnish the services of the individual referred to as "Artist" in the attached Exhibit "A," upon and subject to all of the terms and conditions set forth in said Exhibit. Notwithstanding the fact that, as a matter of convenience, Exhibit "A" is drafted in the form of an agreement between Artist and us, it is understood and agreed that you are supplying Artist's services to us, that we are utilizing said services in accordance with the terms and provisions of said Exhibit "A," and that you are granting us all rights stated therein. Notwithstanding anything to the contrary contained herein, you agree that the credit, if any, accorded to Artist pursuant to Exhibit "A" shall continue to be accorded to Artist, and that you will receive no credit in connection therewith. You agree to cause Artist to comply with all of the terms and conditions hereof. We shall have, and you hereby grant to us, all of the rights to Artist's services and the results and proceeds thereof, the benefits of all warranties, representations and indemnities, and all other rights which are granted to us in Exhibit "A," to the same extent as though Artist had executed said Exhibit "A," and we were the employer-for-hire of Artist.

2. You represent and warrant that you are a bona fide corporation established for a valid business purpose within the meaning of the tax laws of the United States; that you are licensed to do business in the state in which you are incorporated; that Artist is under an exclusive written contract of employment with you for a term extending at least until the completion of all services required of Artist hereunder, which contract provides for payment to Artist of an amount not less than the minimum compensation per year required under any applicable law as a requisite for injunctive relief and gives you the right to loan or furnish the services of Artist to us as herein provided; and that you are a party to all guild or union agreements applicable hereto which may be in effect from time to time and which are by their terms controlling with respect to the subject matter of this agreement. You further acknowledge that the foregoing representations and warranties will be relied upon by us, among other reasons, for determining whether or not it is necessary to make withholdings for U.S. federal and state taxes from monies being paid to you hereunder, and you agree that if withholdings are not made from said payments, you and Artist will indemnify us against all loss, cost, damages, liabilities and expenses (including reasonable attorneys' fees) relating thereto and which may be suffered by us on account of any claim of breach of any warranty or representation made by you hereunder.

3. It is agreed that you are the employer of Artist with respect to Artist's services here-

under and that you will discharge all the obligations of an employer whether imposed by law (including, without limitation, taxes, unemployment and disability insurance, compensation insurance and social security), applicable union rules or regulations requiring payments to Artist, or otherwise. In connection therewith, you agree to cause Artist to comply with any and all requirements relating to the Immigration Reform and Control Act of 1986, including, without limitation, Artist's completion, execution and submission of a Form I-9. You and Artist will indemnify us against all loss, cost, damages, liabilities and expenses (including reasonable attorneys' fees) arising out of any claim of breach of your obligations in this paragraph.

4. Notwithstanding that you are furnishing Artist's services to us, for the purposes of any and all applicable Workers' Compensation statutes, an employment relationship exists between Artist and us, such that we are Artist's special employer and you are Artist's general employer (as the terms "special employer" and "general employer" are understood for purposes of Workers' Compensation statutes). The rights and remedies, if any, of Artist and Artist's heirs, executors, administrators, successors and assigns, against us and/or our officers, directors, agents, employees, successors, assigns or licensees, by reason of injury, illness, disability or death arising out of or occurring in the course of Artist's rendition of services hereunder shall be governed by and limited to those provided under such Workers' Compensation statutes, and neither we nor our officers, directors, agents, employees, successors, assigns or licensees, shall have any other obligation or liability by reason of any such injury, illness, disability or death. If the applicability of any Workers' Compensation statutes to the engagement of Artist's services hereunder is dependent upon, or affected by, an election on the part of you or Artist, such election is hereby made by each of you in favor of such application.

5. We shall pay directly any amounts due any applicable guild's pension and/or health and/or welfare funds as the employer's share of the contribution(s) required to be made to such funds in respect of Artist's services hereunder; provided, however, that we shall not in any event be obligated to pay an amount in excess of the amount we would have been obligated to contribute on account of Artist's services hereunder had we employed Artist directly.

6. If you or your successors in interest should be dissolved or otherwise cease to exist or for any reason whatsoever fail, be unable, neglect or refuse to perform, observe or comply with any or all of the terms and conditions of Exhibit "A" and/or this agreement, Artist may, at our election, be deemed a direct party to Exhibit "A" until completion of the services required of Artist thereunder, upon the terms and conditions set forth therein. In the event of a breach or a threatened breach of this agreement or Exhibit "A" by you and/or Artist, we shall be entitled to seek legal, equitable and other relief against you and/or Artist, in our discretion. We shall have all rights and remedies against Artist that we would have if Artist was a direct party to Exhibit "A." We shall not be required to resort first to or exhaust any rights or remedies that we have against you before exercising our rights and remedies against Artist.

AGREED TO AND ACCEPTED:

(Lending Company)

("you," "your")

By______________________________
Authorized Signatory

Fed. Id. #: ______________________

AGREED TO AND ACCEPTED:

(Production Company)

("us," "our," "we")

By ______________________________
Authorized Signatory

ARTIST'S INDUCEMENT

In order to induce ______________________ ("Producer") to enter into the foregoing agreement with ____________________ ("Lender"), and for other good and valuable consideration, receipt of which is hereby acknowledged, the undersigned hereby consents and agrees to the execution and delivery of said agreement by Lender and hereby agrees to render all the services therein provided to be rendered by the undersigned, to grant all the rights granted therein and to be bound by and duly perform and observe each and all of the terms and conditions of said agreement regarding performance or compliance on the undersigned's part, and hereby joins in all warranties, representations, agreements and indemnities made by Lender and further confirms the rights granted to Producer under said agreement and hereby waives any rights of droit moral or similar rights which the undersigned may have. The undersigned further waives any claim against Producer for wages, salary or other compensation of any kind pursuant to said agreement or in connection with the motion picture and the exercise by Producer of rights therein or derived therefrom (provided, however, that such waiver shall not relieve Producer of any of its obligations to Lender under said agreement), and the undersigned agrees to look solely to Lender for any and all compensation that the undersigned may become entitled to receive in connection with the said agreement.

Dated as of ____________, 200__

____
("Artist")

HIRING DIRECTORS

While there are many examples of independent and specialty pictures being directed, produced, and written by the same individual, this sort of multitasking is hardly the standard. More likely, you will find yourself involved in demanding and often Byzantine negotiations for the services of even the most enthusiastic and easygoing would-be auteur/director.

Since the director is one of the first persons engaged on a motion picture (after the writer) and generally is the last person to complete services on a motion picture (other than the producer), the negotiation of the director's deal involves a broad range of issues. Generally, the status of the director, his experience, the budget, and nature of the production and the resolution of who ultimately is in control, will set the tone for the negotiation of the terms and conditions in the director's agreement. This chapter includes a form of director agreement and we also discuss the major issues.

Directors Guild of America (DGA)

When you hire your director a threshold question is whether your director's agreement will be subject to the Directors Guild of America. Directors who are members of the DGA are forbidden from working for producers who are not signatories to the DGA. If you sign with the DGA, the director, the assistant directors, the unit production manager, and certain other production staff must be DGA members and there can be an additional cost for hiring these personnel on guild terms and conditions, as well as the downstream obligation to pay guild residuals to the directors.

Typically, independent producers sign with the DGA on a picture-by-picture basis. The DGA, like other guilds, seeks to take a security interest in the project to make sure that their directors get paid. It also has rules that govern most aspects of the working arrangements for directors and other DGA members. The DGA Web site at *www.dga.org* is a good way to access up-to-date, detailed information.

Conditions Precedent

Customarily, two and sometimes three major conditions precedent, or contingencies, must occur prior to the obligation to use the director's services and, more importantly, pay his compensation. First, the producer must have a signed written agreement with the writer of the screenplay and the owner of the underlying rights, if any. Only after you have acquired all the necessary rights to produce the picture can serious negotiations with the director begin.

A second condition precedent, which is common in director agreements, but is generally resisted by representatives of directors, is a requirement that the producer has obtained all the necessary financing for the motion picture project. Directors' representatives do not like to see these types of conditions precedent in directors' agreements, as they serve to delay payment of compensation and the official commencement of the director's engagement. But these conditions are often the reality of producing independent films and are common in directors' agreements and should be noted and dealt with accordingly.

A third condition precedent of the director deal may be the requirement that you have engaged one or a number of principal cast members and have approved the final screenplay, the production budget, and the production schedule.

Director's Services

In many cases, the director is brought onboard the project as soon as the writer is engaged and is asked to supervise the further writing, development, and general shape of the project to suit his and the producer's vision. The director may also be asked to supervise preparation of a budget based on the screenplay, to conduct and assist in location surveys, to actively participate in the casting process, and to assist in obtaining a completion bond based on the budget and the screenplay.

These services are referred to as development services or preproduction services. It is common to pay a director a modest development fee for these services, which is applied against the full directing fee when the picture is made. Once the star, the cast, the final screenplay, the budget, the production schedule, and the locations have been approved, the director is required by the director agreement to direct the picture in accordance with the screenplay, the approved budget, and the production schedule. Additionally, the director is often responsible for supervising the editing of the picture in accordance with the postproduction schedule and the anticipated delivery date for the final, locked cut of the motion picture.

The director will also be required to supervise the shooting of any retakes, the recording of the soundtrack, process and special effects shots, added scenes, looping, dubbing, the preparation of the titles, and sometimes the theatrical trailer and will customarily participate in publicity tours and interviews and make festival appearances.

The issue of how much time a director will have for preproduction and postproduction is generally a subject of negotiation. Depending on the budget of the picture and when the director is actually engaged, it is customary to have an approximately eight-week preproduction period prior to the commencement of principal photography, during which time all of the necessary preparations will take place for the production. Directors like to have as much time as possible for actual shooting of the film. Negotiations often result in giving directors a specific number of days to shoot and include a specific period of time to edit the film and deliver a director's cut.

The DGA Basic Agreement provides for a minimum of ten weeks from the time of completion and delivery of the film editor's first assembly of the picture for a director to create and deliver his cut. Of course, many independent films that are produced are not subject to the DGA and as a result, it is prudent to negotiate a specific postproduction period within which to deliver a director's cut, so that the budget and postproduction schedule are not exceeded.

The question of the director's exclusivity will also be negotiated. Typically, directors are engaged on a nonexclusive, but first-priority, basis during preproduction; exclusive during production and postproduction through the delivery of the director's cut; and then nonexclusive thereafter. Generally, the director's representative will try to insist that after the completion of principal photography, the director's services are nonexclusive, but first-priority, rather than exclusive.

The Pay-or-Play and the Pay-and-Play Issue

As is customary in actors' deals, directors generally like to be engaged on a pay-or-play basis and prefer even more to be engaged on a pay-and-play basis. Pay-or-play means that the director is entitled to get his compensation whether or not the producer uses the director's services or even makes the movie, subject of course to the director's breach, disability, death, or events of force majeure. Pay-and-play means that the producer is not only obligated to pay the director, but must also use the director's services in connection with the picture. From a financier's point of view and a producer's point of view, the pay-and-play provision is particularly dangerous, especially if there are creative differences, production is not on schedule and on budget, or if other problems involving the director arise.

Depending on the bargaining position, stature, and leverage of the director, producers can customarily negotiate pay-or-play provisions, which are contingent on the full financing of the picture and usually the engagement of one or several of the cast. However, banks, completion guarantors, and producers generally resist or at least limit the pay-and-play provision by at most guaranteeing that the director will have the opportunity to direct at least the first three days, the first week, or the first two weeks of principal photography prior to the producer having the ability to terminate the director for breach or exercise a pay-or-play right for creative or other reasons. The pay-and-play provision is of course always subject to the director's death, disability, and events of force majeure.

Director's Compensation

Director's compensation is customarily dependent on the budget or the director's prior quotes and accordingly varies to a large degree. The DGA Basic Agreement provides for a minimum compensation. Currently, on films budgeted between $3.5 million and $6 million, the director must be guaranteed not less than 13 weeks of work for total pay of $99,313, plus a minimum back-end fee of $55,000 if and when the film reaches a break-even profit status.

For movies budgeted $100,000 to $1,500,000, the minimum is 13 weeks at $9,587 per week for a total of $124,631. Movies under $500,000 require an 11-week guarantee at $8,435 per week, with a minimum of $92,785 for the movie.

Since many independent films are not produced under the DGA Basic Agreement, we have negotiated director's agreements on independent films that start as low as $10,000 for all services and go up to well over a million and a half dollars. Richard Donner, the director of such large-budget, star-driven films as *Maverick*, the Lethal Weapon series, and *Conspiracy Theory*, reportedly earns $6 million up front against 5% to 15% of the gross receipts of his films. However, his pictures often have budgets exceeding $60 million and commercial expectations are for robust business in theatrical and ancillary markets. Superstar directors like Robert Zemeckis reportedly get $10 million up front against 15% of the gross receipts. In the case of Woody Allen, who makes films that normally cost less than $15 million, a *New Yorker* article pegged his cash compensation at $450,000 against 15% of the gross. Allen serves additionally as writer and often star of his pictures, and his presence virtually guarantees that name actors will work for less than their normal rates in supporting roles. Further down the budget scale, it is not uncommon for independents like John Sayles and Nick Gomez to work for a nominal five figure up-front fee and an even larger chunk of the back-end proceeds. And, as is well documented in this age of Sundance rags-to-riches stories, most micro-budget debut filmmakers—who often serve as producers of their own work—decline to take a fee on their pictures and instead provide for deferments for themselves and key cast if, and hopefully when, the film gets picked up for distribution.

The cash compensation for director services is generally paid over a schedule as follows: 20% during the preproduction period (provided the conditions precedent have been satisfied), 60% over the course of principal photography, 10% on delivery of the director's cut, and 10% on delivery of the answer print or the delivery of the locked picture to the distributor. Sometimes, payments are also made on the completion of dubbing or scoring. These payment periods are subject to negotiation and the director's representative generally wants the compensation paid earlier, and the producer wants to hold monies back, pending final delivery of the completed film.

Deferred Compensation

When the negotiated cash compensation does not meet the director's current quote for working on a picture, a deferred compensation provision will be negotiated which will get the director up to his cash compensation or his current quote plus whatever increase, if any, the particular artistic demands or commercial prospects of the picture entail. We touched on this kind of fee deferral in the financing discussion. The point at which the deferred compensation is payable is generally the subject of heated negotiation, as the term "profits" can have many definitions. We explore the subject of calculations of profits in Chapter 14, Profits.

Directors want any deferred compensation paid as soon as possible and with as few possible priorities (i.e., for investors, distributors, producers, and the like) before the director's deferred compensation kicks in. The point at which deferred compensation is payable to the director is dependent on their stature and will also vary based on the type of picture being produced and how it is financed. When private investors fund the entire movie, a director's deferred compensation will generally start to be paid after the investors have recouped their initial investment plus whatever premium has been negotiated on top of the investment. Sometimes this will be negotiated as a point after which the investors have recouped 125% to 175% of their investment.

On a studio motion picture, deferred compensation is sometimes payable at the point at which the studio receives two and one half times the negative cost of the picture or at the point in time immediately prior to the payment of the net profits of the picture. Generally, the director's deferred compensation will be paid pro rata and pari passu with any other deferred compensation payable in connection with the picture, such as that of the producer, writer, or leading actors. "(Pro rata and pari passu" means that the deferrals are pooled and paid out proportionately at the same time.)

Director Credit

In DGA pictures, the "directed by" credit is rarely the subject of much negotiation, simply because The Director's Guild—long an advocate of the director's innate "authorship" of a motion picture—has legislated it in its collective bargaining agreement with its signatory companies. The director's credit must be the last credit to appear in the main titles (where the credit to the main creative elements go) on the screen in a size no less than seventy percent of the nonartwork title of the picture. Additionally, the directed by credit is required to appear in all paid ads subject to customary distributor limitations and exclusions. Directors also try to negotiate an additional credit known as the "film by" or possessory credit (currently the subject of considerable debate between the DGA and the Writers Guild of America), which usually appears as one of the first credits on screen and one of the first credits in paid ads. Customarily, this film by credit will appear above the title both onscreen and in all paid ads and be the same size as the production credit (e.g., A Joe Blow Production).

Credits on Non-DGA Films

Where the DGA is not involved, it is important to remember to carefully negotiate the credit provisions and specify when and where and in what form these credits will appear. The film by credit is considered particularly prestigious and will not generally be routinely granted to first-time directors by studios. On non-DGA pictures, you must negotiate whether or not the credit will appear on posters, billboards, on the video box artwork, and on soundtrack album covers or liner notes.

Generally, the size of the director's credit is a certain percentage, somewhere between 50% and 100%, of the size of the picture's regular title and anywhere from 15% to 35% of the size of the artwork title is paid ads. In ads, the regular title is generally the title used in the so-called billing block (which is discussed in Chapter 9, Hiring Actors) and the artwork title is the stylized graphic version of the title.

Codirector credits have become more prevalent in the past few years. They are not permitted under the DGA Basic Agreement unless the directors are siblings (where the credits have read, for instance, simply "A Hughes Brothers Film" or "A Farrelly Brothers Film") or a specific waiver is granted by the Guild. It is important to negotiate and determine whose name goes in first position both on screen and in paid ads when codirector credits are involved.

Approvals, Controls, Final Cut

As a general rule, the producer or production company will have the complete and unconditional right to cut, edit, add to, subtract from, arrange, rearrange, and otherwise revise the picture in any manner in their sole discretion. The producer also retains total access to all phases of production and postproduction, including all rights to view the dailies, the rough cut, and all subsequent cuts of the picture. Although the producer maintains these rights, the director will complete at least an initial cut of the picture. Under the DGA Agreement, this cut is referred to as the "DGA cut" or the "director's cut." Under the DGA Agreement, negotiation determines who has cutting rights after delivery of the director's cut.

Some prominent directors have been able to negotiate final cut for themselves, but this rare event only happens when the director is also one of the film's producers or when a director agrees to provide a final cut, which must contractually meet a specified MPAA rating and length. Other directors are not able to negotiate for final cut for the theatrical release version of the film, but may attempt to negotiate for the right to create a "special edition" or "special director's cut" specifically for the film's release on home video, laserdisc, or DVD.

Certain high-power producer/directors—the Oliver Stones, George Lucases, and Steven Spielbergs of the world—generally have long (even unlimited) periods of time to prepare and deliver the release version. As for the rest of the world, the director's cutting period will vary depending on the budget of the picture. Typically, the time used to prepare the director's cut has been carefully allotted and budgeted, as there are release requirements and bank loans with interest running that have to be repaid. Hollywood is replete with stories of first-time directors who were unable to deliver a sensible product in the time allotted or abused their rights to create a director's cut. Not long ago, director Tony Kaye, a respected commercial and video director, was embroiled in a dispute with New Line Productions over the editing of his debut picture *American History X.* The press has documented Kaye's displeasure of New Line's revisions of his DGA cut. However, New Line's right to change the editing of the picture were perfectly within the DGA Basic Agreement, as well as their contract with Kaye. Still, the editing, revision, alteration, or modification of a director's original vision, regardless of the legal and collective bargaining controls, remains a touchy subject in Hollywood. Producers and studios are loath to interfere in the cutting process.

The editing of the picture brings up several contractual negotiating points. Directors often ask to have at least consultation and sometimes approval over the location of the editing and postproduction of the picture. In the independent financing arena, postproduction may indeed take place almost anywhere in the world. As a result of various financing and production subsidy programs, producers often require certain services to be performed, facilities to be used, or monies to be spent in those jurisdictions that provide either government or other sources of financing. Canada, France, the U.K., and Germany are particularly popular places to perform postproduction services as a result of the incentives, financing opportunities, and subsidies available in those territories. Directors may or may not want to travel to those locations, so it is important to agree on where the postproduction, editing, and additional effects and sound work will be performed.

It is also customary to specify in a director's agreement that the picture, when completed, will be delivered with a specified MPAA rating. Usually that rating is to be no more restrictive than R. Additionally, it is customarily specified that the picture, when delivered, will be no less than 95 minutes and no more than 110 minutes in length. This time frame is necessary to meet certain territorial and broadcast time requirements, as well as to conform to the budget, make less expensive prints, and also so that it will not affect the number of daily screenings the picture can have in theaters.

Because many directors like to test the movie before live theatrical audiences before they deliver their final director's cut to the producer, it is also customary to negotiate, if the budget permits, one or two paid public previews to assess the audience reaction to the picture, as well as allow additional cutting periods beyond each preview to cut the film in response to the previews. Although the DGA mandates one preview, directors will ask for two cuts and two previews, although many independent films have neither the budgets to perform those previews nor a director willing to subject his vision to judgment by an audience.

Directors are also asked, in many cases, to deliver a "television version," which will satisfy the prevailing United States network and cable broadcast standards and practices departments and enable the picture to be broadcast into homes with children on those outlets, as well as on foreign-network television.

Often, directors request that they be involved in the supervision of any and all additional cuts and edits of the picture that are required for airline versions, nontheatrical versions, laserdiscs, and DVD release of the picture, and any other versions that are required to be made for ancillary exploitation of the picture in various media formats.

Directors generally want at least full and meaningful consultation and sometimes negotiate for approval of the individuals engaged for the director of photography, art director, assistant directors, production designer, editor, and composer of the picture, as well as locations and other key creative decisions affecting the picture. The producer will customarily retain the final approvals with respect to all of the foregoing.

The producer will want to have a clause that indicates that the director has approved the budget and will direct the picture and postproduce and edit the picture in accordance with the budget. Additionally, both the completion guarantor and the producer will require a letter signed by the director that states specifically that he has reviewed the budget and the schedule and that he will be able to deliver the picture on time and on budget. As a result, if the picture appears to be beyond schedule and over budget, the guarantor will have additional leverage with the director, by means of asking the director to reduce his salary or furnish a portion of his salary toward a the budget of the picture.

Depending on the budget of the film, the director will usually request that he have available to him for exclusive use an office and an assistant or secretary (at least during the preproduction phase and the production phase until the picture wraps). In many independent films, this luxury is simply not available. On modest budget films, the negotiation will generally focus on the number of weeks that the assistant will be available to the director during the production and thereafter during postproduction.

Suspension and Termination

Suspension and termination clauses in any motion-picture contract are important, but due to the nature and influence of the role of the director, suspension and termination clauses must be carefully negotiated. Most director agreements allow the director to be suspended, or if applicable, terminated in the event of the director's incapacity, death, the occurrence of events of force majeure, or any willful or negligent failure or refusal or neglect by the director to report to work and render director services in accordance with the terms of the directing agreement.

Additional causes for termination, which customarily appear in director's agreements, include the picture being more than 10% overbudget or the production schedule being more than 10% behind. Another clause that is beginning to appear more and more in the suspension and termination sections of the director's agreements is the right to suspend or terminate for the inability or failure to render services by reason of the ingestion or injection of, or intoxication by, drugs or liquor. Directors' representatives resist this clause, but they do appear to be relatively common in director agreements. One of the ways that directors' representatives can limit the harshness of these restrictions is to negotiate a cure period, which allows the director somewhere between 24 and 72 hours to cure (fix) any material breach of the agreement. Additionally, depending on the length of the production schedule, directors will customarily have five to ten days of disability or incapacity before their services can be suspended or terminated for illness, sickness, or some other incapacity.

It should be noted that if the picture is properly insured, most of the costs and expenses incurred in connection with the director's incapacity should be covered under the insurance policy, which could require shutting the picture down for the duration of the incapacity.

Effect of Suspension

If the director is suspended for breach, disability, or force majeure, the agreement will remain in effect for the duration of the suspension. As a result, the director will not be allowed to render services for any other entity in the entertainment industry during the suspension. During the suspension, payments are terminated until the lifting of the suspension. The director's representatives will argue that in the event of a suspension of the director for an event of force majeure, the producer should have to suspend all other personnel in connection with the picture as well. It is also customary to provide that, in the event of force majeure for more than eight consecutive weeks, either party, the producer or the director thereafter, has the right to terminate the agreement. In the event that the director terminates the agreement, the producer customarily has the right within one week of the notice of termination to reinstate the director and retain the right to his services (but the producer must pay the director's salary).

Effect of Termination

Generally, if the director is terminated for any sort of material default or breach, no further sums, either cash or contingent compensation, are payable. In some cases, agreements specify that if the director had been previously paid any money, either the director must return the sums paid or the producer is entitled, in addition to any other rights and remedies it may have, to bring an action to recover the amounts paid to the director. The theory underlying this position, from the producer's point of view, is that the essence of the agreement is that the director complete and deliver all materials of the picture and that the fee to the director constitutes payment for all services and materials to be delivered and is not allocable to portions of the movie as the same are completed and delivered to producer. The director's representatives will argue that the director is entitled to the same proportion of the negotiated fee as the proportion of the total services that the director actually performed. The party with more leverage will usually prevail.

If the termination is based on an event of force majeure or disability, the director is entitled to receive and retain all compensation that has been due or is accrued prior to the termination for disability or force majeure.

It is usually agreed that if the director is suspended for disability or force majeure and ultimately the picture is completed, then the deferment and contingent compensation are based either (1) on the same percentage that cash salary actually paid prior to termination bears to the total cash salary contracted for, or (2) on that proportion of the footage actually directed by the director, which appears in the picture, bears to the total amount of footage in the picture as actually released. Sometimes this amount is reduced by one half of the contingent compensation, if any, payable to the director who actually completes and delivers the picture.

Director and Producer's Remedies

The financing entities, banks, and completion guarantors, as well as the studios require a provision that states that the only remedy available to the director for the producer's breach would be an action at law for damages. The provision provides that in no event would the director be entitled to terminate the agreement, rescind the agreement, obtain an injunction against the distribution or exploitation of the picture, or seek and obtain any other equitable relief. This is one of the few deal-breaker provisions in boilerplate, and producers and studios never waive it. On the other hand, the producer who will have invested considerable sums and services in connection with the production of the picture, generally has a provision in the director agreement that allows the producer to seek an injunction against the director, if the director chooses not to honor the agreement or attempts to work for some other entity during the exclusive period.

Remakes, Sequels, Prequels, and Television Productions

Directors are usually "tied" to productions derived from the picture they direct, such as remakes, sequels, prequels, and television productions. This tie, however, is generally subject to the following conditions: a) the director did not breach the agreement; b) the director promptly completed and delivered the picture in accordance with the budget and the shooting schedule; c) the director is then available and ready, willing and able to perform directing services; and d) that he is then active as a director in the motion picture or television business. If the director meets such conditions, he is accorded a first negotiation and sometimes the last refusal to render services as the director of a remake, sequel, prequel, or television movie or pilot for a television series based on the picture. In a situation where the director has written the script as well, and the parties do not want to spend a lot of time negotiating what would happen on future projects based on the film, producers and directors sometimes agree that the right to develop and produce any remakes, sequels, prequels, and television series is frozen and there is a so-called Mexican standoff, unless and until an agreement is made by the parties for the services or passive payments to the original writer/director of the picture. There is usually a provision, which is included in the remake and sequel clause, which provides that in the event the picture is a theatrical remake or sequel, then the floor of the financial terms of the agreement would be the terms of the initial agreement that engaged the director for the first picture. It is extremely important to specify that this floor applies only to theatrical remakes and sequels, as we have encountered situations where the negotiated floor was a blanket floor for all productions and where a director received significant compensation on the initial theatrical motion picture and the floor for the negotiation of the director's fee on the television pilot (which would necessarily be produced for far less money than the theatrical feature) would obviously be way out of line for the budget of the television pilot.

Works Made for Hire; Waiver of Moral Rights

In the United States it is customary for the director's agreement to include a clause which states that the director has performed all services as "works made for hire" for the producer and that all rights in and to the director's work, including the copyright, will automatically vest in the producer as the author of the motion picture in accordance with the U.S. copyright law. This clause is required to preserve the producer's or the financing entity's ownership rights in the picture under U.S. law.

It is also customary for the director agreement to include a waiver of moral rights. Moral rights are predominant in Europe but at this time are not extensively recognized in the United States. Moral rights are the rights considered to be innately ascribed to the creator of a work of art. These rights entitle an artist to maintain the integrity of his work and limit a studio's right to modify a film or produce remakes and sequels. However, because of the way motion pictures are financed in the United States by banks, completion bonds, other lending institutions, and studios, the concept of moral rights is often unacceptable and most directors' agreements include a moral rights waiver.

Transportation and Expenses

When a director must travel more than 50 miles from his principal place of residence to render services, a provision will be included in the director's contract to provide for first-class transportation (required under the DGA) as well as a first-class hotel, per diem, and transportation to and from the set and to and from the airport. The per diem will generally be a function of the director's prior quotes and the cost of staying at the location. Sometimes, the agreement will specify that the director's expenses will be those included in the budget of the picture. On studio pictures, directors often negotiate provisions that provide for transportation and expenses to all major premieres, preview screenings, screenings, and debuts at major festivals and markets such as Cannes, Sundance, Berlin, and New York and directors ask for and obtain the right to bring guests to these functions as well. On large-budget movies, directors also attempt to negotiate provisions that provide them with trailers equal in size and amenities to those accorded the stars.

Publicity Services and Publicity Controls

Because the director is considered the auteur of the motion picture in many territories around the world and because the press and festivals generally want to interview the director, director agreements have provisions that require them to perform reasonable publicity and promotional services in connection with the picture at no additional cost other than travel expenses and per diem, subject to their current availability. The producer will also obtain the right to use the director's name, likeness, photograph, and biography in connection with the advertising and promotion of the motion picture, so long as the director is not depicted as using, endorsing, or promoting any product, commodity, or service without his consent.

On the other hand, directors' agreements have restrictions against the director issuing any publicity or statements that are derogatory to the picture. The director's agreement will almost always have a provision that states that the producer will have the right to control any and all publicity relating to the picture other than the director's incidental reference to the picture and the fact that he directed it, in his own personal publicity releases.

When dealing with directors who are also actors or are for whatever reason more visible in the artistic community than is the norm, producers may have to bend on certain publicity provisions. Kevin Costner, Clint Eastwood, and Mel Gibson, all of whom have directed major studio pictures in which they have starred, are known to be meticulous in their negotiation of publicity appearances, as excessive interviews and press junkets may negatively impact their separate acting careers. In any event, these individuals often negotiate only a few key appearances on the major shows as opposed to agreeing to participate in a multiday, full-scale junket in support of the picture. As a rule, when dealing with an actor/director, the producer should carefully negotiate appearances and interviews to maximize the visibility of the picture without marring the director's public image.

Insurance Coverage

Director's agreements require that the director submit to a medical exam so that the director can be insured against losses arising out of the director's incapacity or disability as well as for purposes of obtaining a completion bond. Not long ago, the press reported that legendary Italian director Michelangelo Antonioni had failed his insurance-required medical exam, and as a result was forced by the producers of his new film to appoint a back-up director, in case he was incapacitated for any reason. Most agreements provide that unless the producers can obtain an insurance policy at a reasonable or budgeted premium, then the producer may terminate the agreement. The director, on the other hand, often will ask for a provision giving him the right to have his own personal doctor present during any examination, as well as to get a second opinion in the event that an examination renders the director uninsurable. The director will also ask for a provision that allows him to pay any extraordinary premium or cover an extraordinary deductible in the event that the director cannot be insured at customary premiums within the budget of the picture. The director will also seek a provision that provides that the producer will name the director an additional insured in the production's general liability insurance policy and the producer's errors and omissions insurance policy and provide the director with a certificate of coverage under those policies. The coverage of the director would be subject to applicable deductions, deductibles, and exclusions and would only cover claims or liabilities arising out of actions within the scope of actions, duties, and services under the director's agreement.

Videocassette, Laserdisc, Videodisc, and 35mm Print

The DGA Basic Agreement guarantees the director a videocassette copy of the film, but a major director will want a provision that provides that the director will be entitled to a free copy of the picture on videocassette, laserdisc, videodisc, and DVD, when each such device becomes commercially available. Major directors will negotiate for the right to retain a free 35mm print of the picture. Before agreeing to this, the producer will require the director to sign the producer or distributor's customary antipiracy/private use lending agreement, which provides that the picture is being lent to the director and is not to be released or otherwise copied or used for anything other than the private, noncommercial use of the director.

No Quote Deal/Confidentiality

Occasionally, directors' agreements provide that the terms and conditions of the agreement are strictly confidential and will not be quoted to any third party unless required by law. This provision benefits the director and the producer or studio where the director has agreed to work for less than his normal fee or the studio has broken certain studio precedents or policies to land a certain director.

Perhaps the most challenging aspect of negotiating, drafting, and executing the director's agreement is the sheer weight and importance of the task. In hiring the director—and engaging in active discussions over the points discussed above—the producer is closing the deal for an individual who has to be his key artistic partner during the making of the film. In this regard, director's agreements are often the most sensitive agreements negotiated on a given motion picture. The potential for budget overages, bruised egos, or the director feeling his artistic credibility being undermined before a reel of film is shot, is high.

Director Agreement (Form for DGA Director)

As of ____________

(Name of Director)
c/o **(Agency)**

Re: (Name of Production Company)/ "(Name of Picture)"/(Name of Director)

Dear ____________:

This will confirm the agreement ("Agreement") between __________________ ("Director"), whose Social Security number is ___________ and who is a citizen of ____________, and ___________________ ("Producer") regarding Director's directing services in the motion picture now entitled ___________________ (the "Picture") as follows:

1. Conditions Precedent. All of Producer's obligations hereunder are expressly conditioned upon:

1.1 Agreement Signature. Signature by Director of this Agreement.

1.2 Lender and Director providing Producer with all documents which may be required by any governmental agency or otherwise for Director to render services hereunder, including without limitation, an INS Form I-9 completed to Producer's satisfaction, together with Director's submission of original documents establishing Director's employment eligibility.

1.3 Lender and Director providing Producer with all documents necessary to evidence Director's status as a member in good standing with the DGA.

2. Guaranteed Compensation.

2.1 Development Fee. ___________ Dollars ($_____), payable one-half on fulfillment of the Conditions Precedent and one-half on Producer's election to proceed to production or abandon.

2.2 Production Fee. ________ Dollars ($_____), (less the Development Fee) payable 20% over preproduction, 60% over the period of principal photography, 10% upon completion of dubbing and scoring and 10% upon complete delivery of the Picture in accordance with Producer's standard delivery specifications.

3. Contingent Compensation. 5% of 100% of Net Proceeds, if any, derived from the Picture. Net Proceeds shall be defined, paid and accounted for in accordance with Producer's agreement with the worldwide distributor of the Picture, or, if there is no worldwide distribution, in accordance with Producer's standard definition of

Net Proceeds. Director shall have customary accounting and credit rights.

4. **Services/Location.**

4.1 Services. The Guaranteed Compensation will cover all development and production services as are customarily rendered by directors of first-class, theatrical motion picture projects and as required by Producer commencing on the date designated by Producer and continuing until the completion of all required services hereunder; it being agreed that principal photography is contemplated to commence on or about _____________. Director shall render exclusive services in connection with rehearsals, preproduction, photography, trailers, promotionals and other film or tape material to be exhibited in connection with the Picture and otherwise in connection therewith until Producer secures delivery of Director's cut of the Picture; thereafter, Director's services shall be rendered on a nonexclusive but first-priority basis until completion of the answer print. Lender will also make Director available, upon Producer's request, for publicity and promotional activities.

4.2 Location of Principal Photography Services. _______________ area.

4.3 Location and Travel Expenses.

(a) One first-class round-trip air transportation (if available and if used), from Los Angeles to location.

(b) Ground transportation to and from the airports and set.

(c) DGA scale per diem.

(d) Living accommodations (i.e., One first-class hotel room or equivalent accommodations).

(e) Office/Dressing Facilities (i.e., while Director is rendering services at a location, Producer shall provide Director with a trailer at a cost within the limits of the Producer approved budget).

5. **Credit/Likeness.**

5.1 Credit. Subject to any applicable guild or union requirements, if Director performs all of the obligations hereunder and is the director of the Picture, Producer shall accord Director credit on screen and in paid advertising in accordance with the DGA Basic Agreement.

5.2 Prospective Cure. Producer will exercise reasonable efforts, after receiving written notice from Director, to cure prospectively on any materials thereafter created any failure to accord credit in connection with this Paragraph, it being understood that Producer shall have no obligation to recall or cease the use of materials created before Producer is so notified.

6. **Additional Provisions.**

6.1 Promotion and Publicity Services. Subject to Director's professional availability, Director will be available for and to participate in interviews and other customary events to help promote the Picture. If Director is requested to travel for such purpose, Director will then be advanced or reimbursed for expenses.

6.2 Cutting Authority/Consultation. ________________ (Name of Producer executive with final cut) shall, in the ordinary course of business, have final cutting authority for Producer. Director shall have a right of consultation regarding key crew, key locations and schedules, provided, however, in the event of any disagreement, Producer's decision shall be final. In the event Director is unavailable at such times and places as required by Producer, such approvals and consultation rights, if any, shall be deemed waived.

6.3 Videocassette/DVD. Director shall receive for Director's own personal use one complimentary VHS or DVD copy of the Picture.

6.4 DGA. Producer shall be a signatory to the DGA Basic Agreement and shall make all pension, health and welfare payments in accordance with the DGA Basic Agreement.

6.5 Insurance. Director shall be added as an additional insured on Producer's errors and omissions and general liability insurance policies, subject to the terms and conditions of such policies.

6.6 Subsequent Productions. Provided Producer produces the Picture, Director directs the Picture, Lender and Director are not in material breach hereof, the Picture's negative cost does not exceed 110% of the Approved Budget, the Picture is delivered in accordance with the mutually approved delivery schedule, Director is then actively engaged as a director in the motion picture industry and Director is available to render directing services as, when and where reasonably required by Producer, then, if Producer desires to produce a sequel, prequel, remake or television production of the Picture (collectively, "Subsequent Production") within five years after the initial domestic release of the Picture and subject to network approval in the event of a television production, Producer will negotiate in good faith with Director concerning Director's services with respect to the first Subsequent Production on terms to be negotiated in good faith and in accordance with industry standards for comparable engagements. If such negotiations do not result in an agreement within twenty days from the commencement thereof, Producer shall have no further obligation to Director under this subparagraph. The provisions of this subparagraph apply to Director personally and not to any heirs, executors, administrators, successors or assigns of Director. Director's right with respect to each Subsequent Production shall be a "rolling right" as such term is commonly understood in the entertainment industry with this deal as the floor as to each subsequent production in which Director is the director.

6.7 Notices and Payments. The addresses of the parties for notices and payments hereunder shall be:

(a) Director: as provided above

(b) Producer: **(Name of Producer)**
(Name of Production Company)
c/o **(Attorney/Agent)**
(Address)

All payments due or payable to Director from Producer herein may be made by check to Director or its agent at the above address and the receipt by such agent shall be good and valid discharge of all such indebtedness.

7. Additional Terms and Conditions. The balance of this agreement shall be the attached Terms of Personal Services Engagement (TOPSE 1.0), subject to those changes, if any, mutually agreed to in writing by the parties after good faith negotiations within customary parameters in the motion picture industry for comparable engagements with a director of Director's stature. Unless and until the parties hereto enter into a more formal agreement, this letter shall constitute a binding agreement between the parties, shall supersede any prior or contemporaneous agreements and may not be waived or amended, except by a written instrument signed by the parties hereto.
If the foregoing does not accurately reflect your agreement, please contact me immediately. Otherwise, please arrange to have your client sign this agreement and return it to me.

Very truly yours,

(Signed by Producer or Producer's attorney)

ACCEPTED AND AGREED:

____
("Director")

(Name of Production Company)

By: ___________________________

WELCOME TO HOLLYWOOD
NET
GROSS

HIRING ACTORS

In this chapter we will review the process of hiring casting directors and actors, some of the important provisions of the Screen Actor's Guild ("SAG") Basic Agreement, and the various deal terms that should be included in actor deals.

Casting Director

Casting directors are among the first workers hired on a production, since often it is necessary to get the cast in place to secure the financing. Their job is to be familiar with actors who can fill the roles in the film, make recommendations to the director and producer, assist in auditions, and negotiate the deals for actors other than the stars.

Casting director deals, unlike director or producer deals, are made on a weekly basis; that is, the casting director is hired to work for only a specified number of weeks. That time period is usually equal to the time between when the casting director is hired and shooting starts. In some instances, but only in the independent world, casting directors agree to do the casting with the hope that the financing will come together. Generally, they want a guaranteed fee whether or not the picture goes forward. Typical fees to casting directors in the independent world are $10,000 on the low side to $125,000 on the extremely high side. Sometimes they have a portion of their fee guaranteed and the balance contingent on the picture going forward.

Casting directors customarily receive a "Casting By" credit in the main titles of the picture. This is often the first credit after the main credits to the actors. Casting directors also often get paid ad credit when the so-called billing block is used. We discuss the billing block later in this chapter.

It is absolutely crucial that the casting director coordinate with the producer, director, and the producer's lawyers with respect to commitments that are made on behalf of the production company. This is particularly necessary with respect to credit. Credits to actors have become extremely complicated, especially in the independent world where there are frequently ensemble casts and where credit can often be accorded alphabetically or in order of appearance. It is very easy to inadvertently give different actors credits that conflict.

We provide a sample casting director agreement at the end of this chapter.

Actors

Swifty Lazar was a legendary agent who made many of the biggest deals in Hollywood, but with one notable exception, he avoided representing actors. The exception arose in a bet he made over breakfast with Humphrey Bogart. Swifty bet Bogie that he could get him six movie deals by lunch. He succeeded and Bogie bestowed him with the nickname "Swifty," a moniker Swifty hated. Swifty did not like representing actors because he thought they were narcissistic and whiny, but he loved entertaining with actors and was famous for his Oscar party and his private dinners with the biggest stars in Hollywood. This schizophrenic feeling towards actors is common in Hollywood. Many people find them difficult and some undoubtedly are. But if you do not like actors, do not be a producer. You will be miserable. It is also critical that you cultivate a personal relationship with your stars. Do not try to rely on your relationship with the manager or agent, who oftentimes will be your enemy rather than your ally. Actors need to have confidence in you and the picture. Do not keep them in the dark.

The Screen Actors Guild

A threshold question for the independent film producer is whether the picture will use professional actors who are members of the Screen Actors Guild (SAG) or whether the production will use nonunion actors. Virtually all professional motion picture and television actors in the United States are members of SAG and, as such, are forbidden from working for a company that has not signed up with SAG and agreed to abide by all of the provisions of one of the Screen Actor Guild agreements. The basic agreement is aptly called the Screen Actors Guild Codified Basic Agreement. It is the collective bargaining agreement negotiated between the union and the Alliance of Motion Picture and Television Producers (AMPTP), that bargains on behalf of the major studios and other producers. The SAG Codified Basic Agreement covers most pictures shown at movie theaters.

There are several other SAG agreements, including the Low-Budget Agreement, Modified Low-Budget Agreement, Experimental Film Agreement, and Student Film Letter, which can apply to certain productions. These agreements are alternatives to the Basic Agreement and are designed to help beginning and low-budget filmmakers use SAG talent. They tend to relax some of the minimums and other provisions that shoestring-budgeted producers find difficult to meet. These agreements, however, are designed to recapture the money and benefits the actors waived if the film becomes a commercial success. So there are potential trade-offs. If you want to utilize one of these SAG agreements, consult with experienced filmmakers and attorneys to weigh the short-term benefits against potential long-term costs. Details of the agreement are available on the SAG Indie Web site, *www.sagindie.org*.

As of 2004, the SAG Low-Budget Agreement can be utilized for pictures with a total budget of under $2,000,000 ($3,000,000 if the project meets certain diversity casting criteria) that are entirely shot in the United States and have initial release in movie theaters. It provides for a lower minimum pay rate for actors ($466 for a day player compared to $617 under the Basic Agreement). It also reduces the overtime rate and covers fewer extras.

The Modified Low-Budget Agreement can be utilized where the total budget is less than $500,000 (or up to $750,000 if the project meets diversity casting requirements), the picture is shot in the United States, and the picture is initially released in theaters. The minimum rates are even than the SAG Low-Budget Agreement.

Each of these two special agreements is conditioned on the picture having an initial theatrical release. The theatrical release need not be nationwide, but it cannot be a sham. Mark recently worked on a picture where release in one theatre (paid for by the producer) sufficed. If the picture does not get a theatrical release, but is sold to television instead, then the performers must retroactively be upgraded to the terms of the Basic Agreement. In addition to having to pay higher minimums, the so-called consecutive employment provisions of the SAG Basic Agreement will apply. Those provisions require that a producer pay actors consecutively from the first day they act until the last, whether or not they worked each day. Not all actors work every day of the schedule. After all, actors would have a hard time getting work elsewhere for one day out of a week. That is the notion behind the consecutive employment restriction. That restriction is lifted on these two special SAG Agreements if the picture has an initial theatrical release, but goes back into effect if it does not. So, in addition to the higher minimums of the Basic Agreement, the producer must also pay for those intervening days.

In addition to the foregoing two theatrical agreements, SAG offers three other agreements that apply to very low-budget pictures destined for very limited release. The first is the Limited Exhibition Agreement. It is applicable to pictures with budgets of under $200,000, which are exhibited only in very short runs in art house cinemas or on educational or public television or non-commercial basic cable network, as experimental or independent producer telecasting. Rates are extremely low but special provisions apply, so make sure you understand all of the conditions before signing up.

The Experimental Film Agreement applies to pictures shot in the United States with budgets under $75,000. Distribution is limited to film festivals. Any other use requires making a new deal with SAG and with each professional performer.

The final SAG agreement is the Student Film Agreement. It is limited to pictures of up to 35-minutes running time with a budget not exceeding $35,000 and a maximum of 20 shooting days over six calendar weeks. Only students enrolled in an accredited educational institution qualify, and exhibition is essentially limited to the classroom and at student film festivals. Any other exploitation requires a renegotiation with SAG and all the performers.

Whichever SAG agreement you pursue, you must contact SAG and start the signatory procedure a minimum of 30 days before photography starts. The process involves supplying SAG with detailed information and proof of chain of title. In the last few years, we have found SAG to be increasingly demanding and difficult in the signatory process for independent productions. The process must be completed before the actors can start to work. In fact, actors are required to call "Station 12" at SAG before they report for work to get confirmation that the production company has completed its affiliation with SAG. If the production is not clear with Station 12, the actors cannot work. Any actor who violates these restrictions and works for a nonguild company—even a not-quite-signed company—can face union discipline that can include fines and expulsion.

The SAG Basic Agreement covers

1. Minimum pay for actors
2. Working conditions
3. Credits
4. Residual payments for videocassettes, television, and the like.

The agreement also establishes a mandatory arbitration procedure to resolve many of the disputes that can arise. To obtain a copy of the SAG Basic Agreement or alternative low-budget agreement outlined above and to initiate the process of signing the production company, you can contact SAG.

SCREEN ACTORS GUILD (SAG)
www.sag.org
5757 Wilshire Boulevard
Los Angeles, CA 90036
Tel: (323) 954–1600
or
360 Madison Avenue
12th Floor
New York, NY 10017
Tel: (212) 944–1030

While not light bedtime reading, it will be valuable for you to go through the SAG Basic Agreement. You will find very specific requirements about rehearsals, dressing rooms, nudity, publicity stills, overtime, and many other practical considerations that you must be familiar with.

One consideration, which does not appear clearly in the SAG Basic Agreement, needs to be pointed out. As a condition of allowing a production company to sign with SAG, the union requires the company to post a cash bond with SAG to ensure that the actors are paid their salaries. The size of the bond is tied to the projected cast payroll and is usually around 40% of the cast budget. The SAG bond is returned, sooner or later, to the producer after principal photography has been completed and the actors are paid. You will have to include the bond in your budget and cash flow projections. While SAG does return the bond if you have paid all your actors, it takes quite a bit of time for SAG to actually confirm payment and release the bond. Also, if any actors pursue claims, SAG will hold up return of the bond until the claim is arbitrated.

If the production company is a SAG signatory, then all the actors, professional singers, dancers, stunt performers, airplane and helicopter pilots, stunt coordinators, and puppeteers on the production must be SAG members. Also, extras in Hawaii, Las Vegas, Los Angeles, New York City, San Diego, and San Francisco are under SAG jurisdiction and producers are required to hire a certain number of SAG extras before they can hire nonguild extras. There are some minor exceptions such as children under the age of four. This means that you cannot just hire actors who are already SAG members under the SAG Agreement and ignore the agreement for nonmembers. The provisions apply to all the actors whether they are SAG members or not.

If a performer is not a SAG member when they are hired, they must become a member by the 30th day after the performer first works in the motion picture industry.

Like the other entertainment guilds, the Screen Actors Guild has staff available to guide neophyte producers in their dealings with SAG and its members. Of course, the staff's first loyalty is to the union, then to individual members, but they understand that without producers, there are no acting jobs, so they provide helpful guidance to producers. Nevertheless, some people believe it is safest to approach guild personnel with hypothetical questions without giving out the name of the production, the producers, the director, and the production company.

You should note that SAG sets the minimum requirements for actors, which cannot be waived without SAG permission. Actors, however, are free to negotiate for terms better than the SAG minimum requirements.

The Star Deal

Making the star deal is perhaps one of the most crucial negotiations in the financing and production of a motion picture. In today's name-driven marketplace, closing a deal with a star has become the critical step toward getting a film into production. As we have explained, this is primarily because the star commitment—with all of its accompanying visibility, hype, promotional and worldwide market value, along with the various and sundry press releases—can be the trigger that sets the financing and production in motion. The terms and conditions of the star deal can be the determining factors in obtaining a commitment to finance a picture, the ultimate green lighting of a picture, as well as the release date of the picture and in shaping how and to whom the picture will be marketed, distributed, and promoted.

The actor is the only creative element that appears in front of the camera and on the screen as well as in the advertising, promotion, marketing, and publicity materials. Additionally, the star is generally expected to be the individual who will travel all over the world in support of the picture's release. Like it or not, the star is invariably the "face" of the movie. Accordingly, much of the negotiation has to do with the manner of how the actor's name, likeness, image, and photograph are marketed and sold, as well as what the star's rights and responsibilities are after shooting has concluded.

Deal Terms

The principal deal terms for any actor's deal are

1. Role
2. Compensation
3. Start date
4. Guaranteed work period
5. Credit
6. Perquisites

Role

The role is the part the actor will play. Sometimes, scripts are significantly rewritten from the draft the actor first reads. To protect their clients, star's representatives sometimes ask that the actor has the right of approval over material changes in the role or has the right not to do the part if it is materially changed. Producers like to retain flexibility and do not like to give this approval as part of the contract. The reality is that it is easier to make the proverbial horse drink water than to make your star play a part he or she does not want to play. You must be very careful in changing the role as it is set forth in the script that the actor saw before committing. We have seen numerous instances where stars have sought to withdraw using script changes as an excuse.

Compensation

Compensation is the fixed fee, sometimes sweetened with a profit participation, for stars. The range of these fees is immense, with a few top Hollywood stars deals now at $25 million guaranteed per picture. However, in the indie world stars are rarely, if ever, paid their studio quote, so you must be clever in crafting a deal where you can afford both the guaranteed fee and the increased back end that makes the deal attractive.

Start Date

Oftentimes, the producer does not know the exact start date for principal photography when the actor deal is made. Preparation time or the availability of locations can keep the date floating. At the same time, the actors need to know when they are going to work and are not going to sit around indefinitely without being paid. This gets to be a tricky issue. The SAG Basic Agreement has a concept of an "on or about" start date, such as, "Actor's start date is on or about May 10." But the term technically applies only to performers covered under Schedules B and C of the SAG Basic Agreement, not stars, who are covered by Schedule F. They are performers whose pay falls within certain ranges. For them, provided the actor gets the contract at least seven days before the starting date, "on or about" allows the producer a latitude of 24 hours, exclusive of Saturdays, Sundays, and holidays either prior to or after the date specified in the contract. Only with a SAG waiver can the producer get more flexibility. In our example, the start date could be May 9, 10, or 11. The producer, of course, could start later, but would have to start paying the actor as of May 11.

For higher paid actors—those currently earning $40,000 or more for the picture, there is no definition of "on or about" and its meaning is uncertain. In a dispute it could be interpreted the same as for Schedule B and C performers or much more loosely as starting sometime around the date. Since the start date is the day when the actor goes on the payroll, it matters. The best practice is not to have the contract just say "on or about," but to define it such as "on or about May 10" (i.e., within one week prior to or after such date).

The Work Period

The work period is generally divided into three classifications of work to be performed. The first is the preproduction period where the actor may be required to participate in rehearsals, wardrobe fittings, hairdressing and make-up tests, photographic and recording tests, readings, conferences, publicity stills, and interviews. The second is the production services period, which generally includes acting services during principal photography, as well as any stunts, trick shots, singing, playing musical instruments, and other services required to be performed in the actor's role in the picture, as well as appearing in documentary or "making of" featurettes and the electronic press kit, which may be used to help promote the picture in conjunction with its release. Depending on the contract and the negotiation of the terms, production services may also include services performed during retakes and added scenes, which are required after the completion of scheduled principal photography. The third classification is the postproduction services period, which generally includes services required for looping, dubbing, recording of the soundtrack, and additional services that may be required for trailers and foreign versions as well as publicity services. In some agreements, retakes, added scenes, and trick shots are included in the postproduction section of the contract.

A typical star deal will be negotiated to include a flat-fee (e.g., $1,000,000) for a specified period of preproduction, i.e., two weeks of rehearsal, wardrobe fittings, make up and hair appointments; ten weeks of principal photography, plus two additional "free weeks" (in the event principal photography is extended or the actor services are required for a period of time longer than anticipated); and three to five "free" looping, dubbing, and postproduction days. The finer points of the negotiation will deal with what happens if the services required of the actor go beyond the contracted period during principal photography and what will each day of overage services cost. In our example above, will an overage week cost $100,000 (one million divided by ten weeks) or $83,333 (one million divided by 12 weeks)? Additionally, if the producer needs the services of the actor beyond five days of looping and dubbing, will the producer have to pay the actor $83,333 a day, or will the actor do those additional days at SAG scale? If the actor travels, will the travel day or days be included in the compensation package, or will they be treated as extra workdays and paid at the full rate? Will the services required of the actor be "consecutive" workdays or weeks, or can they be "nonconsecutive" or split up? Can there be a gap between the preproduction/rehearsal period and the production period or must the actor be paid for any interim period between the preproduction/rehearsal period and the production period? All of these points will be specifically delineated in the contract so that presumably there will be no misunderstanding as to exactly how much the actor will be paid for what services.

Credits

Everyone knows what screen credits are: the names and credits that appear on the movie (onscreen) and in its advertising (paid ads). Onscreen credits are divided into the opening or main title credits—which appear at the beginning of the movie—and the end credits, which appear at the end. Occasionally, a filmmaker will petition the guilds for permission to omit the opening credits and all the credits will appear at the end. *Apocalypse Now* was an early example. The most hotly negotiated elements of screen credits are position and size.

To some extent, the position of many credits is preordained. The DGA requires that the director credit appear as the last card immediately preceding principal photography. The WGA Agreement provides that only a single producer card can intervene between the writer credit and the director credit. The International Alliance of Theatrical and Stage Employees (IATSE) Basic Agreement, which governs employment of many below-the-line staff positions, mandates that the director of photography credit appear on a separate card immediately adjacent to the group of cards for producer, writer, and director, with an executive producer or coproducer credit possibly slipped in between the producer and writer credit.

Per the IATSE Basic Agreement, the art director is on a separate card adjacent to the director of photography. The editor credit also goes on a single card and must be in the main titles if the director of photography credit and art director credit are in the main titles. The customary, but not mandatory, position is immediately prior to the art director.

So, on union pictures much of the main title structure is already mandated. Composers usually receive their credit in the main titles, but that is a matter of negotiation, as are the actor credits. The SAG agreements do not require any main title credits for actors or limit their number although there is a requirement for crediting actors in the end titles.

Since actors are on their own in negotiating the position of their credit, we will outline the options from top down. Having credit on a separate card means that no other credit can appear on screen while that credit appears. Separate cards are considered far more prestigious than shared cards. Getting the first screen credit among actors, of course, is the most desirable and it is considered a particular status symbol to have your credit—and no other actors—appear before (or "above") the title such as: Tom Cruise in *Mission Impossible.*

Sometimes the main title acting credits are divided into starring and costarring credits. This is an arbitrary division. Costars frequently share cards. On occasion, rather than appear at the midpoint in a long set of actor credits, an actor will opt to take the last acting credit in the form of "special appearance by" or "and starring Jerry Mathers as The Beaver." We can tell countless war stories where producers or casting directors promised different actors conflicting credits. These usually result from an unexpected change in the cast; someone is replaced by a bigger or lesser star. But often it is just a matter of confusion; Nicole Kidman is offered credit to immediately follow Tom Cruise. Ben Affleck is guaranteed not less than second position among the cast, and Tom Cruise gets credit in first position. Since both Ben and Nicole cannot be second, the credit must be renegotiated.

Once the order of credits is determined, the size is to be considered—and size matters. The most desirable is to be in the largest typeface—no one larger—and to guarantee that the size will not be smaller than a percentage of the size of the title of the movie. Another approach is to tie to the size of credits for nonactors. The director is the top choice because the DGA Agreement has very specific requirements for the size of the director credit. This tying approach works reasonably well on screen where there normally is little variation in the size of names, but, as discussed below, it becomes very complicated in advertising.

In addition to size, the duration that the credit appears on screen is sometimes negotiated—usually not a specific length of seconds but typically of a duration no shorter than the longest time devoted to another person's credit. Lawyers for big actors also want to ensure that the style, typeface, color, and boldness of their client's credit is not less favorable than any other star.

Screen credits are actually simple compared to other credit issues for advertisements. Credits can appear in newspaper advertising, on television and radio, on billboards, on the theater marquee, in press kits, and publicity releases and on merchandising, videocassettes, and soundtrack albums. These categories are usually broken down into paid ads, written publicity, merchandising, home video devices, and soundtrack albums. On deals for stars, the credit is negotiated for each category. You can imagine the complexity since the same credit considerations figure into the deals for writers, producers, director, and others, as well as for each actor. To simplify the process, studios came up with what they call the billing block. It is a multipurpose list of all the necessary credits in appropriate order and relative size. It is usually set in a very, very skinny typeface. It is slapped on the end of newspaper and TV ads, billboards, soundtracks, and videos to satisfy the various paid ad requirements.

A paid ad is advertising that the distributor or studio purchased. It, for example, would not include a review of the picture. Even when a producer agrees to give credit in paid ads, it will exempt a list of ads called "excluded ads." The lists vary, but typically include radio and television ads and small newspaper ads of less than eight column inches, among others.

Perquisites

Perquisites, in entertainment parlance, are travel and accommodation arrangements and other amenities. For local shoots, these are relatively simple; dressing facilities and sometimes transportation from home to the set. On location, the list is much longer and can include travel from home to airport, airport to hotel, and hotel to set; rental car; hotel accommodations; and per diem (a nonaccountable allowance computed on a daily basis and designed to cover the cost of meals and sundry miscellaneous expenses). In Hollywood, the per diem ranges from the current SAG minimum of $35 to the medium level of $100, and up to the star level of $3,500 per week plus hotel.

Many stars have special needs that are negotiated into their agreements in order that their lifestyles are comfortable and they are ready to work without additional, unneeded distractions. Many big stars negotiate to have a personal assistant on the payroll, mostly to meet their various business and creative needs. Additionally, stars with children will typically negotiate for the right to bring their children to the location at the expense of the production, along with their nanny, housekeeper, or baby-sitter. Since stars have to keep in shape, they will negotiate that a gym facility or special exercycle be made available or other special training needs be covered while on location, including a trainer. Major stars are concerned with their personal safety and security and will sometimes negotiate provisions that allow their security personnel to travel with them and have their salaries covered by the production. Some stars also have special dietary needs and requirements and can negotiate provisions concerning special food for on-set consumption or for a cook, who is made available to the star while on location at the expense of the production.

In the more exotic category, we would place the demand we saw for matching black Range Rovers on location for a star and his boyfriend/assistant, one of which was rejected because its window tint did not match the other. In a Western, we encountered an actor who demanded that his horse be washed twice a day to stave off an allergic reaction. We also negotiated for new wigs, on a weekly basis, for a bald star.

Obviously, the budgets of most independent films require Spartan perquisites even for stars, but it is helpful for the producer to understand what the actors are accustomed to.

Dressing Facility

Negotiations for dressing facilities are notorious. Stars want to be comfortable and have as many amenities and conveniences as possible while they are waiting to be photographed and preparing to perform. Trailers and dressing facilities come in numerous sizes, shapes, and degrees of luxury, and you can be sure that the star's representative will be well-versed in all of the lingo on this count. The typical star dressing facility will be a large trailer fully equipped with a bed, kitchen, shower, living area, satellite television, VCR, stereo, and cellular telephone. Sometimes, the budget for a film will not be able to accommodate all of these amenities. As a result, variations are sometimes negotiated or a provision that states that the star will receive the best available dressing facility within the parameters of the budget is placed in the contract. Another provision customarily negotiated concerning dressing facilities is a restriction that states that no other actor will receive a more favorable dressing facility.

Another issue that comes into play is the condition that the dressing facility not be shared with any other actor. Sometimes, large trailers are split in half in what are customarily and affectionately known as "two-bangers," which provide separate facilities in each compartment, but which only require one driver rather than two. This is a way of saving money and still providing reasonably comfortable dressing facilities.

On tighter budgets, stars will sometimes agree to use what is called a "honeywagon," where one driver will tow a trailer that includes three, four, or five rather small dressing facilities, again, saving on transportation costs. While stars generally do not prefer honeywagons, they will sometimes agree to them to accommodate the budget of the picture, provided that no other actor is provided with a more favorable dressing facility.

Still Approvals

While stars need and want to have their names, photographs, and likenesses publicized in order to continue promoting their careers, they also need to control the nature and scope and use of their image—whether that image be a picture, a portrait, a caricature, or even a computer-generated visual effect, in connection with a motion picture and the many ancillary avenues of exploitation that picture offers.

As a result of a newfound caution in this age of nude celebrities on the Internet and fully computerized actors that live and breathe like real-life monsters, ghosts, and bad guys; stars' representatives very carefully negotiate the still and likeness rights—often as vigorously as for the negotiations for the cash and contingent compensation.

With respect to stills, stars are typically accorded the right to approve 50% of the still photographs submitted to the actor for use in connection with the promotion, marketing, and publicity of the picture. When a star appears with one or more other persons in a still, generally, the star will be required to approve at least 65% to 75% of the stills submitted. The approval process can take quite some time, so producers generally require that the approvals be exercised within five business days or, in the event of exigent circumstances, three business days. It is customary to include a clause that provides that the failure to receive notice of disapproval will be deemed approval of the stills submitted.

Likeness Approval

The star will also want the right to approve any nonphotographic likenesses that are drawn, electronically manipulated, or otherwise created for use in connection with the advertising, publicity, promotion, and exploitation of the picture. The producer would be required to submit such likenesses for approval, and the star generally has a five- or three-business-day period to approve or disapprove. Often, those likenesses are not approved and what is built into likeness approval clauses is that the star will have the opportunity to review at least three different submissions of a likeness. For example, once an artist has approved the nose, hair, eyes, and dimension as presented, then he would not be able to disapprove those items that had been previously approved. Likewise, approval clauses require the producer to try to redo the likeness keeping the artist's comments in mind, and after another two or three passes the likeness is deemed approved.

Merchandising, Soundtrack Album

Merchandising items such as toys, T-shirts, posters, clothing, greeting cards, and the like, have become a major ancillary revenue source in the motion picture business. In many cases, the revenue from such films as *E.T.* , *Batman*, *Spiderman*, *Harry Potter* and *Titanic* can amount to hundreds of millions of dollars, and in extraordinary cases can exceed the box-office revenue. Stars are accustomed to participating in this merchandising revenue stream when the stars' photographs or likenesses appear on specific merchandising items.

Low-level stars' participation in merchandising revenue is usually 5% if only their likeness appears or 2.5% if others also appear. This can escalate for bigger stars to 15% of merchandising revenues after the deduction of various distribution fees and expenses. Merchandising distribution fees are negotiable but are customarily in the 50% range. Similarly, when a star's voice is used on a soundtrack album, either in dialogue or in a song, the star will negotiate a soundtrack album royalty.

In indie star deals where the leverage is with the actor, it is very common for the star to have outright approval over the use of their image and voice in merchandising and soundtrack albums. Merchandising and soundtrack album rights are usually more valuable in studio pictures than indie pictures, so the stakes are lower for the indie producer.

Commercial Tie-Ins and Endorsements

Another restriction that stars want to place on their name, likeness, and photograph involves their use in connection with any commercial products, endorsements, or promotional tie-ins with restaurants (e.g., McDonald's Happy Meals), goods and services, and the like. No such uses are allowed without the expressed written consent of the star, which may be refused for any reason.

Doubles, Dubbing, Outtakes, Nudity

In order to further protect their image, stars require the approval of the use of a body double, unless the double has been engaged as a specialty or stunt performer. As with makeup and hair personnel, stars generally have doubles with whom they work regularly.

Additionally, if the star's voice is to be dubbed in his native language, then the star will require at least the first opportunity to perform any such dubbing. The dubbing issue becomes more important when the star is multilingual. When the star is well-known in a foreign territory and, for example, performs his role in English for the movie, he certainly would not want his voice dubbed by another actor in Spain, if he were originally from Spain. With international coproductions becoming more prevalent, the dubbing issue has become more important in recent years.

Outtakes are sequences shot for the film that are not used in the final cut. Many stars now restrict the use of any outtakes for any reason without their prior written consent.

Negotiations concerning nudity are a serious, important concern among actors and involve a series of rather extensive protections concerning the use of nude, sex, or simulated sex images. The SAG Basic Agreement carefully outlines protections for actors asked to perform scenes involving nudity or sexual acts. They start with a requirement that the performer get notice of any required nudity or sex acts prior to the first audition or interview. The actor then must approve appearing nude or in a sex act in writing. If the producer plans to use a double for the nude or sex scenes, that also requires the performer's written consent. The consent must include a general description of the nudity and type of physical contact required in the scene. If the performer has consented but later chickens out, the producer can use a double and still retains the right to use footage already shot.

During shooting, the set must be closed to all persons having no business purpose being there, and there can be no still photography without prior written consent of the actor.

Premieres and Previews

A typical provision in the star deal will have the star and a companion being invited to the North American premiere screening of the film and perhaps the European premiere of the picture. These provisions invariably include provisions for first-class transportation, accommodations, and a per diem allowance. Many actor's representatives now negotiate provisions that concern the star not only being invited to the premiere but also to previews, as well as film festival screenings of the picture.

Videocassette, Videodisc/DVD, 35mm Print

A customary provision for stars includes a free copy of the picture on videocassette, videodisc/DVD, and laserdisc when they are commercially available, subject to the signing of an antipiracy private use lending agreement. Major stars can sometimes negotiate for a free 35mm print of the picture, subject to the same antipiracy and private use restrictions as for directors.

Insurance Matters

Most star agreements have a provision that requires that the stars submit to a physical exam for insurance purposes. Generally, the exam is provided by a doctor engaged by the production's insurance carrier or the producer. The star will also want to have his or her personal physician present during any such examination to explain or otherwise challenge any erroneous medical reports that may be furnished by the carrier-appointed physician. The star will also want a special provision in his or her agreement that provides that in the event the insurance carrier has a special exclusion, deductible, or extra premium as a result of the star's medical condition, the star would be allowed to pay that additional premium, cover that deductible, or otherwise deal with any insurance problems that exist. The star will want to be an additional insured on the Producer's errors and omissions insurance and general liabilities insurance policies.

Tax Matters

Many countries have tax withholding statutes that can significantly reduce the cash compensation payable to the star for services rendered in those particular territories. A relatively common request from stars' representatives is a tax indemnity provision whereby the producer is required to cover or indemnify the star from any of those tax withholdings that exceed U.S. withholding. The terms and conditions of such a tax indemnity are highly detailed and specialized and require expert tax advice from international tax specialists. Indie producers usually want to avoid the risk of a tax indemnity and resist them, although they will assist the actor in limiting withholding in the local jurisdiction. Tax considerations can lead to separate, bifurcated acting contracts whereby the actor is employed as an individual in the shooting location (rather than through his loan out) to make sure that any local withholding is credited against his U.S. taxes.

Favored Nations

In the entertainment law context as opposed to the international trade context, "favored nations" means that the provisions granted to one party are at least as favorable as the best provisions granted to anyone else. For example, if an actor gets favored nations on his dressing facility with other actors on the picture, then that actor's dressing facility has to be as good (or better) than any other actor's. On independent low-budget pictures, it is common for all the stars to agree to a favored nations deal. Typically, no one makes their usual salary. They can accept that, but they do not want to be shortchanged compared to other actors. If you make this kind of arrangement, be careful and think it through. If one of the actors has special needs—for example, kids who travel with her—make it clear to all the actors up front that the favored nations does not extend to extra airfares and hotel rooms. Above all, resist any temptation to make a secret deal to pay or treat one person better than the others. We worked on a picture where a producer thought if he violated favored nations with a confidential side letter he kept in his drawer, he would be safe. Suffice it to say we disabused him of this notion immediately. People talk on the set and in the make-up rooms. You are certain to be found out. Your credibility will be destroyed and you will deserve the inevitable lawsuit you will face.

Conclusion

In the last several years, landing a star has become more important than ever for producers who work outside of the studio system to finance films. Once the star has accepted to take the role in principle, a delicate and intricate balancing act begins. The above set of guidelines should be helpful in the relentless give and take that is the negotiation process for the star deal. With any independent picture, the collaborative, sometimes scrappy nature of a lower budget, the fiercely refined vision of the director and the screenplay he has chosen to film and the seemingly unending mechanics of the contract negotiation can, if properly coordinated, result in a film that makes sense financially and is artistically and critically acclaimed. How the star—and his deal—fit into this apparatus is a challenge that only the best producers meet with any regularity. Consultation with an agent, manager, or experienced entertainment attorney in making these deals is essential to avoid the many pitfalls and roadblocks that can ensue.

Casting Director Agreement

As of ____________ (Date)

(Casting Director Name)
(Address)

Re: **(Production Company)**/"**(Project Name)**"/Casting Services

Dear _____________:

This will confirm the agreement between ____________________ ("Producer") and you (jointly and severally "Artist"), respecting Artist's services as casting director in connection with the United States casting for the motion picture currently entitled ____________________ (the "Picture") on the following terms and conditions:

1. Engagement. Producer hereby engages Artist to personally render all services required by Producer as casting director in connection with the Picture, as more specifically set forth below, and Artist hereby accepts such engagement.

2. Commencement Date. Such services shall commence on the date hereof for a period of ____ week(s). Artist's services hereunder shall be on a nonexclusive basis, and Artist shall not, during the term hereof, render services for any third party or on Artist's own behalf which will materially interfere with Artist's services hereunder.

3. Services.

3.1 Artist shall render all services customarily rendered by casting directors of first-class feature films and in accordance with the terms of Exhibit "A" (attached hereto and incorporated herein by this reference), which terms are hereby specifically agreed to by Artist, plus any other services required by Producer to complete Artist's casting services hereunder, including, without limitation the following:

3.1.1 Artist shall assist the director, producer(s) and executive producer(s) of the Picture in making suggestions and in conducting interviews and readings for the roles for the major American actors.

3.1.2 Artist shall not be permitted to authorize a role or a screen test, or sign any agreement on Producer's behalf, without Producer's written approval.

3.1.3 Artist shall submit all credit provisions to Producer for approval before submission to third parties. Once approved, all credit clauses shall conform to Producer's approved standards, which shall be separately approved by Producer's attorney. There shall be no main title screen credit and/or paid ad credit given unless Producer's written consent is first obtained, in which event Producer's attorney shall draft all such paid ad provisions.

3.1.4 Artist shall furnish Producer with a written list of all required screen and advertising credits.

4. Rights.

4.1 Artist agrees and acknowledges that Artist's services hereunder are rendered specifically for inclusion in an audiovisual work, and such services and the results and proceeds thereof are a work made for hire under the copyright laws of the United States. Accordingly, Producer shall solely and exclusively own Artist's services and all of the results and proceeds thereof (including, but not limited to, all rights, throughout the universe and in perpetuity, of copyright, trademark, patent, production, manufacture, recordation, reproduction, transcription, performance, broadcast and exhibition by any art or method now known or hereafter devised), together with all so-called moral rights in and/or to all of the results and proceeds of Artist's services hereunder. If and to the extent Producer is not automatically deemed the author and owner of Artist's services hereunder and the results and proceeds thereof, Artist hereby assigns and transfers to Producer, in perpetuity and throughout the universe, all rights (including all rights of copyright) in and to same, without reservation, condition or limitation. If Producer shall desire to secure separate assignments of or for any of the foregoing, Artist shall execute the same upon Producer's request therefor; and Producer shall have and is hereby granted the right and authority and power, which power is coupled with an interest, to execute, in Artist's name and as Artist's attorney-in-fact, all such assignments which Artist fails to promptly sign after Producer's request therefor.

4.2 All rights granted or agreed to be granted to Producer under this agreement shall vest in Producer immediately and shall remain vested whether this agreement expires in normal course or is terminated for any cause or reason.

4.3 Producer shall always have the right to use and display Artist's name, likeness and biography for advertising and publicizing and otherwise in connection with the Picture or any rights or elements therein or based thereon. However, such advertising may not include the direct endorsement of any product (other than the Picture) without the written consent of Artist. The exhibition of all or part of the Picture by any manner or medium, even though a part of or in connection with a commercially sponsored program, shall not be deemed an endorsement of any nature.

5. Compensation. Upon condition that Artist fully performs all services and obligations required hereunder, Producer shall pay to Artist (at the above address) as compensation in full the flat "pay-or-play" sum of Thirty Thousand Dollars ($30,000), which shall accrue and be payable as follows:

5.1 ____________ Thousand Dollars ($________) promptly following Artist's execution and delivery to Producer of this agreement;

5.2 ____________ Thousand Dollars ($________) promptly following Artist's completion of services required by Producer hereunder.

6. Independent Contractor. As an independent contractor, Artist represents and warrants that Artist has the right to enter into this agreement and that Artist will pay all unemployment, disability, insurance, social security, income tax and other withholdings, deductions and payments required by law with respect to Artist's services hereunder. In addition, in connection with Artist's services hereunder, to the extent that Artist furnishes the services of any other persons, or incurs any overhead or other similar expenses, same shall be Artist's sole responsibility and shall be at Artist's sole cost and expense, and, with respect to the services of such other persons, Artist shall have all obligations of employers with respect thereto, including, without limitation, payment, payroll deductions and withholdings, employer's taxes and worker's compensation insurance.

7. Business Expenses. Offices and assistant shall be provided by Incognito Entertainment. Producer shall advance or cover reasonable out-of-pocket business expenses incurred directly in connection with Artist's services hereunder; provided such business expenses are approved in writing by Producer, which approval shall not be unreasonably withheld or delayed.

8. Credit. Subject to any union and/or guild restrictions and provided that Artist fully complies with Artist's obligations, representations and warranties and is not in breach hereunder, Artist shall be accorded main title screen credit in all paid ads in which the billing block appears as the first credit following the actor's credits ("Artist's Credit"), in substantially the form: "Casting by: ____________________" (Casting Director Name). Subject to the foregoing, the size, position, placement and all other matters with respect to any credit to be accorded to Artist shall be at Producer's sole discretion. No casual or inadvertent failure by Producer, nor any failure by third parties, to comply with these provisions shall constitute a breach of this agreement. Upon written notice from Artist that Artist's Credit does not conform to this paragraph, Producer shall prospectively cure any such failure to accord credit; it being understood, however, that such cure shall apply only to subsequently prepared materials, and in no event shall Producer be obligated to recall any materials.

9. Remedies Cumulative. All remedies accorded herein or otherwise available to Producer shall be cumulative, and no one such remedy shall be exclusive of any other. The commencement or maintaining of any action by Producer shall not constitute an election on Producer's part to terminate this agreement or Artist's engagement hereunder nor constitute or result in the termination of Artist's engagement hereunder unless Producer shall expressly so elect by written notice to Artist. The pursuit of any remedy under this agreement or otherwise shall not be deemed to waive any other or different remedy which may be available under this agreement or otherwise, either at law or in equity. Notwithstanding anything in this agreement to the contrary, in the event of a breach by Producer of any of the terms or provisions of this agreement, Artist shall not be entitled to withdraw any of the rights herein granted, rescind this agreement or seek injunctive or other equitable relief; Artist's only remedy shall be the right to seek recovery of monetary damages in an action at law.

10. Satisfaction of Producer's Obligations. Producer shall have no obligation to produce, complete, release, distribute, advertise or exploit the Picture, or to use the results and proceeds of Artist's services in the Picture, if produced, or to utilize Artist's services in any manner; but nothing in this paragraph shall relieve Producer of its obligation to pay the compensation set forth herein, subject to, and in accordance with, the terms and conditions of this agreement.

11. Assignment. Producer may assign this agreement or all or any part of Producer's rights hereunder to any person or entity, and this agreement shall inure to Producer's benefit and to the benefit of Producer's successors and assigns.

12. Publicity. Artist will not furnish or authorize any advertising material or publicity (other than publicity primarily concerning Artist which makes incidental, nonderogatory mention of Artist's services, the Picture and/or Producer) of any form relating to the Picture, Artist's services or Producer (or its operations or personnel) or any distributors or broadcasters of the Picture.

13. Force Majeure. If the preparation or production of the Picture is materially hampered, interrupted or prevented due to inclement weather, an act of God, war, riot, civil commotion, fire, casualty, strike, labor dispute, act of any federal, state or local authority, death, disability or default of any member of the cast or of the crew, including, without limitation, the director, or for any similar or dissimilar reason beyond Producer's control, Producer shall have the right to suspend this agreement. Producer's election to suspend this agreement shall not affect Producer's right thereafter to terminate this agreement. If, as a result of one or more events of force majeure, Producer suspends this agreement for four consecutive weeks or more, then Producer may terminate this agreement by written notice given at any time during the continuation of such suspension.

14. Warranties. Artist hereby warrants that, to the best of Artist's knowledge (or that which Artist should have known in the exercise of reasonable prudence), all material created, submitted and/or contributed by Artist hereunder for or in connection with the Picture shall be wholly original with Artist and shall not infringe upon the copyright of, or violate the right of privacy of, or constitute a libel or slander against, or violate any common law rights or any other rights of any person or entity; and that Artist is not under any obligation or disability, created by law or otherwise, which would in any manner or to any extent prevent or restrict Artist from entering into and fully performing this agreement. Artist hereby agrees to indemnify Producer and all distributor(s) and broadcaster(s) of the Picture, and each of their officers, employees, directors, successors, agents, licensees, sponsors and assigns from and against all cost, expense, damage, loss and liability (including attorneys' fees) arising out of or in connection with any claims, demands, actions and holdings arising out of any breach of Artist's warranties, representations and/or agreements hereunder.

15. Artist's Unique Services. Artist acknowledges that Artist's services, and the rights granted to Producer herein, are of a special, unique, extraordinary and intellectual character that give them peculiar value, the loss of which cannot be reasonably or adequately compensated in damages in an action at law and that a breach by Artist of this agreement will cause Producer irreparable injury. Accordingly, Artist acknowledges that Producer shall be entitled to injunctive and/or other equitable relief to prevent a breach of this agreement by Artist, which relief shall be in addition to any other rights or remedies that Producer may have, whether for damages or otherwise.

16. Video. Producer shall supply Artist with two (2) videocassettes of the Picture upon their commercial availability.

17. Premiere Tickets. Artist shall be provided with two (2) tickets to the initial United States celebrity premiere of the Picture, if any.

18. Standard Terms and Conditions. This agreement is subject to standard terms and conditions for comparable agreements, including, without limitation, the following: wage control; this agreement constituting and merging the parties' entire agreement; limitation of provisions which are illegal or inconsistent with any applicable union or guild agreements; no modifications, amendments or other agreements unless in a writing signed by both parties; article headings for convenience only; application of California law; exclusive jurisdiction of the courts located in Los Angeles, California; the prevailing party in any action being entitled to attorneys' fees and costs and expenses; Producer's right to suspend, extend and/or terminate in the event of Artist's disability or default; and customary credit exclusions and exceptions. The parties understand that this agreement, supplemented by such terms and conditions, shall serve as a fully binding and effective agreement.

Very truly yours,

(Production Company)

By: ______________________________

Its: ______________________________

ACCEPTED AND AGREED:

____

(Casting Director)

Social Security #______________________

Exhibit "A"
Casting Procedures

(References in this Exhibit "A" to "Casting Director" shall mean and include "Artist")

1. A cast budget will be given to Casting Director, and Casting Director shall comply therewith. Any changes must be approved in writing by Producer.

2. All deals shall be negotiated by Producer unless Producer advises Casting Director otherwise.

3. Casting Director shall not authorize a role or a test or submit to a third party (or sign) any agreement without Producer's written approval. No tests shall be conducted without Producer first obtaining a signed deal memo.

4. On all deals negotiated by Casting Director, Casting Director will first issue an internal draft deal memo, to be approved by and submitted only to Producer, not to any third parties. All such deal memos shall be submitted to Producer and Producer's attorney, who will draft the formal documents.

5. Casting Director must immediately advise Producer prior to engagement of a minor so that court approval can be arranged and trust accounts established, if necessary. Casting Director must obtain a signed parental agreement (a form copy of which may be obtained from Producer) and the names and addresses of both parents, and indicate whether the parents are presently married to each other, as this affects the approval requirement in certain states.

6. Casting Director acknowledges awareness of, and agrees to comply with, the Equal Opportunity provisions of the SAG/AMPTP Agreement in furnishing all of the services required hereunder, and Casting Director shall cooperate with Producer in placing minorities (including, without limitation, handicapped persons) in applicable roles. Casting Director shall prepare any reports or lists required in connection therewith.

NOTE: For compliance with the foregoing casting procedures contact

____.

(Attorney Name, Address and Phone)

Actor Agreement

____________ (Date of Agreement)

(Name of Actor)
c/o **(Agent)**
(Address)

Re: **Name of Production Co. - "Name of Picture" - Name of Actor (Actor)**

Dear __________________: **(Name of Agent)**

This will confirm the agreement ("Agreement") between ____________________ ("Artist"), a citizen of the United States and ______________________ ("Producer") regarding Artist's acting services in the role of "______________________" in the motion picture now entitled "______________________" (the "Picture").

1. Conditions Precedent.

1.1 Artist providing Producer with all documents which may be required by any governmental agency or otherwise for Artist to render services hereunder, including without limitation, a valid United States passport (if applicable), an INS Form I-9 completed to Producer's satisfaction, together with Artist's submission of original documents establishing Artist's employment eligibility.

1.2 [Additional condition]

2. Compensation.

2.1 Guaranteed Compensation. Provided Artist is not in material breach or default hereunder and subject to Producer's receipt of this agreement fully executed by Artist, Artist shall be paid ________ Dollars ("Guaranteed Compensation"), payable in equal weekly installments on Producer's regular payday one week in arrears over the period of Artist's initially scheduled services in principal photography of the Picture. Overages for services in addition to those set forth in Paragraph 3.2 below shall be paid at the rate of ________ Dollars per day. The Guaranteed Compensation buys out all overtime, holidays and other like terms to the maximum extent permissible under the applicable SAG Agreement.

2.2 Reuse. Producer shall have the unlimited right in perpetuity to exploit the Picture theatrically, on television, Internet, home video and the ancillary rights therein in any and all media whether now known or hereafter discovered throughout the universe, and in the event Producer exercises any of such rights, and unless provided for in this Agreement, Artist shall receive additional compensation only in the minimum amounts required by the applicable provisions of the applicable SAG Agreement.

2.3 Union Payments. Producer shall, on behalf of Artist, make all employer contributions to the Screen Actors Guild of America Pension Plan and Health and Welfare Plan in accordance with the terms thereof, required by reason of Artist's services and the compensation payable to Artist for such services hereunder.

3. Services/Location.

3.1 Start Date. Artist's services in connection with principal photography will commence on or about ________(start date) (i.e., one (1) week either side).

3.2 Services. The Guaranteed Compensation will cover ____ free prep days for wardrobe, rehearsal and makeup (which days may be nonconsecutive), ____ consecutive weeks of principal photography; ____ additional free consecutive weeks of principal photography; all holiday days (if applicable); ____ free travel days and ____ free post days for reshoots, added scenes, looping and dubbing (which may be consecutive or nonconsecutive at Producer's discretion; provided, if such days are nonconsecutive such days shall be subject to Artist's professional availability). Subject to Paragraph 6 below, Artist shall be available, subject to Artist's professional availability, upon Producer's request, for publicity and promotional activities.

3.3 Location of Principal Photography Services. (Location city and state.)

4. Credit.

4.1 Credit. Artist will receive credit on screen, on a separate card, in the main titles, below the title of the Picture, in the ________ position among all principal actors, equal in size and style to all other principal cast members.

5. Perquisites.

5.1 Dressing Facility. During Artist's principal photography services, Producer shall provide Artist with private first-class dressing facilities with customary first-class amenities.

6. Additional Terms.

6.1 Promotion and Publicity Services. Subject to Artist's professional availability, Artist will be available for interviews and other customary events to help promote the Picture. If Artist is requested to travel for such purpose, Artist will then be advanced or reimbursed for first-class travel and expenses for Artist.

6.2 Stills/Likeness Approval. Artist shall approve (not to be unreasonably withheld or delayed) not less than fifty percent (50%) of all submitted publicity stills for the Picture in which Artist appears alone and seventy five percent (75%) for group stills, with such stills to be provided in groups. Artist will be required to provide Artist's disapproval within three (3) business days after delivery to Artist or Artist's representative (unless Artist is advised that marketing exigencies require a sooner response), or approval will be deemed given.

6.3 Videocassette. Artist shall be furnished (free of charge) with one VHS videocassette promptly following commercial availability, for Artist's private noncommercial use.

6.4 Merchandising. Producer shall be entitled to use Artist's name, voice, likeness and other personal attributes in merchandising or commercial tie-ups based on Artist's role or character subject to a royalty to be paid Artist equal to 5% of 100% of Producer's net merchandising revenues less customary fees and expenses, reducible by all royalties paid to any other actors whose name or likeness appears in the same merchandise to a floor of 2.5% of 100%. Notwithstanding the foregoing, there shall be no merchandising or commercial tie-ins associated with alcohol, tobacco, weapons or hygiene products.

6.5 Notices and Payments. All notices and payments to Artist hereunder shall be made and paid in care of ____________________ (name of agent) at the address set forth above and Artist hereby authorizes Producer to make all such payments in the above-described manner. All notices to Producer hereunder shall be sent to ____________________ (production company or its lawyer's address).

6.6 SAG. Artist shall be a member in good standing in the Screen Actors Guild, and any services of Artist rendered hereunder shall be subject to the applicable SAG Agreement. Producer is now or prior to commencement of principal photography shall be a signatory to the SAG Basic Agreement or other SAG Agreement, which shall be applicable to the Picture.

7. **Balance of Terms and Conditions.** The balance of this agreement shall be Producer's Terms of Personal Services Engagement-Actor ("TOPSE-A"), a copy of which is attached. Unless and until the parties hereto enter into a more formal agreement, this letter together with TOPSE-A shall constitute a binding agreement between the parties, shall supersede any prior or contemporaneous agreements and may not be waived or amended, except by a written instrument signed by the parties hereto.
If the foregoing does not accurately reflect your agreement, please contact me immediately. Otherwise, please arrange to have your client sign four (4) copies of this agreement and return them to me.

Very truly yours,

____

(Signor of letter agreement)

ACCEPTED AND AGREED:

____
("Artist")

("Producer")

By: ____________________________________

Its: ____________________________________

Terms of Personal Services Engagement - Actor

1. **General.** These Terms of Personal Services Engagement-Actor (1.0) ("TOPSE-A") are incorporated into the principal agreement to which they are attached ("Agreement"). The individual rendering personal services pursuant to the Agreement is referred to herein as "Artist." If Artist's services are furnished by a corporation loaning services, that corporation is referred to herein as "Lender." The entity engaging Artist's services under the Agreement either directly or through Lender is referred to herein as "Producer," and the motion picture or pictures in connection with which Artist is engaged is referred to herein as the "Picture." In the event of express inconsistency between the Agreement and TOPSE-A, the Agreement shall prevail.

2. **Services.** Artist shall render all services required hereunder at such place or places as required by Producer from time to time during the term thereof. Artist shall render all services under the supervision, direction and control of Producer, in a diligent and conscientious manner, and to the best of Artist's ability, and comply with all of Producer's instructions, directions, requests, rules and regulations (including those relating to matters of artistic taste and judgment). Except as otherwise expressly provided to the contrary in the Agreement, Artist shall render his services exclusively and solely for Producer during the entire term hereof. Artist agrees, if and when requested by Producer, to report to wardrobe fittings, hairdressing, makeup, publicity interviews, publicity photography, story conferences, song conferences, production conferences, making of stills, retakes, looping, dubbing, added scenes, transparencies, process shots, trick shots and the like and for changes in and/or foreign versions of the Picture and for no additional compensation therefor. If any such services would conflict with any of Artist's existing professional commitments, then Artist shall give Producer timely notice of same, in which case Artist shall cooperate to the fullest extent with Producer in becoming available to render such services. No additional compensation whatsoever shall accrue or be payable to Artist including without limitation to the generality of the foregoing, for any services rendered at night, on Sundays or holidays or after the expiration of any number of hours of services in any period.

3. **Services Unique.** Artist acknowledges that rights granted to Producer and Artist's services hereunder are of a special, unique, unusual, extraordinary and intellectual character giving them peculiar value, the loss of which cannot be reasonably or adequately compensated in damages, and that a breach by Artist may cause Producer irreparable injury and damage. Accordingly, without limiting or waiving any other rights or remedies of Producer, Producer shall be entitled to seek injunctive or other equitable relief to prevent such breach and to prevent Artist from performing services for himself, or any person other than Producer.

4. **Results and Proceeds.** Producer shall own, in perpetuity, throughout the universe, all right, title and interest in and to the Picture, the elements thereof, and the results and proceeds of Artist's services hereunder and all materials produced thereby or furnished by Artist, of any kind and nature whatsoever, to the maximum extent permitted by any applicable guild or union agreement and free and clear of any and all claims

for royalties and other compensation except as specifically set forth in the Agreement. Artist acknowledges that any and all results and proceeds of Artist's services hereunder shall be a work made for hire for Producer, specially commissioned for use as part of a motion picture or other audiovisual work. Producer shall have the right to adapt, change, revise, delete from, add to or rearrange the Picture or any part thereof, and Artist waives throughout the universe the benefit of any law, doctrine or principle known as "droit moral" or moral rights of authors or any similar law, doctrine or principle however denominated, to the maximum extent permitted in each applicable jurisdiction. Producer shall own the Picture produced hereunder and all rights whatsoever therein, including, but not limited to, all copyrights, throughout the world and in perpetuity and in all elements thereof and shall have the right to sell, lease, license and otherwise exploit such rights and elements, as Producer may determine in its sole discretion. Artist's grant includes all rights regarding the renting, lending, fixing, reproducing and other exploitation of the Picture conferred under any applicable laws, directions or regulations, including without limitation, those of the European Union ("EU").

5. Representations and Warranties; Insurance; FCC; Indemnity. Artist hereby represents, warrants and agrees as follows:

(a) Artist is free to enter into the Agreement and is not subject to any obligation or disability which will or might prevent Artist from keeping and performing all of the conditions, obligations, covenants and agreements to be kept or performed hereunder; and Artist has not made, and will not make, any agreement, commitment, grant or assignment, nor do any act or thing which might interfere or impair the complete enjoyment of the rights granted and the services to be rendered to Producer.

(b) All ideas, creations and literary, musical and artistic materials and intellectual properties ("materials") furnished by Artist hereunder, shall be wholly original with Artist except materials in the public domain and that neither the materials nor the use thereof will infringe upon or violate any right of privacy of or constitute a libel, slander, or any unfair competition against, or infringe upon or violate the copyright, common law rights, literary, dramatic, photoplay, right of publicity, or any other rights of any third party. The foregoing is subject to and limited by Article 28 of the WGA Basic Agreement, if applicable.

(c) If and only if expressly required by Producer in connection with the services to be performed by Artist hereunder, Artist will become, at Artist's sole cost and expense and will remain throughout the term hereof, a member in good standing of the properly designated labor organization or organizations (as defined and determined under applicable law) representing persons performing services of the type and character that are to be performed by Artist hereunder.

(d) Artist shall indemnify and hold Producer, any licensee or distributor of the Picture, and the shareholders, directors, officers, agents, employees, successors, licensees and assigns of any of the foregoing, harmless from and against any and all liability, loss, damage, costs, charges, claims, actions, causes of action, recoveries, judgments, penalties and expenses, including attorneys' fees, which they or any of them may suffer by reason of the services rendered or the use of any materials furnished by Artist hereunder, or any breach of any representation, warranty or agreement made by Artist in the Agreement.

(e) Producer may secure any type of insurance covering Artist, insuring Producer or its designees. Artist will assist Producer prior to principal photography in procuring such insurance by submitting to customary examinations (with Artist to have the right to have Artist's physician present at such exams) and by filling out required applications. If Producer is unable to procure such insurance covering Artist at normal rates and without special exclusions, Producer may terminate Artist's services hereunder and be relieved of any further obligation to Artist hereunder. From the date three (3) weeks before the scheduled start of principal photography until completion of all services required of Artist hereunder, Artist will not ride in any aircraft, other than as a passenger on a scheduled flight of a United States or major international air carrier maintaining regularly published schedules, or engage in any extra hazardous activity, without Producer's prior written consent in each case.

(f) Producer and Lender acknowledge and agree that the following sums are in consideration of, and constitute equitable remuneration for, the rental right included in the rights herein granted: (i) an agreed allocation to the rental right of 3.8% of the fixed compensation and, if applicable, 3.8% of the contingent compensation provided for in this agreement; and (ii) any sums payable to Lender with respect to the rental right under any applicable collective bargaining or other industry-wide agreement; and (iii) the residuals payable to Lender under any such collective bargaining or industry-wide agreement with respect to home video exploitation which are reasonably attributable to sale of home video devices for rental purposes in the territories or jurisdictions where the rental right is recognized. If under the applicable law of any territory or jurisdiction, any additional or different form of compensation is required to satisfy the requirement of equitable remuneration, then it is agreed that the grant to Producer of the rental right shall nevertheless be fully effective, and Producer shall pay Lender such compensation or, if necessary, the parties shall in good faith negotiate the amount and nature thereof in accordance with applicable law. Since Producer has paid or agreed to pay Artist equitable remuneration for the rental right, Artist hereby assigns to Producer, except to the extent specifically reserved to Artist under any applicable collective bargaining or other industry-wide agreement, all compensation for the rental right payable or which may become payable to Lender or Artist on account or in the nature of a tax or levy, through a collecting society or otherwise. Artist shall cooperate fully with Producer in the collection and payment to Producer of such compensation. Further, since under this agreement Producer has paid or agreed to pay Artist full consideration for all services rendered and rights granted by Artist hereunder, Artist hereby assigns to Producer, except to the extent specifically reserved to Artist under any applicable collective bargaining or other industry-wide agreement, all other compensation payable or which may become payable to Artist on account or in the nature of a tax or levy, through a collecting society or otherwise, under the applicable law of any territory or jurisdiction, including by way of illustration only, so-called blank tape and similar levies. Artist shall cooperate fully with Producer in connection with the collection and payment to Producer of all such compensation.

6. **Producer's Controls.** As between Artist and Producer, Producer shall have full and exclusive budgetary, financial creative and business control over the Picture. Artist shall not at any time without Producer's prior written approval had and obtained in each case (whether before, during or after the term hereof), make any public statements or release or authorize any information, advertising or publicity relating to the engagement hereunder, the Picture, or Producer or Producer's personnel or operations, provided Artist can make incidental nonderogatory references in personal publicity.

7. **Name and Likeness.** Producer shall have the perpetual right and may grant to others the right, to disseminate, display, reproduce, use, print, publish and make any other uses of Artist's name, sobriquet, voice, signature and/or likeness (whether or not taken from the Picture) and biographical material concerning Artist as news or information matter in connection with advertising, publicizing and exploiting the Picture, Artist's services hereunder, including but not limited to, the right to use and authorize others to use the same in the credits of the Picture, in trailers, in commercial tie-ups and in all other forms and media of advertising and publicity and in connection with novelizations and other publications and in connection with the advertising and/or merchandising of any product, commodity or service or series; provided that Artist shall not be represented as endorsing any products or services without Artist's prior consent. Producer contemplates filming and exploiting films, including, without limitation, "behind-the-scenes" or "making-of" productions (jointly and severally, "Promotional Rights") about the development and production of the Picture. Artist hereby agrees to participate in and consents to such filming and exploitation (including, without limitation, use of any film clip footage from such Picture and behind-the-scenes photography and filmed interviews with Artist (but excluding any depiction of Artist in the nude without Artist's approval) and hereby grants to Producer, in perpetuity and throughout the universe, the right to use Artist's name, voice and likeness in connection with such Promotional Rights for no additional consideration, inasmuch as the compensation payable to Artist under this Agreement for the Picture shall be deemed to include compensation for all rights granted pursuant to this paragraph. Producer shall have exclusive merchandising and commercial tie-in rights in connection with Artist's role and/or character in the Picture are granted to Producer. Notwithstanding the foregoing, there shall be no merchandising or commercial tie-ins associated with alcohol, tobacco, weapons or hygiene products.

8. **Producer's Breach.** Notwithstanding any contrary provision hereof, or the operation of law, the Agreement shall not be terminated because of a breach by Producer of any of the terms, provisions or conditions contained herein unless and until Artist has given Producer written notice of any such breach and Producer has not within a period of ten

(10) business days after receipt of such notice from Artist cured such breach. Artist's rights and remedies in any event whatsoever shall be strictly limited, if otherwise available, to the recovery of damages in an action at law, and in no event shall Artist be entitled to rescind this Agreement, revoke any of the rights herein granted, or enjoin or restrain the production, broadcast, distribution or exhibition of the Picture, or any other motion picture, remake, sequel, television Picture or derivative production based thereon.

9. No Obligation to Use. Producer shall have no obligation to produce, release, broadcast or otherwise exploit the Picture, or to use Artist's services or the rights granted hereunder in connection therewith or otherwise, and Producer shall be deemed to have fully satisfied its obligations by paying to Artist the Guaranteed Compensation due Artist pursuant to the terms of the Agreement.

10. Credit. Except as expressly provided to the contrary in the Agreement, Producer shall determine, in its sole discretion, the manner, form, size, style, nature and placement of any credit given to Artist, subject only to the provisions of applicable guild or union agreements. No inadvertent failure of Producer to comply with the provisions hereof with respect to credit, no failure, error or omission in giving credit due to acts of third persons, nor the omission of credit where the exigencies of time make the giving of credit impracticable, shall constitute a breach of the Agreement. In the event of a breach of this paragraph, Artist's remedies, if any, shall be limited to the right to recover damages in an action at law and in no event shall Artist be entitled to terminate or rescind the Agreement, revoke any of the rights herein granted or to enjoin or restrain the distribution or exhibition of the Picture.

11. Notices; Payments. All notices, accountings and payments ("notices") which either Producer or Artist shall be required to give hereunder shall be in writing and shall be served by United States mail to the address specified in the Agreement or at such other address which either party may hereafter give by written notice, or by facsimile or by personal delivery. Service of any notice, statement or other paper upon either party shall be deemed complete if and when the same is personally delivered to such party, upon receipt by such party of a facsimile (with facsimile confirmation), or upon its deposit in the continental United States in the United States mail, postage or prepaid registered or certified mail, return receipt requested, and addressed, as the case may be, to the party which is the recipient at its address in the Agreement.

12. Suspension; Termination. If Artist fails, refuses or is unable for any reason whatsoever to render any of Artist's services hereunder, if there is a material change in Artist's physical appearance such that Producer in its sole discretion determines that Artist can no longer play Artist's designated role or perform the services required herein, or if Producer's development and/or production of the Picture hereunder is interrupted or materially interfered with by reason of any governmental law, ordinance, order or regulation, or by reason of fire, flood, earthquake, labor dispute, lockout, strike, accident, act of God or public enemy or by reason of any other cause, thing or occurrence of the same or any other nature not within Producer's control ("Force Majeure"), Producer shall have the right (i) to terminate the Agreement (whether or not Producer has theretofore suspended the Agreement as hereinafter provided) and Producer shall have no further obligation to Artist hereunder (except to pay accrued but unpaid compensation in the event of Force Majeure), or (ii) at Producer's option, to suspend the Agreement for a period equal to the duration of any such failure, refusal, or inability or the occurrence of any events of Force Majeure, and no compensation shall be paid or become due to Artist hereunder for such period. No suspension shall relieve Artist of his obligation to render services hereunder when and as required by Producer under the terms hereof, except during the continuance of a disability of Artist. Unless the Agreement shall have been previously terminated as provided herein above, any such suspension shall end promptly after the cause of such suspension ceases, and all time periods and dates hereunder shall be extended by a period equal to the period of such suspension.

13.

(a) **Waiver.** No waiver by either party hereto of any failure by the other party to keep or perform any covenant or condition of the Agreement shall be deemed to be a waiver of any preceding or succeeding breach of the same or any other covenant or condition. Neither the expiration nor any other termination of the Agreement shall affect the ownership by Producer of the results and proceeds of the services rendered by Artist hereunder or any warranty or undertaking on the part of Artist in connection therewith. The remedies herein provided shall be deemed cumulative and the exercise of any one shall not preclude the exercise of or be deemed a waiver of any other remedy, nor shall the specification of any remedy hereunder exclude or be deemed a waiver of any rights or remedies at law, or in equity, which may be available to Producer, including any rights to damages or injunctive relief. All rights granted to Producer are irrevocable and without right of rescission by Artist or reversion to Artist under any circumstances whatsoever, and Artist's rights and remedies shall be limited to the recovery of damages. Artist shall not have the right to enjoin or restrain the production, distribution, exhibition or other exploitation and the elements thereof of the Picture.

(b) **Assignment.** Producer shall have the right to assign all or any part of its rights under the Agreement to any person, but no such assignment shall relieve Producer of its obligations hereunder unless the assignment is to a major or minimajor studio, a network, a Company acquiring substantially all the assets of Producer, a parent of Producer or a financially responsible party who assumes Producer's obligations in writing. Artist shall not have the right to assign the Agreement or any of Artist's rights hereunder. This agreement will be binding upon and inure to the benefit of Producer's respective licensees, successors and assigns.

(c) **Jurisdiction.** The laws of the State of California applicable to agreements executed and to be wholly performed within the State of California shall apply to the Agreement. The parties agree and consent to the jurisdiction of the courts of the State of California and agree to venue in courts located in Los Angeles County,

California. In the event there shall be any conflict between any provision of the Agreement and any applicable law or applicable guild or union agreement, the latter shall prevail, and the provision or provisions of the Agreement shall be modified only to the extent necessary to remove such conflict and as so modified the Agreement shall continue in full force and effect.

(d) **Guild/Union.** Producer shall have the right to the maximum extent permissible under such applicable guild or union agreements, to apply all compensation paid to Artist on account of Artist's services under the Agreement as a credit against any and all amounts which may be required under such collective bargaining agreements to be paid to Artist for Artist's services, the results and proceeds thereof, the rights granted by Artist hereunder and the exercise thereof and for any other reasons whatsoever. If, pursuant to such collective bargaining agreements, Artist is entitled to any payment in addition to or greater than those set forth herein, then any such additional or greater payment made by Producer shall, except to the extent expressly prohibited by such collective bargaining agreements, be considered as an advance against and deducted from any such sum which may subsequently become payable to Artist hereunder. If, in determining the payments to be made hereunder, there is required any allocation of the compensation paid to Artist as between Artist's various services, Artist agrees to be bound by such allocation as may be made by Producer in good faith.

(e) **Withholdings.** Producer may deduct and withhold from the compensation payable to Artist hereunder any union dues and assessments to the extent permitted by law and any amounts required to be deducted and withheld under the provisions of any statute, regulation, ordinance, order and any and all amendments thereto heretofore or hereafter enacted requiring the withholding or deduction of compensation. If, pursuant to Artist's request or authorization, Producer shall make any payments or incur any charges for Artist's account, Producer shall have the right to deduct from any compensation payable to Artist hereunder any charges so paid or incurred, but such right of deduction shall not be deemed to limit or exclude any other rights of credit or recovery or any other remedies that Producer may have. Nothing herein above set forth shall be deemed to obligate Producer to make any such payments or incur any such charges.

(f) **Directed Withholdings.** If Producer is directed, by virtue of service of any garnishment, levy, execution or judicial order, to apply any amounts payable hereunder to any person, firm, corporation or other entity or judicial or governmental officer, Producer shall have the right to pay any such amounts in accordance with such directions, and Producer's obligations to Artist shall be discharged to the extent of such payments. If because of conflicting claims to amounts payable hereunder, Producer becomes a party to any judicial proceeding affecting payment or ownership of such amounts, Artist shall reimburse Producer for all costs, including attorneys' fees, incurred in connection therewith.

(g) **Entire Agreement.** This instrument constitutes the entire Agreement between the parties and supersedes all prior agreements and understandings, whether written or oral, pertaining thereto and cannot be modified except by a written instrument signed by Artist and an authorized officer of Producer. No officer, employee or representative of Producer has any authority to make any representation or promise in connection with the Agreement or the subject matter hereof which is not contained herein, and Artist agrees that Artist has not executed the Agreement in reliance upon any such representation or promise.

(h) **IRCA.** All of Producer's obligations hereunder are conditioned upon and subject to Artist's delivery to Producer of a completed and certified Employment Eligibility Verification (Form I-9) in compliance with the Immigration Reform and Control Act of 1986.

(i) **Further Documents.** Artist agrees to perform such other further acts and to execute, acknowledge and deliver such other further documents and instruments, including, without limitation, certificates of authorship and certificates of engagement with respect to all material furnished by Artist hereunder, as may be necessary or appropriate to carry out the intent hereof and to evidence Producer's ownership of the results and proceeds of all services rendered pursuant hereto, and Artist hereby appoints Producer as Artist's attorney-in-fact, which appointment is irrevocable and coupled with an interest, with full power of substitution and delegation, to execute any and all such documents which Artist fails to execute within five business days after Producer's request therefor and to do any and all such other acts that Artist fails to do after Producer's request therefor.

(j) **Lender's Obligations, Representations and Warranties, and Dissolution.** If the Agreement is entered between Producer and a corporation ("Lender") which furnishes the services of Artist, Lender represents and warrants that it is duly organized and presently in good standing in its state of incorporation; has a valid agreement with Artist under which Lender has the right to enter the agreement and grant Producer any and all of the services and rights granted hereunder and make all of the representations, warranties and agreements made by Artist. Producer shall pay Lender all compensation that would have been payable to Artist hereunder if Producer had directly employed Artist and Producer shall not be obligated to make any payments whatsoever to Artist. Artist's services shall be rendered as Lender's employee and Lender agrees to fully perform all such obligations and indemnifies Producer from all claims, liabilities and expense (including, without limitation, attorneys' fees) for or in connection with withholding and/or payment of any sums required to be paid by an employer to any governmental authority or pursuant to any guild or union health, welfare or pension plan or on account of any other so-called fringe benefits or workers' compensation premiums. Artist represents and warrants that Artist is familiar with the terms hereof and agrees to be bound by same, and agrees to look solely to Lender for all compensation or other consideration in connection with the rights granted and services to be rendered hereunder. If Lender or Lender's successors in interest should be dissolved or otherwise cease to exist or for any reason whatsoever fail, be unable, neglect or refuse to perform, observe or comply with any or all of the terms and conditions of the Agreement and/or this Agreement, Artist may, at Producer's election, be deemed a direct party to the Agreement until completion of the services required of Artist thereunder, upon the terms and conditions set forth therein. In the event of a breach or a threatened breach of this Agreement or the Agreement by Lender and/or Artist, Producer shall be entitled to seek legal, equitable and other relief against Lender and/or Artist, in Producer's sole discretion. Producer shall have all rights and remedies against Artist that Producer would have if Artist were a direct party to the Agreement. Producer shall not be required to resort first to or exhaust any rights or remedies Producer has against Lender before exercising Producer's rights and remedies against Artist.

14. Worker's Compensation. For the purpose only of determining the applicability of Workers' Compensation statutes to Artist's services under the Agreement if the Agreement is entered between Producer and Lender, an employment relationship exists between Producer and Artist, Producer being Artist's "special employer" and Lender being Artist's "general employer." In this regard, Lender agrees (a) that the rights and remedies of Artist and Artist's heirs, executors, administrators, successors, licensees and assigns against Producer, its officers, agents and employees (including any persons whose services are furnished to Producer by any corporation or other entity under an agreement granting Producer the right to supervise, control and direct such person's services ["other special employees"]) by reason of any injury, illness, disability or death of Artist which falls within the purview of applicable Workers' Compensation statutes and which arises out of and in the course of Artist's services under the Agreement will be limited to the rights or remedies provided under such Workers' Compensation statutes; (b) that Producer, its officers, agents and employees will have no obligation or liability to Lender or Artist by reason of any such injury, illness, disability or death; (c) that neither Lender nor Artist, nor any of Artist's heirs, executors, administrators, licensees, successors or assigns will assert any claim by reason of any such injury, illness, disability or death against any other corporation or entity which furnishes to Producer services of any other special employee; and (d) that to the extent required by law, Lender has and, at all times during the term of Artist's engagement and services hereunder, shall maintain workers' compensation insurance covering Artist . Lender and Artist hereby agree to defend, indemnify and hold Producer and any person or entity claiming under or through Producer, harmless from and against all claims, demands, liabilities, losses, costs (including reasonable attorneys' fees) and expenses (other than any claims, demands, etc. under applicable Workers' Compensation statutes) arising in connection with any such injury, illness, disability or death. Lender, Artist and Producer hereby make any election necessary to render Workers' Compensation statutes applicable to Lender's engagement to furnish the services of Artist hereunder.

Screen Actors Guild, Inc. Minimum Freelance Contract Continuous Employment - Weekly Basis - Weekly Salary - One (1) Week Minimum Employment

THIS AGREEMENT, made this ______________ (date), between __________________ (Production Company), hereinafter called "Producer," and ____________________ (Name of Actor), hereinafter called "Performer."

1. **Photoplay, Role, Salary and Guarantee.** Producer hereby engages Performer to render services as such in the role of ________________, in a photoplay, the working title of which is now __________________, at the salary of $_____________ ($_____________ per week). Performer accepts such engagement upon the terms herein specified. Producer guarantees that it will furnish performer not less than __________ weeks of employment. (If this blank is not filled in, the guarantee shall be one (1) week.)

2. **Term.** The term of employment hereunder shall begin on _______________, on or about ______________1, and shall continue thereafter until the completion of the photography and recordation of said role.

3. **Basic Contract.** All provisions of the collective bargaining agreement between Screen Actors Guild, Inc. and Producer, relating to theatrical motion pictures, which are applicable to the employment of Performer hereunder, shall be deemed incorporated herein.

4. **Performer's Address.** All notices which the Producer is required or may desire to give to Performer may be given either by mailing the same addressed to Performer at _________________ or such notice may be given to Performer personally, either orally or in writing.

5. **Performer's Telephone.** Performer must keep the Producer's casting office or the assistant director of said photoplay advised as to where Performer may be reached by telephone without unreasonable delay. The current telephone number of Performer is __________________.

6. **Furnishing of Wardrobe.** Performer agrees to furnish all modern wardrobe and wearing apparel reasonably necessary for the portrayal of said role; it being agreed, however, that should so-called character or period costumes be required, Producer shall supply the same.

7. **Arbitration of Disputes.** Should any dispute or controversy arise between the parties hereto with reference to this contract or the employment herein provided for, such dispute or controversy shall be settled and determined by conciliation and arbitration in accordance with the conciliation and arbitration provisions of the collective bargaining agreement between Producer and Screen Actors Guild, Inc. relating to theatrical

motion pictures, and such provisions are hereby referred to and by such reference incorporated herein and made a part of this agreement with the same effect as though the same were set forth herein in detail.

8. Next Starting Date. The starting date of performer's next engagement is ______________.

9. Performer may not waive any provision of this contract without the written consent of Screen Actors Guild, Inc.

10. Producer makes the material representation that either it is presently a signatory to the Screen Actors Guild collective bargaining agreement covering the employment contracted for herein or that the above referred to photoplay is covered by such collective bargaining agreement under Section 24 of the General Provisions of the Producer-Screen Actors Guild Codified Basic Agreement of 1998.

IN WITNESS WHEREOF, the parties have executed this agreement on the day and year first above written.

(Production Company)

("Producer")

____

By________________________________
Authorized Signatory

____________________________ **("Performer")**

Date of Birth (if minor) ________________

Rider to Screen Actors Guild, Inc. Minimum Freelance Contract

dated ______________________________, 200_, between ________________ ("Producer") and ________________________________ ("Performer"), with regards to the production now entitled "____________________" ("Picture").

1. (If applicable) Provided Performer is not in breach hereunder and appears recognizably in the Picture and subject to the policies of the initial domestic broadcaster and to any applicable guild or union agreements, Producer agrees to accord Performer credit on positive prints of the Picture substantially as follows: (Credit Provisions).
All other aspects of any such credit shall be determined by Producer in its sole discretion. Any casual or inadvertent failure and any failure of persons other than Producer or because of exigencies of time, to comply with the provisions of this paragraph shall not constitute a breach of this agreement.

2. Producer shall have the exclusive right to use and to license the use of Performer's name, sobriquet, photograph, likeness, voice, signature and/or caricature (collectively, "name and likeness") and shall have the right to simulate Performer's name and likeness by any means in and in connection with the Picture and the advertising, publicizing, exploitation and exhibition thereof in any manner and by any means.

3. The results and proceeds of Performer's services hereunder shall constitute a work made for hire (it being acknowledged that the results and proceeds of Performer's services are specially ordered and commissioned for use as part of an audiovisual work), and Producer shall be the sole and exclusive owner and author thereof. Producer shall have the right, but not the obligation, to use, adapt, change, alter, delete from, add to or rearrange such results and proceeds or any part thereof, to combine the same with other works and to use, distribute, exploit and advertise any and all of the foregoing in any manner in any and all media, whether now known or hereafter devised; it being agreed that Performer hereby waives all so-called moral rights. Without limiting the generality of the foregoing, Performer hereby assigns to Producer and authorizes Producer to exploit in its sole discretion in perpetuity throughout the universe, all rights (including all rights of copyright) in and to the results and proceeds of Performer's services hereunder.

4. Nothing herein shall be deemed to obligate Producer to use Performer's services or the results of such services, in the Picture or to produce, release or distribute the Picture or to continue the release and distribution of the Picture if released or to otherwise exploit any rights granted to Producer hereunder. Producer shall have fully discharged Producer's obligations hereunder by payment to Performer of any compensation guaranteed in the principal agreement.

5. Performer shall report, if and when required by Producer, for wardrobe fittings, hairdressing, make-up, publicity interviews, publicity photographs, story conferences, song conferences, production conferences, making of stills, retakes, looping, added scenes, trailers, transparencies, process shots, fixed shots and the like and for changes in and/or

foreign versions of the Picture, and Performer shall be paid therefor only if and to the minimum extent required by applicable collective bargaining agreements (it being agreed that the compensation provided in the principal agreement is in full consideration of all such services).

6. To the extent permitted by any applicable collective bargaining agreement, the compensation provided in the principal agreement is in full consideration of all of Performer's services (including, without limitation, travel days, any services performed at night, on Saturdays, Sundays or holidays or in excess of any particular number of hours in any work week, and unworked holidays shall not count as work days for the purpose of calculating any guaranteed period of work). Performer's services in principal photography shall commence upon the Start Date and shall continue thereafter until completion of all services required of Performer hereunder (the "Exclusive Period"). Performer's services hereunder shall be exclusive during the Exclusive Period.

7. Producer may assign its rights hereunder in whole or in part to any person or entity. This agreement shall inure to the benefit of Producer and its successors and assigns.

8. If Performer shall commit a felony or fail, refuse or neglect or threaten to refuse to render services or fulfill Performer's obligations with respect to the Picture for any reason whatsoever, including, but not limited to, default, sickness, disability, unavoidable accident or death of Performer, Producer shall have the right to suspend this agreement while such event continues and/or to terminate this agreement. If the preparation or production of the Picture is materially hampered, interrupted or prevented due to inclement weather, an act of God, war, riot, civil commotion, fire, casualty, strike, labor dispute, act of any federal, state or local authority, death, disability or default of any member of the cast or any principal member of the crew or for any other reason beyond Producer's reasonable control, Producer shall have the right to suspend this agreement while such event continues and/or to terminate this agreement. Producer's election to suspend this agreement shall not affect Producer's right thereafter to terminate this agreement. If Producer suspends this agreement, Performer's services and the accrual of compensation hereunder and the running of any periods herein provided for, shall likewise be suspended. If Producer elects to terminate this agreement, the compensation, if any, theretofore accrued to Performer hereunder, when paid, shall be deemed payment in full of all compensation payable to Performer, and thereafter Performer and Producer shall be released and discharged from any and all further obligations which each may have to the other hereunder.

9. Producer may secure any type of insurance covering Performer, insuring Producer or its designees. Performer will assist Producer in procuring such insurance by submitting to examinations and by filling out applications. If Producer is unable to procure cast insurance covering Performer at normal rates and without special exclusions, Producer may terminate Performer's services hereunder and be relieved of any further obligation to Performer hereunder.

10. If there is any inconsistency between this agreement and the terms of any applicable collective bargaining agreements, then the terms of such collective bargaining agreements shall control, this agreement shall be deemed modified to the minimum extent necessary to resolve the conflict, and this agreement, as thus modified, shall remain in full force and effect. Producer shall be entitled to the maximum benefits permitted to Producer under any such collective bargaining agreements for the minimum payments required, except as may be otherwise specifically provided in this agreement. To the maximum extent that any such collective bargaining agreement requires compensation to Performer in addition to the amounts provided for herein, Producer agrees to pay and Performer agrees to accept the minimum additional scale compensation so required. To the maximum extent permitted under any such collective bargaining agreement, the amounts payable to Performer hereunder shall be considered an advance against and prepayment of any and all amounts payable under such agreement and vice versa.

11. Performer will not furnish or authorize any advertising matter or publicity of any form relating to the Picture, Performer's services in connection therewith, Producer or its operations or personnel or any exhibitors of the Picture to any person or entity other than Producer and its respective agents and employees, without the prior written approval of Producer in each case.

12. A waiver by either party of any of the terms and conditions of this agreement in any one instance shall not be deemed or construed to be a waiver of such terms or conditions for the future or of any subsequent breach thereof. Producer's remedies and rights contained in this agreement shall be cumulative and the exercise of any remedy or right shall not be in limitation of any other remedy or right. Performer agrees that if Producer breaches this agreement, the damage, if any, caused Performer thereby will not be irreparable or otherwise sufficient to entitle Performer to injunctive or other equitable relief. Performer agrees that no breach by Producer shall entitle Performer to rescind this agreement, to restrain Producer's exercise of any rights hereunder, to enjoin Producer's use of the results and proceeds of Performer's services hereunder or to restrain the exhibition or exploitation of the Picture or any elements thereof; in the event of any breach hereof by Producer, Performer's sole remedy shall be an action for damages.

13. Performer warrants and represents that Performer will not pay or agree to pay any money, service or other valuable consideration, as defined in the Federal Communications Act, for the inclusion of any matter in the Program and that Performer has not accepted and will not accept or agree to accept any money, service or other valuable consideration (other than payment to Performer hereunder) for the inclusion of any matter in the Program. Performer will, during or after the completion of services hereunder, complete standard Federal Communications Act report forms, promptly upon request.

14. This agreement contains the entire understanding of the parties hereto relating to the subject matter herein contained, and all prior agreements between the parties have been, by this reference, merged herein. No representations or warranties have been

made other than those expressly provided for herein. This agreement may not be altered, modified, changed, rescinded or terminated in any way except by an instrument in writing signed by the parties hereto. This agreement shall be governed by and construed in accordance with California law as if this agreement were executed and performed fully in California, regardless of where execution and performance hereunder may actually occur, and the parties hereto hereby submit to the exclusive jurisdiction of the courts located in Los Angeles, California.

15. Performer represents and warrants that Performer is free to enter into this agreement and is not subject to any obligation or disability which will or might prevent Performer from keeping and performing all of the conditions, obligations, covenants and agreements to be kept or performed hereunder; that Performer has not made and will not make any agreement or commitment, which could or might be inconsistent or conflicting with this agreement and has not done and will not do any act or thing, which could or might impair the value of or interfere with Producer's enjoyment of the rights granted and the services to be rendered by Performer hereunder; that Producer shall at all times have first call upon Performer's services during the term hereof; and that Performer is and will remain throughout the term hereof a member in good standing of any and all guilds and unions (including Screen Actors Guild) governing Performer's services hereunder. Performer agrees to indemnify any broadcaster or distributor of the Picture and Producer, its successors and assigns and their shareholders, directors, agents, officers, employees, licensees, successors and assigns of each of the foregoing and each of them from and against any and all liability, loss, damage, cost and expense, including reasonable attorneys' fees, which Producer or any of the foregoing may suffer by reason of the use of any materials or services furnished by Performer hereunder, any acts or words spoken by Performer in connection with the production, rehearsal, exhibition or other use of the Picture and/or the rights granted by Performer hereunder (unless such acts or words have been expressly requested or supplied by Producer) and/or any claim, demand, action or holding inconsistent with any representation, warranty or agreement made by Performer in this agreement.

ACCEPTED: ACCEPTED:

(Name of Production Company)

("Producer")

By ____________________________ ____________________________

Authorized Signatory ("Performer")

Day Player Agreement

Performer May Not Waive Any Provision of This Contract Without the Written Consent of Screen Actors Guild, Inc.

SCREEN ACTORS GUILD
DAILY CONTRACT
(DAY PERFORMER)

For Theatrical Motion Pictures

Company ______________________ Date ________________________

Date Employment Starts ___________ Performer Name _____________

Production Title __________________ Address ____________________

Guaranteed Number of Days _________

Production Number ________________ Telephone (___) ____________

Role ____________________________ Social Security No. ___-___-___

Daily Rate $_______________________ Legal Resident of ________ (state)

Weekly Conversion Rate $____________ Citizen of U.S.? ____ Yes ____ No

COMPLETE FOR "DROP AND PICK-UP" DEALS ONLY: Firm recall date on __________________ or on or after ____________________ (i.e., date specified or within 24 hours thereafter). ("On or after" recall only applies to pick-up as Weekly Performer.)

As ______ Day Performer______ Weekly Performer

The employment is subject to all of the provisions and conditions applicable to the employment of Performer contained or provided for in the Screen Actors Guild Codified Basic Agreement (the "SAG Agreement") as the same may be supplemented and/or amended.

Performer _____ does _____ does not hereby authorize Producer to deduct from the compensation hereinabove specified an amount equal to ___________ percent (___%) of each installment of compensation due to Performer hereunder and to pay the amount so deducted to the Motion Picture and Television Relief Fund of America, Inc.

Special Provisions: The attached Rider is incorporated herein.

PRODUCER: PERFORMER:

____________________________ ____________________________

By ____________________________

Its ____________________________

Production time reports are available on the set at the end of each day. Such reports shall be signed or initialed by Performer.

Attached hereto for Performer's use is Declaration Regarding Income Tax Withholding.

NOTICE TO PERFORMER: IT IS IMPORTANT THAT YOU RETAIN A COPY OF THIS AGREEMENT FOR YOUR PERMANENT RECORDS.

Rider to Screen Actors Guild Daily Contract (Day Player)

dated ________________, 20__, between ______________________ ("Producer") and ________________________ ("Performer") with regard to the motion picture currently entitled "_______________________" (the "Picture").

1. (If applicable) Provided Performer is not in breach hereunder and appears recognizably in the Picture and subject to the policies of the initial domestic distributor and to any applicable guild or union agreements, Producer agrees to accord Performer credit on positive prints of the Picture substantially as follows:

____.

All other aspects of any such credit shall be determined by Producer in its sole discretion. Any casual or inadvertent failure, and any failure of persons other than Producer or because of exigencies of time, to comply with the provisions of this paragraph shall not constitute a breach of this Agreement.

2. Producer shall have the exclusive right to use and to license the use of Performer's name, sobriquet, photograph, likeness, voice, signature, and/or caricature (collectively, "name and likeness") and shall have the right to simulate Performer's name and likeness by any means in and in connection with the Picture and the advertising, publicizing, exploitation, and exhibition thereof in any manner and by any means.

3. The results and proceeds of Performer's services hereunder shall constitute a "work-made-for-hire" (it being acknowledged that the results and proceeds of Performer's services were created within the scope of Performer's employment hereunder), and Producer shall be the sole and exclusive owner and author thereof. Producer shall have the right, but not the obligation, to use, adapt, change, alter, delete from, augment, or rearrange such results and proceeds, or any part thereof, to combine the same with other works, and to use, distribute, exploit, and advertise any and all of the foregoing in any manner in any and all media, whether now known or hereafter devised; it being agreed that Performer hereby waives all so-called moral rights. Without limiting the generality of the foregoing, Performer hereby assigns to Producer and authorizes Producer to exploit in its sole discretion in perpetuity throughout the universe, all rights (including all rights of copyright) in and to the results and proceeds of Performer's services hereunder. To the extent that the laws of the European Union and its member countries provide for rental, lending, or similar rights, Performer hereby irrevocably transfers and assigns to Producer all such rights throughout the universe and confirms that five percent (5%) of the compensation payable to Performer hereunder is allocated as equitable remuneration for such rights.

4. Nothing herein shall be deemed to obligate Producer to use Performer's services, or the results of such services, in the Picture, or to produce, release, or distribute the Picture or to continue the release and distribution of the Picture if released, or to otherwise exploit any rights granted to Producer hereunder. Producer shall have fully dis-

charged Producer's obligations hereunder by payment to Performer of any compensation guaranteed in this Agreement.

5. Performer shall report, if and when required by Producer, for wardrobe fittings, hairdressing, make-up, publicity interviews, publicity photographs, story conferences, song conferences, production conferences, making of stills, retakes, looping, added scenes, trailers, transparencies, process shots, fixed shots, and the like, and for changes in and/or foreign versions of the Picture, and Performer shall be paid therefor only if and to the minimum extent required by applicable collective bargaining agreements (it being agreed that the compensation provided in this Agreement is in full consideration of all such services).

6. To the extent permitted by any applicable collective bargaining agreement, the compensation provided in this Agreement is in full consideration of all of Performer's services (including, without limitation, travel days, any services performed at night, on Saturdays, Sundays or holidays, or in excess of any particular number of hours in any work week, and unworked holidays shall not count as work days for the purpose of calculating any guaranteed period of work). Performer's services in principal photography shall commence upon the Start Date and shall continue thereafter until completion of all services required of Performer hereunder (the "Exclusive Period"). Performer's services hereunder shall be exclusive during the Exclusive Period.

7. Producer may assign its rights hereunder in whole or in part to any person or entity. This Agreement shall inure to the benefit of Producer and its successors and assigns.

8. If Performer shall commit a felony or fail, refuse, neglect, or threaten to refuse to render services or fulfill Performer's obligations with respect to the Picture for any reason whatsoever, including, but not limited to, default, sickness, disability, unavoidable accident, or death of Performer, Producer shall have the right to suspend this Agreement while such event continues and/or to terminate this Agreement. If the preparation or production of the Picture is materially hampered, interrupted or prevented due to inclement weather, an act of God, war, riot, civil commotion, fire, casualty, strike, labor dispute, act of any federal, state or local authority, death, disability, or default of any member of the cast or any principal member of the crew, or for any other reason beyond Producer's reasonable control, Producer shall have the right to suspend this Agreement while such event continues and/or to terminate this Agreement. Producer's election to suspend this Agreement shall not affect Producer's right thereafter to terminate this Agreement. If Producer suspends this Agreement, Performer's services and the accrual of compensation hereunder, and the running of any periods herein provided for, shall likewise be suspended. If Producer elects to terminate this Agreement, the compensation, if any, theretofore accrued to Performer hereunder, when paid, shall be deemed payment in full of all compensation payable to Performer, and thereafter Performer and Producer shall be released and discharged from any and all further obligations which each may have to the other hereunder.

9. Producer may secure any type of insurance covering Performer, insuring Producer or its designees. Performer will assist Producer in procuring such insurance by submitting to examinations and by filling out applications. If Producer is unable to procure cast insurance covering Performer at normal rates and without special exclusions, Producer may terminate Performer's services hereunder and be relieved of any further obligation to Performer hereunder.

10. If there is any inconsistency between this Agreement and the terms of any applicable collective bargaining agreements, then the terms of such collective bargaining agreements shall control, this Agreement shall be deemed modified to the minimum extent necessary to resolve the conflict, and this Agreement, as thus modified, shall remain in full force and effect. Producer shall be entitled to the maximum benefits permitted to Producer under any such collective bargaining agreements for the minimum payments required, except as may be otherwise specifically provided in this Agreement. To the maximum extent that any such collective bargaining agreement requires compensation to Performer in addition to the amounts provided for herein, Producer agrees to pay and Performer agrees to accept the minimum additional scale compensation so required. To the maximum extent permitted under any such collective bargaining agreement, the amounts payable to Performer hereunder shall be considered an advance against and pre-payment of any and all amounts payable under such agreement, and vice versa.

11. Performer may not waive any provision of the SAG Agreement without the written consent of the Screen Actors Guild, Inc. ("SAG").

12. Performer will not furnish or authorize any advertising matter or publicity of any form relating to the Picture, Performer's services in connection therewith, Producer or its operations or personnel, or any exhibitors of the Picture to any person or entity other than Producer and its respective agents and employees without the prior written approval of Producer in each case.

13. A waiver by either party of any of the terms and conditions of this Agreement in any one instance shall not be deemed or construed to be a waiver of such terms or conditions for the future, or of any subsequent breach thereof. Producer's remedies and rights contained in this Agreement shall be cumulative, and the exercise of any remedy or right shall not be in limitation of any other remedy or right. Performer agrees that if Producer breaches this Agreement, the damage, if any, caused Performer thereby will not be irreparable or otherwise sufficient to entitle Performer to injunctive or other equitable relief. Performer agrees that no breach by Producer shall entitle Performer to rescind this Agreement, to restrain Producer's exercise of any rights hereunder, to enjoin Producer's use of the results and proceeds of Performer's services hereunder, or to restrain the exhibition or exploitation of the Picture or any elements thereof; in the event of any breach hereof by Producer, Performer's sole remedy shall be an action for damages.

14. This Agreement contains the entire understanding of the parties hereto relating to the subject matter herein contained, and all prior agreements between the parties have been, by this reference, merged herein. No representations or warranties have been made other than those expressly provided for herein. This Agreement may not be altered, modified, changed, rescinded, or terminated in any way except by an instrument in writing signed by the parties hereto. This Agreement shall be governed by and construed in accordance with California law as if this Agreement were executed and performed fully in California, regardless of where execution and performance hereunder may actually occur, and the parties hereto hereby submit to the exclusive jurisdiction of the courts located in Los Angeles, California.

15. Performer represents and warrants that Performer is free to enter into this Agreement and is not subject to any obligation or disability which will or might prevent Performer from keeping and performing all of the conditions, obligations, covenants, and agreements to be kept or performed hereunder; that Performer has not made, and will not make, any agreement or commitment which could or might be inconsistent or conflicting with this Agreement and has not done, and will not do, any act or thing which could or might impair the value of, or interfere with Producer's enjoyment of, the rights granted and the services to be rendered by Performer hereunder; that Producer shall at all times have first call upon Performer's services during the term hereof; and that Performer is and will remain throughout the term hereof a member in good standing of any and all guilds and unions (including SAG) governing Performer's services hereunder. Performer agrees to indemnify any broadcaster or distributor of the Picture, and Producer, its successors, and assigns and their shareholders, directors, agents, officers, employees, licensees, successors, and assigns of each of the foregoing, and each of them, from and against any and all liability, loss, damage, cost, and expense, including reasonable attorneys' fees, which Producer or any of the foregoing may suffer by reason of the use of any materials or services furnished by Performer hereunder, any acts or words spoken by Performer in connection with the production, rehearsal, exhibition, or other use of the Picture and/or the rights granted by Performer hereunder (unless such acts or words have been expressly requested or supplied by Producer) and/or any claim, demand, action, or holding inconsistent with any representation, warranty, or agreement made by Performer in this Agreement.

AGREED AND ACCEPTED:

____

("Performer")

AGREED AND ACCEPTED:

____

("Producer")

By ________________________

Its ________________________

PRODUCER DEALS AND OTHER PRODUCTION AGREEMENTS

There are several types of producers: producers, executive producers, coproducers, and others. There is a Producers Guild of America (PGA) that has, until recently, tried to impose some standards on who is entitled to producer credit, but until recently it has had little impact and inconsistency abounds. However, the PGA and the studios are doing their best to limit producer credits, and the Academy of Motion Picture Arts and Sciences has limited the Best Picture Oscar to two producers. However, the effort, for now, has not impacted the independent world to any measureable degree. In trying to understand producer deals, it is worthwhile to discuss functions first and then talk about the labels.

Every picture has to have a boss or team of bosses who make the key decisions. This boss may need to clear decisions with the financiers or the director or star, but he or she is the key decision maker. In the feature film world, these people normally get credit as "producer" and in recognition of their contribution, the Motion Picture Academy only allows producers on stage to accept the Oscar for best picture. In the television world, these people normally get credit as "executive producers" and producer is regarded as a more lowly credit. Typically, in the feature film world the producer is not only the maker of the film, but also the originator—the person who found the book or script, shepherded the project through development and found the cast. Sometimes, these originator and moviemaker functions are split and the picture has an originator or "creative producer" and a movie-making or "line producer." Where this happens, the line producer reports to the creative producer in normal situations. Most large studio pictures divide these functions, although it is common for both the creative producer and line producer to receive credit as producer.

On some pictures, the director or star has an individual who works closely with them on all their projects. Sometimes, these people are partnered in a company with the creative talent or they may be the personal manager. Quite often, these individuals also receive credit as producer. With independently financed pictures, the financiers may also get producer credit. As you can see, it is easy to have three or more producers and still have other important people involved in the production. That is where credits like executive producer, coexecutive producer, etc., come in handy, and they are doled out as necessary.

In terms of prestige in the feature world, executive producer credit ranks second to producer credit. Coexecutive producer takes the third spot. Typically, all of these credits appear in the main titles. Coproducer credit is considered fourth rank and often runs in the end credits. Associate producer is end rank and usually appears in the end titles.

There are no laws that limit you to this list of labels. "Supreme Producer" and "Big Cheese" are fine, if you can bear the embarrassment. About the only restraint on your creativity, if this is where you elect to exercise it, is the Directors Guild's claim to exclusive say over the use of any credit involving the word "director."

This discussion about functions and their relationship to credits is important to understand some of the key deal points in agreements with producers of any ilk. A fundamental issue is the time commitment the producer must make to the picture. Entertainment deals usually put that commitment at one of three levels.

The highest level is "exclusive services," which means that the person is expected to be rendering full-time, in-person services on the picture and not trying to do anything else at the same time. Line producers are exclusive during prep and photography. "First priority" means the person can do whatever else they want, but if the picture needs them, they must be immediately available. This is the appropriate level of commitment for a creative producer.

The third level of commitment is nonexclusive. That means that the individual will not be required on location and their involvement is largely passive. This level of service is appropriate for someone who, for example, optioned a book and took it to a big-time creative producer. They will make a deal for a fee if the movie is made and will want a credit, which could range from executive producer to coproducer, but their services will not be essential during production.

It is important to understand the function in order to have the right level of services and also the right compensation for producers. Producer fees are freely negotiable and can range from a few thousand dollars to over one million, but anyone will want and deserve more money if they render exclusive services than if they do not have to commit that level of time. Generally, producer fees are a flat amount for the entire picture and payments are spread over prep, production, and postproduction. Occasionally, they are computed on a weekly basis so if the production takes longer than anticipated, the fee increases.

Producer deal points are: function, credit, and level of services. Cover those and work out travel and perquisite terms and you have made your producer deal.

The producer form at the end of this chapter is readily adaptable to deals for all varieties of producers, as well as for some other production staff.

Other Production Personnel Deals

Budgets on films are traditionally broken down into the "above-the-line" elements and "below-the-line." In terms of personnel, the writer, director, cast, and producers are above-the-line elements. Everyone else on the picture is below-the-line. This encompasses people like the editor, composer, and director of photography, as well as everyone in the lighting, sound, camera, and transportation departments. Despite the wide range of responsibilities, the deals for production personnel all share the same issues: you must specify the services, set the pay, address credit, and fix travel and per diem costs.

There are a few other issues that you should consider. The first is the guaranteed term of employment. Your shoot may be scheduled for four weeks, but you may want the flexibility to replace the sound staff, or someone else midway without being obligated to pay for the whole shoot. You must be very clear with your production staff on this point. Are they hired "at-will," which means they can be replaced at any point, "week-to-week," which guarantees them pay for the balance of the week if they are fired midweek, or "run of the show," which guarantees them payment for the entire picture?

There are several unions, most significantly IATSE and the Teamsters that represent many production staff workers. If you utilize members of these unions, you will be required to sign a collective bargaining agreement that will govern many aspects of the employment and also residuals.

Finally, some categories of film crews normally utilize their own tools and equipment when they work on a shoot. For these employees, you will also pay a weekly "box rental" to cover the use of their equipment. The form crew agreement at the end of this chapter is appropriate for staff such as the lighting and camera departments. The form producer agreement discussed earlier can be adapted to cover the editor, director of photography, and similar positions.

Working With Animals

Animals are not members of SAG, although we have a lawyer friend who once tried to negotiate residuals for an orangutan he represented. In the absence of an animal union, the American Humane Association (AHA) is very active in working with film producers to ensure the proper care and use of animals on sets and in productions. They have very comprehensive guidelines, which you can obtain from the American Humane Association, 15366 Dickens Street, Sherman Oaks, CA 91403. Their toll-free number is (888) 301-3541 and their fax is (818) 501-8725. The e-mail address is info@ahafilm.org and the Web site is *www.ahafilm.org.* There is no charge for the American Humane Association's services.

Producers are not legally required to follow the AHA guidelines, but there are three factors that influence producers to use the guidelines and fully cooperate with the AHA. First, there is a Federal Animal Welfare Act, which requires exhibitors of animals to have appropriate U.S. Department of Agriculture permits. Professional movie industry animal trainers have these permits, and they are very protective of their animals' welfare. Often animal trainers insist that producers who use their animals fully adhere to the American Humane Association guidelines.

The second reason is that the Producer/Screen Actors Guild Codified Basic Agreement contains a section on the humane treatment of animals. It does not require that producers fully follow the AHA guidelines, but it does say that, "producers should cooperate with the Hollywood office of the American Humane Association. Producers believe it is important for this liaison to continue in the interest of assuring responsible, decent, and humane treatment of animals." Producers are obligated under this section to notify the American Humane Association prior to the commencement of any work involving an animal and advise it of the nature of the work to be performed. They also must make script scenes involving animals available to the AHA and allow representatives of the AHA to be present at any time during the filming when animals are used. These provisions will apply if your company uses professional actors and is a signatory to the SAG Agreement.

The third reason for fully adhering to the AHA guidelines is to be able to use their official "end credit disclaimer," which goes on screen and states, "no animals were harmed...."

The AHA guidelines are very specific and very strict. They require that a veterinarian knowledgeable in the species of animal be available in case of any emergency. You must provide that veterinarian's name, address, and telephone number to the AHA. Also, a veterinarian must be present at all times during the rehearsal and filming of scenes in which stunts or special effects create a risk of injury to animals (e.g., racing scenes, stampedes, etc.).

The guidelines limit the use of sedatives and other drugs and specific handling techniques. They allow the animal handler to remove all personnel from the set during animal stunts or whenever wild animals are performing. An AHA representative and the animal handler must inspect the set and working areas prior to each day's filming to identify hazards or environmental conditions that could injure an animal. There are also specific sets of regulations for use of dogs, cats, birds, horses and livestock, fish, and insects. For example, a fish may not be out of water for longer than 30 seconds without prior approval from the AHA. Fish must be rotated so that no fish is used more than one time in a row and no fish can be used more than three times in one day. Section 805.3 in the guidelines implores producers to make sure that when bugs are used, they collect them all after they've been used in filming.

Producer Agreement

(Date) __________

(Name of Artist)
(Artist's Address)

Re: **(Production Company)/ ("Picture")/(Artist)/(Capacity, e.g., Coproducer)**

Dear ____________________ **(Artist):**

This agreement is made and entered into as of the date written above, by and between ___________ ("Producer") and __________ ("Artist") concerning Artist's services in connection with the project presently known as ___________ (the "Picture"). The parties hereto agree as follows:

1. **Employment.** Provided Artist is available when and where reasonably required by Producer, Producer shall engage Artist as ____________ (capacity) for the Picture, and Artist accepts such employment, upon the terms and conditions herein contained.

2. **Term.** Artist's services hereunder shall be nonexclusive during development and first priority during production, provided, however, that any services which Artist may render for third parties or on Artist's own account during nonexclusive periods shall not materially interfere with the timely performance of Artist's services and obligations hereunder.

3. **Compensation.** As full and complete consideration for all of the undertakings and services of Artist and all rights and materials herein purchased, granted and agreed to be granted and upon the condition Artist shall fully and faithfully complete all services that may be required hereunder and provided that Artist is not in breach or default hereof, Producer agrees to pay to Artist, and Artist agrees to accept, the following:

3.1 A development fee of __________________ ("Development Fee"), payable promptly following execution hereof. Said Development Fee shall be fully applicable against the Production Fee as defined below.

3.2 Provided the Picture is produced, a fee of ______________ ("Production Fee") (less the Development Fee), payable promptly following the completion of principal photography of the Picture.

3.3 Producer shall have the unlimited right to rerun the Picture on television, make foreign telecasts thereof and release the Picture theatrically and in any and all supplemental markets anywhere in the world and otherwise exploit the Picture in all media throughout the universe, and, in the event Producer exercises any such rights, Artist shall receive no additional compensation therefor, except as expressly set forth herein.

3.4 Nothing herein shall be deemed to obligate Producer to use Artist's services, or the results of such services in the Picture, to produce, release or distribute the

Picture or to continue the release and distribution of the Picture if released or to otherwise exploit any rights granted to Producer hereunder. Producer shall have fully discharged Producer's obligations hereunder by payment to Artist of the Compensation set forth herein.

4. **Credit.** In the event that the Picture is produced by Producer and provided Artist performs all of Artist's services hereunder and on the condition that Artist is not in breach or default hereof and subject to customary approvals of the studio, network and/or other similar parties, Producer shall accord Artist screen credit on positive prints of the Picture in substantially the form ___________ (credit). All other matters relating to credit shall be determined by Producer in its sole and exclusive discretion and subject to the standards and operating policies and practices as established and determined by the network, studio or similar party. No inadvertent or casual failure by Producer or any failure by a third party to accord the credit provided herein shall be deemed a breach of this Agreement.

5. **Travel.** If Producer requires Artist to render services on the Picture more than one hundred (100) miles away from Artist's principal residence (a "Distant Location"), Producer shall furnish Artist with round-trip transportation and, while Artist is at such Distant Location at Producer's request, reasonable hotel accommodations and ground transportation to be negotiated in good faith with Producer's customary parameters for comparable engagements.

6. **Miscellaneous.** The balance of this agreement shall be Producer's Terms Of Personal Services Engagement (TOPSE 1.0), a copy of which are attached, subject to those changes, if any, mutually agreed in writing by the parties. This letter shall constitute a binding agreement between the parties, shall supersede any prior or contemporaneous agreements and may not be waived or amended, except by a written instrument signed by the parties hereto.

Very truly yours,

____

AGREED AND ACCEPTED:

____

(Name of Artist)

Social Security No. _______________

Date of Execution: _______________

(Production Company)

By: ___________________________

Its: ___________________________

Terms of Personal Services Engagement (TOPSE 1.0)

1. General. These Terms of Personal Services Engagement (1.0) ("TOPSE 1.0") are incorporated into the principal agreement to which they are attached ("Agreement"). The individual rendering personal services pursuant to the Agreement is referred to herein as "Artist." If Artist's services are furnished by a corporation loaning services that corporation is referred to herein as "Lender." The entity engaging Artist's services under the Agreement either directly or through Lender is referred to herein as "Producer," and the television motion picture or pictures in connection with which Artist is engaged is referred to herein as the "Picture." In the event of express inconsistency between the Agreement and TOPSE 1.0, the Agreement shall prevail.

2. Services. Artist shall render all services required hereunder at such place or places as required by Producer from time to time during the term thereof. Artist shall render all services under the supervision, direction and control of Producer, in a diligent and conscientious manner, and to the best of Artist's ability, and comply with all of Producer's instructions, directions, requests, rules and regulations (including those relating to matters of artistic taste and judgment). Except as otherwise expressly provided to the contrary in the Agreement, Artist shall render Artist's services exclusively and solely for Producer during the entire term hereof. Artist agrees, if and when requested by Producer, to report to all development, preproduction, principal photography and postproduction activities, publicity interviews, publicity photography, story conferences, song conferences, production conferences, making of stills and the like and for changes in and/or foreign versions of the Picture and for no additional compensation therefor. If any such services would conflict with any of Artist's existing professional commitments, then Artist shall give Producer timely notice of same, in which case Artist shall cooperate to the fullest extent with Producer in becoming available to render such services.

3. Services Unique. Artist acknowledges that rights granted to Producer and Artist's services hereunder are of a special, unique, unusual, extraordinary and intellectual character giving them peculiar value, the loss of which cannot be reasonably or adequately compensated in damages and that a breach by Artist may cause Producer irreparable injury and damage. Accordingly, without limiting or waiving any other rights or remedies of Producer, Producer shall be entitled to seek injunctive or other equitable relief to prevent such breach and to prevent Artist from performing services for himself, or any person other than Producer.

4. Results and Proceeds. Producer shall own, in perpetuity, throughout the universe, all right, title and interest in and to the Picture, the elements thereof and the results and proceeds of Artist's services hereunder and all materials produced thereby or furnished by Artist, of any kind and nature whatsoever, to the maximum extent permitted by any applicable guild or union agreement and free and clear of any and all claims for royalties and other compensation except as specifically set forth in the Agreement. Artist acknowledges that any and all results and proceeds of Artist's services hereunder shall be a work made for hire for Producer, specially commissioned for use as part of a motion picture or other audiovisual work. Producer shall have the right to adapt, change, revise, delete from, add to or rearrange the Picture, or any part thereof and Artist waives throughout the universe the benefit of any law, doctrine or principle known as "droit moral" or moral rights of authors or any similar law, doctrine or principle however denominated, to the maximum extent permitted in each applicable jurisdiction. Producer shall own the Picture produced hereunder and all rights whatsoever therein, including, but not limited to, all copyrights, throughout the world and in perpetuity and in all elements thereof and shall have the right to sell, lease, license and otherwise exploit such rights and elements, as Producer may determine in its sole discretion. Artist's grant includes all rights regarding the renting, lending, fixing, reproducing and other exploitation of the Picture conferred under any applicable laws, directions or regulations, including without limitation, those of the European Union ("EU").

5. **Representations and Warranties; Insurance; FCC; Indemnity.** Artist hereby represents, warrants and agrees as follows:

(a) Artist is free to enter into the Agreement and is not subject to any obligation or disability which will or might prevent Artist from keeping and performing all of the conditions, obligations, covenants and agreements to be kept or performed hereunder; and Artist has not made and will not make any agreement, commitment, grant or assignment, nor do any act or thing which might interfere or impair the complete enjoyment of the rights granted and the services to be rendered to Producer.

(b) All ideas, creations and literary, musical and artistic materials and intellectual properties ("materials") furnished by Artist hereunder, shall be wholly original with Artist except materials in the public domain and that neither the materials nor the use thereof will infringe upon or violate any right of privacy of or constitute a libel, slander or any unfair competition against or infringe upon or violate the copyright, common law rights, literary, dramatic, photoplay, right of publicity or any other rights of any third party.

(c) If and only if expressly required by Producer in connection with the services to be performed by Artist hereunder, Artist will become, at Artist's sole cost and expense and will remain throughout the term hereof, a member in good standing of the properly designated labor organization or organizations (as defined and determined under applicable law) representing persons performing services of the type and character that are to be performed by Artist hereunder.

(d) Artist represents that Artist is aware that it is a criminal offense under the Federal Communications Act of 1934, as amended ("Communications Act"), for any person, in connection with the production or preparation of any television Picture to accept or pay money, service or other valuable consideration for the inclusion of any plug, reference or product identification or other matter as a part of such Picture unless such acceptance or payment is disclosed in the manner required by law. Artist further understands that it is Producer's policy not to knowingly permit the acceptance or payment of any such consideration and that any such acceptance or payment will be cause of immediate dismissal, it being Producer's intention that the Picture shall be capable of being broadcast without the necessity of any disclosure or announcement which would otherwise be required by Section 317 or Section 507 of the Communications Act. Artist represents, warrants and agrees that Artist has not paid or accepted and will not pay or accept any money, service or other valuable consideration for the inclusion of any plug, reference or product identification or any other matter in the Picture and that Artist has no knowledge of any information relating to the Picture which is required to be disclosed by Artist under Section 507 of the Communications Act. Artist further agrees that Artist will promptly deliver to Producer, upon request, such affidavits and/or statements as Producer may require with respect to said Section 507.

(e) Artist shall indemnify and hold Producer, any licensee or distributor of the Picture, any station or network telecasting the Picture, each sponsor and its advertising agency, and the shareholders, directors, officers, agents, employees, successors, licensees and assigns of any of the foregoing, harmless from and against any and all liability, loss, damage, costs, charges, claims, actions, causes of action, recoveries, judgments, penalties and expenses, including attorneys' fees, which they or any of them may suffer by reason of the services rendered or the use of any materials furnished by Artist hereunder, or any breach of any representation, warranty, or agreement made by Artist in the Agreement.

(f) Artist shall be added as an additional insured on Producer's errors and omissions and general liability insurance policies, if any, subject to the terms and restrictions of such policies. Producer may secure any type of insurance covering Artist, insuring Producer or its designees. Artist will assist Producer prior to principal photography in procuring such insurance by submitting to customary examinations (with Artist to have the right to have Artist's physician present at such exams) and by filling out required applications. If Producer is unable to procure such insurance covering Artist at normal rates and without special exclusions, Producer may terminate Artist's services hereunder and be relieved of any further obligation to Artist hereunder. From the date three (3) weeks before the scheduled start of principal photography until completion of all services required of Artist hereunder, Artist will not ride in any aircraft, other than as a passenger on a scheduled flight of a United States or major international air carrier maintaining regularly published schedules or engage in any extrahazardous activity without Producer's prior written consent in each case.

(g) Producer and Lender acknowledge and agree that the following sums are in consideration of and constitute equitable remuneration for, the rental right included in the rights herein granted: (i) an agreed allocation to the rental right of 3.8% of the fixed compensation and, if applicable, 3.8% of the contingent compensation provided for in this agreement; and (ii) any sums payable to Lender with respect to the rental right under any applicable collective bargaining or other industry-wide agreement; and (iii) the residuals payable to Lender under any such collective bargaining or industry-wide agreement with respect to home video exploitation which are reasonably attributable to sale of home video devices for rental purposes in the territories or jurisdictions where the rental right is recognized. If under the applicable law of any territory or jurisdiction, any additional or different form of compensation is required to satisfy the requirement of equitable remuneration, then it is agreed that the grant to Producer of the rental right shall nevertheless be fully effective, and Producer shall pay Lender such compensation or, if necessary, the parties shall in good faith negotiate the amount and nature thereof in accordance with applicable law. Since Producer has paid or agreed to pay Artist equitable remuneration for the rental right, Artist hereby assigns to Producer, except to the extent specifically reserved to Artist under any applicable collective bargaining or other industry-wide agreement, all compensation for the rental right payable or which may become payable to Lender or Artist on account or in the nature of a tax or levy, through a collecting society or otherwise. Artist shall cooperate fully with Producer in the collection and payment to Producer of such compensation. Further, since under this agreement Producer has paid or agreed to pay Artist full consideration for all services rendered and rights granted by Artist hereunder, Artist hereby assigns to Producer, except to the extent specifically reserved to Artist under any applicable collective bargaining or other industry-wide agreement, all other compensation payable or which may become payable to Artist on account or in the nature of a tax or levy, through a collecting society or otherwise, under the applicable law of any territory or jurisdiction, including by way of illustration only, so-called blank tape and similar levies. Artist shall cooperate fully with Producer in connection with the collection and payment to Producer of all such compensation.

6. Producer's Controls. As between Artist and Producer, Producer shall have full and exclusive budgetary, financial creative and business control over the Picture. Artist shall not at any time without Producer's prior written approval had and obtained in each case (whether before, during or after the term hereof), make any public statements, release or authorize any information, advertising or publicity relating to the engagement hereunder, the Picture, or Producer or Producer's personnel or operations, provided Artist can make incidental nonderogatory references in personal publicity.

7. Name and Likeness. Producer shall have the perpetual right and may grant to others the right, to disseminate, display, reproduce, use, print, publish and make any other uses of Artist's name, sobriquet, voice, signature and/or likeness (whether or not taken from the Picture) and biographical material concerning Artist as news or information matter in connection with advertising, publicizing and exploiting the Picture, Artist's services hereunder, including but not limited to, the right to use and authorize others to use the same in the credits of the Picture, in trailers, in commercial tie-ups and in all other forms and media of advertising and publicity and in connection with novelizations and other publications and in connection with the advertising and/or merchandising of any product, commodity or service or series; provided that Artist shall not be represented as endorsing any products or services without Artist's prior consent. Producer contemplates filming and exploiting films, including, without limitation, "behind-the-scenes" or "making-of" productions (jointly and severally, "Promotional

Rights") about the development and production of the Picture. Artist hereby agrees to participate in and consents to such filming and exploitation (including, without limitation, use of any film clip footage from such Picture and behind-the-scenes photography and filmed interviews with Artist (but excluding any depiction of Artist in the nude without Artist's approval) and hereby grants to Producer, in perpetuity and throughout the universe, the right to use Artist's name, voice and likeness in connection with such Promotional Rights for no additional consideration, inasmuch as the compensation payable to Artist under this Agreement for the Picture shall be deemed to include compensation for all rights granted pursuant to this paragraph.

8. Producer's Breach. Notwithstanding any contrary provision hereof or the operation of law, the Agreement shall not be terminated because of a breach by Producer of any of the terms, provisions or conditions contained herein unless and until Artist has given Producer written notice of any such breach and Producer has not within a period of ten (10) business days after receipt of such notice from Artist cured such breach. Artist's rights and remedies in any event whatsoever shall be strictly limited, if otherwise available, to the recovery of damages in an action at law, and in no event shall Artist be entitled to rescind this Agreement, revoke any of the rights herein granted or enjoin or restrain the production, broadcast, distribution or exhibition of the Picture or any other motion picture, remake, sequel, television Picture or derivative production based thereon.

9. No Obligation to Use. Producer shall have no obligation to produce, release, broadcast or otherwise exploit the Picture or to use Artist's services or the rights granted hereunder in connection therewith or otherwise, and Producer shall be deemed to have fully satisfied its obligations by paying to Artist the fixed compensation due Artist pursuant to the terms of the Agreement.

10. Credit. Except as expressly provided to the contrary in the Agreement, Producer shall determine, in its sole discretion, the manner, form, size, style, nature and placement of any credit given to Artist, subject only to the provisions of applicable guild or union agreements. No inadvertent failure of Producer to comply with the provisions hereof with respect to credit, no failure, error or omission in giving credit due to acts of third persons nor the omission of credit where the exigencies of time make the giving of credit impracticable, shall constitute a breach of the Agreement. In the event of a breach of this paragraph, Artist's remedies, if any, shall be limited to the right to recover damages in an action at law and in no event shall Artist be entitled to terminate or rescind the Agreement, revoke any of the rights herein granted or to enjoin or restrain the distribution or exhibition of the Picture.

11. Notices; Payments. All notices, accountings and payments ("notices") which either Producer or Artist shall be required to give hereunder shall be in writing and shall be served by United States mail to the address specified in the Agreement or by facsimile or by personal delivery or at such other address which either party may hereafter give by written notice. Service of any notice, statement or other paper upon either party shall be deemed complete if and when the same is personally delivered to such party, upon receipt by such party of a facsimile (with facsimile confirmation) or upon its deposit in the continental United States in the United States mail, postage or prepaid registered or certified mail, return receipt requested and addressed, as the case may be, to the party which is the recipient at its address in the Agreement.

12. Suspension; Termination. If Artist fails, refuses or is unable for any reason whatsoever to render any of Artist's services hereunder, or if Producer's development and/or production of the Picture hereunder is interrupted or materially interfered with by reason of any governmental law, ordinance, order or regulation or by reason of fire, flood, earthquake, labor dispute, lockout, strike, accident, act of God or public enemy or by reason of any other cause, thing or occurrence of the same or any other nature not within Producer's control ("Force Majeure"), Producer shall have the right (i) to terminate the Agreement (whether or not Producer has theretofore suspended the Agreement as hereinafter provided) and Producer shall have no further obligation to Artist hereunder (except to pay accrued but unpaid compensation in the event of Force Majeure), or (ii) at Producer's option, to suspend the Agreement for a period equal to the duration of any such failure, refusal, or inability or the occurrence of any events of Force Majeure, and no compensation shall be paid or become due to Artist hereunder for such period. No suspension shall relieve Artist of Artist's obligation to render services hereunder when and as required by Producer under the terms hereof, except during the continuance of a disability of Artist. Unless the Agreement shall have been previously terminated as provided herein above, any such suspension shall end promptly after the cause of such suspension ceases, and all time periods and dates hereunder shall be extended by a period equal to the period of such suspension.

13.

(a) **Waiver.** No waiver by either party hereto of any failure by the other party to keep or perform any covenant or condition of the Agreement shall be deemed to be a waiver of any preceding or succeeding breach of the same or any other covenant or condition. Neither the expiration nor any other termination of the Agreement shall affect the ownership by Producer of the results and proceeds of the services rendered by Artist hereunder or any warranty or undertaking on the part of Artist in connection therewith. The remedies herein provided shall be deemed cumulative and the exercise of any one shall not preclude the exercise of or be deemed a waiver of any other remedy, nor shall the specification of any remedy hereunder exclude or be deemed a waiver of any rights or remedies at law or in equity, which may be available to Producer, including any rights to damages or injunctive relief. All rights granted to Producer are irrevocable and without right of rescission by Artist or reversion to Artist under any circumstances whatsoever, and Artist's rights and remedies shall be limited to the recovery of damages. Artist shall not have the right to enjoin or restrain the production, distribution, exhibition or other exploitation and the elements thereof of the Picture.

(b) **Assignment.** Producer shall have the right to assign all or any part of its rights under the Agreement to any person, but no such assignment shall relieve Producer of its obligations hereunder unless the assignment is to a major or minimajor, a network, a Lender acquiring substantially all the assets of Producer, a parent of Producer or a financially responsible party who assumes Producer's obligations in writing. Artist shall not have the right to assign the Agreement or any of Artist's rights hereunder. This agreement will be binding upon and inure to the benefit of Producer's respective licensees, successors and assigns. No additional compensation whatsoever shall accrue or be payable to Artist including without limitation to the generality of the foregoing, for any services rendered at night, on Sundays or holidays or after the expiration of any number of hours of services in any period.

(c) **Jurisdiction.** The laws of the State of California applicable to agreements executed and to be wholly performed within the State of California shall apply to the Agreement. The parties agree and consent to the jurisdiction of the courts of the State of California and agree to venue in courts located in Los Angeles County, California. In the event there shall be any conflict between any provision of the Agreement and any applicable law or applicable guild or union agreement, the latter shall prevail, and the provision or provisions of the Agreement shall be modified only to the extent necessary to remove such conflict, and as so modified, the Agreement shall continue in full force and effect.

(d) **Guild/Union.** Producer shall have the right to the maximum extent permissible under such applicable guild or union agreements, to apply all compensation paid to Artist on account of Artist's services under the Agreement as a credit against any and all amounts which may be required under such collective bargaining agreements to be paid to Artist for Artist's services, the results and proceeds thereof, the rights granted by Artist hereunder and the exercise thereof and for any other reasons whatsoever. If, pursuant to such collective bargaining agreements, Artist is entitled to any payment in addition to or greater than those set forth herein, then any such additional or greater payment made by Producer shall, except to the extent expressly prohibited by such collective bargaining agreements, be considered as an advance against and deducted from any such sum which may subsequently become payable to Artist hereunder. If, in determining the payments to be made hereunder, there is required any allocation of the compensation paid to Artist as between Artist's various services, Artist agrees to be bound by such allocation as may be made by Producer in good faith.

(e) **Withholdings.** Producer may deduct and withhold from the compensation payable to Artist hereunder any union dues and assessments to the extent permitted by law and any amounts required to be deducted and withheld under the provisions of any statute, regulation, ordinance, order and any and all amendments thereto heretofore or hereafter enacted requiring the withholding or deduction of compensation. If, pursuant to Artist's request or authorization, Producer shall make any payments or incur any charges for Artist's account, Producer shall have the right to deduct from any compensation payable to Artist hereunder any charges so paid or incurred, but such right of deduction shall not be deemed to limit or exclude any other rights of credit or recovery or any other remedies that Producer may have. Nothing herein above set forth shall be deemed to obligate Producer to make any such payments or incur any such charges.

(f) Directed Withholdings. If Producer is directed, by virtue of service of any garnishment, levy, execution or judicial order, to apply any amounts payable hereunder to any person, firm, corporation or other entity or judicial or governmental officer, Producer shall have the right to pay any such amounts in accordance with such directions, and Producer's obligations to Artist shall be discharged to the extent of such payments. If because of conflicting claims to amounts payable hereunder, Producer becomes a party to any judicial proceeding affecting payment or ownership of such amounts, Artist shall reimburse Producer for all costs, including attorneys' fees, incurred in connection therewith.

(g) Entire Agreement. These terms of Personal Services Engagement (TOPSE 1.0) and the principal agreement to which they are attached constitutes the entire Agreement between the parties, supercedes all prior agreements and understandings, whether written or oral, pertaining thereto and cannot be modified except by a written instrument signed by Artist and an authorized officer of Producer. No officer, employee or representative of Producer has any authority to make any representation or promise in connection with the Agreement or the subject matter hereof which is not contained herein, and Artist agrees that Artist has not executed the Agreement in reliance upon any such representation or promise.

(h) Lender's Obligations, Representations and Warranties, and Dissolution. If the Agreement is entered between Producer and a corporation ("Lender") which furnishes the services of Artist, Lender represents and warrants that it is duly organized and presently in good standing in its state of incorporation; has a valid agreement with Artist under which Lender has the right to enter the agreement and grant Producer any and all of the services and rights granted hereunder and make all of the representations, warranties and agreements made by Artist. Producer shall pay Lender all compensation that would have been payable to Artist hereunder if Producer had directly employed Artist and Producer shall not be obligated to make any payments whatsoever to Artist. Artist's services shall be rendered as Lender's employee and Lender agrees to fully perform all such obligations and indemnifies Producer from all claims, liabilities and expense (including, without limitation, attorneys' fees) for or in connection with withholding and/or payment of any sums required to be paid by an employer to any governmental authority or pursuant to any guild or union health, welfare or pension plan or on account of any other so-called fringe benefits or workers' compensation premiums. Artist represents and warrants that Artist is familiar with the terms hereof and agrees to be bound by same and agrees to look solely to Lender for all compensation or other consideration in connection with the rights granted and services to be rendered hereunder. If Lender or Lender's successors in interest should be dissolved or otherwise cease to exist or for any reason whatsoever fail, be unable, neglect or refuse to perform, observe or comply with any or all of the terms and conditions of the Agreement, Artist may, at Producer's election, be deemed a direct party to the Agreement until completion of the services required of Artist thereunder, upon the terms and conditions set forth therein. In the event of a breach or a threatened breach of this Agreement or the Agreement by Lender and/or Artist, Producer shall be entitled to seek legal, equitable and other relief against Lender and/or Artist, in Producer's sole discretion. Producer shall have all rights and remedies against Artist that Producer would have if Artist were a direct party to the Agreement. Producer shall not be required to resort first to or exhaust any rights or remedies Producer has against Lender before exercising Producer's rights and remedies against Artist.

(i) **IRCA.** All of Producer's obligations hereunder are conditioned upon and subject to Artist's delivery to Producer of a completed and certified Employment Eligibility Verification (Form I-9) in compliance with the Immigration Reform and Control Act of 1986.

(j) **Further Documents.** Artist agrees to perform such other further acts and to execute, acknowledge and deliver such other further documents and instruments, including, without limitation, certificates of authorship and certificates of engagement with respect to all material furnished by Artist hereunder, as may be necessary or appropriate to carry out the intent hereof and to evidence Producer's ownership of the results and proceeds of all services rendered pursuant hereto, and Artist hereby appoints Producer as Artist's attorney-in-fact, which appointment is irrevocable and coupled with an interest, with full power of substitution and delegation, to execute any and all such documents which Artist fails to execute within five business days after Producer's request therefor and to do any and all such other acts that Artist fails to do after Producer's request therefor.

14. Worker's Compensation. For the purpose only of determining the applicability of Workers' Compensation statutes to Artist's services under the Agreement if the Agreement is entered between Producer and Lender, an employment relationship exists between Producer and Artist, Producer being Artist's "special employer" and Lender being Artist's "general employer." In this regard, Lender agrees (a) that the rights and remedies of Artist and Artist's heirs, executors, administrators, successors, licensees and assigns against Producer, its officers, agents and employees (including any persons whose services are furnished to Producer by any corporation or other entity under an agreement granting Producer the right to supervise, control and direct such person's services ["other special employees"]) by reason of any injury, illness, disability or death of Artist which falls within the purview of applicable Workers' Compensation statutes and which arises out of and in the course of Artist's services under the Agreement will be limited to the rights or remedies provided under such Workers' Compensation statutes; (b) that Producer, its officers, agents and employees will have no obligation or liability to Lender or Artist by reason of any such injury, illness, disability or death; (c) that neither Lender nor Artist, nor any of Artist's heirs, executors, administrators, licensees, successors or assigns will assert any claim by reason of any such injury, illness, disability or death against any other corporation or entity which furnishes to Producer services of any other special employee; and (d) that to the extent required by law, Lender has and, at all times during the term of Artist's engagement and services hereunder, shall maintain workers' compensation insurance covering Artist . Lender and Artist hereby agree to defend, indemnify and hold Producer and any person or entity claiming under or through Producer, harmless from and against all claims, demands, liabilities, losses, costs (including reasonable attorneys' fees) and expenses (other than any claims, demands, etc. under applicable Workers' Compensation statutes) arising in connection with any such injury, illness, disability or death. Lender, Artist and Producer hereby make any election necessary to render Workers' Compensation statutes applicable to Lender's engagement to furnish the services of Artist hereunder.

Crew Agreement

Date: ________________ Production Company: ____________________

Picture: ______________________

Employee:	Position:
Social Security#	Account:
Address:	Approx Start Date:
	Daily Rate (If applicable)
	Weekly Rate (If applicable)
Phone/Fax #:	Guarantee:
	Overtime:
Lender:	Additional Terms:
Tax ID#	
In case of emergency contact (Include name and phone numbers): ______________________	______________________ ______________________ ______________________

This deal memo and Employee's services are subject to and must provide no less than the minimum terms of the applicable collective bargaining agreement, if any and upon satisfactory proof of applicant's identity and legal ability to work in the United States, as required by the Immigration Reform and Control Act.

1. Rate. If a daily rate is indicated, services are guaranteed for a period of one day. If a weekly rate is indicated, services are guaranteed for a period of one week. There is no other guarantee of the period of services. Hours paid for "Idle" days and "Travel only" days shall be computed per the applicable collective bargaining agreement and not be subject to the hours guaranteed above. Overscale wage rate (if indicated above) shall remain in effect during the entire period of employment even if the minimum rates of the applicable collective bargaining agreement changes; however, that at no time shall the rate paid be less than the minimum rate applicable. Time cards must reflect hours worked, not hours guaranteed and must be turned in at the end of the last day of the production week.

2. Overtime/Premium Pay. No seventh day, holiday or in-town eighth day work will be paid unless authorized in advance by the Unit Production Manager. No overtime prior to company call or after wrap may be worked, nor any forced calls incurred without the UPM's prior approval.

3. Withholding. Withholding taxes will be applied to all amounts paid for per diem, mileage, box or kit rentals or for any nonaccountable expense reimbursements in excess of IRS guidelines.

4. Drugs/Alcohol. Use of alcohol or drugs during working hours shall be cause for immediate dismissal.

5. Purchases/Rentals/Expenses. All purchases and rentals must be accompanied by Producer's purchase order or check request, and only those petty cash expenses accompanied by original receipts will be reimbursed.

6. Box Rental, Recoverable Items. Box or other authorized rental payments will be prorated for any partial week worked. A complete list of items included in rental shall be attached as an addendum to this deal memo. Employee is responsible for all recoverable items purchased and these must be reconciled with Producer's accounting department during wrap. All recoverable items will be collected at wrap.

7. Photos. No personal photography is permitted on or around the set. Employee shall not issue nor permit others to issue information or statements (written or otherwise) concerning the Picture or any person or entity connected therewith.

8. Voice/Likeness. Employee irrevocably grants Producer and its successors and assigns the right to photograph and make motion pictures and sound recordings of Employee's voice and likeness and to reproduce the same in any manner and any medium whatsoever, in perpetuity and throughout the universe, without further compensation.

9. Credit. Subject to applicable collective bargaining agreements and full and complete rendition of Employee's services hereunder, Employee shall receive screen credit in the end titles; all other aspects of Employee's credit shall be at Producer's sole discretion; any casual or inadvertent failure and any failure of persons other than Producer or because of exigencies of time, to comply with the provisions of this paragraph shall not constitute a breach of this agreement. In no event shall Employee be entitled to equitable or injunctive relief.

10. Damages Exclusive Remedy. In the event of a breach by Producer, Employee's sole remedy shall be an action at law for damages. In no event shall Employee be entitled to equitable or injunctive relief.

11 No Obligation. Nothing herein shall be deemed to obligate Producer to use Employee's services or the results of such services, in the Picture or to produce, release or distribute the Production or to continue the release and distribution of the Picture if released or to otherwise exploit any rights granted to Producer hereunder. Producer shall have fully discharged Producer's obligations hereunder by payment of the minimum compensation required hereunder, if any.

12. Default/Disability/Suspension/Termination. If Employee is charged with a felony or fails, refuses or neglects or threatens to refuse to render services or fulfill Employee's obligations with respect to the Picture for any reason whatsoever, including but not limited to, default, sickness, disability, unavoidable accident or death of Employee, Producer shall have the right to suspend this agreement while such event continues and/or to terminate this agreement. If the Picture is materially interrupted due to inclement weather, an act of God, war, riot, civil commotion, fire, casualty, strike, labor dispute, act of any federal, state or local authority, death, disability or default of any member of the cast or any principal crew member or for any other reason beyond Producer's reasonable control, Producer shall have the right to suspend this agreement while such event continues and/or to terminate this agreement. Producer's election to suspend this agreement shall not affect Producer's right thereafter to terminate this agreement. If Producer suspends this agreement, Employee's services and the accrual of compensation shall likewise be suspended. If Producer elects to terminate this agreement, the compensation, if any, accrued to Employee as of the date of termination, when paid, shall be deemed payment in full of all compensation payable to Employee, and thereafter Employee and Producer shall be released and discharged from any and all further obligations which each may have to the other hereunder.

13. Warranties. Employee represents and warrants that Employee is free to enter into this agreement and is not subject to any obligation or disability which will or might prevent Employee from keeping and performing hereunder; Employee will not make any agreement inconsistent with this agreement. Employee's services shall be first call during the term hereof. Each party shall indemnify the other and the directors, agents, officers, employees, licensees, successors and assigns of each of the foregoing and each of them from and against any and all liability, loss, damage, cost and expense, including reasonable outside attorneys' fees, which either may suffer by reason of any claim inconsistent with any representation made by either party in this agreement.

14. Entire Agreement. This agreement contains the entire understanding of the parties and supersedes all prior agreements (whether verbal or written) between the parties. No representations or warranties have been made other than those expressly provided for herein. This agreement may not be altered, modified, changed, rescinded or terminated in any way except by an instrument in writing signed by the parties hereto. This agreement shall be governed by and construed in accordance with California law as if this agreement were executed and performed fully in California, regardless of where execution and performance hereunder may actually occur, and the courts located in Los Angeles, California shall have exclusive jurisdiction of all cases and controversies.

AGREED TO BY EMPLOYEE:

By: ______________________
(Employee's signature)

AGREED TO BY PRODUCER:

By: ______________________
Authorized Signatory

Thank You,
Siskel & Ebert
HOLLYWOOD
Rini

LOCATIONS

Today, virtually all independent pictures and most studio pictures are shot on location. Some photography still takes place on studio lots, but the days are gone when most pictures were shot on large sound stages or on studio lots with their building façades and streets. As an independent producer, you either make your own arrangements for locations or you hire a location scout who specializes in knowing a large number of suitable locations.

Film Permits

Some producers try to shoot guerrilla style; by simply showing up and shooting. For a tiny crew and a few hours of shooting, you may get by, but it is far preferable to make formal arrangements and know that you have the location for the time you need it. These arrangements may involve getting a film permit, and you will need a location agreement.

Los Angeles, New York, and some other cities and states require filmmakers to get filming permits before they can legally shoot on public or private property. The requirements vary and you should contact your state film commission as a first step. It can advise you of requirements and help you to meet them.

We will outline the permit process in Los Angeles so you will have an idea of what requirements you might face elsewhere.

In Los Angeles, a county ordinance mandates a temporary use permit (a filming permit) for all location shooting. The Entertainment Industry Development Corporation (EIDC) was formed to assist production companies by serving as its liason in getting the necessary permit and approvals. Their address is 7083 Hollywood Boulevard, 5th Floor, Hollywood, CA 90028; telephone (323) 957-1000; fax (323) 463-0613. You can print an application from their Web site *(www.eidc.com)*. The application requires information about the production and an EIDC production coordinator can assist you with completing it.

The starting point for getting a permit is providing EIDC with proof of insurance. They require a certificate of liability insurance from an approved carrier that shows a minimum of $1 million in coverage. Both LA County and EIDC must be additional insureds. This is something your insurance broker will handle for you.

As of this writing, there is also a nonrefundable $450 fee to EIDC for processing the application.

If you plan to use Los Angeles County property such as parks, beaches, courthouses, or jails, there are additional location fees.

Also, there are fees for personnel who may be required. For example, if you shoot in a courthouse, county sheriffs are usually assigned. At county beaches, lifeguards are assigned to monitor the production. Depending on the location, cast and crew size, and activities (f/x, helicopter landings, etc.), Los Angeles County Fire Safety Officers may also be assigned.

While this may seem to be a burden of requirements, the process is essentially one stop and EIDC coordinates with other governmental units. Other cities and states have their own requirements. Many are simpler than Los Angeles, which sees high-density shooting. The California Film Commission, for example, offers a one-stop permit for a variety of state facilities: museums, parks, office buildings, etc., and there is no charge for the permit or location. The only cost to the production company is the reimbursement of employment time for park rangers or other state employees who are assigned.

Location Agreements

Location agreements are different from film permits. Permits come from governmental authorities. Location agreements are with the owners of properties where you plan to shoot. The key to location agreements is to understand that they are two agreements wrapped in one document. One component is a lease or rental agreement that is not unlike one used in renting an apartment. It gives you the right to take possession of the property for a fixed term of time for a fee. How you can use the property is limited by the agreement. The second component is the consent to photograph the property and use the photographs in your picture. This aspect is very similar to the rights you get in a prop release or an appearance release form for a bystander that allows you to take his photograph and use it in the picture.

We supply a location release form at the end of this chapter. Some landlords frequently rent their property as a location or are tied to a location finding service and have their own form that they want you to sign. Their form, of course, protects them as its top priority. If you encounter one of these "your form vs. their form" situations and need the location, you can work from the landlord's form, but anticipate that it may need some amending. Compare their form to ours to see what they forgot to put in.

From the filmmaker's point of view, there are several key issues that must be addressed in location arrangements.

1. Dates. Make certain you have access for loading in and for wrapping. Typically, rates are lower for nonshooting days. Try to get an out for bad weather. If you cannot shoot, you do not want to pay and will need the landlord to give you other dates. Generally, the landlord does not want to give rain checks, so you will have to work something out ahead of time.
2. Insurance and Damages. The landlord will want a certificate that proves that you have liability insurance, in case of personal injury at the location. Your insurance broker can provide it if you leave enough lead time. You will be responsible for damage to the property and theft. Film crews make the proverbial bull-in-a-china-shop look dainty. If you use someone's home, you should be prepared for claims of damage. Shooting a video or a roll of "before" pictures can protect you against bogus complaints, but if your crew does some damage, you must repair it or pay for the fix. The location owner may require you to indemnify and hold it harmless against any liabilities arising in connection with your use. You should review those agreements with your insurance broker to make certain your policies cover this.
3. Parking. Determine what you need and arrange for it. Big productions with trucks and lots of crew can choke a neighborhood. You may have to rent parking space and run shuttles. Neighbors can get very cranky over night shoots and even more so if they cannot park near their homes. That leads to them turning up their radios very loud, calling the city, or finding other ways to disrupt the shoot. Diplomacy is crucial.
4. Constructed Sets. Sometimes filmmakers reconstruct part of a location building on a stage. Interiors of houses can get cramped for shooting so exteriors can be shot on location and interiors on a stage. If you reproduce someone's property on a stage, you must make certain the location agreement gives you that right.

   Sometimes the construction occurs on the location and the landowner wants to keep it. We worked on a well-known feature that used a Montana location that overlooked a river. The production built a large, ornamental pavilion that the landowner wanted to keep. The production was happy to leave it, but it had not received any building permits or inspections and was not up to code. The production left it after the landlord signed an acknowledgment and assumed all liabilities. Set construction is not designed for the ages and if you leave construction behind, you have to protect yourself.

5. The Landlord. Make certain that the person you are making the location arrangements with has the authority. For example, someone who leases a warehouse—even on a long-term basis—may not have the right under the lease to grant you the right to shoot there. You may sneak through, but to avoid problems, ask the questions. Our form makes the person who signs represent that they have necessary authority.

Location Agreement

Property Owner: Picture: ______________________

Name: ______________________ Production Company: ______________

Address: ______________________ Address: ______________________

______________________ ______________________

______________________ ______________________

Phone: ______________________ Phone: ______________________

Your signature in the space provided below as owner or agent, will confirm the following agreement ("Agreement") between you as the property owner ("Owner") and the production company identifiable above ("Producer") regarding use of your property (the "Premises") described below in connection with the production of the above referenced motion picture (the "Picture").

1. Rights. Owner hereby grants to Producer the exclusive right during the Term (as defined below) hereof to enter upon and to utilize the Premises described below and to bring onto the Premises such personnel and equipment as Producer deems necessary in connection with the production of the Picture. This Agreement allows the Producer to enter upon the Premises with personnel, materials, vehicles and equipment, erect and construct sets and props, store sets and props, conduct activities upon and photograph and record at the Premises (including, without limitations, to photograph and record both the real and personal property, all of the signs, displays, interiors, exteriors and the like appearing therein, if any) for the period specified below.

2. Premises. As used herein, the term "Premises" refers to the premises located at: ______________________________ including the grounds at said address and all buildings and other structures located thereon, together with access to and egress from said Premises.

3. Term. The term hereof ("the Term") shall commence on or about ______________________ and shall continue until ______________________, unless modified by the parties. Producer personnel may, prior to the commencement of the Term, enter, visit, photograph or otherwise inspect the Premises to plan and set up for production without additional charge at reasonable times and with reasonable notice to Owner. The Term shall be subject to modification due to weather conditions or changes in production schedules. If a force majeure event continues for longer than two days or if the Premises are thereafter deemed uninhabitable, this Agreement shall terminate and the parties shall have no further obligation hereunder other than for payment fees for use prior to the date of the force majeure event.

4. Fee. As compensation for use by Producer of the Premises during the Term, Producer shall pay Owner the following rate ("Fee"):

______________________ Prep days @ $__________________

(Dates: __________________)

______________________ Hold days @ $__________________

(Dates: __________________)

______________________ Shoot days @ $__________________

(Dates: __________________)

______________________ Strike days @ $__________________

(Dates: __________________)

5. Representations and Warranties. Owner represents and warrants that (a) Owner has the right and authority to make and enter into this Agreement and to grant Producer the rights set forth herein; (b) the consent or permission of no other person or entity is necessary; and (c) Owner shall take no action, nor allow or authorize any third party to take any action which might interfere with Producer's authorized use of the Premises. Owner's sole remedy in the event of a dispute hereunder shall be an action at law for damages. Owner shall indemnify Producer for any breach of the representations and warranties of this paragraph.

6. Reentry. If, following the Term, Producer requires additional use of the Premises for retakes or other scenes, subject to Owner's approval, Owner shall permit Producer to reenter and use the Premises at the rate specified in Paragraph 4 above.

7. Election Not In Use. Producer may, at any time, elect not to use the Premises by giving Owner notice of such election, in which case neither party shall have any further obligation hereunder except if such election is within twenty-four (24) hours of commencement of the Term, Producer agrees to pay Owner twenty-five percent (25%) of the total compensation specified in Paragraph 4 above.

8. Condition of Premises After Use. Producer agrees to leave the Premises in substantially the same condition as when received by Producer, excepting reasonable wear and tear. Promptly following the expiration of the Term and, if applicable, promptly upon the completion of any additional use by Producer of the Premises, Producer shall remove from the Premises all structures, equipment and other materials placed thereon by Producer.

9. Producer's Indemnification of Owner. Producer agrees to indemnify and hold Owner harmless from damage to the Premises and property located thereon and for personal injury occurring on the Premises during the Term and from any liability and loss which Owner may incur by reason of any accidents, injuries, death or other damage to the Premises directly caused by Producer's negligence in connection with its use of the Premises. In connection therewith, Owner agrees to submit to Producer in writing, within five (5) days after the expiration of the Term (including any additional use by Producer of the Premises) a detailed listing of all claimed property damage or personal injuries, if any, arising out of or resulting from such use, and Owner shall permit Producer's representatives to inspect the property so damaged. Owner hereby waives, on behalf of Owner and Owner's insurance carrier, all rights of subrogation on any claim(s) arising under any and all insurance policies in effect during the Term of this Agreement insuring any of Owner's property on the Premises.

10. No Obligations. Nothing shall obligate Producer to photograph, to use such photography or to otherwise use the Premises. Producer shall have the right to photograph, record and depict the Premises and/or any part or parts thereof, accurately or otherwise, as Producer may choose, using and/or reproducing the actual name, signs, logos, trademarks and other identifying features thereof and/or without regard to the actual appearance or name of the Premises or any part or parts thereof, in connection with the Picture and any other Picture produced by Producer hereunder. Producer shall have the right to construct a set duplicating all or any part of the Premises (including, but not limited to, any signs and the interiors of said Premises) for the purpose of completing scheduled work or for filming retakes, added scenes, advertisements or promotions.

11. Producer's Ownership of Photography, Limitations on Owner's Remedies. Owner acknowledges that, as between Owner and Producer, Producer is the copyright owner of the photography and/or recordings of the Premises and that Producer, its successors and assigns the irrevocable and perpetual right, throughout the universe, in any manner and in any media to use and exploit the films, photographs, and recordings made of or on the Premises in such manner and to such extent as Producer desires in its sole discretion without payment of additional compensation to Owner. Producer and its licensees, assigns and successors shall be the sole and exclusive owner of all rights of whatever nature, including all copyrights, in and to all films, Pictures, products (including interactive and multimedia products), photographs and recordings made on or of the Premises and in the advertising and publicity thereof, in perpetuity throughout the universe. Owner hereby acknowledges that neither Owner nor any tenant or other party now or hereafter having an interest in the Premises, has any interest in Producer's photography or recording on or of the Premises nor any right of action, including without limitation, any right to seek injunctive relief against Producer, its successors and/or assignees or any other party arising out of any use of said photography and sound recordings. In the event of breach of this agreement by Producer, your rights and remedies shall be limited to the right, if any, to obtain damages at law and you shall have no right to seek or obtain injunctive or other equitable relief or to rescind or terminate this agreement or any of Producer's rights hereunder.

12. General Terms. Producer may assign or transfer this Agreement or all or any part of its rights hereunder to any person, firm or corporation; Owner agrees that it shall not have the right to assign or transfer this Agreement. This agreement shall be binding upon and inure to the benefit of the parties hereto and their successors, representatives, assigns and licensees. This document sets forth the entire understanding between Producer and Owner and may not be altered except by another written agreement signed by both parties.

APPROVED AND ACCEPTED:

"Owner":

____

NOTE: If an agent signs on Owner's behalf please complete the following:

I, ____________________, warrant and represent that I am the authorized agent and representative of the above named owner of the premises, and I have been expressly authorized by Owner to license Producer to use the Premises and grant to Producer all the rights granted to Producer under this Agreement, and I have, by my signature above, bound Owner to the terms and conditions of this Agreement.

____

Agent for Owner

____

Agent's Address

____

Print Name

____

Agent's Telephone Number

RELEASES

You may find that you use things in your picture that are owned, copyrighted, trademarked, or otherwise protected by other people. Getting permission to use them is the role of the releases we discuss next. Permissions to use copyrighted music are covered in Chapter 13, Music in Film.

Prop Releases

The conservative view is that anything that appears in a film and is protected by copyright must be cleared. That is, you must get a signed release from the owner of the copyright. This owner may be different from the owner of the thing. If you rent a house as a location and there is a poster on the wall, the owner of the house may own that particular copy of the poster but probably does not own the copyright and does not have the authority to give you a release to use the poster in your picture.

If your use of a copyrighted work is fleeting and incidental, you may fall within the "fair use" doctrine and your use may be okay, but the safest course is to get permission. Lest you think we are going overboard, we refer you to a case called *Ringgold v. Black Entertainment, Inc.,* where a court found federal copyright infringement when a poster entitled "Church Picnic Story Quilt" appeared for 26 seconds in the background of a sitcom. Artwork is a chronic problem area. So are book jackets and magazine covers, which are invariably copyrighted. Prop houses can supply or make up fake books, magazines, and household goods that do not need to be cleared.

You must be diligent to prevent something from inadvertently appearing. One of us negotiated a small cash settlement on a legal claim where a jogger in the background of a scene wore a copyrighted T-shirt from a charitable organization. We do not know if a court would have found the film to be a copyright infringement, but the producer did not want the embarrassment of being sued by a charity.

Trademarks that appear in a picture do not have to be cleared, with two exceptions. If your picture is being made for television, complicated FCC rules and network policies sharply limit the appearance of trademarks. The second exception is if the portrayal is disparaging. For example, if the movie contains a running joke about what a lemon a car is, you are inviting trouble from an auto manufacturer. Of course, some manufacturers want to have their logos portrayed and will provide free items and money for product placement. That is discussed in Chapter 5 in the section "Product Placement."

The generic prop release at the end of this chapter can be used for virtually any prop or set dressing you want to use.

Using Clips

Using excerpts or clips from someone else's movie or television program in your picture is a clearance nightmare. It is complicated and expensive because you may have to make multiple deals to clear a single clip, and even when you get permission it is generally of a very qualified kind. Frankly, we discourage you and our clients from using clips. Still, we know there are times when a picture demands it, so we will outline what is involved in clearance.

You need permission from the owner of the copyright in the clip. Often, that is a Hollywood studio or a network. There is a tidy side business in licensing clips and they have staffs that make the arrangements. There are also companies that are in the footage licensing business. If you need a shot of the Eiffel Tower or a roaring lion, they can take care of you. Here are several large stock footage libraries:

STOCK FOOTAGE LIBRARIES

Archive Films
Tel: (800) 876-5115
www.archivefilms.com

Film & Video Stock Shots
Tel: (888) 436-6243
www.stockshots.com

Grinberg Film Libraries
Tel: (213) 464-7491
www.grinberg.com

Paramount Stock Footage Library
Tel: (323) 956-5510

Twentieth Century Fox Film Library
Tel: (310) 369-2763

Clip footage is usually priced per minute of running time and you have to bear the costs of duplication.

Sometimes, the process is not so simple. Some pictures have been sold to different distributors for different territories. Since you want your picture to be able to be seen throughout the world, you must make certain the copyright owner you deal with controls the clip licensing rights throughout the world, or you may have to deal with several distributors.

Getting permission from the owner of the worldwide rights in the clip is step one. If the clip has music in it, background or source, you will have to get a synchronization and public performance license from the music publisher for the music. If the music came from an album, you probably will need a master license from the record company and permission from the musical act. There may also be payments required to be made to the American Federation of Musicians (AFM). If you are trying to save money and if you must use the clip, try to avoid the use of any music. If the actors in the clip were members of SAG or another union, you will need written consents from every actor in the clip and must make certain payments to them and their pension fund. There are also payments to the WGA writer, the DGA director, and fringe payments to their guilds.

If the clip is from a nonguild production, like news footage (without the announcers who are probably guild members) or an independent production, you do not have to worry about the SAG, DGA, and WGA issues, but you need the consent of the owner of the footage and may need consents from people who appear in the clip. If the people are politicians or other public figures in the news, or if the producer of the footage had them sign broad agreements during the original shooting, you probably can forego them.

Because of the complications in clearing film clips, they are normally excluded from coverage on your errors and omissions insurance policy unless you take specific steps—including getting the releases outlined above—to have them covered.

Crowds and Background Extras

Often, producers who shoot on location find themselves filming crowds or have a stray passersby appear deep in the background when they are shooting. When the person appears only fleetingly and in the background, no signed release is required. The obvious exception is if the shot is disparaging or invades a right of privacy. Showing someone who is appearing to smoke marijuana in a concert crowd could prompt a claim. The classic example is a New York case over a picture in a newspaper that showed a romantic couple strolling arm-in-arm. It did not seem offensive to the photographer, but it was to the couple when their respective spouses saw it in the paper. It never hurts to get a release signed. Take a look at the form included at the end of this chapter.

When you know there will be a crowd, the customary practice is to post audience or crowd signs prominently that indicate filming is taking place. An example of that language appears below.

Crowd Release

(Post outside of entry doors or on perimeter of filming area.)

By entering and by your presence here, you consent to be photographed, filmed and/or otherwise recorded. Your entry constitutes your consent to such photography, filming and/or recording and to any use, in any and all media throughout the universe in perpetuity, of your appearance, voice and name for any purpose whatsoever in connection with the production presently entitled: ______________________
You understand that all photography, filming and/or recording will be done in reliance on this consent given by you by entering this area.
If you do not agree to the foregoing, please do not enter this area.

Prop Release

Name: ______________________	Picture: ______________________
Address: ______________________	Production Company:
______________________	______________________
______________________	Address: ______________________
Phone #: ______________________	______________________
Fax #: ______________________	Phone#: ______________________
	Fax #: ______________________

Your signature in the space provided below will confirm the following agreement ("Agreement") between you ("Owner") and the production company named above ("Company") regarding use of the material described below (the "Material") as set dressing in connection with the production of the above-referenced motion picture (the "Picture").

____

[Description of items to be used]

____

You hereby grant to Company and its licensees and assigns the irrevocable right to use the Material in and in connection with the Picture (and any and all versions thereof) and the distribution and exploitation of the Picture or any part or version thereof in any and all media whether now known or hereafter devised, throughout the universe, in perpetuity.

If the Material appears in the Picture as exhibited, Company shall pay you a one-time license fee of $_________________________ as consideration for all rights granted herein.

You understand that Company is relying on this agreement in the preparation, production and distribution of the Picture. You acknowledge that you have not been induced to sign this release based on any statements or promises not set forth in this release and will not bring or participate in any claim or lawsuit against Company, its licensees, employees, assigns or related parties based upon the use of the Material.

You warrant and represent that you own or control all rights necessary to make the grant of rights made hereunder; that use by the Company will not infringe upon or violate the right of any person or entity and that Company will not be required to make any additional payments by reason of its use of the Material. You warrant that you have the full right to enter into this agreement and that no other party's consent to the use of the Material is required. You agree to indemnify and hold Company harmless from and against all claims, damages, liability and expense arising out of any breach of any warranty or agreement made by you hereunder.

Notwithstanding anything to the contrary contained herein, Company has no obligation to use the Material or any part thereof.

APPROVED AND ACCEPTED:

____

("Company")

By ________________________________

By ________________________________

("Owner") Authorized Signatory

Print Name: ___________________________

Date: ________________________________

MUSIC IN FILM

Film is simultaneously a visual and aural medium. The combination of visual and aural gives the medium a power that exceeds images or sound alone.

Rock and roll changed music in film markedly. Prior to Bill Haley's *Rock Around the Clock*, virtually all film scores were written and conducted by classically trained composers who were influenced by the great European composers of the 17th through 19th centuries. These composers used large orchestras that provided rich multilayered sounds. During the height of the studio era in the '30s and '40s, each major studio had its own orchestra.

Things are different now—film music is driven by pop influences and technological changes, especially the use of digital synthesizers. More and more filmmakers who seek to emulate the mood of a particular period now license the use of songs and recordings (witness *Forrest Gump*). And composers who used to have to use an 80-piece orchestra can emulate that sound at low cost with the use of digital synthesizers in their home studios.

How important is music in film? In terms of its relative weight in the budget, music averages 2% to 5% of the budget at major studios and rarely exceeds 5%. Since the average budget is $50 million, the music costs for a studio feature frequently exceed $1 million. However, if the music is done well, it can have an incredible effect on the film's impact on viewers. If you doubt this, look at a DVD and mute the music. The film becomes emasculated.

Music can have a direct and immediate impact on your ability to sell your film. We were involved in a film entitled *The Spitfire Grill*, a touching film with no stars and a rather tragic ending. After the film was completed, the producers realized the score did not have the impact they wanted. They screened the film for James Horner (before he won an Oscar for "My Heart Will Go On" from Titanic), who agreed to rescore the film. *Spitfire*, with Horner's music, was subsequently screened at the Sundance Film Festival, became the object of a bidding war for distribution rights, and reportedly sold for twice its cost.

At the same time, our experience is also that the contribution of music to a film can be exaggerated and can be the subject of much hype. When a project is submitted to us during development and the emphasis is the music (unless it is a music-based project, such as *Evita*), oftentimes the producers are trying to put a music Band-Aid on a story sore—and the sore is usually beyond healing. Just because Sting wants to do the score for your film does not make it a project that is capable of raising financing.

Licensed Music

One great feature of music is that it is very malleable. It can be put in and taken out during postproduction with relative ease. It loses its malleability, however, if it is vital to the action or story line or if the performance of the song is shot live. But you must be careful. Music must be "cleared" in order for you to use it in a film. There is no such thing as fair use of music in a film—you cannot drop in two seconds of a song and claim under copyright law that the use is so insignificant that you do not need permission from the copyright owner.

The bottom line is that the music must be cleared in order for you to distribute your movie. It makes no sense to spend millions of dollars on developing, shooting, and editing a movie and then be stuck with a useless property because the music is not cleared. You should also realize that unless the music is cleared up front you will lose all your negotiating leverage and could be held up for exorbitant fees. You should also realize that among the legal weapons in the arsenal of music owners is the injunction, whereby a court can prohibit your distribution of the film—and if you violate the order you can go to jail!

Let us say you want to use the Beatles song "Hey Jude" in your movie. Whose permission do you need? First of all, you must understand a few basics of copyright. A recording embodies two separate copyrights—the copyright in the song—what the copyright law calls a "musical work"—and the copyright in the recording—what the copyright law calls a "sound recording." If you use a recording, you must clear both the musical work and sound recording. In some cases, you also need permission from the recording artist or songwriter. Finally, if the recording was done under the jurisdiction of a music union (which is quite common), you may be contractually obligated to clear the use with the recording artist and have to pay what are called "reuse" or "new use" fees, which equal the original session fees. This can become very expensive when you reuse an orchestral piece.

We strongly recommend that you use a music clearance company to sort all this out.

When you use a preexisting song or recording, you acquire what is called a "license" (permission) to use the song or recording. You do not buy the copyright in the song or recording. Generally, the license is nonexclusive—that is, the owner of the song can license it for use in other movies.

MUSIC CLEARANCE COMPANIES

Jill Meyers Music Consultants
1551 Ocean Avenue, #260
Santa Monica, CA 90401
Tel: (310) 576-1387
Fax: (310) 576-6989

Copyright Clearninghouse
405 Riverside Drive
Burbank, CA 91506
Tel: (818) 558-3480
Fax: (818) 558-3474

Arlene Fishbach Enterprises
430 California Avenue, #14
Santa Monica, CA 90403
Tel: (310) 451-5916
Fax: (310) 393-5313

Fricon Entertainment
1048 S. Ogden Drive
Los Angeles, CA 90019
Tel: (323) 931-7323
Fax: (323) 938-2030

Evan M. Greenspan
11846 Ventura Blvd., #140
Studio City, CA 91604
Tel: (818) 762-9656
Fax: (818) 762-2624

The Winogradsky Company
11240 Magnolia Blvd., #104
North Hollywood, CA 91601
Tel: (818) 761-6906
Fax: (818) 761-5719

Composers

Music can be written specifically for a film. There are composers, many classically trained, who score films. Clearance is usually not an issue when you hire a score composer, since it is common for the producer to own the music. Thus, the producer can not only put the music in his own film but can license that music for other uses, such as in a soundtrack album and even in other pictures.

How do you find a composer? Movie studios have music departments that have relationships with the major film music agencies. You can also approach composer agents directly. Generally, the composer is hired during postproduction, not before. Directors are intimately involved in the selection of composers. A composer deal is a hybridized deal that covers creative services, music publishing, and a record deal. The up-front deal points can be negotiated by you or your lawyer, with the composer directly or through his agent or lawyer. Because of the complexity of composer deals, you are usually best served by having your lawyer handle the negotiations.

The fundamental structure of film composing deals has changed radically in the last twenty years, especially in the independent film area. Under the traditional studio model, the composer was paid a creative fee to write and conduct the score, and the studio covered the score costs, including the orchestra. Today, the majority of composer deals, especially in the independent world, are structured as so-called package deals. Package deals mirror the practice in the recording industry, in that the composer's creative fee, like the recording artist's fee, is built into a budget—but rather than an album being recorded, the film score is being recorded. The basic advantage to you as a producer is that you cap your costs, and there are no surprises. This is especially important in postproduction, when there is little, if any, money left.

Whether the deal is structured in a traditional manner or as a package, you must start out by defining the scope of the composer's job. This is usually done in terms of the number of weeks the composer has to write the score, the length of the score, and the scope of the instrumentation (synthesized, acoustic, or orchestral). If you commission an orchestral score, the costs can be prohibitive—if you commission a synthesized score, the cost will be less.

Another fundamental deal point is where the score will be recorded. It is more convenient for the score to be recorded where you are doing postproduction. However, in some cases, producers chose to record the score overseas to take advantage of nonunion status of the musicians and other cheaper attendant costs.

All studio scores are done under the jurisdiction of the American Federation of Musicians (AFM). Technically, the AFM does not have jurisdiction over the basic writing of the score; however, it does have rates for orchestration, which are typically folded into the creative fee. Many independent pictures are done outside AFM jurisdiction. The major reason why producers seek to avoid the AFM is that the AFM also legislates minimum session fees for the musicians who perform, and, like SAG, WGA and DGA, mandates that residuals (additional payments) be paid if the film is exploited in television and in home video, as well as additional payments for the soundtrack album release.

Who owns the score? In the studio model, the studio always owns the score. In the independent world, the range is from the producer owning the score to the composer owning the score and only granting a license for use of it in the film. We worked on a picture that was scored by a prominent composer who typically charged several hundred thousand dollars to do a score. On our film, he only made $20,000, but kept the ownership of the score, its recording, and all royalty income.

When a producer owns the score, the producer owns the music publishing rights to the score. Music publishing is an anachronistic term. The term publishing emanated from sheet music being distributed—thus, the music was published. A more accurate term for music publishing these days is music exploitation, since there are numerous ways music is distributed to the public. Today, the main sources of income for music publishers are public performance, mechanical (record royalties), and synchronization income, not the sale of sheet music.

Music Income

Again, we must turn to the Copyright Act to understand how these sources of income work. One of the exclusive rights that the song owner enjoys is the right to publicly perform the song, i.e., control over whether a song is performed (live or recorded) in a public setting, including on radio, television, concert halls, and yes, even in a Gap Store. Music publishers and composers are represented by so-called public performance societies, which license the public performances. The two most prominent performing rights societies in the United States are ASCAP and BMI, which each have hundreds of millions of songs in their repertoire and generate hundreds of millions of dollars in public performance income per year. Each has both songwriter and music publisher members, and the collected fees are paid to composers and music publishers after deduction of administrative fees.

Because of some antitrust cases, there is no public performance income generated from movie theaters in the United States; however, substantial revenue can be generated overseas from public performance in movie theaters. For a film, public performance revenue is also generated when the picture is exhibited on television (including network and pay) but not on home video. Again, there is a distinction overseas where fees are paid to composers in some countries for the use of their films in home video devices.

Another income source for the song owner is mechanical royalties, which are generated when there are record sales. In the United States, mechanical royalties are calculated on a flat rate per selection; overseas it is typically done on a percentage of the wholesale or retail price. The current (2004) per selection rate in the United States is about 8¢ per song for each album sold.

If a film composer retains the publishing and has ten songs on a soundtrack album, the film composer can look forward to approximately 80¢ per album sold if the full statutory rate applies. If you acquire the publishing from the composer, you would get half or 40¢ per album and the composer would get the other half. However, studios and smart independent producers borrow a convention from the recording industry and typically negotiate for a so-called controlled composition rate, which traditionally is three-quarters of the statutory rate. This reduced rate applies to songs the composer writes or controls. At the current level, this rate is approximately 6¢ per selection, so the mechanical royalties for ten controlled compositions on a soundtrack album would be 60¢ per album.

Music income from the sound recording is different. There are no public performance royalties payable in the United States for use of sound recordings. Income is derived from master license fees, which allow preexisting recordings to be put in a film and from royalties from sales of soundtrack albums. The income from soundtrack albums, as for recording artists, is computed on a royalty basis. The composer's royalty is a percentage of the suggested retail list price of the recording. The current range of the recording royalty for composers is 3% to 6% of retail on the low side and 12% to 14% on the very high side. How does this translate to dollars? It can be very complicated, but when you boil it all down, the major record labels at this time pay approximately 12¢ per CD copy for each 1% of retail. On a 12% of retail deal, the composer would receive approximately $1.44 per album sold. Thus, on a million-selling album, a composer with a 6% of retail deal would receive approximately $600,000 in artist royalties, and a composer at 12% of retail would receive approximately $1,440,000 in royalties.

However, this is the gross royalty, and there are many deductions from it. The first is proration. If there are cuts on the soundtrack album other than those of the composer, the royalties will be reduced. If the composer has only five of ten cuts, then the royalty will be halved. Another deduction is costs that can be recouped by the producer or the record company before the composer royalty is paid. Some deals provide that all recording costs are recouped against the composer's share. Composers with more clout can typically limit the recouped cost to so-called conversion costs, which are the costs of converting the recordings from use in the film to use in the soundtrack album. These costs are always recouped from the composer's first royalties. Under our hypothetical, if the costs recoupable against the composer's royalty are $720,000, even if the album sells a million units, the composer with a 6% royalty will get paid nothing. You, as the producer, however, will be able to recoup these costs and hopefully put them in your pocket.

Other Composer Issues

In addition to financial issues, another major issue is what credit will be granted to the composer and where in the credits it will appear. There are probably more variations of film composers' credits than any other credit. We have seen "Composed By," "Music Composed By," "Music Composed and Orchestrated By," "Music Composed and Recorded By." and other variations, with the most common form being "Music By." Typically, this credit is in the main titles (where the credits are for the other main creative forces, such as the writer, director, producers, and star actors).

Another major issue regarding credit is whether the credit appears in paid ads. All prominent film composers receive paid ad credit. The real issue is in what paid ads must the credit appear. Almost without fail, the credit is included in the billing block portion of paid ads, when all the other main creative elements are listed. In most billing blocks, all the credits are the same size, with the exception of star actors who may have credits bigger than anyone else's or additional credits outside the billing block.

Another hotly contested deal point is whether the composer has to be paid again if his music is used in another film. If the composer owns the score, this is a given. Even when giving up the publisher's share of revenue to the producer, some high-end composers receive a separate and additional creative fee when their score is used in another film. This is the exception, however, and most studios and even independent producers are able to use the music in other films without payment to the composer. A middle ground is to allow the music to be used in sequels and remakes without a fee, but otherwise the composer is paid. In any event, the composer will receive the writer's share of public performance revenue, so there is some money to be made.

As evidenced by our experience on *Spitfire Grill*, scores may be thrown out. What obligations does the producer have to the composer in such event? Almost without fail, by contract, you are allowed to throw the score away and not use it. You in effect pay-or-play the score. Some composers will negotiate a reversion of the rights to the score to the extent it is thrown out. A trickier question is what is done with the composer's credit. The standard at this time is that if more than 50% of the background score is recorded and written by the composer, the composer gets his composer credit, and if there is less, he does not get credit, at least in the main titles. Typically, when there is a relatively modest amount used in the film the composer receives end title credit in the form "Additional Music By." If the composer's recordings are not used in the soundtrack album, no royalties are payable. However, high-end composers sometimes are guaranteed one or two cuts on the soundtrack album.

Theme Music

Enough about composers. What if you want to hire Sting not to do the score but rather to write and perform a pop song to be used over the main title credits? Assuming Sting is interested, there are myriad legal and business issues to contend with.

The first legal issue that must be sorted out when dealing with a recording artist/songwriter is whether he is under any contractual commitments that could preclude you from using his recording and songwriting services. Almost without fail, prominent recording acts/songwriters are signed to major record labels, and many are signed to music publishing deals. In such cases, you must get permission from the record label and the music publisher in order to use the recording artist/songwriter's services. The most adroit way of getting label permission is to promise the soundtrack album to the label. Sting's label would be loath to have his recordings used in a prominent way in a film, and for the soundtrack album to be distributed by a different label. Music publishers often grant permission for use of songwriter's services on a film but almost without fail will insist that a portion of the music publishing (either ownership and/or revenue) not be acquired by the studio or producer. In terms of the mechanics of the negotiation, once the recording artist/songwriter is interested, his representatives will typically "clear" the situation with the recording label and music publisher.

Assuming there is no problem with the label or the music publisher, you then have to negotiate a deal. Typically, these are package deals that range from $25,000 to hundreds of thousands of dollars. The producer wants to acquire as many rights as he can. The record label and the music publisher want the exact opposite—they want to preserve as many rights as they can. At a minimum, the studio or producer will have the right to use the recording in the movie in all media in perpetuity, including in advertisements and maybe even an MTV-type video. As in composer agreements, the recording artist receives a record royalty stated as a percentage of the suggested retail list price and will seek to keep a portion of the publisher's share of music publishing revenue. Another hotly contested area is so-called singles rights. For example, Celine Dion's "My

Heart Must Go On" appeared not only in the soundtrack album for the film Titanic, but also on Celine's solo album.

With respect to ownership of the recordings, we were involved in Stevie Wonder's *The Woman in Red*, which had an Academy Award winning single "I Just Called To Say I Love You." In that deal, Stevie kept the ownership of the recordings and the ownership of the songs. To some studios, especially Disney, this is absolutely anathema. Even when Disney hires recording acts/songwriters of the stature of Elton John and Phil Collins, reportedly Disney still ends up owning half the publishing.

Let us assume that instead of hiring Sting you want to use one of his preexisting recordings. The license to use Sting's recording is called a "master use" or "master recording" license. Typically, this license is granted by the record company that owns the recording. There are two fundamental issues, scope of use and price. The scope of use has to do with how prominently the recording will be used in the film. If it is used in a prominent way, such as in the main titles, you pay more. If you use the entire song, instead of a short snippet, you pay more. Additionally, if you want to use the song prominently in advertising materials, such as the trailer, you pay more. In the license, the grant of rights will be to use the recording in the film and in all media in perpetuity. This contrasts to the television industry, in which master use and synch licenses are for a stated term, such as seven years.

Another tricky area when it comes to master use license is the artist's consent. In many cases, prominent recording artists have the contractual right under their recording agreements to veto the use of their recordings for uses outside of records, such as in films, television productions, or commercials. Even when they do not have this right contractually, record labels often inquire as to whether the artist objects. In some cases, the record label will insist that the studio or producer negotiate separately with the artists in order to get the consent, so you may have to pay an additional fee to the artist. The bottom line is that if the prominent recording artist/songwriter does not want their recording used in a film, it is probably not going to happen.

Let us assume that you have been diligent and have negotiated a license with the record label and have gotten the artist's consent. Is your clearance job done? No. You still must clear publishing rights in the song and for that you must secure a "synchronization and performance" license. "Synchronization" means that you are putting the song in the film in time relation to the action. In addition to the synchronization license, in the United States you must receive a license to publicly perform the song in theaters, since they are not licensed by ASCAP and BMI. The other issues involved in synchronization licenses are identical to those in master use licenses. The price is determined by the scope and prominence of the use. Typically, the price of a synchronization license and master use license are identical. In many cases, this is mandated by so-called favored nations clauses whereby the record label wants to make sure that the music publisher is not paid more and vice versa.

A warning regarding titles—there has been a recent trend of studios and producers to use well-known music titles as the titles of their film. If you are going to use a title of a well-known song as the title of your film and want to use that song in your film, you are going to pay a separate and additional charge for the use of the title. If you want to use a well-known title and are not going to use the song, you need to get an opinion from a copyright lawyer that the use is permitted.

Occasionally, songs are the basis of a movie story. We were involved in a case in which ABC wanted to use the song "Like a Virgin" as the basis of a film, but failed to acquire the rights in writing. If you want to use a song as the basis for your story, that is a separate and additional right that must be cleared.

Music Supervisors

Thirty years ago music supervisors did not exist. This was for two fundamental reasons. First, the number of independent pictures was negligible. Second, virtually all the music decisions were made by the in-house studio music department and the key music decision was basically who to hire as the composer. However, with the emergence of independent films and the emergence of the use of "period" recordings and contemporary music acts, music supervisors became an important cog in the music process.

What do music supervisors do? Their services include music clearance, assisting in negotiating soundtrack albums deals, assisting in the negotiating of performing and writing agreements, assisting in selection of the composer, suggesting outside or source music to be included in the soundtrack of the picture, and perhaps even creating music cue sheets. Music supervisors do not handle formal music licensing agreements, although they customarily send out so-called quote letters for licenses from record companies and music publishers. Often, music supervisors are hired because of their strong connections in the pop music world, a world that film producers rarely visit. In addition to their relationships with music performers, music supervisors have continual relationships with record companies that distribute soundtrack albums, and they can help get acts to perform for the soundtrack and help get a soundtrack album deal.

The amounts paid to music supervisors range from almost nothing to hundreds of thousands of dollars. It is common, however, for the music supervisor to participate in music revenues from the soundtrack album and in some cases, from the publisher's share of music publishing. With respect to participation in soundtrack album revenue, the first issue is whether the music supervisor will participate in the advance. Producers try to resist this whenever possible because often, the entire advance from the record company is used up creating music for the film. However, high-powered music supervisors usually do get a chunk of the advance.

In addition to possible participation in the advance, music supervisors receive a record royalty on the entire album. This royalty can range from .5% to 2%. Often, there are royalty escalations based on the number of sales.

Probably the most important issue with respect to the royalty is whether the producer gets to recoup his recording costs and advance before paying the music supervisor. We recently did a survey of studio practice in this regard and found that virtually all studios try to recoup both the advance and the costs before paying the royalty. However, in some instances, superstar music supervisors negotiate for a royalty that starts at a much earlier point.

With respect to music publishing, the music supervisor can sometimes receive anywhere from 10% to 50% of the publisher's share of music publishing royalties. With respect to credit, music supervisors usually get credit in the main titles of the picture, on the soundtrack album, and sometimes in paid ads and video packaging.

Soundtrack Albums

There are basically two kinds of movie soundtrack album deals. There are those that are released by major labels with major acts, which typically have very wide distribution and substantial exploitation and marketing budgets. At the other end of the spectrum is the release of soundtrack albums by so-called boutique labels, which are typically orchestral, have no exploitation and marketing budgets, and typically sell very few units. However, some of the biggest selling orchestral records of all time are movie soundtrack albums (witness John Williams' *Star Wars*).

The negotiation of most movie soundtrack album deals is very straightforward. The label pays an advance against the royalties payable to the movie production company. The movie company pays royalties to the artist out of its aggregate royalty. Advances can range from nothing to several million dollars when there are substantial pop acts and a major movie. Royalties range from 12% to 20% of the retail price of the album. Assuming that each 1% of royalty is equal to 12¢, the royalty to the movie company can range from $1.44 to $2.44 per album. However, before the royalties are paid, the label will recoup its advance from the aggregate royalty.

One issue in soundtrack deals is the term of the label's right to exploit the album. When labels pay a substantial advance, they insist on perpetuity. If there is no advance, the label's rights might be limited to ten to 20 years. Another issue is territory. A label should only acquire rights in the territories in which it distributes. Most major record albums are distributed on a worldwide basis.

Labels sometimes insist on a commitment from the film's distributor that the picture will be released in a minimum number of theaters for a minimum number of weeks. Movie producers and distributors always resist this. However, it is a certainty that major labels like to deal with major studios that have substantial distribution arms. It is extremely unlikely that a picture without distribution would get a soundtrack album deal, especially one with a substantial royalty.

Synchronization and Performance License

DATE:	PUBLISHER CREDIT FOR CUE SHEET:
LICENSOR:	TYPE & DURATION OF USE:
LICENSEE:	TERRITORY:
PICTURE:	LICENSE FEE:
COMPOSITION:	PUBLISHER'S OWNERSHIP SHARE: 100%
BY:	

1. **Right.** In consideration for the payment of the License Fee promptly following the signing of this agreement, Licensor hereby grants to Licensee, its successors, licensees and assigns the following nonexclusive and irrevocable rights throughout the Territory in perpetuity:

(a) the right to record the Composition in synchronization or timed relation with the Picture and copies thereof in any manner, medium, form or language to make copies of such recordings and to import such recordings and copies into and exploit them in each country of the Territory in accordance with the terms, conditions and limitations contained in this license;

(b) the right to distribute, publicly perform, sell, lease, broadcast, exhibit and otherwise use and exploit all versions and copies of the Picture with the Composition contained therein in any media and by any means now known or hereafter devised (including without limitation in the theatrical, nontheatrical, television [all forms including pay-per-view] and home video media);

(c) the right to utilize the Composition or excerpts therefrom, in or out of the context in which the Composition has been recorded in the Picture, in any media for the purpose of advertising, promoting or publicizing the Picture (including without limitation in trailers, spots and commercials).

2. **Performing Rights.** Licensee agrees that it shall not authorize the performance of the Composition in the Picture in the United States by means of television unless the broadcaster or exhibitor has a valid small performing rights license for the Composition from a performing rights society or from Licensor, unless Licensee has obtained such a license directly from Licensor and with respect to the theatrical or television performance of the Composition in the Picture in any country outside of the United States where small performing rights licenses are required for such use, unless the performance shall have been cleared by the applicable performing rights society in accordance with such society's customary practice and subject to payment to such society of such

society's customary fees for such performance, unless Licensee has otherwise obtained a valid license for such use directly from Licensor.

3. **Reservation of Rights.** This license does not authorize or permit any use of the Composition not expressly set forth herein, all rights not expressly granted herein being reserved to the Licensor.

4. **Warranties and Indemnities.** Licensor warrants and represents that it has the right to grant this license and that the use of the Composition by Licensee as contemplated by this agreement will not violate the rights of any person or entity. Licensor will indemnify and hold Licensee harmless from any and all claims, liabilities, losses, damages and expenses arising from any breach or alleged breach of Licensor's warranties or representations under this license.

5. **Cure/Remedies.** No failure by Licensee to perform any of its obligations hereunder shall be deemed a breach hereof unless Licensor has given written notice of such failure to Licensee does not cure such nonperformance within thirty (30) days after receipt of such notice. In the event of a breach of this agreement by Licensee, Licensor's rights and remedies shall be limited to its right, if any, to recover damages in an action at law and in no event shall Licensor be entitled to injunctive or other equitable relief.

6. **Binding Effect.** This license shall be binding upon and shall inure to the benefit of the parties and their respective successors, licensees and/or assigns.

7. **Applicable Law and Jurisdiction.** This license has been entered into in and shall be interpreted in accordance with the laws of the State of California, and any action or proceeding concerning the interpretation and/or enforcement of this license shall be heard only in the State or Federal Courts situated in Los Angeles. The parties hereby submit themselves to the jurisdiction of such courts for such purpose.

IN WITNESS WHEREOF, the parties have executed the foregoing license as of the day and year set forth above.

LICENSOR: ______________________________

FEDERAL ID #: ______________________________

BY: ______________________________

TITLE: ______________________________

LICENSEE: ______________________________

BY: ______________________________

TITLE: ______________________________

MASTER USE LICENSE

_______________ ["we", "us", "our"]

____

____

Dated as of ____________________

____

c/o

Atten:

Gentlemen:

You ("Producer") are producing a motion picture entitled "________________________" (the "Producer") and have requested our permission to utilize the master recording of the musical composition entitled "_________________" ("_____") (the "Recording") embodying the performance of the artist professionally known as ____________________ (the "Artist"), as provided hereinbelow. The following shall confirm our understanding and agreement regarding the use of the Recording in connection with the Picture:

1.

(a) The "Territory" shall be the world.

(b) The use of the Recording hereunder shall be a featured background source.

(c) The "Term" of this license shall be for the remainder of the current term of the United States copyright in the sound recording (and in the renewal term thereof, if any) to the extent owned or controlled by ____________ [us].

2.

(a) Subject to Producer fulfilling all of the terms and conditions hereof, we hereby grant to Producer the following rights:

(i) the non-exclusive right and license to re-record, reproduce and perform excerpts from the Recording, on (1) time, not to exceed one minute thirty seconds (1:30) in playing time, solely as provided in Paragraph 1(b) above, in the soundtrack of and in timed relation with the Picture for the sole purpose of exhibiting the Picture in motion picture theaters, on aircraft and ships at sea, and by means of broadcasting, exhibiting, distributing and telecasting the Picture on commercial television, and on pay, cable and subscription television systems throughout the Territory.

(ii) the non-exclusive right and license to cause or authorize the reproduction of the Recordings as embodied in the Picture on videocassettes and videodiscs ("Videogram(s)") serving to reproduce the Picture in its entirety. The rights granted pursuant to this subparagraph 2(a)(ii) include the right to manufacture, reproduce, distribute, advertise, sell, lease and license such Videograms throughout the Territory. The term "Videogram" as used herein specifically means an audio-visual device intended primarily for "Home Use" (as such term is commonly understood in the recording industry), but shall specifically exclude audio-visual devices which embody audio-visual material together with audio-only material (e.g., CD/Video), CD Rom and other interactive software.

(iii) the non-exclusive right and license to reproduce or perform any part of the Recording in air, screen and television trailers or television and radio advertisements solely related to the Picture; provided that the Recording is used only in the same context as the Recording appears in the Picture.

(b) Notwithstanding anything to the contrary contained herein:

(i) Any use by Producer of the Recording other than as described in Paragraph 2(a) above without the express prior written authorization of us is prohibited.

(ii) The Recording and all master recordings, duplicates and derivatives thereof, and all copyrights and rights therein and thereto shall remain the sole and exclusive property of us and/or the underlying rights holder, subject to the rights of Producer pursuant to the terms of this agreement.

(iii) This license does not include any right or authority to utilize the Recording in connection with any manufacture or sale of phonograph records, tapes or other types of sound-only reproduction or to use the Recording separately or independently from the Picture or this license.

(c) All rights not specifically set forth herein are expressly reserved by us (including, without limitation, the right to use or reproduce the Recording as embodied in the Picture in so-called "interactive" media or devices now or hereafter known).

3. In consideration of the rights granted herein, Producer shall pay to us a non-returnable, non-recoupable sum in the amount of ______________________ Dollars (U.S.$__________) promptly following the complete execution of this agreement.

4.

(a) Producer warrants, represents and agrees that it will obtain all requisite consents and permissions with respect to its use of the Recording as contemplated hereunder, including, without limitation, the consent and permission of the copyright owner(s) of the musical composition embodied in the Recording and the consent and permission of all applicable unions and guilds. Producer shall be solely responsible for and shall pay, with respect to its use of the Recording as contemplated hereunder: (i) all monies required to be paid to the copyright owner(s) of the musical composition embodied in the Recording; (ii) any payments required to be paid pursuant to any applicable collective bargaining agreement, including, without limitation, any and all so-called "re-use" and "new use" fees and "conversion costs"; (iii) all costs relating whatsoever to the Picture or Videogram, including, without limitation, any with respect to manufacturing, promotion, advertising, distributing and selling same; and (iv) all applicable taxes and duties by reason or Producer's activities hereunder. Producer hereby indemnifies and holds us harmless from any and all claims, liabilities, losses, damages and expenses, including, but not limited to, attorneys' fees and costs arising out of or in connection with any breach of Producer's warranties, representations or covenants under this agreement, or in any way resulting from or connected with Producer's use of the Recording.

(b) We warrant only that we have the right to grant the license specified in Paragraph 2 hereof, and this license is given and accepted without any other representation, warranty or recourse, express or implied, except for our agreement to repay the consideration set forth in Paragraph 3(c) above if, as the result of a final non-appealable judgment having been entered against us in a court of competent jurisdiction, it is determined that we have breached said warranty. Our aggregate liability to Producer shall not exceed the amount of consideration actually paid by Producer to us hereunder.

5. Producer shall accord us screen credit with respect to the Recording on the negative and all positive prints of the Picture and of the Videogram, in the form of:

"____"

Such credit shall be the same size and given the same prominence as all other credits to parties furnishing master recordings for use in the Picture. Producer will require compliance with the foregoing screen credit requirements in all agreements for the broadcast and exhibition of the Picture and with respect to the Videogram.

6. Producer shall not have the right to use the name (except as provided in Paragraph 5 above), likeness or any other identifying feature of Artist without our prior written consent, including, without limitation, for advertising, publicity or promotion purposes.

7. Producer may not assign or license any of the rights granted herein without our prior written consent. Any such assignment shall not relieve Producer of any of its obligations hereunder. We may, at our election, assign this agreement to any third party. This agreement shall inure to the benefit of and be binding upon us and Producer and our and their respective successors, permitted assigns and representatives.

8. This agreement sets forth the entire understanding between us and Producer with respect to the subject matter hereof and no amendment to or modification, waiver, termination or discharge of this agreement or any provision hereof shall be binding upon us or Producer unless confirmed by a written instrument signed by Producer's authorized signatory and our authorized signatory. No waiver of any provision of or default under this agreement shall affect Producer's or our right, as the case may be, thereafter to enforce such provision or to exercise any right or remedy in the event of any other default, whether or not similar. This agreement shall be deemed to have been made in the State of ______________ and its validity, construction, breach, performance and operation shall be governed by the internal laws of the State of ____________ applicable to contracts to be performed wholly therein. Both parties agree that only the ____________ court shall have jurisdiction over this agreement and any controversies arising out of this agreement shall be brought by the parties to the Supreme Court of the State of ___________, County of ____________, or to the United States District Court for the ____________ District of ____________, and they hereby grant jurisdiction to such court(s) and to any appellate courts having jurisdiction over appeals from such courts.

9. All notices and other items from one party to the other hereunder will, unless otherwise designated in writing, be addressed to each party at the respective addresses set forth on the first page of this agreement. Copies of all notices to us shall be sent to ______________________________, ______________________________, Atten: ________________. Any such notice will be deemed complete when said notice (containing whatever information may be required hereunder) is deposited in any United States mailbox (as certified or registered mail) with postage prepaid, addressed as aforesaid. The date of mailing shall constitute the date of notice.

10. Upon Producer's written request, we shall deliver or cause to be delivered to Producer one (1) duplicate master recording of the Recording for Producer to use in connection with the rights granted herein. Producer shall promptly reimburse us for our actual out-of-pocket costs of duplicating, shipping (and insuring) the duplicate master recording requested by Producer hereunder.

Very truly yours,

____

("we", "us", "our")

By________________________

Its________________________

Federal I.D. ____________

ACCEPTED AND AGREED:

____
("Producer")

By___________________

Its___________________

Composer Agreement

As of __________ (Date)

(Composer Attorney)
(Address)

RE: **(Production Company)** - "**(Picture Title)**" - ("**Composer**")

Dear _________:

I am writing to confirm the terms of the agreement between __________________ ("Company") and _________________ ("Composer") (Social Security No.: _______________) in connection with the Picture, including any prequels, sequels, spinoffs and/or remakes thereof:

1. **Services.** Composer shall compose, record, produce and deliver an original musical score in accordance with instructions from Company ("Score") for the Picture. Composer's services shall not include orchestration or conducting. The Score, the record mixes of the Score ("Score Masters"), and all results and proceeds of Composer's services hereunder are collectively referred to as the "Work."

2. **Non-Score Musical Works.** If Company desires Composer to write and produce non-Score musical works, Company shall negotiate with Composer in good faith.

3. **Term.** The term hereof shall commence upon the dates set forth above and shall continue until satisfactory completion of Composer's services, during which time Composer's services shall be nonexclusive first priority. The Work is to be delivered to Company no later than ________ (Date) (delivery and acceptance of the Work is acknowledged).

4. **Compensation.**

(a) **Composing Fee.** The Composing Fee of ____________ Thousand Dollars ($_____) shall be payable to Composer as follows:

(i) ________ Thousand Dollars ($_____) on commencement of services (receipt of which is acknowledged);

(ii) ________ Thousand Dollars ($_____) promptly following Company's designated "spotting" date for the Picture;

(iii) ________ Thousand Dollars ($_____) promptly following delivery to and acceptance by Company of the Work.

(b) **Songwriter/Composer Royalties.**

(i) **Print:** 10¢ per instrumental/vocal copy and 12 1/2% on folios;

(ii) **Mechanical:** 50% of net income;

(iii) **Synchronization:** 50% of net income;

(iv) **Performance:** 50% of net income (i.e., 100% of the writer's share which Composer shall collect directly from ASCAP); and

(v) **Other:** 50% of net income derived from other sources, if any.
All such royalties with respect to the Score shall be reduced proportionately to take into account any cowriting (including lyricist) services.

(vi) If Company contracts with a third party to collect music publishing income, it shall use good faith efforts to require such third party to pay Company "at the source." In any event, Company (and its affiliated companies) shall not charge an administration fee or overhead with respect to music publishing income, and except for direct out-of-pocket costs, Composer shall be paid Composer's royalties based on 100% of income paid to Company.

(c) **Publishing Royalties.** Fifty percent (50%) of the "publisher's share" of music income.

(d) **Record Royalties.**

(i) Composer shall receive an "artist royalty" of 7% for Score Masters, pro rata, and a "producer royalty" of 3% for Score Masters, pro rata, of the retail price (or its wholesale equivalent) of the soundtrack album derived from the Picture ("Album"), subject to a reduction in the event that another artist, producer or other third party is entitled to a royalty therefor and calculated in the same manner as Company's royalties and subject to the same reductions, deductions and category variations.

(ii) Royalties will be payable after recoupment of conversion costs from Composer's net artist royalties. Following such recoupment, Composer's artist royalties and Composer's producer royalties will be paid prospectively.

(iii) Company shall use its best efforts to have the record company directly account to and pay Composer. Composer shall be accounted to semiannually.

(e) Deferment. __________ Thousand Dollars ($________) payable pari passu with the deferment payable to ________________. The deferment to ______________ shall be payable once Company recoups the cost of the Picture, any financing costs and out-of-pocket costs for customary distribution expenses, such as residuals but no distribution fees or overhead to Company (or its affiliated companies).

5. Rights of Company. The Work shall be a work made for hire for Company and Company shall own 100% of the copyright thereof and all of the results and proceeds of Composer's services. Company shall have the exclusive worldwide right in perpetuity to own and administer the Work and to use the Work on a royalty-free basis in the Picture and any prequels, sequels, spinoffs and/or remakes thereof.

6. Credit.

(a) Screen. If more than 50% of the background music is Score, the Composer shall receive credit in the main titles on a separate card (or in the end titles on the equivalent of a separate card if the writer, producer and director credits are only in the end titles) substantially as follows: "MUSIC BY ________________" (Composer Name).

(b) Paid Ads. If more than 50% of the background music is Score, the Composer shall receive credit substantially as "MUSIC BY ________________" (Composer Name) in all paid advertisements produced by or under Company's control in which any other person receives credit (other than actors, writers, director and producers), subject to Company's customary exclusions set forth in Company's distribution agreement(s).

(c) Screen and Paid Ads. If 50% or less of the background music is Score, the parties shall negotiate an appropriate credit for Composer in good faith.

(d) Soundtrack Album: If more than 50% of the music on the Album is Score Master, then Company will direct the record distributor to accord front cover credit worded as in Paragraph 6(a) above and back cover and label credit in the form "Produced By ____________________" (Composer Name). In the event 50% or less of the recordings on the Album is Score Masters, then Company will direct the record distributor to accord Composer a "Written By" credit on the back cover or in the liner notes for each applicable track on the Album. Credits shall apply to all configurations on the soundtrack album.

(e) Cure. All other characteristics of the aforementioned credits will be at Company's sole discretion and no casual or inadvertent failure to comply with such provisions shall be deemed a breach hereof; provided Company shall promptly prospectively cure the same.

7. Non-AFM. Company is not an AFM signatory. The Work is not to be recorded under AFM or any other guild jurisdiction.

8. Travel Expenses/Per Diem. To be negotiated in good faith within the context of the budget for the Picture.

9. Errors and Omissions Insurance: Composer to be covered at Company's cost.

10. Picture/CD Copies. Company shall provide Composer with two (2) videocassettes of the Picture and five (5) CDs upon commercial availability.

11. Score Copies. Composer may retain the originals of the Score for Composer's personal use; provided, however, that if such Score is needed for delivery by Company to a distributor, then Composer shall deliver such Score to Company. Notwithstanding Composer's retention of the originals of the Score, Company shall own the copyright in the Score, and under no circumstances shall Composer exploit the Score in any media.

Until such time, if ever, a more formal agreement is prepared, this deal memorandum shall govern the terms of the agreement between the parties hereto. Please have Composer acknowledge his agreement to the foregoing by having Composer sign and return four (4) originals of this letter agreement and the attached Certificate of Authorship to me.

When signed by Composer, this letter agreement and the attached Certificate of Authorship shall constitute a binding agreement between the parties.

Sincerely,

____

(Attorney Name)

AGREED TO AND ACCEPTED BY:

(Production Company)

By: ____________________________

Its: ____________________________

____

(Composer Name)

Composer Certificate of Authorship

For One Dollar ($1.00) and other good and valuable consideration, the receipt and sufficiency of which is hereby acknowledged, I hereby certify that I will write an original musical background score ("Score") intended for use in the theatrical motion picture tentatively entitled ____________________ ("Picture"), at the request of ____________________ ("Company") pursuant to a contract between Company and me dated as of ________________ ("Agreement"). (The Score and all other results and proceeds of my services hereunder and under the Agreement are hereinafter referred to as the "Work".) I hereby acknowledge that the Work has been specially ordered or commissioned by Company for use as part of a contribution to a collective work or as part of the Picture, that the Work constitutes and shall constitute a work made for hire as defined in the United States Copyright Act of 1976, as amended, that Company is and shall be the author of said work made for hire and the owner of all rights in and to the Work, including, without limitation, the copyrights therein and thereto throughout the universe for the initial term and any and all extensions and renewals thereof and that Company has and shall have the right to make such changes therein and such uses thereof as it may deem necessary or desirable all pursuant to the terms and conditions of the Agreement. To the extent that the Work is not deemed a work made for hire and to the extent that Company is not deemed to be the author thereof in any territory of the universe, I hereby irrevocably assign the Work to Company (including the entire copyright therein), and grant to Company all rights therein, including, without limitation, any so-called Rental and Lending Rights and Neighbouring Rights pursuant to any European Economic Community directives and/or enabling or implementing legislation, laws or regulations (collectively, "EEC Rights"), throughout the universe in perpetuity, but in no event shall the period of the assignment of rights being granted to Company hereunder be less than the period of copyright and any renewals and extensions thereof.

Company's rights hereunder shall include (but at all times subject to the terms and conditions of the Agreement), without limitation, the rights to authorize, prohibit and/or control the renting, lending, fixation, reproduction, performance and/or other exploitation of the Work in any and all media and by any and all means now known or hereafter devised, as such rights may be conferred upon me under any applicable laws, regulations or directives, including, without limitation, all so-called EEC Rights. I hereby acknowledge that the compensation paid hereunder and under the Agreement includes adequate and equitable remuneration for the EEC Rights and constitutes a complete buyout of all EEC Rights. In connection with the foregoing, I hereby irrevocably grant to Company, throughout the universe, in perpetuity, the right to collect and retain for Company's own account any and all amounts payable to me with respect to EEC Rights and hereby irrevocably direct any collecting societies or other persons or entities receiving such amounts to pay such amounts to Company.

I hereby waive all rights of droit moral or "moral right of authors" or any similar rights or principles of law which I may now or later have in the Work. I warrant and represent that I have the right to execute this Certificate, that the Work is and shall be new and original with me and not an imitation or copy of any other material and that the Work is and shall be capable of copyright protection throughout the universe, does not and shall not violate or infringe upon any common law or statutory right of any party including, without limitation, contractual rights, copyrights and rights of privacy or constitute unfair competition and is not and shall not be the subject of any litigation or of any claim that might give rise to litigation (only as a result of my breach of my representation, warranties, or covenants hereunder), including, without limitation, any claim by any copyright proprietor of any so-called sampled material contained in the Work. I shall indemnify and hold Company, the corporations comprising Company, and its and their employees, officers, agents, assignees and licensees, harmless from and against any losses, costs, liabilities, claims, damages or expenses (including, without limitation, court costs and attorneys' fees, whether or not in connection with litigation) arising out of any claim or action by a third party which is inconsistent with any warranty or representation made by me in this Certificate or in the Agreement, and which is reduced to a final, adverse nonappealable judgment or settled with my consent, such consent not to be unreasonably withheld. I agree to execute any documents and do any other acts which may be required by Company or its assignees or licensees to further evidence or effectuate Company's rights as set forth in this Certificate or in the Agreement. Upon my failure promptly to do so, I hereby appoint Company as my attorney-in-fact only for such purposes (it being acknowledged by me that such appointment is irrevocable and shall be deemed a power coupled with an interest), with full power of substitution and delegation.

I further acknowledge that in the event of any breach by Company of this Certificate, I will be limited to my remedy at law for damages (if any) and will not have the right to terminate or rescind this Certificate or to enjoin the distribution, exploitation or advertising of the Picture or any materials in connection therewith, that nothing herein shall obligate Company to use my services or the Work in the Picture or to produce, distribute or advertise the Picture and that this Certificate shall be governed by the laws of the United States and the State of California applicable to agreements executed and to be performed entirely therein.

Company's rights with respect to the Work may be freely assigned and licensed and its rights shall be binding upon me and inure to the benefit of any such assignee or licensee.

IN WITNESS WHEREOF, I have signed this Certificate effective as of______ (Date).

____

(Composer Name)

Social Security #: _______________

Performing Rights Society: _____________________________

Payment Address: ___________________________________

____

(Production Company)

By _______________________________

Its _______________________________

Music Supervisor Agreement

As of ____________ (Date)

(Production Company Name)

Re: "(Picture Name)"/(Name/Company of Music Supervisor)/Music Supervisor Agreement

Dear ________:

This will confirm the agreement ("Agreement") between __________________ ("Supervisor") and __________________ ("Producer") regarding Supervisor's services as Music Supervisor for the theatrical motion picture presently entitled __________________ (the "Picture").

1. Services. Supervisor shall render, on a nonexclusive, first-priority basis, all services customarily rendered by music supervisors in connection with the Picture, including the clearance of existing music; assisting in negotiation of a soundtrack album deal; assisting in negotiation of performer agreements; assisting in the preparation of music cue sheets and the selection of the composer; with the understanding that such services shall be performed on a regular, in-person basis in a diligent and conscientious manner, to the best of Supervisor's ability, and no services performed for any third party during the term hereof shall materially interfere with Supervisor's services to be performed hereunder. Under Producer's control and supervision, Supervisor shall assist in the negotiation and documentation of all music licenses and agreements required by Producer, including agreements with artists whose performances are embodied in the soundtrack and/or the soundtrack album and including any soundtrack album agreement if requested to do so by Producer, using "quote letters" supplied and/or approved by Producer. The formal music licensing contracts will be documented by Producer.

2. Compensation. Provided that Supervisor is not in material breach or default hereunder and further provided that Supervisor fully performs all material services required by Producer in connection with the Picture, Producer shall pay compensation to Supervisor in the following amounts, which amounts shall be payable as follows:

(a) A music supervisor fee of $100,000, payable

(i) $20,000 on signature hereof.

(ii) $26,666 on commencement of principal photography.

(iii) $26,667 on commencement of spotting.

(iv) $26,667 on completion of services.

(b) If Producer enters into a soundtrack album agreement with a third party

("Record Distributor"), Supervisor shall be entitled to receive additional compensation equal to 10% of the gross advance (whether characterized as an advance, advance plus recording costs or a recording fund) actually received by Producer, if any, as a result of such agreement, not to exceed $75,000. Supervisor's percentage shall be payable from 100% of the first monies from the advance received by Producer from the Record Distributor.

(c) If the box office gross for the picture in the United States and Canada, as reported by EDI, equals or exceeds $25 million dollars, Supervisor will be paid an initial $25,000, payable within 30 days after such box office bench mark is achieved.

3. **Soundtrack Album.** Provided that Supervisor is not in material breach or default and further provided that Supervisor fully performs all material services required by Producer in connection with the Picture, Producer shall cause the Record Distributor, if any, to pay to Supervisor a record royalty of 1% of the suggested retail list price ("SRLP") of U.S. net sales through normal retail channels ("USNRC") of the soundtrack album, escalating prospectively to 1.5% at 500,000 USNRC net sales and further escalating prospectively to 2% of SRLP at 1,000,000 USNRC net sales. In all other respects, the royalty payable to Supervisor shall be subject to the same proportionate category variations, exclusions, deductions, reductions and adjustments (but excluding escalations based on sales) as those applicable to Producer's agreement with Distributor (including, without limitation, terms relating to foreign sales, singles sales, record club sales, PX sales, bonus records, midpriced records, budget records, direct sales, discounts, packaging, sales plans, reserves, extended play rate, multiple albums, free goods). Notwithstanding the foregoing, Supervisor's royalties are predicated upon Producer retaining a "net" royalty spread of 4% of SRLP or more (i.e., the difference between the "all-in" royalty rate under the soundtrack album agreement and the royalty rate payable to all artists and other producers, engineers or mixers participating thereon, excluding Supervisor) but excluding nonartist parties engaged by Producer (e.g., the director and any executives, etc.). To the extent that the "net" spread to Producer is less than 4%, Supervisor's record royalties shall be reduced by 100% of such difference, but in no event shall Supervisor's royalty be less than 1%. Supervisor royalties shall be paid on a prospective basis only after USNRC net sales in excess of 350,000 units. Supervisor shall have customary audit rights of Producer's books and records regarding the soundtrack album, and, if Producer audits the Record Distributor, Supervisor shall receive its pro rata share of the net recovery. Notwithstanding the foregoing, Supervisor shall not be entitled to a royalty with respect to any "story teller" books or other items of merchandising which are distributed by the Record Distributor.

4. **Credit.** Provided that Supervisor is not in material breach or default

(a) Producer shall accord screen credit to Supervisor on a separate card in the opening credit sequence, in substantially the following form: "Music Supervisor— ________________" (Name); provided, however, that if any guild prohibits the wording of such credit, or if the wording or placement of such credit will trigger additional credits to be placed in the main titles, then the parties will mutually agree upon an appropriate alternate credit (or placement), with Producer's decision controlling in the event of a dispute.

(b) Supervisor shall be accorded credit on all soundtrack album recordings to read "Music Supervisor—__________________" (Name). Similar credit shall appear on (a) all other types of audio recordings including but not limited to CDs (enhanced CDs are deemed to be audio-only), cassettes, singles and EPs.

(c) Supervisor shall be accorded in the form "Music Supervisor—__________________" (Name) in all paid ads (subject to customary exclusions), on one sheets and if the billing block appears, on the packaging of video cassettes and video discs.

(d) If Supervisor serves as the actual producer of any Master Sound Recordings embodied in the soundtrack album, Producer shall accord credit to Supervisor in substantially the form "Produced by __________________" (Name), it being understood that such credit may be shared and the order of the "Produced By" credit shall be in Producer's sole discretion. Supervisor's credit, however, shall be in the same size and prominence as the other individuals receiving "Produced By" credit. Subject to the foregoing, Producer shall have no obligation to accord credit to Supervisor with respect to the individual Master Sound Recordings; however, if Producer does accord credit to other individuals with respect to Master Sound Recordings not produced by Supervisor, then Supervisor shall receive like credit, in the same size and prominence as those others receiving "Produced By" credit with respect to the individual Master Sound Recordings.

5. **Supervisor's Costs.** Supervisor shall not be required to, nor shall Supervisor, provide or incur any recording costs in connection with the Picture or any soundtrack album derived therefrom, excepting only such usual and customary costs and expenses, if any, as are typically incurred by music supervisors in the normal performance of their services. Producer agrees to reimburse Supervisor for reasonable, out-of-pocket expenses which are directly related to the performance of Supervisor's services hereunder, including long-distance telephone calls, messenger charges and faxes; provided, however, that any such expenses in excess of $200 shall be subject to Producer's prior written approval.

6. **Travel Expenses/Per Diem.** If applicable, to be negotiated in good faith.

7. **E&O Policy.** Supervisor shall be added as an insured to Producer's E&O policy, if any, subject to the terms, limitations and conditions of such policy.

8. **Indemnity.** Producer shall indemnify Supervisor from all claims not arising from Supervisor's breach of this agreement.

9. Entire Agreement. This agreement, includes the entire understanding between the parties and supersedes all prior agreements, understandings and memoranda with respect to the subject matter hereof.

IN WITNESS WHEREOF, the parties hereto have executed this agreement as of the day and year first above written.

(Production Company Name)
("Producer")

By: ______________________________

Its: ______________________________

By: ______________________________
(Music Supervisor Name)

PROFITS

Since most independent films are underfinanced and most of the people working on them are underpaid, producers use the incentive of profits or "points" to lure investors, talent, and others to participate in the picture. Your job in making these deals is complicated by the cynicism that surrounds Hollywood accounting. Most people regard it as an elaborate cheat. We are going to go into this topic in some depth because it is complex.

Profit Definitions

When you first think about it, profits do not seem complex. It is easy to understand what profits are: you see how much money you took in from sales; you subtract your costs, and what is left is profit. Even in Hollywood, this is how profits are defined. The art and negotiation revolve around the definition of revenue and the definition of costs.

It is simplistic to think that there are easy and obvious definitions of revenue and costs and that the Hollywood variations are just manipulations and tricks to cheat people out of their share of the "real profits." You must realize that the accounting rules that companies use when dealing with the IRS and their shareholders are very different from profits reported to participants, which are defined by contract, not accounting rules. These contractual definitions usually run many pages, and they appear as exhibits to long-form agreements. Studio definitions do have some aspects that we find unfair, but whether you are giving shares of profits or getting them, there are some hard issues to address. Here is an introduction to the main ones that arise in customary Hollywood profit formulas.

Revenue

The starting point for most profit definitions is what is usually labeled "gross receipts." The most fundamental issue lurking in this term is whose receipts? When you buy a ticket to see a movie, the theater takes your money. Is this box office revenue the same as gross receipts? Or are gross receipts only the portion of the box office money that the theater gives to the distributor of the film? Or are gross receipts the portion of the money that the distributor passes on to the production company? What if the same company owns both the production company and the distributor or owns both plus the theater? Should gross receipts be the same?

This problem of defining whose gross receipts becomes more complicated when the same movie goes to other media and other territories such as foreign television. Are the broadcaster's advertising revenues from commercials that run with the movie defined as gross receipts? Or are gross receipts just the license revenue paid by the broadcaster to a foreign subdistributor who acquired the rights from the U.S. distributor? Or are they what the U.S. distributor got?

Competent definitions of revenue must very clearly specify the level in the distribution chain where revenue is computed. Most profit definitions define revenue as money that reaches the hands of the company in the United States that grants the profits. But you have to know where that company stands in the distribution chain to know what that means. Since independent films, by definition, are not owned by distributors, the independent producer's revenue is different from the distributor's revenue and that distinction will impact any profit arrangements you make on your independent film.

The second issue that affects profits is the kinds of revenue that are included and the kinds that are not. Typical profit definitions exclude certain items called "off-the-tops," which include taxes, collection costs, and trade association payments. They also exclude revenues from licensing portions of the picture as stock footage, money donated to charities (for example, the proceeds of a benefit screening), and proceeds from lawsuits. Also excluded are refunds, credits, discounts, adjustments, deposits subject to refunds, and advance payments until earned. Revenue from merchandising, soundtracks, and books may or may not be included. Revenue from sequels is generally not included. Maybe that is reasonable, maybe not.

The third fundamental issue in defining revenue is what we call "fair pricing." The issue is obvious when a vertically integrated company licenses to a different division. When Disney Pictures grants ABC a license to broadcast one of its movies, the amount of money the ABC Broadcasting division of the Walt Disney Company pays to the Disney Pictures division of Walt Disney Company impacts mainly the profit participants in the picture; not the Walt Disney Company, since both companies are under the same roof. The less ABC pays, the less revenue and the less money for the profit participants. Who can say what is the fair price?

Fair pricing can also be a problem even in situations where there is no self-dealing. When a group of pictures is licensed at one time, there is an opportunity to distort revenue. For example, if Universal Pictures agreed to license Showtime the pay television rights to all of an upcoming slate of fifteen pictures for $30 million, the deal could be structured several ways. Each picture could be licensed for $2 million and show $2 million in revenue. Or some pictures could be considered better prospects and separate prices allocated to each. Or the allocation could be based on the budget. Is a picture that costs $80 million worth four times as much as one budgeted at $20 million? Another pricing technique is to allocate retroactively based on how the pictures do at the box office. That sounds fair but it might not correspond to the ratings the pictures get when they run on Showtime. Does this mean ratings are the best method of allocation? Finally, there is the possibility that a portion of the $30 million fee is allocated to "exclusivity"—the agreement of Universal not to sell the pictures to HBO. Do the profit participants in the pictures get a share of that revenue? What is fair?

A final major issue in determining revenue is how the profit definition treats security deposits and advances. It is common, for example, for a foreign broadcaster to pay a percentage of the license fee when a deal is made even though it will have to wait for the theatrical release and home video distribution to be completed before it can broadcast the film. The studio has received the deposit, but most profit definitions exclude it from gross receipts, at least until the picture can be broadcast. It is then considered to be "earned." During the interim, the studio has the advance and it keeps charging interest on unrecouped production and distribution expenses. Most studio definitions go even further. Taking our television license example, let us assume that the license was for up to ten runs over four years for a license fee of $1,000,000, and the fee was payable $100,000 on signing and $900,000 18 months later when the broadcaster was allowed to start its runs. Most studio accounting departments would allocate the $1,000,000 over the permitted ten runs and would not consider anything earned until the runs occurred. So for example, if the broadcaster ran the picture once as soon as it was permitted, the studio would regard the first $100,000 as earned at that point and report it as gross receipts. Remember the studio would have collected the full $1,000,000 by then. If the picture ran again a year later, another $100,000 would be reported. If the broadcaster only ran the picture five times during its license period, the studio would report $100,000 for each run as it occurred and only report the remaining $500,000 when the four-year license term expired and the broadcaster forfeited the right to take its last five runs.

Costs

What a picture "costs" is an even thornier problem than the question of how much revenue it generates. Most definitions of costs break them down into five categories: distribution fees, distribution expenses, financing costs, production costs (including overhead), and profits to third parties.

Distribution Fees

These are costs attributed by distributors to arrange the licensing or sale of the picture and they are normally calculated as a percentage of gross receipts, with different percentages assigned for different revenue sources. The variation in percentages is designed to take into account the difficulty and expense of making the sale. For example, it is simpler to sell U.S. television rights to a single network like Lifetime than to make many separate sales to independent TV stations around the country, so the distribution fee for a television network sale is usually less than for syndicated sales.

Distribution fees are often internal costs. That is, the distributor is not paying the fees to someone else; it essentially is paying itself for the costs of its sales force and general sales operation, so they are somewhat arbitrary. These fees also do not fluctuate as the revenue changes. Just because one picture generates ten times more revenue than another does not prove that it was ten times as hard to sell—but the participant bears ten times the distribution fee.

Sometimes there are subdistributors involved who have made deals with the primary distributor giving them rights to make sales in certain territories or certain media. These subdistributors are paid by deducting distribution fees for themselves from the revenue they generate. This can lead to compound distribution fees. A subdistributor may license rights to a picture in Russia for $100,000 and take a 30% distribution fee with $70,000 going to the primary distributor. If the profit definition allows the primary distributor to also take a 30% distribution fee (after all it found the subdistributor), it could take its fee (an "override" fee) on the $70,000 (or even worse for profits, on the $100,000), leaving $49,000 (or $40,000 if the override fee is on $100,000) in revenue after deducting the distribution fee. Sometimes, deals call for the primary distributor to absorb any subdistributor distribution fees from its fee or call for a cap on the combined distribution fee of the primary distributor and any subdistributors.

Distribution fees are the most malleable component in calculating costs. Studios often have a variety of kinds of profits definitions with different labels they can offer to people who work on a picture. Often, these differ from each other just in the distribution fees. The difference between "modified gross profits" and "net profits" may simply be a reduced distribution fee—a simple but crucial difference.

The typical distribution fee charged by major studios on U.S. theatrical distribution is 30%. Fees for foreign theatrical distribution generally range from 35% to 40%. The domestic fee is usually 30% for nontheatrical distribution, such as airlines. For carriers based outside the United States, the fee is 35% to 50%.

Distribution fees for U.S. television typically are, pay—20% to 30%; network—15% to 30%; syndication—30% to 40%. The fee is usually 35% to 40% for foreign television.

On home video sales of videocassettes and DVDs, instead of charging a distribution fee studios usually include a royalty equal to 20% of the wholesale cost in gross receipts. This is the equivalent of an 80% distribution fee, although the studios do bear manufacturing and marketing costs. The convention of only crediting 20% of wholesale to gross receipts began when the studio licensed their product to third-party home video distributors and typically received only 20% of wholesale. Studios now all distribute home videos themselves, and their margin is far in excess of 20% of wholesale. Still, with the rapidly escalating costs of production and distribution, studios insist on the artificial 20% of wholesale convention.

Distribution Expenses

The second traditional category of costs is distribution expenses or distribution costs. These are the costs of marketing and distributing the completed picture, excluding the salaries of salespeople. Unlike distribution fees, most but not all of these costs are paid to outside third parties and so are less controversial. The distributor shares the profit participant's desire to pay as little as possible for these items. However, some distributors do charge a 10% to 15% distribution expense overhead charge on top of the actual distribution costs to cover the costs of their staffs in managing and administering the marketing and advertising of the film.

For theatrical films, the largest and fastest-growing of these expenses is advertising. The cost of a television and newspaper advertising campaign is eye-popping and can exceed the cost of making the film. Some studios charge a fee for administering the ad purchases and designing the ad campaign and calculate it as a percentage of the ad expenditures. If an overhead fee is charged, try to limit it to the actual advertising creative costs rather than the entire set of all distribution expenses. Unquestionably, they have staff involved in advertising campaigns, but this is another internal cost that the studio pays itself and therefore is somewhat arbitrary. The cost of making the film prints shown in theaters (over $2,000 each), shipping and storage of prints, publicists and publicity junkets, guild residuals, costs of dubbing into foreign languages, traveling to foreign territories, market fees, posters, billboards, the building and breakdown of booths at markets and conventions, and out-of-pocket sales costs like expensive lunches in Cannes also fall into the distribution expense category.

Financing Costs

Financing costs are rightfully met with some skepticism by profit participants. Most profit definitions allow production companies to charge their costs of getting financing for the picture. For independent pictures, these are the frighteningly real costs of getting a loan: interest, points, and legal fees to bank lawyers that we discussed in connection with production loans. For billion dollar studios, these are not the actual costs—they do not have to go to a bank and get a loan for each picture they make. They have their own cash flow, as well as enormous credit facilities as financial resources. Instead of making a reasonable effort to approximate their real costs of financing, they put a formula into the profit definition that inflates their real cost of money. Typically, studios charge the movie interest at one to two points over U.S. prime rate or worse, 125% of prime, but to the extent they do borrow money, they actually get far better rates. They also often use questionable policies to start interest running on production costs before they have even been paid and to keep the interest running long after they have received offsetting revenue. Time is the profit participant's mortal enemy as interest often works like quicksand to pull the picture deeper and deeper into debt. Much negotiation revolves around when interest starts and ends as well as the rate.

Production Costs

Production costs are what you normally think of as the costs of making the movie. They include the script, the actors, the director, crew, film, camera rentals, lighting, set construction, flaming car crashes, the cost of personal trainers and massages for the star, and the myriad other factors that go into making the film. They are sometimes called the "negative cost" because they are costs of creating the film negative. Fair pricing issues arise in production costs where the production company or an affiliate supplies a production element like costumes or lighting—as opposed to getting them from an outside supplier. Many studios have what they call their "rate card," which specifies the charge for a studio-supplied item or service. Like car dealer service department rate cards, these are often grossly inflated above their fair market value. There are also some volume rebates that studios keep to themselves, but production costs are pretty clear and reflect actual, out-of-pocket costs. The notable exception is what is termed "overhead." This is an arbitrary percentage of production costs that is added to compensate the production company for a portion of its general administrative and overhead costs; things like its accountants, development executives, office rents, and the like. The range for overhead charges is usually 10% to 15% of the production or negative cost of the film. Sometimes studios charge overhead on interest and interest on overhead, in other words, fiction on fiction.

Third-Party Profits

The final element of cost is profits paid to others. It should be clear by now that not all profit definitions are created equal. Depending on someone's sophistication, negotiating skill, and leverage, one profit definition can start paying money to one participant while another profit definition has not yet hit pay out. When studios pay profits, they write checks to somebody and they like to treat those payments as costs of the film. In fact, it is money that studio has paid out on the film. The result is that the person who has the second-class definition of profits who was just about to break through and get a check, receives an accounting statement that says in effect, "Oops, costs went up again because your compadre just got a check." Overhead and interest run on that cost and the picture oozes backwards again into the quicksand of nonprofitability. This is exactly what happened to Art Buchwald on the infamous and unfunny case *Coming to America.* Eddie Murphy had a topnotch definition of profits sometimes called "adjusted gross"—that eliminated many distribution fees—while Buchwald had a very crummy one—the infamous "net profit" definition. The more Murphy made in profits—and he made in excess of an estimated $20 million—the deeper in the red went Buchwald because Murphy's adjusted gross profits were deducted as an additional cost of the film. Since Buchwald's definition of net profits provided for recoupment of these costs, this profit statement would always show that after deducting the distribution fees, distribution expenses, interest and financing costs, production costs and profits to third parties like Murphy, the picture was still unrecouped.

Revenues less costs, that is all there is to profits. Below are several charts that summarize the points we covered:

SUMMARY OF PROFIT DEFINITION

GROSS RECEIPTS

minus: distribution fees
minus: distribution expenses
minus: financing costs
minus: production cost
minus: third-party profit participations
equals: profits

GROSS RECEIPT COMPONENTS

THEATRICAL GROSS RECEIPTS

plus: home video sales gross receipts
plus: home video rental gross receipts
plus: television gross receipts
plus: miscellaneous gross receipts
equals: gross receipts

CALCULATION OF GROSS RECEIPTS

BOX OFFICE RECEIPTS
excluding: advances, trailer revenue, etc.
minus: theater operator share
minus: off-the-tops such as ticket audit costs and taxes
minus: subdistributor fees
equals: theatrical gross receipts

HOME VIDEO SALES RECEIPTS
excluding: advances
minus: subdistributor fees
minus: guild residuals
minus: 80% for costs
equals: home video sales gross receipts

HOME VIDEO RENTAL RECEIPTS
excluding: advances
minus: subdistributor fees
minus: distribution fee
equals: home video rental gross receipts

TELEVISION LICENSING RECEIPTS
excluding: advances
minus: subdistributor fees
minus: distribution fee
equals: television gross receipts

MISCELLANEOUS RECEIPTS
excluding: advances
minus: subdistributor fees
minus: applicable distribution fee
equals: miscellaneous gross receipts

PROFIT NEGOTIATION ISSUES

GROSS RECEIPTS
treatment of advances
subdistributor fees
deals with affiliates
define gross receipts actually received "at the source"

DISTRIBUTION FEES
fees for different media

DISTRIBUTION EXPENSES
internal charges such as advertising overhead
allocation of costs among different pictures
definition of actual out-of-pocket distribution expenses
establish a minimum and a cap on distribution expenses

FINANCING COSTS
rates
timing for commencement and end of interest

PRODUCTION COSTS
rates for affiliates
overhead charges
determine whether third-party participants are included in production costs

THIRD-PARTY PROFITS
determine whether participant bears third-party profits

Typical Splits of Profits

For many years, it was common for Hollywood studios to give producers 50% of net profits. The number came from the notion that the financier should get half the profits and the creative talent the other half. The producer was expected to share his profits with the writer, director, actors, and other creative types. Thus, the producer deal was referred to as "fifty percent reducible." Of course, you, like Art Buchwald, now know that 50% of net profits under a standard studio definition of profits does not equate to half of the real economic benefit from a movie. But, this formula of making up to 50% of net profits available to creative talent remains common on Hollywood deals.

There are no set rules, but it is common for an author whose book forms the basis for a movie to receive 2.5% of net profits. Screenplay writers typically receive 5% of net if they get the sole credit as writer or 2.5% if they share credit with another writer. Before the days of Spielberg, Coppola, and Lucas, directors received about 10% of net. Similarly, before the 1980s, star actors might receive as much as 10% of net profits. The producer kept around 25% of net profits after being reduced by net profits paid to other creative participants.

Movie profits have become more complicated. Today, rather than one formula for determining profits, there may be several different types of profits on the same picture. We will work through an example that will give you an idea of the main forms. But, before we go into the math, we want to point out one pitfall. Usually, profit participants receive a percentage of the total net profits from the picture. Sometimes, though, they are tricked into getting a percentage of "producer's net profits." If a director gets 10% of the total net profits or "10% of 100%" as it is commonly called, he ends up with 10% of total net profits. If he receives 10% of producer's net and the producer has a typical deal, at best he gets 10% of the 50% the producer has, so his share of the total is 5%. At worst case he gets 10% of what the producer gets after he has paid everyone else—something along the lines of 10% of 25% or 2.5% of the total net profits.

For our example of movie profits, we will assume a movie with the following financial results. The terms are the ones outlined in the previous section. They are used in a loose and generic fashion. In the real world, their meaning and consequently their magnitude would be set by the detailed definition in the net profit agreement:

gross receipts	$10,000,000
distribution expenses	$2,000,000
cost of production	$4,000,000

(without overhead)	
interest	$500,000
overhead on cost of production (15%)	$600,000
distribution fee on gross receipts (40%)	$4,000,000

Using these figures, here is the calculation of the 5% of net profits due the writer C. Dickens:

gross	$10,000,000
distribution fee	($ 4,000,000)
distribution expense	($ 2,000,000)
interest	($500,000)
production costs	($ 4,000,000)
overhead	($600,000)
third party profits	$0
net profits	($1,100,000)
Dickens' share (5%)	($55,000)

Mr. Dickens is still in deficit under his net profit definition and because the production company has not recouped all of its costs, it continues to accrue more interest charges.

The director, S. Eisenstein, had a modified gross profit participation described as "10% at actual breakeven with a 20% fee," which means that the distribution fee is reduced to 20% from 40%. His definition also excluded third-party profits as a cost in computing his share of profits. His profits statement reads:

gross	$10,000,000
distribution fee	($2,000,000)
distribution expense	($2,000,000)
interest	($500,000)
production costs	($4,000,000)
overhead	($600,000)
profits	$900,000
Eisenstein share (10%)	$90,000

Unfortunately for Mr. Dickens, the profits paid to Mr. Eisenstein are an additional cost, so the deficit under the Dickens' definition goes to

$1,190,000, if we ignore interest and overhead on the Eisenstein profits.

Star G. Garbo received the most favorable definition. She received an acting fee of $500,000 (which is included in the $4,000,000 production costs) against 10% of the gross from dollar one. That is a simple calculation:

gross	$10,000,000
10% participation	$1,000,000
less acting fee	($500,000)
profits due Ms. Garbo	$500,000

Because Mr. Eisenstein is not reduced by third-party profits, he keeps his $90,000. The impoverished Mr. Dickens is now $1,690,000 from seeing his first penny.

This is a simplified example for a fictional picture. What follows below is an actual statement from a major studio to the writer on a 1990s hit picture with star actors, writer, and director elements. We have camouflaged it so as not to disclose the name of the picture. Note two things. Because of the writer's stature, he received a reduced and flat distribution fee of 20% for all media to compute his $100,000 deferment and 7% of the net profits. Still, the picture remained over $50,000,000 in the red, and the writer never received a dime.

SAMPLE STATEMENT

MAJOR STUDIO
Photoplay: Big Picture
Statement To: Loanout Company
Accounting From: ____________ to ____________
inception to Date:

ACCOUNTABLE GROSS: SUBJECT TO DISTRIBUTION FEE OF 20%	
United States — Theatrical	$18,100,592
United States — Nontheatrical	$63,144
United States — Pay Television	$9,873,444
United States — Television	$1,500,000
U.S. Armed Forces	$97,011
Canad	$1,055,823
Canada Pay Television	$304,281
Canada Television	$51,511
Foreign Subsidiaries	$26,305,600
Foreign Distributors	$2,110,800
Foreign Pay Television	$12,970,830
Great Britain	$1,748,811
Great Britain Pay Television	$3,750,000
Total	$87,092,198
SUBJECT TO NO DISTRIBUTION FEE:	
Disc	$960,191
Cassette	$10,234,381
Total	$89,286,770
DISTRIBUTION FEES:	
20% of $78,092,198	($15,618,439)
Total Distribution Fees	($15,618,439)
Balance	$73,668,331
DISTRIBUTION EXPENSES:	
Taxes	($1,153,835)
Prints — 35mm	($7,360,732)
Prints — 16mm	($622)
Duping Prints, Titles, Foreign Versions	($1,690,064)

Freight, Duties, Censorship, Checking	($2,000,782)
Advertising	($31,807,450)
Trade Association Fees	($412,000)
Guild Fees	($5,600,553)
Other Television Expenses	($950,400)
Legal Expenses	($6,000)
Other Expenses	($169,100)
Total Deduction	(51,151,537)
Balance	$22,516,794
OTHER DEDUCTIONS:	
Deferments	($240,500)
Gross Participation	($3,590,000)
Cost of Production (Ex-Interest)*	($65,600,880)
Total Other Deductions	($69,431,380)
Breakeven	($46,914,586)
DEFERMENTS:	
$100,000 Payable at Breakeven	
(with 20% Distribution Fee)	(0)
PARTICIPATION:	
7% of Net Proceeds	(0)

* Cost of Production subject to adjustment. Interest included on subsequent statements.

Profits on Independent Pictures

Most independent producers ask talent to work for comparatively low guaranteed fees, and they offer to make up for it with extra money if the picture is successful. Sometimes, that offer comes in the form of net profits, but because of talent's well-justified cynicism about net profits, they are not much incentive. There are four basic forms of financial upside that independent producers use when conventional net profits are not adequate to close the deal:

1. Enhanced profit definitions
2. Favored nations
3. Deferments
4. Box-office bonuses

As we saw in the examples above, changes in some of the components of the profit formula can radically impact the resulting profits. The components most likely to be changed in an enhanced definition are the overhead and the distribution fee. There are many fancy terms used with enhanced profit definitions: "adjusted gross," "modified gross," "rolling breakeven," etc., but in the end the most powerful variables in the calculation are overhead and distribution fee.

Independent producers can be flexible, if they need to or want to be, in adjusting the overhead in the profit definition. Modifying the distribution fee is more difficult because, unlike at a studio where the production company and distributor are the same, on an independent picture an unrelated distributor will charge the production company an actual distribution fee. If your distributor is charging you a 25% distribution fee on theatrical release, you cannot offer your star first dollar gross, unless you can persuade the distributor to assume the obligation to the star and effectively waive its distribution fee on the star's share of theatrical revenue.

Because producers may have not made their distribution deals by the time they negotiate the talent's profit definition and because it seems inherently fair, producers often use another approach to profits. They offer favored nations. That is, they offer a definition as good as the best afforded another defined group of profit participants. Sometimes that group is defined to include all creative elements (usually actors, director, and writer). Sometimes, it includes the producer himself. On very rare occasions, it includes investors, who usually negotiate the best definition of profits.

The third device to improve on a net profit participation is to agree to a deferment. As we noted when we discussed financing, a deferment is a fixed amount of money, often the difference between a creative element's studio quote and what they are guaranteed on an independent picture. The art in negotiating a deferment is to specify the condition under which it is paid. The least favorable for talent is for it to be paid immediately prior to payment of net profits, which makes it only slightly better than a net profit participation. But sometimes deferments are paid out of a revenue stream with reduced overhead and fees. Occasionally they are paid at a fixed point in time such as six months after release of the picture or on home video release.

When stars are particularly dubious about the accounting, they negotiate for a cash bonus to be paid when the picture generates specified levels of U.S. theatrical box office. The box office represented by the trade paper *Daily Variety* is usually the benchmark and, as an example, a box-office bonus for an independent film might take the form of $50,000 payable when the U.S. box office reaches $10 million and another $50,000 for each additional $10 million. These deals are usually structured as all or nothing without proration, so at $9,999,999 in box office, no bonus is payable.

Independent producers should anticipate that they will be asked for some form of enhanced participation and decide early in the process what form it will take. In the heat of negotiating an important deal, it is easier to give a bigger participation than to change the form of participation. So, you could offer to increase the box office bonus to $75,000 per $10 million rather than leave it at $50,000 and start adding some adjusted gross.

SELLING YOUR COMPLETED MOTION PICTURE

We now are going to address the day when you have just come from the lab, paid your final bill, and you have the canister of 95 minutes of 35 mm film in your possession. Now what do you do?

Hopefully, you have utilized some of the techniques and methods described in the previous chapters, you have made a foreign presale of the project prior to it being made, and your distribution arrangement is in place with various distributors who have prebought your project. However, this chapter focuses primarily on the independently financed project that does not have any distribution in place when it is completed. There is no one right time or way to sell your picture. Every picture is unique, and all the maxims and rules are made to be broken. When you are ready to sell your picture, it is a good idea to arm yourself with a team of experts who can help you weave your way among the obstacles to selling your movie and make what may be several distribution deals, licensing deals, and sales agency arrangements. Do not try to do this yourself. It is a process fraught with danger. One wrong move can kill your movie. While engaging a producer's rep is not the only answer, it is highly recommended. Other collaborators can include an experienced marketing consultant, entertainment lawyer, agent, and manager.

Before you embark on selling or licensing your film, you and your representatives should sit down and agree on a definitive plan for the optimal presentation of your film to potential buyers. This plan will depend upon the time of year at which the film is completed, its genre, its budget and its subject matter.

Film Festivals

Presenting your film at a prestigious film festival is one of the best methods of offering your film to distributors. The film festival establishes an even playing field. All the distributors and sales agents have the opportunity to see your film at the very same time in an optimal setting with a large audience. But film festivals are not appropriate for all films. For example, horror films, sci-fi films and martial arts pictures have never been mainstays of the premiere festivals such as Sundance, Toronto, Cannes, Berlin, or Venice, although such films may indeed be invited to specialized genre festivals and showcases. The story is different for dramas, relationship pictures, thrillers, historical films, and art films, all of which have been embraced by the festivals. Not all films can get accepted by the major festivals. Still, many smaller but emerging festivals such as Santa Barbara, South by Southwest, Seattle, Montreal, Mill Valley, The Hamptons, Austin, New Films/New Directors (MOMA in New York), Locarno, Deauville, Edinburgh, San Sebastian, Vancouver, Slamdance, Telluride, and others too numerous to mention, can, under the right circumstances, make excellent launch pads as well.

If you and your representative feel that the festival route is the appropriate strategy to launch your film, you should know there is absolutely no guarantee that your film is going to be accepted. Film festival programming directors have their own personal tastes, and your film may not fit with their vision. Have several alternative contingency plans. Do not embark on submitting your film to a festival without a qualified representative to help it along.

Since many producer's reps spend considerable time traveling to various film festivals and markets and have assisted in securing invitations for their clients' films to festivals in the past, they know most of the film festival artistic directors. The producer's rep is in a key position to follow up directly with festival administration to make sure that the film is properly screened and given the best possible chance to be accepted. Cannes can be an especially fruitful locale in this regard. Artistic directors and administrators from all of the significant film festivals converge in France to scout possible entries for their events later in the year. They have learned that producer's reps are an excellent source for films to be screened at their particular festivals.

Film festivals provide the filmmaker with an opportunity to work with a proactive partner—the festival itself—in the promotion and introduction of the film to its target audience. Festivals have budgets and staffs of professionals and volunteers available to assist the filmmaker in attracting attention to his picture. Most film festivals have publicists available to propagate the picture's message succinctly and with maximum impact both in the print and the electronic press. These publicists, in consultation with the filmmaker and the producer's rep, can be useful allies in arranging press conferences, interviews, and press releases, often at no charge to the filmmaker, since they are engaged by the festival to serve all of the festival's selections. There is generally a separate pressroom where journalists and publicists congregate. There are mailboxes, coffee lounges, and tables set up for promotional materials that can be made available for both media and potential distributors. The festival's publicity releases and news items that appear in the local papers and the occasional national publication are useful additions to the set of press clippings the filmmaker should maintain for use in a complete promotional package about the film.

The festival publicity departments work all the films in the festival and have competing demands on their time. It is a good idea to have your own publicist work in conjunction with the producer's rep and the festival publicist to help direct the strategy for the most effective publicity campaign for your film. Many film festivals invite and pay for media and distributors to attend their festivals. There is usually an extensive catalogue with a description of the films, cast and crew credits, stills, and many times friendly reviews by film festival programmers. When a film is accepted into a festival it is tracked by the distributors and by third-party independent database companies such as Film Finders, which lists films, the principals and credits, and a general synopsis of the film for the purpose of maintaining a definitive information database on the 1,500 to 2,000 new independent pictures in the marketplace at any given moment, for their clients worldwide.

Film festivals often sponsor social events and parties to honor the premiere of a film. The producer's rep can be influential in negotiating with the film festival and coordinating with the staff to ensure that your film is one that receives such special attention as well as a convenient date, time, and location.

It is important to note that a film may screen several times during a festival, and each one of these screenings is a considerable expense that is incurred by the film festival on behalf of the filmmaker. Many film festivals also invite and pay for the travel and living expenses of the director and sometimes the stars during the festival so another considerable expense for the producer can be reduced. The producer's rep can be very instrumental in assisting the producer in negotiating all of these amenities as well as the optimal screening time and venues for the film during the festival. Screening times and dates can be extremely important to the overall plan for the presentation of the film to potential buyers.

For example, screening your film at 8:30 a.m. midweek of a festival is certainly less desirable than a prime 9:00 p.m. Friday or Saturday evening screening that is immediately followed by an exclusive party or reception. The earlier in the festival the picture premieres, the better the opportunity for buzz on the film to snowball by the time the all-important awards ceremony comes around. As important as film festival premieres are, prior to embarking on that route the producer should consult with his advisors and develop a detailed cost-benefit analysis. Expenses for completion, publicity, marketing, as well as those for travel, living, and entertainment for an entourage involved with the film can mount up quickly.

The Cannes Film Festival is the most famous of all the film festivals. It is the single most important annual international conflux of major stars, directors, international sales agents, bank executives and film business entrepreneurs. Consider using or modifying a number of the following techniques to navigate this and other film festivals.

1. THE PINBALL METHOD

The whole point of your Cannes trip is the sheer number of face-to-face business opportunities you can create. The market and festival offer such a range of companies, dealmakers and personalities that a well-planned and executed Cannes stay can benefit your operations for years to come. For the budding dealmaker there are two basic philosophies to make the most out of your trip. The first is the pinball method, which means allowing yourself to roll with the action by putting yourself in places-be it the MTV party, marching up the steps of the Palais at the hot premiere, taking drinks at the bar at the Majestic, moving through the crowded halls of the Carlton Hotel and its many sales offices, dining on bouillabaisse at Tatou while people watching, belting out a Karaoke tune at 4:00 a.m. at La Chunga or mixing with dignitaries at the beach party. At each venue, you will bump into the people you need to get to know or catch up with. Remember though, Cannes is a marathon, so pace yourself.

2. THE MOHAMMED METHOD

A second approach has been perfected by Cannes veterans like Buckley Morris and Brian Kingman of AON/Albert G. Ruben Insurance. It consists of taking a table out on the patio at the Majestic Hotel bar, across the street from the Palais, and simply sitting there-all day long and well into the evening. Eventually, every person you want to meet, do business with, or catch up with, is going to pass through the Majestic Bar. If you have set the stage properly, they will sit at your table. The bottles of Perrier, chilled champagne, playing cards, backgammon board and a bevy of recognizable attractive performers, associates or executives will help reel in future business contacts.

3. HAVE A PLAN

As glamorously casual as Cannes may seem to an outsider, the successful insiders always go into each year's session with a set strategy in place. It helps to make a list of (and if possible, prior to Cannes to set meetings with) the appropriate sales companies, producers, actors, directors, distributors, bankers, financiers and insurance guarantors that you need to meet to make your project a reality.

4. PUTTING IT IN WRITING, BUT BE THERE

Further to this goal and regardless of what you are pushing, have something in writing. Make it short; make it smart. Whatever you do, do not bring a truckload of scripts or a box load of tapes of your completed film to hand out at Cannes: nobody wants to take it, nobody wants to carry it, nobody has time to read it or view it, and nobody wants to have to pack it in their luggage when they leave. Be prepared to pitch your project or completed film on the spot and hand somebody one or two pages that have the critical information (synopsis, attachments, estimated budget or glossy one-sheet with artwork of your completed film and the like) clearly presented. Then follow up with a script or tape stateside. Some sales agents or distributors will take the time to watch (but not carry back) a two- or three-minute trailer of your completed film.

5. REMEMBER: SELLER ARE THERE TO SELL

The international sales agents at Cannes are there to sell movies to buyers, not look for new projects, and unless the company has a special acquisitions department, they do not have the time or the focus to hear pitches until very late in the market when the key foreign buyers have left. Do not pester sales agents for meetings to pitch a project or completed film. Be flexible, take a meeting when you can get one and make sure you follow up with them after Cannes.

6. THE PAVILIONS: WHERE TO MEET AND GREET (AND REST YOUR FEET)

Of course, to pitch and to meet, a newcomer needs to know where the action is in the first place. We recommend that you spend time at the American Pavilion, the German Pavilion and the various European Pavilions. Take the opportunity to meet other filmmakers, directors, writers, producers and the key international dealmakers who are becoming more and more a force in the independent world. You will also run into agents, managers and lawyers—they are all there. The Pavilion circuit runs numerous panels on everything from film financing, to a roundtable of French directors, to digital filmmaking techniques and a one-on-one conversation between Roger Ebert and Harvey Weinstein. The luminaries who attend Pavilion programs run the gamut. The other advantage to the Pavilions is their status as the office away from home for many Cannes attendees. You should take full advantage (for a nominal fee at the American Pavilion) of the meeting tables, computers, mailboxes, Internet access, telephone services, fax machines and other business services that are essential when a deal pops up out of nowhere and requires immediate action. It also does not hurt that at the American Pavilion the Starbucks, Seattle's Best or Feet's Coffee (or whoever is the sponsor for that particular year) and the accompanying insider chitchat—is top drawer. The availability of the trade papers and the Los Angeles Times and New York Times and a constant stream of information also distinguishes the American Pavilion: keeping connected to what is going on both at the Festival and in the business in general is the key to Cannes.

7. Casual and Comfortable

While we are on the subject of Cannes essentials, here is a note on attire: make sure you have comfortable walking shoes or sneakers. Cannes may be the one place on earth where everybody still walks everywhere. Dress in casual clothes, except for the evening premieres and official black tie dinners, and make sure you bring a tuxedo or gown that fits comfortably. Do not wait until you get to Cannes to try it on. The shops on the Rivera are very expensive.

Make sure you make friends with the concierge at the Majestic Hotel and tip him often. The Majestic is right across the street from the Palais and you will inevitably have your briefcase, handbag, dress shoes, marketing materials or something that you want to leave at the concierge's desk. You do not want to walk up the red carpet of the Palais with a bulky suitcase. The gendarmes will embarrassingly refuse to let you enter in front of all the paparazzi and TV cameras.

8. The Hotel Du Cap

A trip to Cannes is not complete without several stops at the Hotel Du Cap, but bring plenty of cash, as they accept no credit cards. Be sure to schedule and make reservations for lunches and late night rendezvous. This is where the major players play. The A-level industry movers, be they producers, directors, stars, executives, bankers or sales agents are all there. Make friends with (and tip generously) the Du Cap's maitre d' so that you are given that strategically placed sunny table when you want to be in the sun next to this year's hot director.

Cannes in general and the Du Cap in particular follow "European time." The serious action starts at midnight and continues until 4:00 a.m. or 5:00 a.m. each morning. Even deep into the night, it has become increasingly difficult to gain access to the Du Cap bar. Arrive early for dinner and spend the entire evening once you have gained access. When you run into a connected colleague, it is a good idea to have him put you on the bar's invited guest list, or in the alternative, bring enough francs to tip the gendarme at the gate.

9. Make Friends with a Publicist

Cannes is a world most visibly driven by hype and heat. It is the Cannes publicists who rule the Festival, control the A-level events, the private black-tie dinners, the guest lists and the other hot tickets. While there is usually a lot of pressure on these hardworking professionals to find tickets and place settings for unexpected additions to entourages, sometimes they really do have extras. Be particularly nice to any publicists you meet and you might get lucky.

10. Bring Your Entertainment Lawyer

Wherever you go, add one more important party to your entourage. Make sure your entertainment lawyer is at your side at all times. In addition to the key business contacts and introductions that your entertainment lawyer is likely to furnish, negotiations at Cannes can take place everywhere, and you never know when a napkin will become a deal memo. Enjoy Cannes and make it a successful and profitable trip for your career.

Industry Screenings: For Connoisseurs Only

An alternative to the film festival screening is the industry or arts organization-sponsored screening such as the Independent Feature Project Sneak Preview series, which takes place in New York and Los Angeles; the American Cinemateque screenings; Film Forum screenings; AFI sponsored screenings; or the Tribeca film screening series. These special industry screenings may be the best venue in which to present your film. An experienced producer's rep knows the programmers and when the screenings are scheduled, and can assist filmmakers in identifying these outlets and help them to be selected. Most distributors track these screenings and have an acquisition representative in attendance. Many of these screenings are advertised in the trades, which can provide additional promotional value for a film. These artistic organizations have publicists who will make the press aware of the new talent on display, and this process can lead to reviews in the trades and occasionally in the newspapers. There is often a question and answer session with the filmmakers after the film, as well as a reception, which gives additional opportunity for them to promote and market films to potential buyers. All of this is paid for by the organization or the sponsor of the series, which is a considerable savings for filmmakers. Exploitation, horror, and sci-fi pictures are often denied these opportunities; most of these organizations are looking foremost for specialized, relationship, or art pictures—teenage slasher films need not apply (unless they are classy or stylized teenage slasher films).

Distributor Screenings: Assembling the Troops

Another approach to the marketing of films to distributors and buyers is the producer-sponsored screening, often wholly coordinated by the producer and the producer's rep. This type of screening can be the most effective way of marketing a film directly to distributors, simply because the filmmaker takes control of the presentation process and does not wait to be invited by a festival or arts organization. In addition, the distributor screening becomes a focused event for distributors, as opposed to a festival premiere, where the filmmaker competes with other entries just to get looked at. Also, for some reason, distributors are more likely to walk out of a festival film than one in a rented screening room. As for the guest list, the producer's rep and the filmmaker may invite as many as 200 domestic and foreign distributors to attend a special screening. These are usually held at screening rooms in New York and Los Angeles roughly concurrently, or—at the most—within a week of each other. It is a good idea to plan these events well in advance and mail, fax, or e-mail invitations at least two to three weeks prior to the screening to lock in the distributors' attendance. It is also a good idea to include a visual cue or stylistic element on the invitations, such as a still or an illustration, along with a description or descriptive tag line that gives the guest some idea of what genre the picture falls into.

Following the mailing, faxing, or e-mailing of the invitations, the producer's rep and the filmmaker should follow up with at least one, if not several, telephone calls to each invitee to assure that a representative of the distributor will attend. Although some advisors differ in this approach, it is conventional wisdom that the distributor screening audience should be well stocked with friends of the film, such as cast and crew members, family, and colleagues who are familiar with the film and will presumably act together as an audience either in laughter, tears, applause, or visible fright at the exact point in time when the filmmaker intended the reaction. The secret thrill of even the most specialized distributor is to find a film that really grabs a big audience, and having a friendly crowd in the theater can easily propagate such a notion. Although this may be a fruitless suggestion, it is a good idea to ask the friends of the film not to clap and cheer during the credits. When a distributor senses that an audience is stacked out of proportion, the overall positive reaction to the film is diminished.

The goal of the screening is to have more than one domestic distributor and more than one foreign distributor in a competitive bidding situation for licensing rights to the picture.

Selective Private Screenings: What Distributors Do Alone in the Dark

A completely different approach is the selective, discreet shopping method. As opposed to inviting the entire roster of film distributors and sales agents to one make-it-or-break-it screening, the rep opts to selectively shop the film to various key distributors, sales agents, and networks by sending the print for their personal and private viewing at their own, on-site screening facilities. This method can be effective, particularly when a distributor believes it is getting an exclusive early viewing of the film. The upside is considerable: the distributor will often take time out of his workday to attend a scheduled screening by himself in his facility and may treat the opinions he develops about the film with a more serious, businesslike attitude than he would at a nighttime event with several hundred people. Also, private screenings afford the rep and the filmmaker an opportunity to be much more selective in who sees the picture—this can be an effective technique if the film has a controversial subject matter or if there is some plot secret that needs to be protected (such as in *The Usual Suspects* or

The Crying Game).

The downside of private screenings is that neither the producer's rep nor the filmmaker will be allowed to attend, and beyond picking up and dropping off the print at the distributor's office, the filmmaker may not have any idea of what went on during the screening. If the film is marketable, this type of presentation should work, but the danger is that the film will be viewed not as it was meant to be—with an audience collectively reacting to the film without interruption or competing agendas. It is well known that some distributors request screenings and then do not show up, skip reels, take phone calls, or read the trades and converse with their colleagues while screening films. But be sure of this: distributors will admit to none of this behavior.

Recruited Audience Screenings: Do Your Research

Sometimes, for unknown reasons, a film may not have attracted the attention of a distributor, film festival, or arts organization. In this scenario, screen the film before a recruited audience in conjunction with a professional film research firm. Teen comedies, horror films, and family films, which aspire to the broadest kind of audience, can generally benefit from these kinds of screenings. Presumably, the film will be screened in a large screening room and, if the filmmaker and the producer's rep feel it is appropriate, the filmmaker should invite distributors to attend. After the screening, attendees fill out a survey, which is designed by a professional marketing research company that specializes in the movie business. A focus group or question and answer session regarding audience reaction to the characters, the story, the structure of the film, and its pacing is designed to guide the filmmakers toward decisions that will fine tune their efforts to make the most engaging picture possible.

The results of the survey are tabulated and a professional report that scores the audience reaction to the movie is issued. This process is very similar to the method used by studios in their testing of movies prior to the locking of the final cut. Assuming the results are positive, they can be used as a device to entice distributors into releasing the movie. Even if a distributor is not convinced, independent producers have used these results to get individual theater owners or theater chains to believe in the movie and contribute to or undertake the expense of advertising and promoting the film when a filmmaker has made the commitment to self-distribute.

There are no right answers on the proper way to present a movie to potential buyers and distributors. Each movie has different elements, is completed at a different time, and seeks a different segment of the general audience. Only in weighing these considerations can the filmmaker arrive at the best strategy for the ideal means of introducing the distribution community to that special motion picture. It is the function of the producer's rep to work closely with the producer to determine which strategy is appropriate for a particular film.

Sending Videotapes and DVDs to Distributors and Sales Agents

There is no question that it is preferable to screen your film in a theater with an audience when trying to sell it to a distributor. But the reality is that there are only so many screenings you can hold and there are going to be distributors who want to see the film but simply cannot or will not attend your screening.

There are many cases where the 35 mm print has not been made (or there is no money to make it) and the only effective way to show the film is by sending either an Avid or other nonlinear edited (NLE) output or a copy from a video master or DVD master, if one is available. We find that in today's marketplace the DVD screening copy is the viewing medium of choice because of the convenience in size and its superior sound and picture quality. Nevertheless, make sure to ask the acquisitions executive which format is preferable. While we acknowledge that is not the optimal presentation of the film, it is much more convenient for acquisition executives to view videocassettes and DVDs when it fits their schedules. It is a bigger commitment for an acquisitions executive to attend a screening than to simply pop a videocassette into the VCR or a DVD into a computer or DVD player. With almost 2,000 independent films competing every year for acquisitions executives' precious time, it just makes more sense to have the videocassette or DVD sent over to the executive, so it can be viewed calmly over the weekend and you can have an answer the next Monday. Do not be afraid to send a videocassette or DVD to a distributor if your situation warrants it, but only after you give the executive a chance to attend a screening.

Publicity and Marketing: From Teaser to Pleaser

The initial screening of the movie is one element in the overall marketing plan for the sale and licensing of a movie. The producer's rep can assist the producer in securing and working directly with a publicist to create the overall publicity plan for the film. These plans may include conducting and arranging press interviews with stars, the director, writer, and producer during a festival; arranging for a feature story about the film; issuing trade press releases; consulting on how and when to make additional announcements to the media concerning the film; arranging press screenings; making sure that critics get to see the film; and coordinating electronic media coverage and appearances on television, radio, and in on-line forums. The producer's rep should have input and insight into all these matters.

An experienced producer's rep can also assist the producer in the preparation of a poster (key art) and a marketing campaign and can help to formulate the most effective overall visual representation for a movie in conjunction with poster designers and graphic artists who specialize in the field.

If a trailer is advisable and budgeted, the producer's rep, in conjunction with the producer and director, will have input into the creation of the trailer and will consult with the filmmakers on the script, the scenes to be selected, the editing, the music, the voice-over, or the narration, as well as the choice of the trailer house that will put the presentation together.

Making the Deal: Read the Fine Print

Essentially, the role of the producer and the producer's rep is to create and stimulate interest and excitement about the film, to maximize that interest, and create competition among distributors. The rep should facilitate the best possible relationship among the producer and the domestic and foreign distributors of the picture. These distributors may or may not be the same entity—and may at times have conflicting agendas.

Once the buyers have been identified, it is advisable to have the producer's rep and an attorney (if the producer's rep is not also an attorney) negotiate all of the terms and conditions of the domestic and foreign distribution arrangements. While this process involves reams of complicated contracts, rights transfers, schedules, and statements, this is also the most rewarding step of the process—in essence, these rigorous negotiations are the final step before the filmmaker and rep see the connection of picture to audience.

The basic terms and conditions of the negotiation include the term of the agreement (the time span it covers), the territories being sold, the rights being conveyed—such as theatrical, television, and video—and what rights are being reserved (which could include nontheatrical rights; music publishing rights; soundtrack rights; book publishing rights; electronic media rights; live stage rights; theme park rights; restaurant rights; radio rights; in-flight and ship at sea rights; and remake, prequel and sequel, and television series rights). Additionally, the basic financial terms of the revenue splits will be negotiated. Will there be an advance? Who pays for prints, advertising, and marketing costs? Will there be a cap on expenses? If so, what is the cap? What will be the distribution fee in each specific media? How will the producer be accounted to and how often? What will be the producer's audit rights? How will withholding and other taxes be treated? What physical and paper delivery items will be required to be furnished to the distributor? How much will those delivery items cost? Can the producer simply deliver the film by providing lab access to the available physical elements of the picture? Will there be a special trust account or escrow account for the holding and dispersal of funds? What are the filmmaker's approvals and consultations with respect to publicity, the marketing campaign, the poster, the trailer and the territorial sales minimums on a territory-by-territory basis? Will the producer be entitled to approve third-party licensing agreements? What is the extent of the warranties and indemnifications for each of the parties? How will disputes between the parties be resolved? In what jurisdiction will these disputes be resolved? Will court proceedings be required? Will termination rights and other remedies be available to the producer? What will happen in the event that the producer or distributor goes bankrupt? Will the terms and conditions of the agreement be kept confidential? Who will control remakes and sequels if the film is indeed successful?

These terms and conditions are complex and involve a considerable amount of negotiation, skill, and experience in the resolution of these issues. An experienced producer's rep or entertainment attorney who specializes in distribution deals will have dealt with most of these issues and will be extremely helpful in meshing the conflicting interests of filmmaker and distributor.

Administering the Deal: The Best Execution You Will Ever Attend

Once the contractual terms are resolved, concluded, and signed, the producer and the producer's rep will still be involved in overseeing the administration of the contract, including review and interpretation of the accounting statements, making sure they are actually furnished, providing assistance in collection of monies due, and conducting audits, if necessary. The producer's rep will continue to actively consult with the producer concerning the distributor's overall marketing, publicity, and distribution strategy for the picture, both domestically and in foreign territories.

There is no one correct method to sell or license your film. The strategy utilized will depend on what stage of completion your film is in and your particular budgetary considerations, what time of year the film is available for the marketplace, genre, subject matter, cast and director, the condition of the market, and a number of other factors. Your film is unique and there are no set rules. Sit down with an experienced advisor and come up with a plan that you each agree upon before you start the process.

DELIVERY

"Delivery" is the start of the distribution life of your film. In almost all distribution agreements, delivery is a defined term, and the producer is deemed to have delivered the picture only when the distributor has received and accepted every item in an extensive list called the "delivery schedule." We find that quite often producers and distributors are sloppy about both the negotiation and implementation of the delivery schedule. On one picture we handled, we worked from a two-page deal memo signed in Cannes, which said the delivery schedule would be "negotiated in good faith." It took six months and numerous drafts before all the thorny delivery issues were worked out and the producer was not paid until the contract was signed and delivery was complete.

As an example of a delivery schedule for an independent film, we are appending a sample Delivery Schedule, which we negotiated with a major studio on a recent worldwide distribution deal. We have modified it to include other items that distributors normally require. It is very representative of the kind of delivery schedule you must fulfill when you deliver your picture to a distributor. Although in this case, the studio was the worldwide distributor of the picture, often one company has U.S. and Canadian rights (domestic rights) while another company is your agent for international distribution rights. You should remember that when you split rights there is the additional cost of delivering items to both your domestic distributor and foreign sales agent (who in turn delivers to the various foreign distributors). You should also note that your completion guarantor also will append a delivery schedule to the completion bond, but it will be simpler than the schedule you work out with the distributor since it will be limited to the "essential" delivery items discussed below. Nonetheless, you could be dealing with three or more delivery schedules on your picture with each requiring some overlapping and some different items.

We cannot overstate the importance of delivery schedules. Distribution agreements often provide for advances, which can be many millions of dollars. And almost always, the advance is tied to delivery of the picture, which makes sense, since the distributor wants to have the asset it is buying in hand.

Additionally, if the distribution rights term is not perpetual but a stated period of years, the term is typically tied to delivery so the sooner you deliver, the sooner you get rights in your film back.

Essentials

In negotiations with distributors, it is smart to try to differentiate the mandatory or essential delivery items from the nonmandatory or nonessential, and to make, for example, 90% of the advance payable upon mandatory delivery and 10% upon complete delivery, which includes all the nonmandatory items as well.

For example, let us say you are going to be paid a $10 million advance for your film and you did not segregate essential from nonessential delivery. And let us also say that signed formal music licenses are required as part of delivery. Let us assume further that you licensed a song from a music publisher with a quote letter but the music publisher waits to issue a formal license until right before delivery. And then the music publisher dies. Try to get your music publisher's signature now. And try to get your money from the distributor. Let us say interest on $10 million is at 10%. That is $2,740 a day in interest; $83,333 a month; and $1 million a year. Every day of delivery delay costs you substantially.

Delivery Schedule Issues

Let us take a look at how the delivery schedule form works. First, it warns you that not only the materials must be sent to the right place (some to New York; some to Los Angeles) but also alerts you to the fact that copies of your transmittal letter must be sent to XYZ Studios' legal department in Los Angeles and its technical services department in New York. Since getting your money probably depends on both the legal department and technical department signing off on delivery, you could be delayed if you delivered an item to one department, but did not advise the other department.

Next, the schedule explains the mechanism for "acceptance" of delivery and "cure." Say you send in your video master, which has been meticulously prepared by a top lab. XYZ Studios sends it to their lab for a QC (quality control check) and it has a scratch. If XYZ Studios tells you within 15 business days, you have to fix it. If they do not notify you of the problem within 15 business days and they later discover it, they have to fix it. To the extent the distributor elects to fix the delivery materials, they usually charge that amount to distribution expenses or reduce your advance.

Section I of the delivery schedule form lists the main physical elements that must be delivered. You should note that this film was partially subtitled.

Section II lists the items to which XYZ Studios has access (i.e., they can make copies but did not actually own the stuff). To the extent you can grant access to materials to allow the distributor to produce its own copies rather than your having to deliver a copy to the distributor, you can save substantial sums. Film materials are usually stored at a laboratory or vault, and a lab access letter, signed by the owner of the film, allows a distributor to reproduce the materials at the lab but not to remove any of the original materials.

Section III lists the audio materials to which XYZ Studios has access.

Section IV. A. lists the video materials to be delivered. Since video is now the largest market in the world and with the advent of DVD, distributors are increasingly focusing on video materials. The financial difference, depending on who pays for what when it comes to delivery video items, can be $50,000 or more. For an informative description and chart of the postproduction and delivery process and a complete glossary of laboratory and postproduction terms, consult the FotoKem Web site at *www.fotokem.com.*

Section IV. B. lists music materials, which, from our experience, is often the most problematic part of delivery. There are many reasons for this. Two fundamental ones are (1) music is the last creative element added to the film; and (2) music documentation is done at the last minute. Getting music licenses signed remains a headache for most producers. They do not want to pay for the license until they know that they are going to use the music. Additionally, they do not want to pay until the licensor signs. The usual compromise with the distributor is that delivery will be accepted if there is a confirmation letter and proof of payment of the license fee.

There are a few things to beware of with stills and publicity material. First, make sure that you have the required number of stills, discounted by the number you must exclude because of rejection by actors. As noted above, virtually all star actors negotiate for "still approval." The norm is that the actor must approve 50% of the stills where the actor appears alone in the still and 75% when part of a group. Actors usually insist that they be given a reasonable number (or, for example, not less than 100) to approve. Normally you send a contact sheet to the actor's publicist or agent. The normal contractual turnaround time is two to five days. The actors cross out the ones they do not like. You must take care of this in advance or it can delay your delivery.

Stars also have approval over their biographies; some directors and producers do as well. You must have approved materials to satisfy your delivery obligations.

Section IV. D. lists contracts, negative cost statements, and other materials that have to be delivered. The production lawyers will have some of this material, but the producer must make someone responsible for assembling the entire package. Among these items is the copyright registration discussed earlier. The form of copyright notice and disclaimer that should go on screen is provided following the sample delivery schedule at the end of this chapter.

Unfortunately, at least one company that is active in the independent world and is owned by a major conglomerate resists acknowledging delivery (and therefore payment), while at the same time it releases products and collects distribution revenue. We have experienced the following with this company:

1. Claims that delivery items were not sent when they were sent numerous times.
2. Claims that papers were lost internally so they needed to be replaced.

To circumvent bogus claims, always send materials by FedEx or have them delivered by a messenger service so there is a signed receipt.

Sample Delivery Schedule

Delivery of the motion picture currently entitled "Indie Pic" (the "Film") by Indie Production Company ("Company") to XYZ Studios ("XYZ") shall not be complete unless and until:

(1) The items listed below are submitted to the applicable department and individual listed below with a copy of a transmittal letter to the XYZ legal department; and

(2) The applicable XYZ department confirms acceptance of such delivery to the XYZ legal department. XYZ shall have a period of twenty (20) business days after submission of an item to inspect the item. If a submitted item is technically deficient, XYZ shall notify company in writing and company shall have ten (10) days following receipt of such notice to correct the deficiency. If XYZ fails to give written notice of a deficiency in a submitted item within such twenty (20) business day period, then the submitted item will be deemed delivered.

I. Materials to be delivered to XYZ.

A.

(1) 35 mm Positive Print: One (1) complete, final, first-class Anamorphic (2.35:1) 35 mm composite positive print, conforming in all respects to the "Picture specifications" set forth in the agreement between Company and XYZ, fully cut, fully color corrected, approved for color in writing by director and director of photography and balanced to release print standards in the color process in which the Film was photographed, titled and assembled from the original fully cut negative and with the fully mixed soundtrack negative "#1" specified in Paragraph III. A. (4) below (such soundtrack to be a Dolby SR stereo soundtrack negative in perfect synchronization throughout with the photographic action thereof). Such print shall be without scratches, spots, abrasions, dirt, cracks, tears or any other damage of any kind whatsoever. Quality of the picture image and of the soundtrack shall conform to the quality established by current practice in pictures made by major motion picture studios in Los Angeles County, California. The print shall have been made on Eastman Kodak safety photographic raw stock (or a stock chosen by the Director or Director of Photography for use in production). The print shall otherwise correspond to American Standards specification Z-22, 36-1947 for cutting and perforating dimensions from 35 mm motion picture positive raw stock. The print shall be delivered on metal reels in metal carrying cases.

(2) 35 mm Anamorphic (2.35:1) Positive Print with Dolby SR Stereo: One (1) new, complete 1 LITE composite color print (with soundtracks), fully color corrected and balanced, which shall be the first print struck from the Internegative specified in II. B. (3) and the soundtrack negative specified in III. A. (4) ("Check Print"). The Check Print shall be without scratches, spots, abrasions, dirt, cracks,

tears or any other damage of any kind whatsoever. The quality of the picture image and of the soundtrack shall conform to the quality established by XYZ's current practice. The Check Print shall be made on Eastman Kodak safety photographic stock (or a stock chosen by the Director or Director of Photography for use in production) and shall be delivered on metal reels in metal carrying cases.

(3) Spotting/Continuity List: Two (2) copies of a complete English language spotting/continuity list of the print of the Film specified in Paragraph I. A. (1) above, including cut-by-cut frame and footage counts of all dialogue, scene descriptions, music starts and stops, lyrics (if any) and translations of all dialogue spoken in other than English. Footages for continuity and spotting lists should be figured on an AB reel basis (2,000 feet).

(4) Shooting Script: Two (2) typewritten copies of the shooting script of the Picture and trailers in the original language and in English conforming in all aspects to the mixed optical track.

(5) A formatted computer disc, which contains the English-language subtitles and the proper spotting of such subtitles (i.e., footage and frame count, clearly defined picture start for each reel, first frame of picture, first/second/third scene changes, the last three scene changes, last frame of picture), fully synchronized with the 35 mm internegative described in Section II. B. 3 below. In addition, two (2) typewritten copies of the English subtitle list with the proper spotting indications, conformed in all respects to the action and dialogue contained in the Picture.

II. Materials to be delivered to BCD Film Laboratories (or such other laboratory designated by XYZ).

Delivery of all or any items of film material listed below shall not be considered complete until laboratory access for such items has been granted exclusively to XYZ for its territories by a written agreement delivered to XYZ, in a form approved by XYZ, which is signed by the laboratory and in which the Production Company (and, if applicable, the completion guarantor and the bank or financier for the film) release all their rights in the film to XYZ for XYZ's territories.

If the Film is photographed with anamorphic lenses, then unless otherwise specified by XYZ in writing, the titles (main, end, translations, locales, dates, etc.) shall be composed in a manner so as to utilize no more than 42% of the 2.35:1 aspect ratio frame area so that the lettering of the titles shall appear in the "safe lettering area" of the television screen in any television exhibition of the Film.

A.

(1) Original Picture Negative: One (1) Super 35 mm wholly original Eastman Kodak (or a stock chosen by the Director or Director of Photography for use in

production) color FULL FRAME picture negative, conforming in all respects to the "Picture Specifications" in the agreement between Company and XYZ, cut, titled, assembled and conformed in all respects to the composite sample positive print specified in Paragraph I. A. (1) above, with such negative to have the XYZ logo attached thereto. The picture negative shall not contain any physical damage and all splices shall be sound, secure and transparent when viewed by transmitted light.

(2) Intentionally Deleted.

(3) Background Material Negative:

(i) The original negative of ALL background material (textless, i.e., without any superimposed lettering) to the main, credit, insert and end titles of the Film and of photographic overlay titles thereof, containing any and all photographic effects present in the titled negative specified in Paragraph II. A. (1) above, such as fades, dissolves, blowups, freeze frames, multiple exposures, etc.

(ii) One (1) Anamorphic (2.35:1) 35 mm print made from the element specified in Paragraph II. A. (3) (i) above.

(iii) One (1) Anamorphic (2.35:1) 35 mm interpositive made from the element specified Paragraph II. A. (3) (i) above.

(4) Screen Test Negatives: The original negative of all artists' screen tests and any picture material not used in the Film, which may be suitable for film library purposes together with detailed schedules thereof and positive prints thereof, if available.

B.

(1) Film Interpositives: Two (2) flat (1:1.85) 35 mm FULL FRAME unsubtitled interpositives made from the original picture negative specified in Paragraph II. A. (1) above (acetate), fully titled and color corrected, capable of reproducing a 1 LITE internegative.

(2) Intentionally Deleted.

(3) 35 mm Internegative: One (1) Anamorphic (2.35:1) 35 mm 1 LITE internegative made from the interpositives specified in Paragraph II. B. (1) above (ester base), with MPAA rating card affixed immediately after the end credits.

III. Materials to be delivered to BCD Film Laboratories (or such other laboratory designated by XYZ). The soundtrack negative shall not contain any physical damage and all splices shall be sound and secure.

Delivery of all or any items of film material listed below shall not be considered complete until laboratory access for such items has been granted exclusively to XYZ for its territories by a written agreement delivered to XYZ in a form approved by XYZ, which is signed by the laboratory and in which the production company (and, if applicable, the completion guarantor and the bank or financier for the film) release all their rights in the film to XYZ for XYZ's territories.

A.

(1) Domestic Dub ("Stems"): One (1) Multiple Track ("stems") magnetic or digital master of final domestic dub used to manufacture the two-track stereo dub or digital print master in perfect synchronization with the original picture negative specified in Paragraph II. A. (1) above.

(2) Foreign Dub (M & E Track): One (1) 35 mm six-track, with Dolby SR noise reduction, music and effects magnetic master, containing stereo music and effects tracks configured left, center, right, surround on tracks 1 through 4, respectively and any special sound elements peculiar to the Film (e.g., grunts, groans, foreign-language dialogue, chanting, etc.) on track 5 and clean mono English-language dialogue on track 6. The effects in this dub must be fully filled and mixed in the same manner as the domestic dub and in perfect synchronization with the original picture negative specified in Paragraph II. A. (1) above. This element may be substituted by a digital element, provided such digital element contains the same specific stereo music and effects elements, with the same respective configuration and mix.

(3) Digital Multitrack Stereo Print Master or Dolby SR Stereo Master: One (1) digital multitrack stereo master (DASH 33/24 or 33/48 master) with collocated Dolby A analog stereo track from which the stereo optical soundtrack negative specified in III. A. (4) has been made and which is in perfect synchronization with the picture negative. The channel assignments shall be as follows: Ch 1 = Left, Ch 2 = Left Center, Ch 3 = Center, Ch 4 = Right Center, Ch 5 = Right, Ch 6 = Left Surround, Ch 7 = Right Surround, Ch 8 = Sub Woofer, Ch 9 = Dolby A Type Stereo Print Master (Left Total), Ch 10 = Dolby A Type Stereo Print Master (Right Total), Ch 11 = Dolby SR Type Stereo Print Master (Left Total), Ch 12 = Dolby SR Type Stereo Print Master (Right Total). Channels 15 through 24 shall be reserved for the Music and Effects tracks specified in Paragraph III. A. (6) below.

If such a license may not be obtained, XYZ will accept a Dolby SR Stereo digital Multitrack Print Master with the following configuration: Ch 1 (Left Total Mix), Ch 2 (Right Total Mix) and which is in perfect synchronization with the picture negative.

If a Dash model #PCM 3348 recorder is used, no material shall be recorded on any channels above channel 24.

(4) Digital Stereo Optical Soundtrack or Dolby SR Stereo: Two (2) 35 mm wholly original, brand new, English language version digital stereo (collocated Dolby A analog stereo soundtrack) optical soundtrack negatives (Eastman 2374 digital sound recording film), or two (2) Dolby SR Stereo optical soundtrack negatives, made from the print master specified in III. A. (3), fully cut, assembled and conformed in all respect to the answer print. The soundtrack negatives shall not contain any physical damage and all splices shall be sound and secure.

(5) Digital Multitrack Stereo Foreign Master or Dolby SR Stereo: One (1) digital multitrack music and effects master or Dolby SR Stereo multitrack music and effects master. The sound effects in this dub must be fully filled and mixed in the same manner as the domestic dub and in perfect synchronization with the picture negative specified in Paragraph II. A. (1) above. The Dialogue Guide Track shall contain a mono mix of the English language dialogue. The Optional, Extra Materials Track shall contain any special sound elements peculiar to the Film (e.g., grunts, groans, shouts, screams, breaths, foreign language dialogue, chanting, etc.).

The channel assignments must be as follows:

If recorded on a master tape with no other material; Ch 1 = Left, Ch 2 = Left Center, Ch 3 = Center, Ch 4 = Right Center, Ch 5 = Right, Ch 6 = Left Surround, Ch 7 = Right Surround, Ch 8 = Sub Woofer, Ch 9 = Extra, Optional Material, Ch 10 = Dialogue Guide Track.

If recorded on the same master tape as the domestic version dub (Paragraph II. A. (3) above); Ch 15 = Dialogue Guide Track, Ch 16 = Extra, Optional Material Track Ch 17 = Left, Ch 18 = Left Center, Ch 19 = Center, Ch 20 = Right Center, Ch 21 = Right, Ch 22 = Left Surround, Ch 23 = Right Surround, Ch 24 = Sub Woofer. Channels 1 through 12 shall be reserved for the Music and Effects tracks specified in Paragraph III. A. (6) below.

If a Dash model #PCM 3348 recorder is used, no material shall be recorded on any channels above channel 24.

(6) Six-Track Dialogue/Music/Effects Master: One (1) 35 mm six-track Digital Master of the complete Picture, with the following configuration: (i) Ch 1 and Ch 2 containing Dialogue Left, Right; (ii) Ch 3 and Ch 4 containing Music Left, Right; (iii) Ch 5 and Ch 6 containing Effects (fully filled) Left, Right (not left total/right total). All elements must be fully synchronized with the materials in items II. B. (1) and II. B. (3) above and able to be used for full Stereo Mix laydown together (dialogue, music and effects) so that, when the six tracks (i, ii, and iii) are used together, the resulting sound is the full and complete Stereo Mix of the Picture.

(7) Dolby License: An executed license agreement in full force and effect between

Company and Dolby Laboratories, Inc. in connection with the Film.

B. Multitrack Recordings: All multitrack recordings of original music score. All multitrack dub downs of original music recordings including record mixes (if such exist) and four (4) audiocassette transfers thereof (in Digital Audio Tape format).

IV. Other Material.

A. Video and Audio Materials: Deliver to XYZ. General video format should contain the following components and shall appear on all masters in the order indicated below: Roll Up: 1 minute minimum/Bars & Tone: 30 seconds—with beep tone for left and right I.D./Slate: 10 seconds/Black: End credits/Black—1 minute exactly/Textless Backgrounds of Main and End titles and any inserts/Black—1 minute.

(1) One (1) D1 NTSC 4x3 full frame unsubtitled master with theatrical stereo on Ch 1 & 2, fully filled music and effects on Ch 3 & 4 and textless backgrounds on the tail.

(2) One (1) D1 NTSC 16x9 unsubtitled master with theatrical stereo on Ch 1 & 2, fully filled music and effects on Ch 3 & 4 and textless backgrounds on the tail.

(3) One (1) D1 NTSC letterbox unsubtitled master with theatrical stereo on Ch 1 & 2, fully filled music and effects on Ch 3 & 4 and textless backgrounds on the tail.

(4) One (1) D1 PAL 4x3 full frame unsubtitled master with theatrical stereo on Ch 1 & 2, fully filled music and effects of Ch 3 & 4 and textless backgrounds on the tail.

(5) One (1) D1 PAL 16x9 full frame unsubtitled master with theatrical stereo on Ch 1 & 2, fully filled music and effects of Ch 3 & 4 and textless backgrounds on the tail.

(6) One (1) D1 PAL letterbox unsubtitled master with theatrical stereo on Ch 1 & 2, fully filled music and effects of Ch 3 & 4 and textless backgrounds on the tail.

B. Music Materials: Deliver to XYZ.

(1) Music Cue Sheets: Six (6) copies of the music cue sheets in standard form showing particulars of all music synchronized with the Film, including but not limited to titles, composers, publishers, applicable music performing societies (e.g., ASCAP, BMI), form of usage (e.g., visual, background, instrumental, vocal, etc.) and timings. The cue sheet shall indicate whether a master use license is required on each outside cue listed on the cue sheet and its source (e.g., record company name).

(2) Sheet Music: All sheet music of the composer's original score and the band parts of such music and all other music written or recorded either for the Film or recordings by any device (e.g., phonograph records, tapes) relating thereto.

(3) Licenses: Duplicate originals (or clearly legible photostatic copies, if duplicate originals are unavailable) of all licenses, contracts, assignments and/or other written permissions from the proper parties in interest permitting the use of any musical material of whatever nature used in the production of the Film including, without limitation, synchronization and master use licenses.

(4) Personal Services Contracts: Duplicate originals (or clearly legible photostatic copies, if duplicate originals are unavailable) of all agreements or other documents relating to the engagement of music personnel in connection with the Film including, without limitation, those for music composer(s) and conductor(s), technicians and administrative staff.

(5) Soundtrack: The fully executed soundtrack album agreement, music publishing or music administration agreement(s), if applicable and the agreement with the music supervisor for the Film, if any.

(6) AFM Contracts: If the Film was produced under the jurisdiction of the AF of M, copies of all contracts for all AF of M members engaged on the Film.

C. Stills and Publicity Material: Deliver to XYZ.

(1) Black and White: No less than two hundred and fifty (250) black and white stills (8"x10") or contact sheets representing no less than two hundred fifty (250) images of scenes from the Picture, clearly labeled and numbered. No less than two hundred fifty (250) black and white negatives, one (1) for each of the images appearing on any contact sheet, clearly labeled and numbered.

(2) Color: Color contact sheets containing no less than five hundred (500) color images, or if not available, no less than five hundred (500) color slides (transparencies) of scenes from the Picture, clearly labeled and numbered. No less than five hundred (500) color negatives, one (1) for each of the stills/slides, clearly labeled and numbered. DELIVER AS SOON AS POSSIBLE.

(3) Synopsis: Four (4) copies of the synopsis of the Film and biographies of the individual producer(s), director(s), stars and leading players thereof (such biographies to be approved in advance of deliver to XYZ by all individual producers, directors, stars and leading players possessing approval rights over such biographies) and all production notes, interviews and other publicity and/or advertising material for the Film as Company has prepared (including all footage owned by Company or which is under Company's control shot for electronic press kits, featurettes, interviews or television specials) in sufficient quantity and variety to enable XYZ adequately to publicize the Film.

D. Contracts and Negative Cost Statement and Other Materials: Deliver to XYZ.

(1) Underlying Rights and Chain of Title: Duplicate originals (or clearly legible photostatic copies, if duplicate originals are unavailable) of all licenses, contracts, assignments and/or other written permissions from the proper parties in interest permitting the use of any literary, dramatic and other material of whatever nature used in the production of the Film including, without limitation, all "chain of title" documents relating to Company's acquisition of all of the rights in the Film being conveyed to XYZ.

(2) Personal Services Contracts: Duplicate originals (or clearly legible photostatic copies, if duplicate originals are unavailable) of all agreements or other documents relating to the engagement of personnel in connection with the Film including, without limitation, those for individual producer(s), the director(s), all artists other than crowd artists and administrative staff.

(3) Negative Cost Statement: IF REQUIRED BY XYZ, a statement of the final negative cost of the Film certified as being true, correct and complete by an officer of Company; and a "top sheet" from the final budget for the Film (signed by the Producer and director) showing the components of negative cost and any adjustments thereto.

(4) Subordination Agreements: Subordination agreements in form and substance satisfactory to XYZ, from any entity to whom Company sold, transferred, assigned, mortgaged, pledged, charged, hypothecated or otherwise disposed of its rights in and to the Film prior to the conveyance to XYZ.

(5) Short-Form Assignment: A signed and notarized Short-Form Copyright Assignment or instrument of transfer, conveying distribution rights to XYZ.

(6) Errors and Omissions Policy: Certificate of Insurance for errors and omissions for the Film.

(7) U.S. Copyright Registration: All documents or materials required for registration in the United States Copyright Office (and elsewhere as required throughout the territory) of any underlying material upon which the screenplay is based or adapted from, the screenplay and the Picture.

(8) Certificate of Origin: IF REQUIRED BY XYZ, one (1) or more Certificates of Origin in XYZ's customary form.

(9) Stock Footage/Film Clips: Valid and subsisting license agreements from all parties having any rights in any stock footage or film clips used in the Film, granting to XYZ the perpetual and worldwide right to incorporate said stock footage in the Film or any portion thereof embodying said stock footage or clips in any and all media perpetually throughout the world.

(10) Intentionally Deleted.

(11) Audio Tapes/Compact Disc: Six (6) audiocassettes or compact discs (if available) of the soundtrack music of the Picture.

(12) Dolby License Agreement: If applicable, an executed license agreement in full force and effect between Company and Dolby Laboratories, Inc. in connection with the Film.

E. Credits, Stock Footage and Other Materials: Deliver to XYZ.

(1) Screen and Paid Advertising Credits: The complete statement of all screen and advertising credit obligations, including duplicate originals (or clearly legible photostatic copies, if duplicate originals are not available) of all contracts or those contractual provisions pertaining to credits pursuant to which any person or entity is entitled to receive screen and/or advertising credits in connection with the Film; together with a proposed layout of the proposed screen and advertising credits in XYZ's standard format and a statement of all dubbing obligations (if any); it being agreed and understood, however, that (a) XYZ shall have final approval, in its sole discretion, of any main screen credit and paid advertising credit obligations; and (b) no such main screen or advertising credits shall be photographed until XYZ has approved in writing all such credits.

(2) Intentionally Deleted.

(3) Dubbing and Editing Obligations: A complete English language statement of all dubbing obligations (if any) and any other third party restrictions and approval rights (including, without limitation, director's editing rights, video mastering consultation or approval rights, etc.), with excerpts from each applicable third party agreement setting forth the precise extent and nature of such obligations, restrictions and/or approval and consultation rights attached hereto.

(4) Main Title Material: All photographic and nonphotographic material used to generate Main Titles, End Titles, inserts, local titles, dates, translations and captions, including but not limited to, intermediates, original negatives, Hi-con units, artwork, etc.

F. Television Version:

(1) One (1) 35 mm color dupe of each reel of the entire Film, of the TV version of the Film in which there is contained all or any part of the alternative scenes and/or dialogue and/or eliminations and/or additions, fully edited and integrated with a graphic indicator to clearly distinguish new material from original materials for the purpose of conforming to standards and practices and length requirements for the United States and foreign television exhibition of the Film. The running time of the television version when projected at twenty-four (24)

frames per second shall be ninety-six (96) minutes.

(2) One (1) 35 mm magnetic two-track Dolby stereo print master, which shall be fully mixed, equalized and conformed in all respects to the final television dub.

(3) One (1) 35 mm magnetic two (2) track Dolby stereo print master, which shall consist of music, one hundred percent (100%) filled sound effects and surrounds and shall be fully mixed, equalized and conformed in all respects to the final television dub.

G. Airline Version: If the television version does not satisfy the requirements for airline standards, a separate airline version shall be delivered as set forth below:

(1) One (1) 35 mm color dupe of each reel of the entire Film, of the Airline Version of the Film in which there is contained all or any part of the alternative scenes and/or dialogue and/or eliminations and/or additions, fully edited and integrated with a graphic indicator to clearly distinguish new material from original materials for the purpose of conforming to standards and practices and length requirements for the United States and foreign television exhibition of the Film. The running time of the Airline Version when projected at twenty-four (24) frames per second shall be not longer than one hundred eighteen (118) minutes.

(2) One (1) 35 mm magnetic two (2) track Dolby stereo print master, which shall be fully mixed, equalized and shall conform in all respects to the final Airline dub.

(3) One (1) 35 mm magnetic two (2) track Dolby stereo print master, which shall consist of music, one hundred percent (100%) filled sound effects and surrounds and shall be fully mixed, equalized and conform in all respects to the final Airline dub

H. Additional Television/Airline Materials:

(1) If the main and/or end titles of the original 35 mm negative of the Film contain any credits relating to a character or a player that does not appear in the TV/Airline Version, or the TV/Airline Version contains a character or player that does not appear in the feature version, then a newly photographed set of 35 mm negative main and/or end titles reflecting the deletions and/or additions shall be manufactured, cut, edited and assembled and conformed in all respects (including, without limitation, length) to the main and/or end titles of the original 35 mm Film negative.

(2) If the main and/or end titles of the original 35 mm negative of the Film contain any credits relating to any musical compositions contained in the original soundtrack, but not contained in the soundtrack of the TV/Airline Version, then a newly photographed set of 35 mm negative main and/or end titles reflecting the deletions and/or additions shall be manufactured, cut, edited and assembled and

conformed in all respects (including, without limitation, length) to the main and/or end titles of the original 35 mm Film negative.

(3) If the music in the television/airline dub is altered in any way from the theatrical dub (deletions, additions, etc.), six (6) copies of the music cue sheets relating to the television/airline dub, in the same manner as indicated in paragraph V. B. (1) below.

(4) The negative of all alternative takes, cover shots or other material integrated into the TV/Airline Version shall be segregated and clearly marked for identification and assembled on one reel and processed into an interpositive. The interpositive will be clearly marked and identified as an "augmentation reel."

(5) If the Picture is in the anamorphic or 1:85 format, one (1) 35 mm optical house negative conformed to the Original Picture Negative, complete with the text of the main, end and narrative titles, suitable for the television format.

(6) A written log of all changes made for the TV/Airline Version will be provided.

I. Work Materials:

(1) The original negative of all cutouts, outtakes, trims and lifts, as well as all other materials photographed or recorded by Company in connection with the production of the Film.

(2) The positive prints of all cutouts, outtakes, trims and lifts, as well as all other materials, i.e., positive prints of the negative specified in paragraph I (1) above.

(3) All soundtrack cutouts, outtakes, trims and lifts.

(4) The 35 mm edited work print (action) and the 35 mm edited work print (sound).

(5) All original production dialogue or other recordings; all dialogue units and predubs; all sound effects units and predubs; all music units and predubs. All material specified in this paragraph I. (5) must be in perfect synchronization with the negative specified in paragraph I. (1) above.

(6) If the postproduction of the Film was accomplished electronically (e.g., videotape, videodisc, etc.), all source materials that were used or created during postproduction.

(7) The original lined or cutting script (with notes) prepared by the script supervisor concurrently with the production of the Film, as well as any other documents, notes, logs or reports prepared by the script supervisor and used during

post productions.

(8) The editor's Code Book indicating the negative key (edge) numbers, the laboratory negative assembly roll number, the production sound roll number for all scenes printed and delivered during the production of the Film and also indicating the Daily Code numbers or a copy thereof.

(9) All camera reports, laboratory film reports or sound recording and transfer reports delivered with the Film materials during the production of the Film or a copy thereof.

(10) A complete and detailed inventory of all editorial film materials (picture and sound) used or manufactured during postproduction of the Film and indicating the contents and carton or box number of each carton or box packed upon completion of the Film. All cartons or boxes shall be clearly labeled with the production title, contents and carton or box number.

(11) If the postproduction of the Film was accomplished electronically (e.g., videotape, videodisk, etc.), a copy (both hard copy printout and computer readable media) of all Edit Decision Lists, logs and other databases created during postproduction.

(12) A complete list of the end credits of the Picture, indicating the noncontractual names, names that may be struck and names that must be included during creation of the end crawl for television.

Copyright Notice and Disclaimer

The following is our suggestion for the copyright notification to appear on screen at the end of your picture:

"This motion picture is protected by copyright laws of the United States of America and other countries. Any unauthorized exhibition, distribution and/or reproduction of all or part of this motion picture or videotape (including the soundtrack) may result in severe civil liabilities and/or criminal prosecution in accordance with the applicable laws.

Copyright © (year of first publication) All Rights Reserved. Country of first publication: United States of America. (Production Company) is the author of this motion picture for the purposes of the Berne Convention and all national laws giving effect thereto."
If your movie is fictional, use disclaimer #1 below. If your movie is inspired by actual events, use disclaimer #2 below, or adapt it to fit your situation. These disclaimers are not legally required and do not grant immunity from being sued, but they put viewers on notice and are helpful.

1. This story is entirely fictional and any similarity of any characters or incidents to the name, character or history of any actual person, living or dead or to any actual event is entirely coincidental and unintentional

OR

2. This story was inspired by actual events and persons. However, some of the characters and incidents portrayed and the names used are fictitious, and any similarity of those fictitious characters or incidents to the name, character or history of any actual person, living or dead, or to any actual event, is entirely coincidental and unintentional.

17

DIGITAL MOVIE MAKING

There is no aspect of independent pictures that is more revolutionary or evolving faster than digital movie making.

The Future is Now: A Historical Perspective

If you are an independent filmmaker with a limited budget and a project without airplane crashes, elaborate locations, or floods or earthquakes; a project that is original and has emotional impact; can benefit from hand-held camera angles and does not require A-list stars; you should seriously consider shooting on a digital format of some kind.

The idea that to succeed in the theatrical marketplace, you must shoot a project on 35 mm film, is quickly disappearing. Examples of successfully launched digital projects in the early years of digital experimentation include the Special Jury Prize winner at the 1998 Cannes Film Festival, Thomas Vinterberg's *The Celebration*, which was subsequently picked up by domestic distributor October Films and released in the U.S. and 35 other countries theatrically. *The Celebration* was shot hand-held by director of photography Anthony Dodd Mantle on a one-chip $1,000 consumer-grade digital camera and then transferred to 35 mm film by Lukkein Laboratories in Holland for its anticipated festival and theatrical play. It has been described as seminal and as influential a picture as D. W. Griffith's *The Birth of a Nation* was in 1907.

Award-winning and critically acclaimed director Lars Von Trier's *The Idiots*, which was shot on a three-chip ($2,000 to $4,000), slightly more professional digital camera, also screened at the Cannes Film Festival in 1998. *The Idiots*, a caustic black comedy set in a hospital, was also picked up by October Films for U.S. theatrical release and played theatrically in several other major territories. Like *The Celebration*, the project was also transferred to 35 mm film for release.

These European pioneers have been joined by an increasing number of American filmmakers. Bennett Miller's Los Angeles Independent Film Festival award winning project *The Cruise*, about a unique and troubled Manhattan bus tour guide, was also shot on a three-chip digital camera, and following its festival success was picked up for worldwide distribution by a U.S. based minimajor, the digitally progressive Artisan Entertainment. In this case, however, the entire picture was shot in natural light by the director himself, who served as a self-contained, one-person crew. Since then, numerous digital motion pictures have since been shot with digital technology, transferred to film, and exhibited in theaters throughout the world, including Robert Rodriguez's *Once Upon a Time in Mexico* starring Johnny Depp and Antonio Banderas, George Lucas' last and upcoming version of the *Star Wars* series, and sections of acclaimed director Steven Soderberg's *Full Frontal*.

Digital Exhibition

October 1998 marked the first-ever satellite theatrical release in five theaters of Stefan Avalos and Lance Wesley's $900 movie *The Last Broadcast*, an all-digitally shot project, which was completely postproduced on a home desktop PC. The project was never transferred to 35 mm film and was released theatrically in digital form directly by satellite by Wavelength Releasing, by means of receiving dishes installed at specially equipped theaters that had digital projection systems. This event was made possible through the collaborative efforts of Wavelength, Cyberstar—A Loral Company, Texas Instruments, Cinemaccanica (France), and Digital Projection Incorporated.

Here is how the process worked: *The Last Broadcast* was digitally shot and mastered, then sent to Cyberstar in Mountain View, California, for encoding, testing for digital image and sound quality, and was then stored on Cyberstar's servers. Cyberstar's transponder dishes transmitted the movie to a satellite that was in fixed orbit 22,300 miles above the Earth. The satellite amplified the signal and sent it back to each theater's receiving dish, where the movie (in pure digital information form) was sent electronically to the theater's computer server. There, it was transferred to Digital Projection's digital projector system, which incorporated Texas Instrument's Digital Mirror Device (which includes a system of 700,000 independent mirror surfaces, none wider than a human hair), which can enhance the quality of images to levels never before seen in conventional projection systems. At a per screen average of approximately $5,000 per week per screen, *The Last Broadcast*, while in theatrical release, performed favorably opposite *Happiness*, its main indie competition in the marketplace at that time.

Following the lead of *The Last Broadcast*, in June, 1999, Twentieth Century Fox released George Lucas's 95% digitally mastered *Star Wars: Episode I—The Phantom Menace* on four digital screens in the United States. This marked the first time a major studio released a film digitally. Unique to distributor Twentieth Century Fox and Lucas's strategy was the fact that the *Star Wars* release was deliberately designed for two different and competing projection systems, one by the Texas Instruments' group and the other by the JVC/Hughes digital projection system. *Variety's* chief critic Todd McCarthy then reported on the two digital projection systems and concluded that the Texas Instruments' system seemed more suited to high-tech productions like *Star Wars*, while the JVC/Hughes system was particularly effective with costumes and skin tones in more low-tech productions such as *An Ideal Husband*, which was released by Miramax and also played digitally at the Sunset 5 Theatres in Hollywood. On July 30, 1999, Disney joined the digital fold by exhibiting its animated feature *Tarzan* on digital projection systems at three theater complexes: the AMC Pleasure Island multiplex at Walt Disney World in Florida, AMC's Media Center North in Burbank, California, and the Edwards Spectrum Complex in Irvine, California. Adding fuel to an already competitive bonfire, Lucas announced that his next *Star Wars* picture would be produced 100% digitally (thereby making future digital exhibition all the more enticing for distributor, producer, and exhibitor alike). Since then, Texas Instruments' Digital Light Processing ("DLP") Systems (which are now available in at least 20 theaters in the Los Angeles metropolitan area and 11 theaters in the New York metropolitan area); Kodak; and Technicolor, which also developed their own digital cinema operating systems; Barco Systems of Belgium, which recently announced a deal to install 20 digital projection systems in one of Singapore's leading exhibitors; ENGWAH; as well as other companies like Microsoft, NBC, JVC Hughes, and Qualcom have jumped into the fray to attempt to compete and ultimately dominate the digital projection field in the coming years.

Despite the extreme interest in digital exhibition, *Variety* reported that as of mid 2004, there were still less than 50 digital projection systems in U.S. cinemas considered technically appropriate for exhibiting mainstream Hollywood movies. Abroad, there were slightly more than 100 digital in cinemas, with less than half in Europe and much of the balance in China, Japan, and Singapore.

In the spring/summer of 2004, *Van Helsing* was shown in 30 digital cinemas globally, while *The Day After Tomorrow* premiered in 25 digital cinemas.

Digital Production

1999 was a pivotal year in the expansion of digital production. At Cannes that year, maverick producer/director Richard Martini (*You Can't Hurry Love*, *Cannes Man)* was seen all over the Croissette (the main street in Cannes that winds along the seashore and leads up to the Palais where competition films at the Cannes Film Festival are shown), hawking his $15,000 (including the cost of all equipment) digital movie *Camera*, with a feature article on hand on his film in *USA Today's* Tech Extra section which was just then beginning to report on the digital revolution. Other digital projects announced that year from established directors—most from the Sundance generation—included films by Tom Noonan (*the Wife, What Happened Was...*), Jon Jost (*All the Vermeers in New York*), Todd Verow (*Frisk*), Miguel Arteta (*Star Maps, Chuck and Buck, The Good Girl*), Jonathan Nossiter (*Sunday*), Gary Winick (*Sweet Nothing, The Tic Code, Tadpole*), and moviemaking's current *enfant terrible* Harmony Korine (*Julien Donkey-Boy*). With these indie directors and George Lucas (who used a $500,000 Sony/Panavision camera to digitally capture *Star Wars: Episode II*) leading the way, this group was recognized as the true groundbreakers of a new era for cinema, one that has already been seriously compared to 1927's arrival of sound. As for the major studios eventual full-bore participation in this revolution, the question was no longer if, but when. Sony and A level directors like Robert Rodriguez, Steven Soderberg, Mike Figgis, and George Lucas continue to keep pushing the studios in that direction. Recognizing the marketability of the digital revolution, the MPAA and the National Association of Theatre Owners (NATO) also established their own initiatives to encourage widespread use of technology and digital projection systems.

Digital Financing/Distribution

With new digital film projects popping up almost as quickly as Web sites, it is not surprising that financing and distribution entities began cropping up soon after the solo filmmakers. Already well-established as a leader in independent financing and distribution at that time, Ted Hope, James Schamus, and David Linde's Good Machine (now known as Focus Films) financed the fourth independently made DOGMA 95 (the manifesto of guidelines that dictated the means of production on *The Idiots* and *The Celebration*) project, *The King Is Alive,* from the group led by Von Trier, directed by Danish commercial director Kristian Levering and cowritten by Anders Thomas Jennsen, who won an Academy Award for his dramatic short *Election.*

In 2000, The Independent Film Channel (IFC) created a digital affiliate of founder Peter Broderick's Next Wave Films (*www.nextwavefilms.com*). The endeavor, known as Agenda 2000, financed and distributed digital productions with an eye toward theatrical release, but with no less than a guaranteed cable release to the approximately 13 million households that subscribe to IFC and its companion arts channel, Bravo. Next Wave had an illustrious launch and financed or completed a number of pictures but ultimately succumbed to corporate cutbacks. Somewhat more successful was an outfit known as InDigEnt. Independently of Agenda 2000, IFC's president, Jonathan Sehring, and indie attorney/producer John Sloss and his client Gary Winnick entered into a ten-picture agreement in 2000. Under the InDigEnt banner, each picture had an average budget of $150,000, was completely financed by IFC, and executive produced by Winnick and Sloss. A number of the films on the InDigEnt slate were released by Lions Gate and Miramax in the United States. They will appear on IFC and an international distribution deal was secured with Danish international sales agent Trust Film Sales. InDigEnt's more recent films include Peter Hedges' *Pieces of April*, Campbell Scott's *Final*, Ethan Hawke's *Chelsea Walls*, Rodrigo Garcia's *Ten Tiny Love Stories*, and Bruce Wagner's *Women in Film*. InDigEnt is still very actve in today's digital production world.

Former Independent Feature Film Market (IFFM) director Sharon Sklar assembled a group of investors under the banner of Blow Up Pictures (*www.blowuppictures.com*) to produce and distribute digital projects. Blow Up announced the financing of its first projects including Miguel Artera's *Chuck and Buck*, which was ultimately released theatrically by Artisan, and Alan Wade's *The Pornographer: A Love Story*. The budgets of these projects reportedly ranged from $50,000 to $1,000,000. Blow-Up Pictures ultimately founded a joint venture with Mark Cuban's HDNET to produce high definition digital pictures in the two million dollar range. Presumably those films are also to be distributed through Cuban's HDNET service along with the Landmark Theatre Chain, which also announced a digital initiative to furnish its 20-city chain with digital cinemas in a joint venture with Microsoft.

In 1998 and 1999, at the height of the Internet explosion, digital World Wide Web distribution companies sprang up at a stunning rate. The range of ventures included the digitally transmitted pay-per-view cartoons at *Ren & Stimpy* creator John Kricfalusi's Internet Cartoon Network (*www.spumco.com*); AtomFilms' minimovies, which were designed to be short enough so that wired office workers can catch them on coffee breaks at *www.atomfilms.com*; the Digital Multiplex, which planned to sell pay-per-view downloads of second-run movies as an offshoot of the on-line game Hollywood Stock Exchange (*www.hsx.com*); and CinemaNow (*www.cinemanow.com*), the Lions Gate/Microsoft/Blockbuster affiliate that has now become the industry leader and which, even back in 2000, claimed to have 1,000 movies in its streaming video library. Some of these Web sites made it and some did not. CinemaNow and AtomFilms are still around. In February 2002, CinemaNow announced a deal to distribute certain MGM films over the Internet and has as of 2004 increased its library to more than 4200 films including deals with other majors such as FOX, Disney, Miramax, Warner Bros, and others.

The convergence of digital audio and video has also allowed bootleggers to sell illegal digital copies of such films with the ease and anonymity that only the Web provides. In the late 1990's, SightSound Technologies (*www.sightsound.com*), an outfit that sought to become the world's largest on line movie

/nloading store and reportedly had at a very early stage in the internet .xplosion 4.5 million subscribers, principally on college campuses, was the first to release a minimajor's first-run theatrical motion picture (*PI*) in the pay-per-view window on-line. SightSound claimed to have solved the bootlegging issues with proprietary encryption technology, which limited the days and numbers of plays depending on the fee paid for the download and required the user to go back to the SightSound.com Web site to relicense the movie before it could be replayed.

Indie producer David Secter, whose movie *CyberDorm* is an offbeat campus comedy about the webcasting phenomenon, initially tested the waters with SightSound was. "The subject and setting make it a good choice for college broadband distribution," noted Secter, "but with no star names they relied on compelling key art and a provocative trailer to drive downloads. They also developed on-campus promotions with SightSound's team of campus reps. Secter also hoped that some of those who saw the movie on the net would be tempted to buy the video or DVD from our Web site." Unfortunately, *Cyberdorm* and Sight Sound were not able to drive large numbers of viewers to download *Cyberdorm.*

Secter accurately predicted that "the indie film festivals would offer large-screen video projection and let producers save the cost of blow-up until/if/when they secure theatrical distribution," which is exactly what happened. Moviemakers, rather than blowing their pictures up to 35 mm initially, put that money into promoting their movies on the Web, on video, and on television. By sidestepping theatrical exploitation and releasing in first run on the Web, digital entrepreneurs may be on to a new business model for the entire industry; that is, using an innovative Web premiere to drive direct video sales and perhaps TV sales, in almost the same way theatrical releases in the '80s and early '90s were used to move VHS units off the video store shelves and promote awareness to generate higher TV license fees.

SightSound sought to announce a major studio exhibition deal, but never successfully concluded one. Sightsound, which was undercapitalized, ultimately decided that it would be better off licensing its technology to third parties than trying to compete in the marketplace.

CinemaNow, buoyed by an investment from Microsoft and Blockbuster, ultimately became the leader of Web companies that were interested in actively acquiring films from producers for exclusive or non-exclusive Internet runs. Web sites like CinemaNow and Atom Films also provide the opportunity for filmmakers to expose their short films to large audiences and develop future opportunities to make long-form projects. These digital sites may also provide new models for digital storytelling in shorter than usual formats.

The major studios also got into the game but haven't yet prospered with their delivery systems and marketing reach. Disney and Fox announced a joint venture to provide digital movies on demand, but that venture fell apart. Warner, Paramount, Sony, Universal, and MGM also planned for digital pay-per-view delivery systems. In one venture that did come together, MGM and Warner licensed a number of titles to CinemaNow, and is now known as MovieLink (*www.movielink.com*). This system offers digital downloading of major studio movies. Again, since downloading still takes a considerable amount of time, the jury is still out on whether or not MovieLink will be successful. In an effort to cover all subscriber preferences, CinemaNow offers both streaming and downloading options to subscribers.

Clearly, the digital movie making age is upon us. Faced with the decision of whether or not to shoot an independent project on digital, here are some of the factors and issues the aspiring digital filmmaker should consider:

Creative and Production Advantages

The filmmakers who have plunged in to make digital films have raved about the creative flexibility that purely electronic production allows. Because of the tremendous cost savings during both production and in postproduction, filmmakers are not burdened in satisfying the bottom-line needs of the studios, banks, insurers, completion guarantors, distributors, and foreign sales companies. With less cash at stake, a filmmaker can take the kinds of risks that have been impossible on even a one or two million dollar film. Movies have been made on digital for the mind-blowingly low sum of $900 (*The Last Broadcast*) and many digital projects have been completed for well under $100,000. Without the suits, studio executives, bankers, and a legion of meddling private investors looking over their shoulders, filmmakers are free to do unheard of things like retain true final cut of their projects; create new structural paradigms with which to tell their stories (allowing the actors to shoot the film themselves), shoot at ratios of 30:1 as opposed to 5:1, as indie filmmakers are often required to do, shoot movies in the spirit of the DOGMA 95 filmmakers, using natural light, 100% hand-held camera work (which allows the line between actors and directors of photography to blur as in *The Blair Witch Project* (see discussion below), shoot vastly more close-ups than in your average picture; complete postproduction largely at home at an unhurried pace as opposed to at an expensive rental facility where time is money (or worse, having to wait to use off-hours and late-night shifts and weekend editing and postproduction services when the equipment is usually down).

Among the early proponents of digital filmmaking was actor turned director Jean-Marc Barr—a performer in such Von Trier films as *Zentropa* and

…aking the Waves. Barr, after directing the all-digital movie *Lovers*, enthusias-…cally described his experience as literally being part of the audience as he shot. He participated in the movie as an actor; the entire cast and crew consisted of seven people, and all of them blended into the production as props. Barr "held his camera as a little bird" throughout the production, which allowed the director a closeness and intimacy with his cast that he never would have had if he had been forced to shoot the picture within the rigid constraints of traditional celluloid photography.

In the digital arena, a director can view rushes instantaneously in color on a relatively inexpensive color video monitor. If the director and actors do not like the work or simply want to make it better, they can, without fear of economic reprisals, shoot again on the spot and cut short the delays of waiting for the traditional development of dailies. Other production problems and political issues can be solved through the use of digital production. Paul Wagner, the director of the award-winning drama *Windhorse*, stealthily shot the movie, which features rare panoramic vistas and intimate undercover scenes of Tibet under the noses of Chinese authorities who ban all Western artists from filming or photographing there. Wagner posed as a tourist and shot his footage with consumer-grade camcorders. While Wagner's ingenuity earned him international acclaim, his efforts also resulted in his being banned from Tibet by the Chinese government (luckily, the ban was issued after the completion of principal photography).

Director Harmony Korine, whose all-film *Gummo* ricocheted between drama, spectacle, and naked reality, pushed himself even further with his next work, the 100% digital *Julien Donkey-Boy.* Korine and cinematographer Anthony Dodd Mantle reportedly used nine different types of cutting-edge electronic cameras, including spy-size and surveillance cameras affixed to, among other things, eyeglasses and clothing, in order to capture actors improvising scenes in public places working off of Korine's original treatment for the film.

In his directorial debut, Ethan Hawke also pushed the limits of digital technology capturing the hallways and rooms of New York's historic hotel in *Chelsea Walls.* Although the film released with great fan fare, as can be gleaned from a number of the reviews, shooting digitally does not always result in commercial success.

Some Disadvantages

There is no question that digital production can help solve a number of creative and production problems, but it would be irresponsible to extol the virtues of digital production without mentioning some of the disadvantages. Clearly, the most glaring drawback that filmmakers will have to deal with is the fact that, upon completion of the movie, a filmmaker is left not with a 35 mm print, but raw digital information—currently limiting the places the film can be shown to video, TV, the Internet, and the still rare digitally-outfitted auditorium. However, most film festivals, distributors, and exhibitors are beginning to shed their long-entrenched prejudices against video and electronic projection systems and the widespread availability of these systems at festival venues is now a reality.

John Cooper, senior programmer of the Sundance Film Festival, has acknowledged that Sundance is continuing to expand its video and digital screening facilities to deal with the onslaught of digital movies that continue to be submitted for competition each year. Virtually every other major festival, supported by the digital projection purveyors, has also followed suit.

Qualcomm, Inc., of cellular telephone fame, in conjunction with Hughes Electronics and JVC invested millions in the development of a digital projection system in anticipation of the huge demand for the retrofitting of 100,000 theaters to accommodate the digital age of electronic cinema. While these systems cost in the $100,000 to $150,000 range, the costs are expected to decrease rapidly. Industry leaders such as George Lucas will push the exhibition community to fall in line as early as possible.

The debate is still ongoing about who will actually pay for the cost of retrofitting, but in recent years the studios have seemingly become resigned to the fact that they will at least bear part of the responsibility as they have established either digital initiative committees and/or digital production and exhibition divisions. For example Sony Digital Studios announced in mid 2004 the availability of its innovative 4k projector which has four times (4096 pixels across and 2160 high) the image resolution of its chief rival Texas Instruments' 2k chip system (2048 pixels across and 1080 high). Landmark Theatres and new owner Mark Cuban have already taken the bull by the horns and set in motion a plan to outfit each of their exhibition locations with at least one digital projection screening room. Veteran producers' representative and marketing consultant Ira Deutchman and his partner, Hi Definition guru Barry Rebo, have also established their own digital exhibition system known as Emerging Cinemas, which will digitally project movies at museums, colleges, and other organizations through the League of Historic American Theatres (LHAT).

For the time being, however, filmmakers will in many cases still have to transfer their digital movies to 35 mm prints, and responsible filmmakers should budget for such a transfer. Depending on the transfer house and the

·cess used, costs can run between $30,000 and $80,000 to complete the ·ansfer from digital to film. (A discussion about various transfer labs will follow.)

Since many digital moviemakers choose to buy their own equipment (which tends to be fragile), another potential disadvantage to the digital route is that producers are not able to call an equipment rental facility and demand a replacement be delivered immediately. Further, repairing even consumer-grade digital equipment on the set is no filmmaker's idea of a picnic. As such, directors and producers in the digital sector advise purchasing backup equipment in case these kinds of problems arise.

Filmmakers must make decisions about the format they shoot in as early as possible. Previously, the two available formats were NTSC, which is traditionally the American standard for electronic shooting and PAL, which was traditionally the European standard. NTSC has 525 lines of vertical resolution and runs at 30 frames per second, while PAL has 625 lines of vertical resolution and runs at 25 frames per second. Since PAL provides a superior resolution and is closer to film that plays at 24 frames per second, PAL can be transferred to film at a 1:1 ratio (frame by frame) with a slowdown that is not perceptible by the human eye. While the sound may require some tweaking in the postproduction process, the conventional wisdom was that with the lower resolution and the visually perceptible six frames per second difference of the NTSC format, the PAL format was far superior to NTSC for digital filmmaking. The problem for American moviemakers was that PAL postproduction and transfer equipment was not widely available in the United States and the transfer process (at least in the then immediate future) would have to be done in Europe. Astute digital entrepreneurs made the decision to purchase PAL cameras and PAL computer equipment and editing systems to be rented out when not being used on their own productions, in anticipation of a high demand for digital movie making in PAL.

Two more formats have been developed over the last few years that have become more widely accepted than either NTSE and PAL. The 24P format uses digital cameras that actually run at 24 frames per second, the same as film and thus the digital movie shot with a 24P camera can be transferred to film at a 1:1 ratio. The results are stunning and most viewers simply cannot tell the difference between a movie shot digitally on 24P equipment and a 35 mm film. While these cameras cost more, many are still affordable for purchase, and the more expensive ones are readily available at reasonable rental rates. Also emerging in the last few years is the Hi Definition format, which ranges from 720 to more than 1080 lines of resolution using ever more expensive cameras, ranging from $60,000 to $110,000, such as the DVPRO HD-P camera or the

Thompson Viper Camera. As these newer and more expensive cameras and viewing formats have become more prevalent, the filmmaker is faced with more choices and more decisions to be made before shooting. Nevertheless, it is usually the best policy, to the extent financially possible, to push the limit on technology and shoot with the most advanced camera and capturing format available. Since the onslaught of Hi Definition, distributors, festivals, programmers, and distributors have become less interested in the older NTSC card and PAL digital video format and more excited about 24p and Hi Definition movies.

Although not a disadvantage per se, another issue that digital moviemakers should be concerned about when making their movies is the tendency to shoot too much footage. It's tempting to overshoot because it is so inexpensive. The filmmaker must keep in mind that storage space on the computer will be an issue and excessive footage may require the purchase of expensive storage capacity. In addition, the filmmaker should consider the extra time and effort in the editing process it takes to review, choose, and combine the best possible footage. Other issues that digital movie makers have concerns about include hot skies, black and white costumes or backgrounds, excessive stripes, and fine lines, all of which may not capture as well on digital. Finally, since digital sound equipment is so precise, digital moviemakers must be vigilant about sound issues because problems with sound cannot be readily corrected and will be audible to the audience.

While consumer cameras that cost as little as $1,000 are an attractive choice and are available in a wide variety, their picture quality is sometimes questionable, especially when bumped up to 35 mm, where excessive stripes and fine lines in the picture can expose the format's limitations in capturing subtle and detailed visuals. Although money is always an issue for indie filmmakers, in today's market, it is advisable to either rent a Hi Definition camera at a local rental facility or make the investment to purchase a consumer grade Hi Definition camera and digital editing system for $7,000 to $15,000.

Camera Equipment

Once filmmakers have chosen the format to shoot in, the fun really begins. In today's market, a filmmaker can outfit himself with the tools of digital production and postproduction for about $7,000 to $15,000, although depending on how sophisticated a director wants to get, the price tag can easily balloon to the $30,000 to $40,000 range.

There are several basic camera choices. The first is the single-chip consumer digital video camera, which can be purchased at Circuit City, Best Buy, and other mass-market electronics stores for between $500 and $1,000.

Thomas Vinterberg used this type of camera to shoot *The Celebration* in the ate 90s. It furnishes excellent images in low-light situations, but it provides the lowest level of overall image quality.

On the next level up are the three-chip digital cameras which furnish sharper image quality and can be equipped with FireWire output systems or digital video capture boards, which allow directors to do most of their editing, mixing and special effects on a home computer. These cameras provide more professional quality, but at prices ranging between $2,000 and $4,700, are still priced within reach of the consumer market. Early digital movies such as Bennett Miller's *The Cruise* and Lars Von Trier's *The Idiots* were shot on these types of three-chip digital cameras. The Sony VX 1000 and the Canon XL-1 were the current cameras of choice.

The third level includes the professional digital video cameras, which provide the best image quality available electronically but are substantially more expensive than the previous two categories discussed. Cameras that cost between $4,000 and $100,000 (but not including the $500,000 Sony/Panavision prototype, which was used to film *Star Wars: Episode II*) are used primarily for broadcast television and major video productions, and include the Sony Digital Betacam. These cameras do not provide FireWire output capability, so editing on a home computer with this type of camera is not an option.

This level also includes the 24p and Hi Definition cameras, which can range anywhere from a low price of $3, 000 up to $110,000. A variety of models are available from Sony, Canon, Thompson and others. A good source to research these various cameras is the Internet as well as Scott Billups' *Digital Moviemaking*, which is published by Michael Weise Productions and is available at bookstores and *www.mwp.com.* While these camera systems are widely available for rent from professional Hollywood equipment houses, prudent low-budget independent filmmakers have purchased instead the three-chip system and performed editing on a home computer. This method not only gives the filmmaker an unparalleled control over the logistics of postproduction, but allows the filmmaker far more time to experiment with, and ultimately fine-tune, his vision of the finished product.

Noncamera Considerations: Testing

Distributors and film festival programmers including Geoff Gilmore of the Sundance Film Festival, universally relate that the production value missing from most independent productions is top-quality sound. When organizing a digital production, filmmakers must make absolutely sure, to provide themselves with the best sound capability affordable. Sound experts can prove to be valuable consultants in this quarter and can provide especially good advice as to whether or not to record directly into the camera with an external mike or into a DAT recorder. For both paths, booms, high-quality mikes and audio mixers are advisable.

It is also extremely valuable to have a color playback monitor on the set that allows a filmmaker to view instantaneously exactly what has been shot and how the color looks. This instant access to "true" dailies (as opposed to traditional films, which employ the "video assist" for an approximate playback of the action) is one of the biggest advantages to digital filmmaking and allows the director to hone performances, cinematography, set design, and other elements in an immediate and unprecedented fashion.

Today's digital filmmaker should be keenly aware of the nuances of the technology he and his director of photography use. Testing should play a key role in the preproduction phase to ensure that the on-set advantages of digital filmmaking work for the nature of the production and that the appropriate lighting system is utilized. This goes especially for the camera package's ability to cope with light levels during the actual shoot and the types of lighting supplements and equipment that may be required. Shooting in actual or available light will enable a filmmaker to have the most flexibility of movements, the most set-ups per day, and the most freedom for improvisation for his performers, but the story and script (night shoots will almost certainly require special lighting equipment) will determine this approach (and the camera technology should be able to beautifully capture it) before any decisions as to lighting issues or equipment are made.

Another note on testing, in addition to extensive lighting tests in varying situations, on-set performance of the digital tools can be enhanced by testing sound recording and synching (in the case of DAT-recorder usage) and by testing the quality of the video-to-film transfer in conjunction with a transfer facility or several transfer facilities. This last test can be accomplished by shooting test footage that approximates the demands of the film and working with various transfer houses to get the best finished 35 mm result. When planning a high-ratio shoot, it is important to test the editing system that the production will be using. Issues of concern include storage capacity, computing power, and hard drive capabilities available for use in the cutting, mixing, special effects, and mastering processes.

The Transfer

If a digital filmmaker has been lucky enough to be accepted at a prestigious film festival that happens to have the requisite high-quality, all-digital projection facilities (as Sundance, Toronto, and many others have similar facilities), and a

…tributor has acquired the movie prior to the transfer process, the filmmaker …ight not have to arrange for the transfer from digital to film at his own expense. *The Last Broadcast* is still in its original digital form. Television and video exploitation do not require a film print. Nevertheless, in order to attract a film festival or distribution deal, a film transfer should be budgeted for.

There are several different transfer processes in development, including such forms as kinescope (developed in the first days of television), trinescope, electronic beam recorder, and the laser film recorder. Based on whether a digital movie has been shot and postproduced in NTSC, PAL, 24p, or High Definition, and depending on whether the transfer will be to 16 mm or 35 mm film, the processes for transfer differ. While a 16 mm transfer is generally about half the cost of a 35 mm transfer ($35,000 as compared to $70,000), filmmakers should seriously consider the 35 mm route. The transfer to the most standard projection format (35 mm) adds more inherent value to the finished film as screening facilities for the 16 mm film format are scarce. The moviemaker should absolutely lock in and fully negotiate the deal with the transfer house before production begins to avoid unexpected problems and cost overruns when the time comes to perform the transfer.

The leading practitioners of digital to film transfers based in Europe are Swiss Effects in Switzerland, Hokus Bogus in Denmark, Colour Film Services in London, Lukkien in the Netherlands, Cincecitta Digitale in Italy, and Gurtler in Germany. The leading U.S.-based transfer houses include DuArt Tape House Digital and Film Craft LAB in New York; FotoKem, Sony Hi Definition Center, Four Media Company, EFILM, Cinesite, the Post Group, and Liberty Livewire in Los Angeles; and Roland House in Arlington, Virginia.

The Blair Witch Project

While technically not a digital movie, *The Blair Witch Project*, the ultimate success story for the guerilla filmmaking model, was shot primarily on a $500 Hi-8 mm consumer video camera purchased at Circuit City (then returned before the 30-day return period had expired), merits special attention because the model utilized by the Orlando-based movie makers applies so readily to the indie digital moviemaking philosophy. *The Blair Witch Project*, a horror "documentary" about footage left by student filmmakers that reportedly vanished in the woods while making a documentary about a legendary witch, was created by Haxan Films, which consisted of writer-directors Dan Myrick and Edwardo Sanchez and producers Rob Cowie, Gregg Hale, and Mike Monello. It was discovered at the Sundance Film Festival, picked up on a preemptive opening night bid by Artisan Entertainment (now Lion's Gate Films) and went on to screen at that year's Directors Fortnight in Cannes where it won the prestigious

Prix de Jeunesse (Best First Film) Award.

Produced and blown-up to 35 mm, reportedly at a total cost of less than $60,000, *The Blair Witch Project* leapt into the mainstream in 1999 when it garnered a rave review from Roger Ebert, who wrote that the movie "is already the third most talked about film of the summer after *The Phantom Menace* and *Eyes Wide Shut*, and may move into second place by mid-June." In an uncommon embrace for such an out-of-left-field film, *The Blair Witch Project* won high praise from such mainstream publications as *The New York Times*, *Rolling Stone*, *Premiere Magazine*, *Entertainment Weekly*, *Newsweek*, and *The LA Weekly*, all several weeks in advance of its release date.

The Blair Witch Project's creators developed a new form of narrative storytelling and experimented by using elements of the celebrated DOGMA 95 digital paradigm. The actors held the camera and shot the movie themselves while they improvised and worked off the treatment written by Myrick and Sanchez. The actors followed the director's notes. The tension, drama, and horror created in the movie were provided, in part, by the directors' late-night unexpected visits to the actors' campsites. The actors were left in the woods to fend for themselves during the eight-day, real-time chronological shooting period, for the express purpose of scaring them to death. The production design consisted only of natural materials—sticks and vine-like twine, for instance—left by the filmmakers and found by the actors in the woods over the course of the shoot.

The moviemakers started with 20 hours of raw footage, edited that down to eight hours of material that worked, and finally after a year of editing, manipulated the work down to its feature-length version. The movie was designed specifically, creatively and for budgetary reasons to have a video look, since the filmmakers could not afford to shoot and process 20 hours of footage on 16 mm or 35 mm film. Incorporating these techniques, a filmmaker could design a project to be shot in a similar manner in a 100% digital format. *The Blair Witch Project*, which reportedly grossed more than $250 million worldwide, perhaps more than any of the rags-to-riches indie success stories of the last ten years, proves that all a digital filmmaker needs to succeed is an ingenious concept and the ability to execute it well.

While some facets of the motion picture industry are clearly seeing the dawn of the digital age as a far-reaching and historical transformation of the way stories are told, at this point, the digital format clearly lends itself to certain types of stories. On the highest end, the rigorous computer effects work of an extravagant production like *Star Wars* demands a digital approach to principal photography. In the most modest budgetary circles, the electronic camera puts cinematic storytelling techniques in the hands of filmmakers that could not have afforded to shoot anything even a few years ago. Yet to transform, ıgh, is the broad middle of the business. Although they've given the green ,ht to movies such as Robert Rodriguez's *Once Upon a Time in Mexico,* major ,tudios and minimajor financier/distributors are still reluctant to green light a 100% digital live-action production (with the exception, of course, of all-digital cartoons like *Antz, Toy Story* and *Monsters, Inc.*). That day may still be up to three years away. While there is a digital revolution in progress, the final outcome is far from being a forgone conclusion, as the exhibitors, distributors, producers, directors, and even the writers who comprise the bulk of this $6.7 billion-per-year industry must radically alter the way they think about and do business to accommodate something that is still seen, in some of the more traditional circles, as simply a trend.

Nevertheless, as evidenced by the overwhelming success of George Lucas's digital innovations and the early pioneers of *The Celebration, The Cruise,* and *Once Upon a Time in Mexico,* digital filmmaking has a definite upside. While critics may bemoan the death of celluloid (Roger Ebert has accused digital projection companies of trying to trick the film-going public into paying nine dollars a head to watch two hours of what is essentially television), there is no doubt that in the coming years digital filmmaking will open more artistic doors than any new technology in the medium's history. At the very least, any filmmaker who has a vision, a new idea, or a fresh approach to storytelling can actually capture and output his movie in a digital setting completely on his own—for the first time free of the hassle and interference of third-party financing and its inherent economic and creative constraints. For the first time in a century, the filmmaker does not have to stop making his movie if the money people suddenly say "Stop" or "No." A new era of movie making has arrived.

KEY ISSUES IN DIGITAL DISTRIBUTION

In today's fast-paced media marketplace new delivery systems for entertainment content are continually emerging. Programming can now be delivered by traditional means like theater, television, and videotape, and by digital methods such as satellite directly to theaters (a theatrical right) and directly to the home by such services as DirecTV (a television right), by digital videodisc (DVD) (a home video right), over the Internet by telephone dial-up, digital subscriber line (DSL), and cable modem (each of which is used to deliver such online streaming services as Atom Shockwave (*www.atomfilms.com*, *www.shockwave.com*), IFILM ((*www.ifilm.com*), Lion's Gate/Trimark's CinemaNow (*www.cinemanow.com*) or through downloading services such as *www.movietrak.com*, a joint venture of MGM, Paramount, Warner Bros., Sony, and Universal. Over the past few years, new digital delivery systems have emerged such as *www.movieflix.com*, *www.unlimited.com*, *www.imovieshare.com*, and *www.internetmovie.com*. The independents seem to be more flexible than the new studio ventures and are readily adaptable to market conditions. Independent producers and sales organizations are ideally positioned to take advantage of new and existing digital distribution opportunities, just as they were able to take advantage of opportunities during the early years of home video.

For purposes of this chapter, digital distribution systems are defined broadly as any delivery system that delivers content directly to the home by means of streaming or downloading, such as telephone dial-up, DSL or cable modem over the Internet or via a private proprietary Internet or closed fiberoptic network delivery system.

The Threshold Issue

A digital distributor wants to exhibit your movie or program ("product") over the Internet on its Web site, over DSL systems, or by means of a private, closed digital delivery system and provides you with its "standard" distribution agreement. Before you decide to proceed, check with your partners, colleagues, and business and legal advisors to determine if digital distribution is an appropriate choice for exposing your product. There are a number of issues to consider in this arena, including your collective analysis as to whether or not theatrical, television, video, ancillary, and international distribution of your product are available options, the costs and expenses associated with traditional distribution methods, and whether or not the genre, subject matter, and quality of your product is appropriate for digital exploitation.

Once you have determined that the digital route is right for your product, here are some key issues to consider:

The Grant of Rights

It is no secret that digital distribution/exhibition outfits are trying to build libraries and assets, so while it is less common today, do not be surprised if your digital distributor hands you an agreement that grants itself all rights, in all media worldwide, not just digital rights. Digital distributors may argue that they spend huge sums to digitize and market your product to enhance its value and that accordingly they should control all exploitation of your product. However, in all likelihood the distributor spends marketing dollars primarily to promote its own Web site or service. Moreover, the cost to digitize programming has been reduced drastically with new technology. Do not be quick to accept digital distributors' claims and give away more rights than you should. Be informed and know the costs and procedures involved in new digital delivery methods, and you will be able to negotiate knowledgeably from a position of strength.

A good number of digital distributors agree to license only digital online exhibition rights for a limited term and allow you to keep the copyright and all other rights in your product. You may wish to split digital rights between a number of distributors: those that utilize only a streaming method of exploitation, those that license digital downloads only, or those involved in traditional exploitation like theatrical, television, and video. Before you agree to grant any or all rights in your product, make sure you feel comfortable with the digital distributor, the individuals involved, their business plan, pricing structure, and marketing strategy for the digital exploitation of your product.

It is important to perform traditional due diligence, including Uniform Commercial Code and related searches, to find out as much as possible about the commercial health and reputation of your digital distributor. Since bankruptcy termination clauses are difficult to draft effectively and in many cases are unenforceable, it may be difficult and costly, if not impossible, to reacquire your digital rights if the digital distributor files for bankruptcy or otherwise becomes insolvent.

Whether or not you grant any additional rights to your digital distributor, make sure you retain as many rights as you can (e.g., your right to sell packaged video products online, such as videocassettes, laserdiscs, DVDs and merchandising items). Also, negotiate a fair advance or split of the revenue; try to retain approvals over any off-line exploitation deals that the digital distributor is allowed to make; retain some input or control over marketing and distribution plans; and if your digital distributor is publicly traded, in addition to obtaining cash and royalties, ask for stock options with a quick vesting schedule so that if the stock in the digital distributor becomes valuable, you can benefit from taking an early risk with them.

Exclusivity

Most digital distributors will ask for exclusive digital exploitation. Because the digital programming market is so new and no leaders have yet emerged, it is risky to grant exclusivity. Your digital distributor may not be around in a year, or it may struggle without exposure. A safe philosophy is to grant a nonexclusive digital license for a limited term. This will allow the market to mature and you will be able to reassess your position after a relatively short window. It will also enable you to enter into other nonexclusive licenses so that your product receives maximum exposure on as many sites or services as possible, which increases your prospects for higher revenue. If you have to grant exclusivity, try to find a digital distributor that has other revenue sources separate and apart from the digital media, which demonstrates a likelihood that it will be around for a while.

Territory

Digital distributors will presumably initially ask for worldwide rights. Nevertheless, many experts claim that technology is available through blocking telephone area codes and registration procedures to limit the territory to the United States or other geographic designations. Since you may prefer to license international rights in a completely different manner, try to get the digital distributor to limit the territory to the United States or to the specific territory in which it is primarily doing business.

Another method of protecting your product from oversaturation or infringing your other territorial distributors' exclusive rights is to limit the language in which the product may be exploited digitally. For example, if you are required to grant digital rights to the German distributor of your product for traditional media as part of your overall German license, try to include a provision that the product can only be made available on the Internet in the German language, dubbed version and not in any other language, and, further, that Internet exploitation will be held back until the German distributor can provide evidence that digital exploitation of your product can be limited to the German-speaking territories. In order to reduce the harshness of such a clause, a proviso can be added that allows that an insubstantial and inadvertent amount of Internet leakage out of the territory is not deemed a material breach of the agreement and additionally that clips of the product for promotional and publicity purposes up to a maximum of two minutes may be exploited digitally in all languages inside and outside the licensed territory.

Licensing Period

Your license term for digital exploitation will first depend on what other rights, if any, you have previously licensed. If you have already had a theatrical release, you may want to try to fit your digital license period into the two- to three-month pay-per-view window prior to video release so as not to infringe upon video and subsequent pay and free television exploitation. If you have had no previous exploitation, try to limit the license period to six to 12 months so that you can reassess the digital marketplace in short order. With technology changing at such a rapid pace, your digital distributor's market share and strategy may be obsolete before the ink on your contract dries. Keep your license periods as short as possible.

Advertising and Promotion

The digital distributor will generally require the right to use the names, voices, likenesses and photographs of the actors and the other creative talent involved in your movie for its own on-line marketing and promotion, and, if they can get it, the right to use those materials to promote their own Web site and their other marketing and promotional activities. You should be careful not to grant rights in this arena to the digital distributor that are not available under your various talent agreements. As is customary in other media, the length or running time of the use of these materials can usually be limited to not more than five minutes or less. The digital distributor will also require the right to create and use its own marketing and publicity tools in connection with the distribution of your movie, including without limitation, the right to produce original segments, trailers, written summaries and synopses, and excerpts of your movie for the purpose of advertising, promoting, and publicizing the picture.

One provision that a producer should at least ask for, but may not be able to obtain, is a commitment on behalf of the digital distributor to advertise, market, and promote the movie in some specified and negotiated manner, such as buying advertising time; using giveaways such as T-shirts, caps, pens, or other merchandise to promote the picture itself at college campuses; or some other promotions that go above and beyond the digital distributor's own constant efforts in marketing its own Web site.

License Fee/Payment Terms/Audit

Most digital startups claim poverty because the market has not yet matured, so obtaining an advance against royalties for a digital license is difficult, if not impossible. If an advance it is not possible, ask for a large share of the gross revenues for downloads, streaming, or other licenses (30% to 50% is obtainable), and try for a share of advertising revenues associated with viewing your product. If the digital distributor insists on deducting certain advertising and promotional expenses, try to limit the amounts that are recoupable against your royalties, as most of those expenses are probably incurred in promoting the site and not your product. If merchandise related to your product is being sold on the site, retain a 30% to 50% share of that revenue as well. In addition to an advance and royalties, consider asking for stock options, and the right to purchase stock at lower than market rates. Specify the minimum rates to be charged for downloads or viewings. Prices for download licenses tend to fluctuate but average $1.95 to $3.95 for a one-day license, $3.95 to $4.95 for a five-day license, and $9.95 to $12.95 for an unlimited use license. Some services license on a subscription basis, where all or most titles in the digital distributor's library are available at a monthly subscription rate. Make sure that it is absolutely clear how your share of the royalties from subscriptions are to be calculated. Make sure you receive not less than quarterly, if not monthly accountings, not later than 60 days after the end of each accounting period. Require detailed accounting statements and obtain the right to audit the digital distributor's books and records. Try to get the digital distributor to pay for the cost of the audit if an audit proves underpayments of more than 5%.

Cross-Links

Make sure you include a provision that requires cross-linking of the digital distributor's site with your official Web site for your company or product. Try to retain the right to exhibit the product on your official site as well as the right to sell merchandise, videos, and DVDs of your product from your own site. The digital distributor will probably reserve the right to discontinue links if your official site is deemed objectionable. Nevertheless, a successful digital launch of your motion picture may well be the impetus to drive video, DVD, and other merchandise sales related to your movie directly from your own official site or affiliated sales sites, such as Amazon.com.

Delivery of Materials

Because the digital distributor will disseminate your product either via streaming or digital downloads in a digital format to the ultimate user, delivering your product to the digital distributor should be a relatively simple process. You will be required to provide the digital distributor with a digital submaster of the product and its trailer. The expense of prints, interpositives and internegatives, and a number of other customary and expensive delivery items required by distributors in other theatrical and video agreements should not be necessary. Additional delivery items that the digital distributor customarily requires are relatively inexpensive to create and include the product's one-sheet, including the title treatment and background information on the product, existing packaging for the product, such as the VHS or DVD jacket, a copy of the soundtrack, a press kit, a selection of stills of the principal cast, a synopsis or a summary of the product, or any other available publicity materials, along with customary chain-of-title documentation. Try to get the territorial distributor to pay for any dubbed or subtitled versions of the product that may be required, at least in the form of recoupable distribution expenses.

The digital distributor should agree to not authorize any copies of the submaster to be made without your prior written consent and should agree to keep the motion picture submaster secure during the license period and agree to destroy any encoded and compressed versions of the movie at the conclusion of the license period.

The digital distributor should have a reasonable period of time (15 to 30 days) to view and determine if the submaster is of acceptable technical quality for digital distribution and will have a reasonable period to request that you satisfy or cure any technical deficiencies with the submaster, which are listed in a technical report compiled after completing a quality control check of your picture. If you are unable to make the changes, then the digital distributor customarily has the right to terminate the agreement.

Piracy/Unauthorized Playback and Duplication

As with any new technology or delivery system, producers and copyright proprietors are fearful that their product will be pirated and that they will lose revenue as a result of their lack of complete control over dissemination of it. This is a normal fear. As digital distribution methods become more widely acceptable, this concern will subside, just as it did following introduction of video. In order to combat such concerns, digital distributors have been developing various types of encryption technology, watermarking, and proprietary software that could substantially reduce the risk of unauthorized use and duplication.

One such company was SightSound Technologies, a digital distributor that licensed only downloads and developed and patented technology that placed a special digital key on the digital submaster, which is downloaded onto an individual's computer. [already referenced in chap. 17, do we need to reintroduce here, or can we do it in such a way that we acknowledge that we've already talked about them?]SightSound claimed that this key allowed the product to be viewed for a specific number of times or specific period of time for which the product is licensed (be it a short window of a few days or an unlimited use period). Once the term has expired, the key would not allow the product to be viewed again, unless and until the user returned to the SightSound Web site (*www.sightsound.com*) to relicense the product. Additionally, should the user copy the product onto a disk and then attempt to view the product on a different computer or on the same computer after the initial license has expired, the key would automatically direct the new user to go to the SightSound Web site to relicense the product for that particular computer.

If this technology worked exactly the way SightSound claimed it to work, and if the technology withstood any patent challenges, SightSound would have an advantage over competitors that have developed equivalent encryption methods as this type of technology goes a long way to ease the fears of producers and copyright owners who wish to protect their products against piracy over the Internet. However, because downloading is so much more time consuming than streaming, and SightSound was undercapitalized, SightSound was unable to attract a substantial market share and establish itself as a leader in digital distribution. Instead it has sought to license its technology to third party content providers

SightSound recently settled a major patent infringement case against CDNow and N2K under which CDNow and N2k acknowledged the existence of SightSound's patents and paid over $3.3 million to SightSound to resolve the litigation.

The Protection of Intellectual Property

Where a digital distributor claims that it has proprietary software or protectable intellectual property (such as SightSound's patents), one would expect to find a provision in a distribution agreement where the distributor would retain its intellectual property rights and the proprietary software that it developed to exhibit motion pictures and other programming digitally, including any patents it claims to hold. You, as the producer, would also reserve all of your rights in and to your product and any other software or intellectual property assets that you might have in connection with the intellectual property you hold or have created in connection with your product.

Residuals and Contingent Payments

Digital distributors are not interested in getting involved with making any contingent payments to cast and talent or assuming any responsibility for residuals. Although the status quo is likely to change with upcoming SAG and WGA negotiations, residuals are not payable at this time to any talent guilds for Internet exploitation of theatrical motion pictures. That probably will change, as each of the guilds is formulating strategies for residuals—not only for Internet exploitation of theatrical and television motion pictures but for product produced directly for initial Internet exploitation.

With respect to contingent compensation payments due to actors, directors, writers, musicians, producers, and other talent, digital distributors generally take the position that these are obligations that the producer has incurred. However, these issues are subject to negotiation. The party with the most leverage tends to prevail. On the music side, performing rights societies such as ASCAP and BMI are already licensing Web sites that perform their members' music. Music publishers, record labels, and performers will be looking at additional payments for the digital exploitation of their music.

Breach/Injunction

As is customary with most motion picture licensing agreements, you can expect to see a provision in the digital licensing agreement that provides for a reasonable notice period for breaches on either side, but that in the event of a breach on behalf of the digital distributor, you waive your right to any injunctive relief, the right to terminate the agreement or to seek recision, the sole remedy being an action at law for damages. The only exception to this provision would be a situation such as described above regarding SightSound, where in the event the encryption software did not work, you would not have the right to seek damages but would have the right to terminate the agreement.

Representations, Warranties, and Indemnities

The customary representations, warranties, or indemnities that are usually found in motion picture licensing agreements also appear in the digital motion picture licensing agreement.

You will represent and warrant that you own and control all rights in and to your movie, you have not violated any laws or regulations, you have complied with all guild and union requirements if applicable, and you have not and will not violate the rights of any third party in connection with the exploitation of your motion picture.

The digital distributor will represent and warrant that it will exhibit your movie in its entirety and will not delete or edit the titles and the copyright notices, it will honor all credit obligations and advertising commitments, and it will not edit or add to your motion picture in any way without your prior written consent. Each party will indemnify and hold the other party harmless from all claims, costs, and expenses (including reasonable attorneys' fees) arising out of a breach of the respective party's representations and warranties under the agreement.

No Sales Guarantees

Since the market for digital movie exhibition is still relatively small, because no one can predict the market potential at this time, and because it is probably a bad idea to make such predictions, one will find a clause that indicates that the digital distributor has not made any guarantees, forecasts, or other estimates, expressed or implied, with respect to the number of transactions, the revenue expected, or the market share to be obtained from the digital exploitation of your movie.

Conclusion

As the computer-owning segment of the entertainment consuming population continues to increase; as digital cable lines, DSL, satellite and other systems continue to converge; and as delivery technology continues to improve; one can expect that the digital delivery of motion pictures will rapidly expand over the next few years. Digital pricing, territorial limitations, development of an appropriate digital exploitation window, the issue of exclusivity, and the appropriate license periods will begin to stabilize and a set of even more specialized standard terms for digital exploitation will emerge.

With the exception of the particular terms discussed above, the digital movie licensing agreement should be substantially similar to most licensing agreements used for other media in the entertainment industry.

Checklist for Licensing Digital Rights

The following is a checklist of issues to consider in licensing digital rights.

1. Definition of Rights Licensed
2. Limitations and Holdbacks on Rights Licensed
3. Language Rights Licensed
4. Exclusivity Issues and Windows
5. Territorial Restrictions and Holdbacks
6. Licensing Period
7. License Fee, Payment Terms, and Audit Rights
8. Stock Options and Vesting
9. Bankruptcy and Insolvency Considerations
10. Cross-Links
11. Delivery and Acceptance of Masters and Materials
12. Destruction of Copies at End of Term
13. Piracy/Unauthorized Duplication
14. Residuals, Contingent Payments, Music Royalties
15. Ownership of Technology and Intellectual Property

THE LAST SCENE AND CLOSING CREDITS

We have now taken you through the development process, the issues concerning copyrights and titles, true stories, satires and parodies, optioning material, and the terms of writers' deals. We have shown you how to negotiate a contract, the key terms of agreements, offers, counteroffers, acceptance, reliance letters, deal memos, formal agreements, and the all-important standard terms and conditions or boilerplate.

We have revealed how to get through the green-lighting process and explored the chicken-and-egg issue, the pay-or-play strategy, and how agents, managers, lawyers, casting directors, producers, directors, festivals, workshops, seminars, and grants all fit into the green-lighting process. We have talked about financing, private funding, equity financing pitfalls, obtaining money from family and friends, presale contracts, international sales agreements, the role of the producer's rep, subsidies, and tax incentives; how talent and producer fee deferrals can be another source of financing; and the importance of soundtrack albums, music publishing, and product placement in the financing process.

We have explained how entertainment lenders can provide production loans and how completion guarantees, foreign sales agency agreements, and distribution agreements fit into the whole picture of the production loan. We have discussed the different types of production entities that may be appropriate for your production including the sole proprietorship, the partnership (general partnership, joint venture, limited partnership), the corporation, and the limited liability company.

We have covered accounting issues, the difference between independent contractors and employees, loan-out companies, insurance, and script clearance procedures. We have dealt with directors, how to hire them, and the key terms of director deals. We have introduced you to casting directors and their importance in the process of getting a film made, and we have addressed the all-important issue of how to hire an actor, the pay-or-play conundrum, the star deal, and the perks.

On the production side, we have dissected producer deals, the Screen Actor's Guild, the Writer's Guild, the Director's Guild Basic Agreements, day player agreements, the crew deal, working with animals, location agreements, film permits, production insurance, crowd scenes, prop releases, and the use of film clips.

We have discussed the key issues concerning composers, source music, theme music, music supervisors, soundtrack albums, music publishing, synchronization, and performance licenses and the importance of music income.

We have battled our way through the ever-elusive definition of profits on a motion picture, how they are defined, how gross revenue is accounted for, the definition of distribution fees, distribution costs, distribution expenses, financing costs, interest, overhead, gross participations, deferments, profit splits, and profit participation statements.

We have toured around the world to film festivals and markets and revealed how to develop strategies to sell your movie through industry screenings, distributor screenings, selective private screenings, recruited audience screenings, and furnishing prints and videotapes or DVDs to acquisition executives. We have discussed strategies for marketing and publicity. We have guided you in analyzing and dissecting the distribution agreement. We have helped to prepare you for the painstaking task of creating all of the necessary delivery items required by a distributor once you have completed your movie.

We have peered into the future and led you through the ever-evolving landscape of digital production and distribution.

If you have made it through this book, there is nothing left for you to do except make your film. Good luck and please do not forget to thank us when you get your Oscar.

Gunnar Erickson
Harris Tulchin
Mark Halloran

Index

Note: Page numbers in **boldface** indicate contracts and agreements.